THE HISTORY. THE CULTURE. THE MACHINES

DISCOVERING
THE
Motorcycle

SINCE 1867

Armand Ensanian

Designed by Lisa Ensanian

Equus Potentia Publishing

Dedication

Dedicated to the loving memory of Jo Ann Ensanian, pictured on the front page on the author's 1947 Indian® Chief. She enjoyed many miles of motorcycling on her Honda 350, as pictured on the last page of this book.

Cover

The ROBRADY designed Vectrix Superbike casting a shadow of America's first powered cycle; the Roper steam Velocipede of 1869.

Published by Equus Potentia Publishing, LLC
www.equuspotentiapublishing.com

The information presented in this publication is true to the best knowledge of the author and the publisher. The author and publisher assume no responsibility for errors or omissions. References, recommendations, and opinions are made without any guarantee by the author or publisher, who disclaims any responsibility for any direct or indirect liability, injury, loss, or damage incurred in connection with the use of the information and images presented in this publication.

The author's use of trademarks in this publication is solely for the purpose of providing factual and accurate information relating to the history of motorcycles and is not intended to imply any affiliation, sponsorship, or endorsement of the publication or its author by such trademark owners.

First published in 2016 in the United States by Equus Potentia Publishing

ISBN-13: 978-0-9963919-0-0
LCCN: 2016913107

Printed in the United States of America

BMW Concept Ninety in collaboration with Roland Sands Design. Photo Courtesy of BMW Motorrad USA

Contents

Foreword

In developed nations like the United States, very few of us ride motorcycles because we have to. We ride because we want to. We ride for the fun, for the freedom, for the opportunity to separate ourselves from the hordes of cars jostling for position on the highway, their anonymous occupants insulated and indifferent to the world around them. Motorcycling requires exposure, and exposure requires assessing and engaging the world around you. In a car, you view the world from a distance, through a television screen. On a motorcycle, there is no screen.

Starting with the first machines at the turn of the last century, riders discovered the singular experience that is motorcycling. While early automobiles were mostly open to the elements, they aspired to cosset and pamper their occupants. The motorcycle was different. It thrust its pilot out into the open, and if there was luxury, it was the luxury of speed and individual control. The appeal of the motorcycle to independent-minded men and women was immediate, and the freedom of two wheels intoxicating. They became enthusiasts, and their enthusiasm was infectious, driving a sport and an industry that has shaped how we live and look at the world.

Armand Ensanian is the consummate motorcycle enthusiast, and perhaps the perfect person to tell the tale of motorcycles and motorcycling. His love affair with motorcycles started as a teenager with a ride up and down the East Coast on a Honda® CB160. He was, to put it lightly, smitten, and since then he's been drawn by every aspect of motorcycling, from its history to the bikes and the people who ride them. A former columnist for *Popular Mechanics* and photojournalist,

Armand is both rider and writer. Motorcycles have been his vocation and his avocation, and he appreciates deeply, enthusiastically, that motorcycles are much more than simply two-wheeled transportation. They are a window to the world, a world Armand has spent his life embracing and exploring.

Discovering the Motorcycle is much more than just a history book or a simple overview of motorcycling. The title is apt, for this is a discovery, a detailed and deeply insightful look at everything that has made and makes motorcycling what it is. The history of motorcycles isn't just about the machines; it's also about the social forces and historic events that have defined our interest in motorcycles. The infamous 1947 Hollister motorcycle "riot" painted motorcyclists as reckless and drunken hooligans, yet the motorcycle has made great contributions to society, employed by the tens of thousands to support troops and ferry messengers across seemingly impenetrable battle lines during World Wars I and II.

The old joke goes that motorcycle racing started as soon as the first and second motorcyclists met, and it's probably not far off the truth. Competition has always been central to motorcycling, and from the earliest days riders pitted themselves against each other at breakneck speeds. The famed board tracks that once dotted the country were the coliseums of a new age, drawing aspiring competitors who tested their nerve against man and machine. The quest to prove who was best on two wheels launched the famed Isle of Man TT and more, and men like Erwin "Cannonball" Baker made daring cross-country endurance runs on "roads" that were little more than cow trails.

Those were heady days, made all the more amazing considering the primitive state of technology in the early years of motorcycling.

The earliest engines were crude devices, and the machines they powered little more than bicycles. Manufacturers were limited by the technology of the time, but they were innovators, adapting and introducing new technologies as they could to make better, faster, more competent machines.

The "standard" was the basic motorcycle recipe for years, but technology fostered increasingly specialized motorcycles. Constantly looking for new ways to apply their passion, riders put new twists on both competitive and recreational riding. Racing technology migrated to the street, creating not only faster, but safer motorcycles. With the advent of small and light off-road bikes, riding in the dirt went mainstream, prompting legions of new riders to head to the country. The personalized choppers of the 1960s and 1970s inspired a new class of factory specials and cruisers, and new categories like adventure touring have energized motorcycling, bringing a new breed of adventure-seeking rider into the fold. Silent and powerful electric-powered motorcycles have suddenly become a reality, tapping into yet another vein of interest and creating new opportunities not just for riding, but for applying technology to the motorcycle.

Yet it's not all about what's new. Seasoned motorcyclists increasingly look to the past for inspiration, and motorcycling's rich history is drawing a fresh generation of enthusiasts who are discovering for the first time the simple, elemental appeal of vintage motorcycles. Their interests have rippled through the industry and manufacturers are paying attention, producing retro-themed motorcycles that appeal to those riders, new as well as old. The motorcycle landscape is richer than it's ever been, and today's rider can choose from a variety of machines yesterday's motorcyclist could never have imagined.

An unwavering enthusiasm for the value of the motorcycle, for its contributions to us individually and culturally, underpins every page of *Discovering the Motorcycle*. A celebration of every aspect of motorcycling, from why we ride to what we ride, from where we started to where we're going, it's a book only an enthusiast could have written.

Richard Backus
Editor-in-Chief
Motorcycle Classics

Photo by Lisa Ensanian

Introduction

Motorcycles are more popular today than they have ever been before. Despite this popularity, far too few know the remarkable story of how they have impacted our society for over one hundred and twenty years. The technological history of the development of the motorcycle is directly connected to monumental achievements in engineering that touch our daily lives. The public image of those who ride them, however, has paralleled our social history, seeing great highs and lows. This book unfolds the story of the motorcycle from its inception. It touches upon every facet associated with motorcycling and many of the noted makers that built the machines that provide us with transportation, sport, and enjoyment.

Individual chapters are devoted to all major aspects of motorcycling, and ultimately weave together a narrative that explains the motorcycle culture itself. The chapters dive into the history of standards, modern sportbikes, vintage classics, choppers and bobbers, off-road machines, touring rigs, bike events, clubs, and racing.

This book can be a valuable resource to those interested in purchasing a bike, as it investigates the diverse array of options out there. It acts as tool, tempering the influence of dealers, trade shows, magazine reviews, and test rides, which are sure to influence a buyer's decision.

Each machine acknowledged herein contributes to our understanding of motorcycling's rich past, exciting future, and many pleasures. The pleasures include the communion with nature and how it satisfies our primal desire for movement, travel, exploration, and escape. It allows us to experience freely our environment from the outside—letting us smell, feel, and adapt to the space that the roads bring us to. It is the closest we will get to flying without taking to the air. But for some, taking to the air is part of motorcycling as so well illustrated by the photograph on the title page of a high-flying Yamaha® motocross bike.

We ride motorcycles for many different reasons. There are those who own a motorcycle for the purpose of enjoying a few private minutes by themselves on a perfect sunny Sunday, releasing the tension brought on during the week. For others it is four-hundred-mile day trips through winding mountain roads, torrential rain, or endless desert highways, challenging their strength, determination, and skills. Some prefer the centaur-like freedom of riding through a forest trail on a dirt bike. And then there are those who are filled with pride as onlookers admire the machine they spent hours accessorizing and detailing. Motorcyclists love their machines. All of these experiences shape the character of the individual in the saddle. How one handles these experiences can influence one's life itself. Motorcycles certainly allow us the opportunity to challenge our abilities while expressing our individuality.

Despite the efforts of the occasional congressman who is looking to restrict where we ride, motorcycles keep growing in popularity. The surge in motorcycle sales over the last few decades can be attributed directly to three things: technology, variety, and baby-boomers. Bikes have come a long way from the kick-start, oil-leaking monsters they used to be. They are now elegant, electric-start, high-tech devices

that require no more maintenance than the modern automobile. Stylistic designs evoke works of mobile art, capable of fulfilling fantasies. Specialized models open roads to those willing to take to adventure, while baby-boomers can finally afford the bike that they had always dreamt of owning. Today, both men and women can enjoy the pleasures they bring without having to be mechanically inclined or particularly athletic.

This book will address all of these topics in its chapters. It was designed to be read in three possible ways: straight through from start to finish, one chapter at a time in no particular order, or just browsing the images with feet up on the coffee table or workbench. The countless pictures, combined with often-lengthy captions, allow the reader to grab little bits of motorcycle knowledge without having to commit special time for reading. Many of the bikes have been photographed in their native condition; often beat up and dirty as one would expect them to be after many years of loyal service. It is, therefore, my wish that as motorcycle enthusiasts gather, they will share the little known facts that appear throughout the text. It will certainly open many motorcyclists' eyes as to the true riches offered within this world, and hopefully inspire further exploration.

In the spirit of the great Australian motorcycle engineer and Vincent designer, Phil Irving, who said, "Know thy beast," it is my hope that through this book the motorcycle enthusiast gains a broader perspective of the machine, its development, and how it does what it does. The special chapter on the development of the internal combustion engine will inspire a greater appreciation of what powers the beast. Countless people and many good companies have devoted all their energies to provide us with these transcendental devices. They can take us anywhere we want to go, and while we're on the way there, we can be anyone we wish to be. That's what motorcycling is all about.

Kawasaki Ninja® ZX™ - 14R ABS
Photo Courtesy of Kawasaki Motors Corporation, U.S.A.

Acknowledgments

Forty-nine years of personal experience in riding, wrenching, and sharing of information between credible resources in the motorcycling world, have resulted in creating this biography of the sport. Certain events and individuals have further inspired this work. Foremost is Floyd Clymer. His passion for motorcycles was clearly evident in his numerous publications from the 1940s through the 1960s, espousing their utility and the adventure they offer. As other children read comic books, I thumbed through the pages of *Clymer's Motor Scrapbooks*, fascinated by illustrations of engines, transmissions, and interesting motorcycles. It was written by *Cycle* magazine that, "Clymer never met a motorcycle he didn't like." I can understand that statement.

Many others have fueled my interest in the history of this great vehicle. This holds especially true for Jerry Hatfield and his life's work in chronicling the history and mechanical evolution of the American motorcycle. A special shout-out to Kevin Cameron of *Cycle World* for educating us over the decades on the technological sorcery behind these wonderful machines, and Wayne S. Grenning for his brilliant and passionate work recounting the history of the internal combustion engine.

Motorcycling's great organizations have brought this sport to the public and encourage legislators to recognize it as a meaningful and respectable lifestyle. Most prominent is the American Motorcyclist Association. While the AMA fights for motorcyclists' rights and sponsors many of the racing events in this country, the Antique Motorcycle Club of America safeguards the history and wealth of knowledge to keep vintage and antique motorcycles alive. Its many public events offer both novice and expert an opportunity to experience the machines that provided transportation and sport for generations past. Many of the pictures in this book are from AMA and AMCA events.

Scores of motorcyclists, manufacturers, designers, fabricators, owners groups, museums, photographers, racing teams, and artists have contributed images for this book. Most are acknowledged within the captions, and website addresses are often given so that the reader can explore their offerings in greater depth. Of great value were the resources of Yesterdays Motorcycles, with their vast library of antique and vintage motorcycles. Special thanks also to auction houses Bonhams and Mecum Auctions for photographs.

In addition, acknowledgment must be given to the many museums exhibiting motorcycles. Two motorcycle museums stand out. The first is the AMA Hall of Fame. Several outstanding photographs of exhibits at the museum are presented in the book, particularly those relating to engines. Gratitude is also given for the wonderful gift provided us by George Barber in his marvelous creation—The Barber Vintage Motorsports Museum. I greatly appreciate being given permission to present photographs of key historical machines and exhibits I had taken at the Barber museum in this book.

Special thanks to Lisa Ensanian. Lisa's design concepts throughout this book have taken it far beyond what I had imagined. Her wonderful cover design is well representative of how motorcycles have evolved since their first appearance. Pictured is the stunning ROBRADY designed Vecrtix electric Superbike concept, casting a shadow of what many of us consider the first true motorcycle—the Roper Velocipede of 1869. Thanks also to Carla Diaz. Carla's guidance inspired a rational view of how to make this book better.

I am especially grateful to Richard Backus. I have been reading Richard's editorials in a variety of magazines over the years, including *Motorcycle Classics* and *Gas Engine Magazine*. His experience as a journalist, editor, and motorcycle enthusiast offered the ideal background to review the book and write the foreword. But Richard did far more than that. His passion for history and detail expanded his contribution to include verifying elusive historical facts and offering well-founded advice on reader perception and style. I thank Richard for all that he has done to help me tell the story of motorcycling better.

I wish to thank Karen for her guidance, never-ending support and motivation during the countless hours I spent behind the keyboard. She has taught me that riding together and dancing are very much the same.

There are so many others to acknowledge that have touched my motorcycle experience throughout the years. But, finally, I offer my warmest thanks to those who read this work and share their passion for motorcycles with others.

Photo by Stephen Covell

THE ANATOMY OF THE MOTORCYCLE

Twist-Grip Throttle – on right handlebar controls engine power. Actuates carburetor or fuel injection system to control the amount of air and fuel entering the engine.

Direction Indicators – turn signals controlled by a switch on the handlebar. Typically located front and rear. Stop light is centrally mounted on the rear fender.

Rear Suspension – Typically a coil spring and shock absorber unit mounted between the upper frame and swing arm. The pivoting swing arm holds the rear wheel. Many bikes have only one centrally located 'mono-shock' under the seat, while others have the more traditional ones on each side.

Final Drive – from the transmission to the rear wheel. It can be a chain, shaft or cogged belt made from rubber and Kevlar.

Carburetors – or fuel injection units with air filters.

Exhaust – pipes and mufflers. Some sportbikes have them tucked under the seat. Off-road bikes keep them high up.

Photo Courtesy of Triumph Motorcycles

Brake Lever – on right handlebar controls the front brake. Bikes since the 1970s have hydraulically operated disc brakes. Older bikes had drum brakes.

Clutch Lever – on left handlebar is used to disengage the engine from the transmission when shifting between gears. Older bikes, particularly American ones, had a foot operated clutch lever.

Headlamps – come in all sizes and shapes

Fuel Tank – for holding the gasoline, and may have had a separate oil chamber on older bikes. Most new bikes store the oil in the engine itself.

Cylinder Head – sits on top of the cylinders. It contains the valves that open and close to allow gas/air in and exhaust gases out.

Frame – holds everything together. Can be made of tubular steel, aluminum or carbon fiber.

Instruments – and warning lights are typically mounted above the handlebars. Many cruisers have the speedometer mounted in the tank. Tachometer tells the engine's revolutions per minute. This is useful for performance bikes with a high red line; maximum recommended rpm.

Transmission – contains gears and shafts that allow the engine speed to be best matched to the road speed for optimum power. Most bikes since the 1970s have the engine and transmission as one unit. Harley-Davidson still uses separate units on their big bikes. The Primary drive connects the engine to the transmission with either chain, gears or cogged belt. The clutch mechanism controls the connection.

Engine – may be anywhere from one to eight cylinders, and sits low in the frame. Some engines are 'stressed members' and act as part of the frame. Others are rubber mounted to minimize vibration.

Footpegs – tend to be centered, below the knee, for standards, set forward for cruisers and set to the rear on sportbikes.

Front Suspension – is made up of two telescoping fork tubes connected to the steering head by a 'triple-tree'. The tubes contain springs and shock absorbing hydraulic oil dampers. Some old bikes, like Indians, used leaf spring front suspensions.

Tires – may be tube or tubeless. Typically spoked wheels require an inner tube, while cast alloy wheels don't. Some off-road bikes have tubeless spoked wheels for easy flat fixes.

Foot Controls – include the rear brake lever on the right and shift lever on the left. Prior to 1975 many British bikes had this reversed. Antique bikes may have had a hand-shift gear change lever by the tank.

Kawasaki Motors Corporation, U.S.A.

Indian Motorcycle International, LLC

Chapter 1

THE WORLD OF MOTORCYCLES

Motorcycles have been part of our lives for over one hundred years. They truly offer something for everyone—be it a light machine for cost-effective commuting, an attention-grabbing show bike, an exhilarating track-ready sportbike, a comfortable touring machine with backrest and stereo, or a surefooted dirt bike that makes riding through the woods a real joy. Necessity, convenience, adventure, or just fun; whatever the reason, motorcycles are here to serve.

Tamara Hayden

Something For Everyone

Motorcycles provide us an experience in movement. Kids love motorcycles because they can launch them high into the air over homemade ramps and land them joyfully into splashing puddles. Young men and women ride motorcycles not only for sport, but as expressions of individuality that go far beyond the two dimensions of social media. Older folks ride because it makes them feel young, brings back memories, and stirs the senses. Racers ride because it challenges their neurological and physical systems in a way that no other sport can. Hard-core bikers ride because it makes them look tough. Adventurers ride because it can take them to wonderful remote places with little effort. There are as many reasons people take to motorcycling as there are motorcycles themselves.

The author's father and uncle play out many a young boys' fantasy: riding a motorcycle. They are aboard Uncle Harry's 1926 Harley-Davidson® JD during the early years of the Depression.

The universal reward of riding motorcycles is intangible. They provide us with transportation to both physical and mental landscapes. A motorcycle ride melts away the frustrations of life in less than a mile. Our view of the world changes as we ride. Motorcycling has that effect because of specific reasons. First, it requires a high degree of concentration. Unlike a car where we would blast the radio, plug in the cell phone, balance a burger on the lap, and steer with one finger, a bike requires both hands, feet, and the brain. Riding creates this mindful experience where all one's attention is on the here and now. Once on the way, every biker gets that strange, warm feeling of independence. No one can touch us; be it the boss, a bad relationship, or debts. A couple of bucks in the tank will take us far enough away to refresh the mental batteries.

Nothing feels better than a ride into the sunset after a tough day. Modern cruisers like this one made by Suzuki® are the product of a hundred plus years of motorcycle development. Photo courtesy of Suzuki Motor of America, Inc.

Late starting riders, like middle-aged adults, have grown into a huge segment of motorcyclists. Most are looking for some kind of "escape" therapy, and likely have longed for a bike for quite some time. Many are now finally in a position to afford one with kids out of college and mortgages paid. Baby-boomers often buy the machines they dreamt of fifty years ago, or modern versions thereof. Harley-Davidson sales attest to this. Their bikes haven't changed much on the surface over the years and may just be the ticket to bring some spark back into one's life. But beneath the surface, there are countless engineering advances that make these machines highly reliable. Harley-Davidson sells nearly half the bikes sold in the United States today. Foreign competition has ramped up with the introduction of many new models.

It's all about feeling young and invincible again for baby boomers getting back on motorcycles. Many prefer the vintage bikes from their youth.

Riding a motorcycle may be a necessity for some. They are less expensive than cars and consume less gas. A cheap, used bike that someone was about to junk is often the first vehicle a suburban or country kid will get to ride on his or her own. There is always an old dirt bike around that has seen generations of riders earn their wings on its torn saddle. As kids grow, so do the bikes. The next level may be a Kawasaki® 250cc enduro with lights. This opens the door to riding on the street and carrying a passenger. Hours will be spent fiddling with the machine, getting the carburetor right and the ignition to fire on time; a great experience to have for future bike ownership.

Many riders are attracted to a bike because of what it does. An example is a fourteen-year-old wishing he had a YZ-250 while watching extreme motocross on TV. Other times, one is attracted to the image that is created, a big marketing theme for many manufacturers. This was not always the case. When I had my first bike, a late 1960s Honda 160, I took it on the road, in the fields, and in the dirt. It didn't do particularly well off-road, but I didn't really care. I wanted the thrill and freedom. I used the same bike to go to work, or take long weekend trips. This was the case with most bikes fifty or more years ago. We used them for everything and anything. We didn't worry about image because we were the image.

Kids have no fear, and take to bikes like bees to honey. Small 50cc and 80cc two-stroke dirt bikes are great learning bikes and easy to handle. They provide enough power to achieve the ultimate thrill—the wheelie.

Those who grew up with motorcycles will most likely keep riding as adults. It wasn't long ago that these two cousins were tearing up the lawn on their dads' dirt bikes.

For those with limited budgets and little parking space, a bike may be a great way to get to work. It is an efficient means to commute, particularly in good climates. Those living in urban environments have long learned of the indispensability of motorcycles for getting around traffic jams. Used bikes are ideal for city folks. There is less concern about that first scratch and the effect rugged urban riding can have on a bike. Apartment dwellers also find inexpensive used bikes less stressful to keep locked up on the street. Craigslist® offers riders in large metro areas tons of bikes for under $2,000.

I pass this Suzuki Savage nearly every day on my way to my office in Queens. This large, single-cylinder 650cc is easy to ride and maintain, while providing affordable cruiser styling. Its low cost and popularity have kept it in the Suzuki lineup for decades. Re-badged as the S40, it makes a perfect commuter or candidate for customizing into a chopper or café racer.

The motorcycle was adopted quickly by police departments for duty. Their low cost, combined with maneuverability, made them ideal in urban environments. New York City started using Indian® motorcycles back in 1905. Both Harley-Davidson and Indian lobbied hard to get the lucrative municipal contracts for motorcycles. Indian's left-hand throttle allowed police to use the right hand to direct motorists.

City bikes have a tough life. This Honda Shadow® was covered in snow and ice by a plow. It did have to wait for things to warm up, but survived.

For others, a motorcycle is part of their work. Motorcycle cops spend hours in the saddle. Many of them ride for pleasure as well. Delis may use motorcycles and scooters to deliver lunch orders, while messenger services depend on bikes for quick runs across town. The military relied on bikes extensively during both World Wars as a means to get messages between units. Dispatch riders risked life and limb as they rode their olive drab machines through mud and snow while being shot at. The utility of motorcycles cannot be overstated.

Military dispatch riders used light bikes like this WWII Indian Model 741 30.50 cubic inch (500cc) Scout® to relay messages between combat units. Note the watertight air intake and filter box, uncommon on civilian bikes of the era.

Harley-Davidson was a major producer of motorcycles during both World Wars. It keeps the historic memory of its military motorcycles alive with the powerful new Softail Slim® S. The 110 cubic inch engine (1,802cc) produces a massive 109 ft-lbs of torque at only 3,500 rpm. Photo courtesy of Harley-Davidson.

An Affordable Means To Get Around

There was a time when motorcycles provided the only affordable means of transportation to most American families. Many a newborn was brought home in a sidecar regardless of rain, snow, or sleet. Riding in bad weather was not an option; it was a necessity. Automobiles built at the beginning of the twentieth century were terribly expensive. At about $200, bikes were much more attainable by the average working man making $700 a year than the exorbitant custom built cars of the day. Automobiles like the Autocar cost $1,750, while others like the Knox exceeded $2,500. Only the wealthy could afford the luxury of owning and maintaining them. Every part was custom built, and unlike today, required hard-to-find specialists that were available locally to repair them.

Early three-wheelers like this 1908 Indian Tri-Car were the forerunners to bikes with sidecars. They provided families affordable mobility at the turn of the twentieth century.

Henry Ford's assembly line manufacturing process changed all that. Cars could be produced quickly and cheaply with interchangeable parts. It wasn't until the inexpensive

Model T Ford's price dropped to under $400 for the basic Runabout by 1915 that America started giving up two wheels in exchange for four. Many motorcycles were left to rust in storage barns and sheds. It was an easy sell because a bike with a sidecar rig cost nearly the same. Folks with a Model T sat within a protective shell, out of the rain and snow, with the security of four wheels beneath them.

Henry Ford's Model T single-handedly changed not only the automobile industry in America, but the motorcycle industry as well. Over fifteen million Model Ts were built during its nineteen-year run between 1908 and 1927. It came in over a dozen configurations, from no doors to four doors. This late 1921 Touring model cost $355, making the purchase of a motorcycle with a sidecar for around $320 questionable as family transportation.

Motorcycles still continue to provide inexpensive transportation to the masses in developing countries throughout the world. Folks earning less in a year than the average American earns in a week cannot afford cars. Bikes and mopeds are handed down from father to son and maintained on a tight budget. As standards of living improve, bikes eventually get replaced with affordable small cars. What happened in this country a hundred years ago is playing out elsewhere in the world today.

A motorcycle is an affordable and privileged means of transportation in many developing countries. Families of three, four, or even five can be transported on small machines. Photo by Tamara Hayden.

Indian was the largest motorcycle manufacturer in the world at the time of the Model T, having sold nearly thirty-two thousand of its red machines in 1913 out of its Springfield, Massachusetts, factory. Ford sold nearly 500,000 Model Ts by that time, taking significant market share away from the one hundred smaller US motorcycle manufacturers looking to make their mark. Motorcycles had to find a new venue. That wasn't difficult. Bikes became the vehicle of choice for sport and recreation.

Bikes As Social Vehicles

For many, motorcycling is the vehicle for social experience in an otherwise impersonal world. It is tangible and real. Quite a few weekend motorcyclists share strong bonds on those early morning adventures to the local coffee shop or a charity ride for a worthy cause. There is endless conversation about what new bits one added to an already gleaming machine. Each person is surrounded by what he or she loves best and friends who share the feeling of joy when riding together on a warm, sunny day. There are no frowns at such events. Even the mean-looking lone biker that one sees on the highway during a morning commute will crack a smile when you say hello. Sharing a passion for motorcycles develops a bond.

Most motorcyclists are social beings and welcome riding with friends.

Motorcycling isn't just for people. Man's best friend can enjoy the ride as well.

Vintage Bikes for Reliving the Past

Motorcycles are time machines, taking us to places our daily frustrations can't find. They allow us to relive images of wild and romantic days past. Today, men and women ride their fast vintage European and Japanese bikes to local pubs, dressed in black leathers, silk scarves, and goggles. This category of bikes manufactured over twenty-five years ago is becoming big all over. It is the ultimate cool in that in this cookie-cutter world of $40,000 choppers, 160 mph sportbikes, and countless big cruisers, relatively few true vintage bikes from the 1950s through 1980s roam the streets as daily riders.

Highway commuting on a forty-five-year-old bike is one thing, but doing it on one sporting a 305cc engine is another. This vintage rider on the Baltimore Beltway is keeping up with 70 mph traffic without a problem on his superb Honda Super Hawk®. Photo by Lisa Ensanian.

Most bikes built over fifty years ago were considered general-purpose "standard" motorcycles. Modifications by owners or specialty shops turned them into street or track racers. European and British bikes were lighter than most American V-twins, allowing easy upgrades to the more advanced alloy engines and frames to make them go fast. That concept has not been lost to time. Customized vintage bikes are big business today. However, most returning enthusiasts will opt to buy the original bikes they rode during their younger days. This includes American Harleys, Indians, and anything imported across either ocean.

Vintage motorcycle gatherings all over the United States bring folks and their families together to reminisce about dream bikes. Note the classic similarity of the mid-1960s BSA A65 Special in the front with the Triumph Thruxton.

27

The popularity of vintage and antique motorcycling has grown exponentially. Nostalgia is not the only reason. Vintage bikes allow the mechanically inclined enthusiast full opportunity to tune and tinker with the machine. Modern bikes, including retros, feature fuel injection and electronic ignition control units. These have replaced simple carburetors and mechanically activated ignition points that were well within the capabilities of the average handy person to maintain. Vintage is not for everyone, though. Old machines, like old folks, take a while to get going, and kick-start pedals do kick back and take a toll on the knee. It definitely helps to be in shape and to have some wrenching skills when diving into this world. Vintage machines will break down, as they did back in their day, and there aren't as many shops around that know much about them.

Puzzled looks on the faces of vintage bike enthusiasts are a common sight as owners and builders try to keep up with the little gremlins that hide in old machinery. This customized vintage Norton® features many unique innovations. Photo by Lori Weiniger.

An impeccably restored American-made 1913 Excelsior Model 7B belt drive V-twin may be far out of reach of most motorcycle enthusiasts despite the fact that it originally cost $250. Current values can exceed $80,000. The Excelsior brand was founded by Ignatz Schwinn, the bicycle tycoon, in Chicago in 1907. It became known for its reliability and quality. Excelsiors gave Harley-Davidson and Indian quite a run for their money on the racetrack, as well as in sales. The bike was displayed at the annual Antique Motorcycle Club of America's Rheinbeck, NY, event.

Bikes from all eras are available for us to buy and ride. Vintage bike rallies and eBay have brought these machines back into our lives. Nearly every summer weekend sees a vintage bike swap meet someplace nearby. Listings can easily be found in classified publications like *Walneck's Cycle Trader,* AMA publications, and classic bike magazines.

Like A Fine Wine

Vintage is defined as twenty-five years or older. Bikes older than thirty-five years have moved into the antique ranks and can easily cost $20,000 or more. Bikes from the 1960s and 1970s, mostly British, can still strain the wallet. A good running mid-1960s Triumph may cost $8,000 or more. Japanese two-strokes and four-cylinder superbikes from the 1970s and 1980s, on the other hand, are much more affordable. These are bikes that any forty-year-old can relate to and are easy to enjoy. The American Motorcyclist Association's annual Vintage Motorcycle Days in Lexington, Ohio, represents perhaps the largest gathering of vintage bikes for sale in the country. Hundreds of sellers of motorcycles from the 1940s through the 1980s offer their machines for sale every July. Fifty acres of parts are spread over the grassy fields for those looking for that elusive bit to bring their machine back to original. In addition, vintage racing, auctions, and seminars by well-known figures in motorcycling fill the eventful weekend.

Vintage swap meets happen all over the country and are great sources for parts, bikes, and expertise. Complete motorcycles can be assembled from acres of parts.

Of the hundreds of great makes of machines that existed in the first few decades of the twentieth century, most have been lost to memory except to the antique bike enthusiast. Motorcycling's deep roots will certainly open the eyes of any new vintage enthusiast as to the fraternity they have just joined and are sure to inspire delving into the classic and vintage world. Many of the marques (as the British would say) presented in these

pages have long since disappeared but are available to anyone wishing to relive the excitement of riding an old machine and experience the challenges thereof.

A clean unrestored 1973 Suzuki GT380 three-cylinder two-stroke like this can be bought for between $1,600 and $2,200. It is a relatively inexpensive way to get on a ready-to-ride vintage bike like the ones we may have had as teenagers.

Motorcycles As Investments

Antique motorcycles have become valued collectibles. Rare models may cost upwards of $300,000 and are slowly slipping into the hands of investors recognizing their equity. Sophisticated auction houses like Bonhams are selling bikes for big bucks to folks that will never put them on the road. One would be surprised that a barn find may very well be worth a hundred grand. Bikes are meant to be ridden, as the slogan "Ride 'em, don't hide 'em" says so well. Not to fear, there are tens of thousands of inexpensive old bikes out there waiting for a caring and willing owner. The Antique Motorcycle Club of America provides great resources for those interested, including a magazine, national meets, and exhibits.

Old bikes like this 1936 Harley-Davidson EL take a lot of skill and patience to maintain. Anyone that is mechanically skilled can enjoy the thrill of bringing a unique and highly collectible machine like this back to life. Properly insured, it represents a worthwhile investment that is not only guaranteed to grow in value, but will offer hours of enjoyable riding. Photo by Stephen Covell.

Hunting for vintage bikes was quite common twenty and thirty years ago. There were plenty of "barn finds" around. With a bit of detective work, one would be able to scout out an old bike beneath a bale of hay or lying in a musty basement. Someone always knew someone who had an aunt living in an old house that had a shed in the back with an old bike. I spent much of my time in my twenties following such leads. It was a great way to spend a weekend, riding around, chasing a pot of gold. Owners back then would typically be happy to make a few dollars and have you remove "the junk." Unfortunately, hundreds of thousands of rusty old bikes were scrapped by their owners during the WWII steel drives. People would have never guessed that those old frames and engines would be worth tens of thousands of dollars in the decades that followed.

Barn finds of antique bikes are getting tougher to locate. Owners are also becoming savvy as to their worth. However, they are still out there. Tom Cotter's fun book, *The Vincent in the Barn*, recounts numerous enjoyable stories of great finds by "motorcycle archeologists," as he calls them. Television shows like *American Pickers* have created greater awareness of the value of rusty old bikes. This has, however, escalated the market price for these relics beyond the average enthusiast's means. True rare finds seem to elude even the best searchers. Of the 242 American motorcycle brands that existed prior to 1988, as recorded by the Antique Motorcycle Club of America, relatively few have survived extinction. Marques like Bayley-Flyer, Comet, Hoffman, Nelk, Pansy, Torpedo, Royal Pioneer, and Victor will rarely be seen. Fortunately, higher volume producers like Indian, Harley-Davidson, Thor, Reading Standard, Excelsior, and others have left us with enough gems to dream about.

Piles of seemingly worthless junk like this sitting in a damp upstate New York basement for over fifty years may have eluded the untrained eye. It cost the author $600 and resulted in a fully restored 1947 Indian Chief®, worth $28,000.

This rusted 1914 Indian being offered at an antique show for $30,000 is definitely not cheap and would be a tough sell to convince the spouse. Fully restored, it may be worth three times as much.

Completely unrestored and original bikes bring a premium. This 1906 Indian sold for around $70,000 at auction. It brings new meaning to "barn find." Photo courtesy of Bonhams Auctions.

Happiness is bringing home an antique engine that may have been scrapped.

A well-restored Indian Chief like this late 1940s model may easily be valued today at $40,000 and represents a more prudent investment than any stock one can buy. Unlike securities, you can ride this investment and enjoy all that it brings. Historical vehicle insurance is also much less expensive.

Café Racer Revival

Café racers are vintage sportbikes custom made from standard British, Japanese, or European machines. Lower handlebars and rear-set foot controls create a racer's crouch, much like the modern sportbike. The name was coined in the 1950s as young British riders raced between truck and coffee stops on modified bikes.

Café racers emulate European racing motorcycles from the 1950s and 1960s. This nice example features the customary low "clip-on" handlebars, light aluminum alloy gas tank, rear-set foot controls, solo racing saddle, better brakes, and race-tuned Triumph engine. Photo courtesy of Skip Chernoff.

Baby boomers with the ability to invest in the expensive modifications required to convert an old Triumph, Norton, Ducati®, or Moto Guzzi® into a café racer, have revived this genre. So popular have café racers become that many manufacturers, like Triumph, Moto Guzzi, and Royal Enfield®, offer new contemporary versions of them. Basically, they are made to look like vintage sportbikes. They look cool and handle better than standard configurations. The downside is the same as with other modern sportbikes; low handlebars and rear-set foot controls don't make good long distance riders. Wrists, necks, and backs will eventually start to hurt, especially when crawling along in slow moving urban traffic. Riding in pain is no fun. Buyers who plan on owning only one bike should be realistic as to what the primary intended purpose of that machine is. When sticking around locally or heading to the track, sportbikes are unbeatable. Taking a trip to Sturgis from Chicago on a café racer can be tough.

Triumph's Thruxton is a modern-day café racer, perfect for a new generation of riders looking to differentiate themselves from the Japanese sportbike crowd. It is for the rider who simply wants a vintage look with modern components that don't require much maintenance. Photo by Mauricio Romero.

Retro Bikes

The choice to relive the past on a modern machine is not limited to café racers. British, Italian, German, and specialized American bike manufacturers are offering retro-styled bikes in standard, scrambler, and race configurations with reliable modern components beneath their traditional styling. Triumph, Norton, Royal Enfield, Ducati, BMW®, and Moto Guzzi are just a few. These are phenomenal machines, providing the appearance of an older bike, with sophisticated suspensions and electronics.

BMW's R nine T is based on thoroughly modern engineering, but designed to reflect vintage simplicity. The bike is targeted at young riders who are looking for a retro cool machine. It is powered by the company's iconic air/oil-cooled two-cylinder four-stroke flat twin engine. A scrambler version with high pipes is also available. Photo courtesy of BMW Motorrad USA.

Kiwi Indian Motorcycle Inc. not only restores bikes and furnishes complete modern reproduction engines, but also builds complete modern reproductions of old Indians like this 1930's Retro Chief. Engine components are far superior to the originals produced in the 1930s. Electric start options are available. Note the modern disc brakes. Photo courtesy of Mike Dunn.

Retro Bikes can go way back. This 1920s styled British bike is made today with a modern engine and good brakes. Photo courtesy of The Black Douglas Motorcycle Co.

The 2006 Ducati Sport Classic Paul Smart 1000LE pictured is a modernized race-replica of the bike Paul Smart rode to victory at the famous Italian Imola 200-mile race back in 1972. The original was a milestone design for Ducati, defining an engineering foundation for most of its future machines. This retro-styled machine is far advanced over the original factory racer.

In 1999, Kawasaki tried its hand at the retro Brit bike game with its handsome overhead cam W650 twin. Unfortunately the introduction of the "re-al-deal" Triumph Bonneville® limited its life to just two years. A new release is offered overseas with an updated 800cc engine to meet the great interest in retro bikes. The W800 is also available in café racer trim.

Scrambling for Market Share

History keeps repeating itself in motorcycle design and marketing. As a younger generation of riders discover the cool bikes of the past, manufacturers build new models to satisfy their tastes. Scramblers are enjoying such a revival. These machines, popular in the 1960s, were originally built for off-road and desert racing. Street versions featuring standard motorcycles with high exhaust pipes soon followed. The scrambler is seeing a strong comeback with several exciting models from Italy.

An example of an early 1970s Ducati 750 SS racer that inspired the retro styling of the Paul Smart 1000LE. Photo by Stephen Covell.

Photo courtesy of Ducati North America.

34

Ducati is giving the retro-vintage buyer some real fun with its line of Scramblers. Introduced for 2015, seven variations are offered. Six are powered by an 803cc 75 hp (horsepower) desmodromic L-twin engine. These beefy machines truly capture the rambunctious character of the scrambler; be it on urban streets or the dirt track. A photo of an original scrambler from the 1960s can be found in the off-road chapter. Photo courtesy of Ducati North America.

Introduced for 2016 is the Moto Guzzi V7 II Scrambler. It offers the rider who would otherwise prefer a standard motorcycle a very trendy alternative. Despite the retro looks, the bike has many advanced features, including fuel injection and anti-lock brakes (ABS). Photo courtesy of Piaggio & C SpA.

A Royal History

Those of us who had Triumphs in the 1960s and 1970s can buy a reliable new Bonneville and feel like we went back in time without the heartache that is typically associated with older machines. Bike enthusiasts will do a double take, wondering if it is an original. Another example is the Royal Enfield line of bikes. They have hardly changed in appearance since the 1950s. Read the case history at the end of the chapter on standard motorcycles to see how this one brand served generations of riders.

This modern Royal Enfield Bullet 500cc single-cylinder motorcycle looks nearly identical to its vintage predecessors from the 1950s. It is a thoroughly modern machine, built in India. Enfield offers a broad range of affordable 350cc and 500cc singles that are available fuel injected, and even come with electric start. The untrained newcomer to vintage bikes should note that the new Enfields are easy to spot. Look for disk brake up front, sprung saddle despite a rear suspension, unit construction engine and transmission, and turn signals.

The Royal Enfield's Bullet engine holds the record for having the longest production run of an individual design, even longer than any specific engine model offered by Harley-Davidson. It thrives today because of its ability to satisfy all the reasons for riding a motorcycle. Through its broad selection of models, the Royal Enfield makes a perfect entry-level retro bike that will be accepted by all enthusiasts.

Sharing the Joy

Acceptance is a noteworthy topic because some motorcyclists of specific segments and makes tend to be somewhat cliquish. This is a social reality that even non-riders know about. Some cruiser riders tend to look down upon sportbike riders and vice versa. Vintage bikes are somewhat immune to this persecution. Italian bikes are also less affected. Everyone secretly wishes they had one. The sad reality is that when I ride a cruiser, I get waves from other cruiser riders, but when I ride my modern sportbike, the number of waves drops significantly from cruiser riders. For some it's all about brand or segment loyalty. For others it's about the love of motorcycles—wherever they came from. Waving has always been an acknowledgment that we value sharing the freedom and joy we get from riding. So, wave to your brothers and sisters on the road.

An International Affair

Motorcycles, regardless of where they are made, have a connection with other parts of the world. Many makers source certain parts from other countries. Examples include the use of electronic components from Japan, Germany, or China, carburetors from Japan, high-end brake components from Italy, and suspensions from Sweden and Japan. To continue this example, little do most Harley-Davidson riders know that the company has a very diverse international history, including Italian and Japanese relationships. This goes back to when the company put the Japanese in the V-twin motorcycle business nearly eighty years ago.

36

Looking to seize sales opportunities abroad, Alfred Rich Child, an independent business agent authorized to represent Harley-Davidson in Japan, licensed rights to Japanese manufacturers to make Harley-Davidson motorcycles. The idea was to have bikes built locally to reduce their cost to Japanese buyers and increase sales globally for the company. Childs even arranged funds and tooling in hopes of launching this new market to compensate for the loss in sales at home due to the stock market crash of 1929. By the early 1930s, Sankyo was one of the companies that built reproductions of the Harley-Davidson VL and RL series flathead motorcycles in 750cc, 1,000cc, and 1,200cc displacements. Trade disagreements abounded, and the looming militarism in Japan put an end to the relationship after four years. Excessively high import tariffs precluded Harley-Davidson to sell their bikes directly.

A rare 80cid Rikuo reproduction of a Harley-Davidson VL. Photo courtesy of Troyce Walls.

The Japanese-made bikes were branded Rikuo (King of Road) and continued to be made under Sankyo through 1949. The brand was later revived by Showa, who produced the larger displacement bikes primarily for police work until production ceased in 1960. It improved on the original model, subsequentially adding a foot shift and hydraulic front forks in the 1950s. Showa went on to produce suspension units for modern Harleys.

At first glance, this 1958 Rikuo RT2 750cc looks like a Harley-Davidson. Closer examination reveals it to be a Japanese reproduction with a 45 cubic inch flathead V-twin engine. It was the last 750cc Rikuo model. This bike is owned by the Barber Vintage Motorsports Museum. Photo courtesy of the American Motorcyclist Association, AMA Motorcycle Hall of Fame.

This nicely restored 1934 Harley-Davidson VL was one of the models copied by the first generation of Rikuos. The 74 cubic inch VL V-twin was introduced in 1930 by Harley-Davidson with great fanfare but proved poorly engineered. Later models greatly improved engine design and reliability.

Bikes for Sport

Motorcycles are sporting machines. Regardless of a bike's age or style, they do require coordination and physical application to make them go. Some are harder to handle than others. Many antique American bikes have a foot-clutch and gear shift lever mounted tank-side. This takes a bit of getting used to. Controls on bikes today are conveniently placed below the toes and within an inch of the fingers on the han-dlebars. Modern sportbikes are the most particular in their ergonomics and responsiveness. They provide young and old riders with precision machines on which to experience chest crushing acceleration and superb road handling. Every motorcyclist, regardless of preferred segment, should ride a sportbike at least a few times to appreciate the best sporting technology available.

Modern sportbikes bring race bred technology to the street. Sensibly used, and with proper training, machines like this awesome Kawasaki Ninja® ZX™-10R superbike can provide an unequalled level of excitement. Photo courtesy of Kawasaki Motors Corp., U.S.A.

Sportbikes made by the top Japanese and British manufacturers are affordable and verge on purebred racing machines. Italian machines may cost a bit more but are well worth the price for those who can appreciate their exotic engineering and afford the maintenance. Young riders are attracted to sportbikes for all the obvious reasons. We'll explore the great variety of options later in the book.

Motorcycle for Competition

Some people ride just to race. Doing it on the street is still popular but dangerous, given the variables of cars, gravel, curbs, and the law. It is best to keep it on the track.

Street racing can be dangerous. The track allows sportbike riders the opportunity to let it all out in a safer environment. Photo of Aprilia® RSV4, courtesy of Piaggio & C SpA.

Professional racing has always been a big part of the motorcycling scene. Many riders don't follow it and are missing out. The sights and sounds of bikes screaming by the stands are pure adrenaline. Reading about the MotoGP races is a motorcycle enthusiast's soap opera. Exotic names, racing in exotic places, on exotic machines abound with drama.

There are also amateur sportsmen and women who live to race on the track, in the mud, up a hill, or down a drag strip. These folks have a passion that is beyond written words. Many are weekend racers who put every dime they can spare into one machine, hoping to challenge themselves and others.

Motorcycle racing is very physically and mentally demanding. Amateur racers feel a great sense of satisfaction in just being able to complete a race and master a course. Many are as expert as pros but choose to make it a hobby rather than a vocation. Recent turns in the economy have made sponsorships a rare privilege.

Hundreds of races throughout the country bring families in their campers together to cheer dad, mom, or kids on to victory. It is only after attending such an event that the average bike enthusiast may consider taking the plunge. Young age and a big financial backer are not requirements; anyone can race, and it doesn't have to be at a Grand Prix. The American Motorcyclist Association (AMA) sponsors many off-road and vintage racing events to get anyone started. If your kids aren't that good at soccer, consider putting them on a dirt bike and rooting them on from the sidelines. It will develop a sense of confidence, coordination, and control that can rival any sport.

For grown-ups, vintage flat track or road racing may just be the ticket to scratch an old itch. AMA-sanctioned vintage races require no more than a handful of rules, safety gear, and an inexpensive old bike set up for the track. This is a very historic type of racing. It has been popular since the 1920s. Oval dirt tracks at carnivals popped up all over the country, allowing both pros and local amateurs a chance to show their stuff.

The flat track racing on the dirt is as popular as ever with AMA-sanctioned vintage racing. Racers use the same machines that roared around fairground tracks decades earlier.

Bikes for Getting Dirty

There is a segment of motorcyclists that hardly ever ride on paved roads. These are the off-road enthusiasts who ride on rough trails, over the desert or through the woods. It is a great way to enjoy the outdoors and the challenges Mother Nature may throw at us. Modern off-road machines are light and powerful and are not the exclusive domain of motocross rac-

ing. Specialized configurations of engines, frames, and suspensions allow us to explore pretty much any terrain.

Despite the millions of open acres of public land, there are forces at work in the government to keep this kind of fun limited to private lands. The American Motorcyclist Association lobbies hard on behalf of all of us who enjoy the freedom of riding off-road. Photo courtesy of Kawasaki Motors Corp., USA.

Light powerful dirt bikes have become the sport machines of choice for the extreme sport rider. They may have started with skateboards, but nothing propels these young folks through the air like a lean and mean alloy framed motocross bike. Freestyle motocross (FMX) competitions and exhibitions are amazing displays of man and machine, often accompanied by alternative music blasting in the background.

Freestyle motocross focuses on the aerobatic skills of the rider. Tricks are judged based on difficulty and wow appeal. Riders will jump more than fifty feet into the air, flip, and defy gravity as they seem to hang above the crowd. Pictured is Spaniard Dany Torres on his KTM® SX® 250. Photo courtesy of KTM North America, Inc.

Extreme sport motorcycling is every mother's fear and many young dirt riders' dream. You can spot the first signs of this craziness in your kids when they start building ramps in the back yard. Just make sure they wear a good helmet and a spine pad.

Motorcycles and Individualism

Motorcycles are about identity. Some folks get a bike just to stand out in a crowd. A bike is a canvas that allows one to express oneself to the world. A teenager may do so with a hot Japanese four-cylinder screamer outfitted with colorful graphics and matching helmet. Boomers on the other hand may choose a glorious $32,000 cruis-

er, fitted with saddlebags, stereo, and lots of chrome goodies. For others, spending every spare dime to buy a one-of-a-kind custom gives them the head-turning attention they seek.

Eye-popping custom bikes like this are not necessarily the most practical, but who cares. They are so much fun to ride. These head-turners are typically powered by a huge V-twin engine that make a lot of noise through its relatively unrestricted exhaust pipes.

Custom bike sales have rocketed in the last decade. Television shows and celebrities posing on exotic hand-built $150,000 bikes provide fantasies that many work hard to fulfill. The chapter on custom bikes reveals a wild and creative world.

Riders acquire the personality of the motorcycle they are riding. Onlookers will thus stereotype them based on their posture. Cruisers offer the classic, relaxed "I don't care" slouch while sport machines are tightly wound and say "catch me if you can."

Rider ergonomics and seating position convey an attitude. Relocating footpegs and handlebars on the very same bike can change the image (and comfort) dramatically. High handlebars are not as uncomfortable as they may seem. They reflect back on the California choppers of the 1960s. Highway bars (forward mounted footpegs) allow the rider on the right to stretch his legs on a long trip.

Sport and racing motorcycle seating position is quite different. Feet are set to the rear, knees up, and body leaning forward to reduce wind resistance. The rider also places more weight onto the handlebars, improving steering response. The downside is that wrists will start hurting when riding for an extended period of time.

Those of us fortunate enough to own a few different bikes get a chance to experience multiple personalities. This occasionally results in a mismatch, like the three-hundred-pound fellow who decides to ride his wife's 250cc Honda Rebel to the local convenience store just because it was in the driveway. His $30,000 custom chopper may have been a better choice once he sees that the 7-Eleven just happened to be the meeting point for a dozen hard-core bikers on a break. They should not judge. Even tough bikers started on something smaller.

A motorcycle can literally be a canvas. This stunning Suzuki Hayabusa® was meticulously airbrushed and painted by Terrence Phillips and Frank Hazen. With matching helmet, it says a lot about the rider. Photo courtesy of Terrance Phillips, CenelaCustoms.com

Motorcyclists like projecting a very specific image they want the public to see. A true sportbike rider will don full leathers, spine pad, carbon fiber protected gloves, and a $600 Arai® helmet. He may be racing around the cloverleaf at the local interchange, but in the mind's eye, he's on the track, battling for position. On the other hand, black leather is a vital part of the café racer and cruiser scene. Motorcycle makers make a big business out of that. They market their extensive line of appar-

41

el to satisfy the image that their riders wish to convey. Ironically, the very image that tainted motorcyclists as deviants and ruffians over fifty years ago is being modeled by contemporary ads.

A motorcycle provides the ideal canvas for expressing oneself. Lawrence towers over his "Knucklehead"-engined bike. It is his interpretation of the immortal old-school chopper. People will spend a hundred thousand dollars on a custom-built bike to capture the essence of a motorcycle like this.

The leather jacket and engineer boots that were once considered symbols of defiance and independence have become the norm—a fashion statement that has lingered since the 1950s. Biker apparel stores under various retail names have popped up all over the country to take advantage of this market. Everyone is in on the act. Catalog houses like Cycle Gear and Dennis Kirk feature extensive lines of "lifestyle" apparel. I was actually asked by a shopper once where I purchased my "stressed" riding jacket. I don't think he believed me when I told him that it was thirty years old and the stress was from use and a few falls.

Bikes Are for Getting Away

Folks like daydreaming about getting away on a motorcycle. The opening scene of the 1969 television show *Then Came Bronson* said it well. Bronson, a disillusioned journalist, is shown heading out of town on a Harley-Davidson 883cc XLH Sportster®. He was searching for the meaning of life after his buddy jumped to his death. The fellow in a station wagon next to him at the stoplight heading to work says, "Man, I wish I was you." Michael Parks, who played the sentient character, said, "Hang in there." The riding scenes were well staged in the idyllic Western landscape and sprinkled with enough reality via the occasional crash to educate the public of the dangers of riding. It certainly helped sell a few Harleys despite the shocking introduction of the Honda 750 that same year. He inspired many to strap a bedroll onto a sissy bar and head for the mountains.

Touring in absolute style and comfort is a great way for you and your mate to get away and see the country. The Honda Gold Wing® has marked its spot as the grandest of all touring bikes. Photo courtesy of Honda Motor Co., Inc.

Motorcycle touring is most enjoyable. There is nothing like riding down a softly winding road, sun kissed and stretched out like an endless ribbon, with only the hum of the motor and the whistling of the wind to remind us that we are not dreaming. The reliability of modern motorcycles has opened this segment up to everyone. You can tour on anything, but those seeking real comfort can opt for one of the many fully equipped bikes that make riding 400 miles a day seem like a run to the grocery store. Despite the impression people have that touring bikes are huge behemoths, there are many surprisingly sporty touring bikes out there. They are appropriately named sport-tourers. Most major manufacturers offer superb examples as part of their catalog.

Touring with friends has become very popular across the United States. It is a great way to have both private time and social enjoyment, while savoring the road ahead. The wonderful variety of bikes in this group ranged between American, Japanese, and German. Note the safe distance between these experienced riders.

Whenever we take to the road, we know people will be looking at us, in envy or disdain. The latter may not be because of an antisocial attitude, but rather in reaction to our arrogant mobility as we lane split through miles of motionless rush hour traffic. Motorcycles can go places cars can't, and that represents freedom. Even

traditional off-road and dual-sport bikes find themselves in urban environments because of their mobility. There is nothing I would rather have if I were a city dweller in the event I needed to get out of town fast during an emergency.

Bikes Are Gaining in Popularity

Bikes are everywhere today. That is a good thing. The greater people's awareness of bikes on the road, the safer those of us that ride will be. Automobile drivers are not initially programmed to see bikes, and it will be years before reliable proximity detectors are installed in every car to help save motorcyclists' lives. Bikes are smaller and present less of a threat to the average SUV. A motorcyclist's defensive driving skills will save his or her life on many days. Riding may be fun but is still dangerous in a world of automobiles.

How much fun is this! Motorcycling on two or three wheels certainly brings happiness. Not all motorcycles are small. This custom 1957 Chevy style trike will certainly attract attention, and hopefully the eye of a daydreaming automobile driver.

The advances in telecommunications have further threatened motorcyclists as devices allow ready texting on social networks, taking the driver's eyes off the road. Riding with the lights on certainly helps to attract attention. Vehicle-to-Vehicle (V2V) communications systems and on-board rider warning systems are improving every year. Robert Bosh LLC designed an ultrasonic sensor system that tells a rider whenever another vehicle is nearby. This is particularly helpful when changing lanes. The range extends to sixteen feet. In the event of an unfortunate crash, BMW's eCall system will alert authorities automatically of the bikes location for quick response.

More bikers on the road create greater awareness that we are sharing the same space. Those claiming that loud pipes save lives may be encouraging restrictive legislation. Noise level laws will ruin it for the rest of us who enjoy a more reasonable rumble resonating from the exhaust. Most of the noise heads out the back of a bike and will be of little use if a car makes a sudden left turn onto the road one is traveling. Left-turn accidents are the most common. A loud exhaust may be helpful when riding in an automobile's blind spot. There is, however, no substitute for defensive riding. Electric bikes without any exhaust noise will certainly require that.

The popularity of motorcycles has encouraged more and more manufacturers to design and build their own brand of motorcycle. The most successful new entries in the United States are Victory Motorcycles® and Indian, both divisions of Polaris® Industries, Inc. Despite Victory's challenging learning curve when it started in 1998, deep pockets and a remarkable corporate commitment have allowed the brand to mature. Fully modern, stylish, and reliable, the Victory has established itself as another great American motorcycle. Polaris' purchase of the iconic Indian brand in 2011 benefited from this experience. Its own Chief and Scout cruiser models launched with great accolades in 2014.

The Indian Chief, as created by Polaris' new Indian Motorcycle team, pays proper tribute to one of America's most iconic motorcycle brands. Photo courtesy of Indian Motorcycle International, LLC.

Korean and Chinese companies are not sitting idle while interest in motorcycles looms. Chinese manufacturer Lifan is making American styled cruisers with smaller displacement V-twin engines at half the price of other makes. Their reliability and quality is improving with each generation and will eventually become competitive as dealer networks emerge. Koreans have also entered the American market, and if history is an indicator, their proven capability of making superb automobiles at affordable prices is sure to carry over to motorcycles.

It seems just about anyone you talk to has either wanted to ride a bike or has ridden sometime in their past. One can detect a small sparkle in the eye when folks talk about their fling with motorcycles. Stories of moms threatening disownment and dads chasing bad-boy boyfriends are not uncommon. Everyone knows someone who had a bike. Ask your grandma if she has ever been on a bike, and the answer will probably be, "Yes."

Motorcycles not only provide transportation, but offer great vehicles for entertainment. Photo courtesy of Harley-Davidson.

The future of motorcycles will be nurtured by the dependence we have on them. Development continues to provide us with better, faster, safer, and nearly maintenance-free machines. Electric motorcycles are an example of that and are slowly emerging as alternatives to gasoline-powered vehicles. They not only satisfy environmental concerns, but provide extraordinary torque and smooth acceleration. Another benefit is that they are quiet. This makes them ideal for backyard fun in the suburbs.

There is perhaps one segment of motorcycles that is near obscurity, but still enjoys a following among a rare few. It is the category of "Rat Bike." Originally these bikes were just abused, dirty machines. They have now evolved into a trashy art form.

Like all good Rat bikes, this one also leaves its mark with a healthy oil puddle.

The Answer Is . . .

So, why do we need, or want, motorcycles? Is it for necessity, parking convenience, work, cheap transportation, lower insurance cost, adventure, or just fun? No doubt, it is for all of the above. As you read on, you'll see more of what this vast world on two wheels has to offer. Three-wheelers are also covered to some extent because of their direct relationship to two-wheeled motorcycles. Scooters and mopeds are not covered because they deserve volumes of their own, but parallel, motorcycle history verbatim. Many of the great motorcycle manufacturers produced these smaller, less expensive machines as well. They are often the only affordable means of transportation for millions of people. The line gets a bit fuzzy between a moped or scooter and a small motorcycle. Typically, wheel diameter, frame configuration, and engine size dictate the classification. Scooters can be very fast and should never be underestimated. This book will stay focused on motorcycles. The following chapters will dig deeper into this wonderful world.

The line between motorcycle and scooter can be a fine one. Power plants may be as large as those found on many motorcycles. They are offered with engines ranging from 50cc to 650cc. Unlike motorcycles, scooter engines are typically part of the rear wheel assembly, mounted under the seat. Wheel diameter tends to average 13 inches, and is no larger than 16 inches. As this photo of the popular Piaggio Liberty so well presents, scooters are defined by a platform below the feet and feature a step-through design. The Liberty comes with ABS, a real plus for urban riders dealing with stop-and-go traffic on wet roads. Photo courtesy of Piaggio & C SpA.

Motorcycles are works of art. Their organic design is not by chance. Every component was created by the minds of artist-engineers. Motorcycles have been exhibited at the finest of galleries but are best when displayed in the environment they thrive in.

Photo by Paul Ensanian

Harley-Davidson

Harley-Davidson

Chapter 2

MOTORCYCLES IN OUR SOCIETY

From its humble beginnings as an affordable means of transportation, motorcycles have contributed immensely to our society. They have become a vehicle for independence, socialization, and belonging. The image of those who ride them has changed over the decades—from the working man able to commute to a job previously out of reach, to outlaw bikers terrorizing towns in the 1950s. Today, most motorcyclists are respectable citizens looking for a few hours of leisure time on the roads we travel.

A Lasting Impression

My first memory of a motorcycle is at a street race in West Berlin, Germany, when I was about five years old. Petrol-powered motorcycles had already been around for sixty-nine years. My uncle, a sports car enthusiast, took me to races frequently. I remember asking him, "Why don't we have one of these?" The answer was predictable: "Too dangerous."

The sixty-two years that followed have taught me that motorcycling is what it is for each individual. People will develop the need to ride based on their own values and experience. When one announces that he or she is buying a motorcycle, loved ones will often question the sensibility of doing so. It can come at any time. Events in our culture are to blame. We are surrounded by motorcycles. The idea to buy one may have been born out of an ad, a movie, or an event like the one in Berlin. It could have been sparked by a casual glimpse of a carefree weekend warrior riding next to the car on the parkway. It could simply have been in reaction to a lousy day at the office.

In reflecting back on history, we can see the impact motorized bicycles have had on our lives. Certain brands of machines seem to follow us through time. Harley-Davidsons endure in the United States, Triumphs in the U.K., and Moto Guzzis in Italy. There was one brand that clearly stood out at the Berlin races. The bikes had a circular logo with blue and white triangles. I was to learn much later that the BMW (Bavarian Motor Works) logo reflected its original

This fuzzy 16mm movie frame of a sidecar race on a Berlin street was taken the day motorcycling made its first impression on me. Prewar and postwar BMW, DKW, Zündapp, and NSUs were racing on the cobbled streets with little but the curb to direct their path. Film by Ara Movsessian.

heritage of being an airplane engine manufacturer during World War I. The logo represented a rotating propeller. After the war, production focused on making motorcycle engines for other manufacturers. The original 500cc flat twin was based on BMW's early airplane engines and shared similarity to the horizontally opposed British-made Douglas. To this day, the "boxer" engine holds a prominent position in the BMW line of products.

A flawless example of BMW's first motorcycle, the R32, made between 1923 and 1926. The "R" stands for Rad, the German word for wheel. It produced a bit over 8 hp with its 494cc two-cylinder engine. The engine's form was inspired by the British Douglas. BMW shared many good ideas with other makers, including leaf spring front suspension from Indian and ABC, and shaft drive from the Belgian FN.

The Motorcycle Appears

Bikes and the people who ride them have always drawn attention. This started the very first time a motorcycle took to the streets, possibly as early as 1867. Massachusetts' inventor Sylvester Roper was working on a grand idea: a powered bicycle. By 1869, he was turning heads as he chugged gently along on his steam-powered bike in Roxbury, Massachusetts. The same scene was taking place in France, as Pierre Michaux rode his steam bike around Paris. Michaux was known for his advanced bicycle design featuring pedals on the front wheel. He adapted a small Perreaux steam engine to one of his bikes, and created a motorcycle. The trend for steam-powered bikes continued with Arizona native Lucius Copeland in 1881. Steam, however, could not compete with the more practical petrol-fueled internal combustion engines. After all, they did not require waiting for water to boil before rolling off.

A replica of Copeland's 1884 steam-powered American Star high-wheeler. The impractical nature of a high-wheeled bicycle prompted Copeland to manufacture three-wheeled steam-powered carriages instead. Photo courtesy of Bonhams.

Not long after Copeland's debut, Gottlieb Daimler's "Einspur" (one track) became the first petrol-powered motorcycle. It created a stir in 1885 as the machine putted along at seven miles per hour on the cobblestone streets of Cannstatt, Germany. Dozens of other inventors followed, amazing people as they rolled their machines out of workshops to test them on public roads. This fascination for anything mechanical, particularly motorcycles, continues today.

A replica of Daimler's motorcycle as seen at the AMA Hall of Fame Museum in Pickerington, Ohio. This machine was built by enthusiasts Jim Carlson, Roy Behner, and Ray Behner. Even though intended as a test-bed for engine development, it is considered to be the first true petrol-powered motorcycle, despite the training wheels.

The advances Daimler and his associate, Wilhelm Maybach, made on the original four-stroke cycle engine, developed by Nikolaus Otto, launched an exciting era in mankind's history. They mobilized the world. We'll look at the evolution of engines in greater detail in the next chapter.

Machines like this internal combustion engine–powered three-wheeler blew minds as it rumbled along on the streets of Mannheim, Germany. Most people could not have imagined horseless carriages. Karl Benz registered the patent for this vehicle on January 29, 1886. As Daimler's company archives state, this "effectively becomes the 'birth certificate' of the automobile." The slow-revolving engine produced only 0.8 hp at 300 rpm. Photo courtesy of Daimler AG.

Bicycles continued their own development. Steel frames fitted with two wheels of equal size appeared around the same time Daimler was experimenting with the Einspur. They were called "safety bicycles" because of their inherent stability compared to the high-wheelers of the day.

Safety bicycles brought mobility to the masses. People were able to commute further to work, or enjoy a casual day pedaling about. These young ladies from around 1900 have bikes that feature solid steel tube frames, chain drive, brakes, and pneumatic tires. The loop frame became popular with motorcycle builders in that it provided a perfect space to nestle an engine. Photo from the Larry Hart Collection, Schenectady County Historical Society, Grems-Doolittle Library.

The marriage of the safety bicycle and a new engine design by the French brought the motorcycle to the people. The development of smaller, lighter engines allowed for this union and resulted in easy to handle motorbikes and tricycles. Of greatest significance were the independent efforts of Peugeot, and the team of Count Albert De Dion and his mechanic, Georges Bouton. The company De Dion and Bouton, formed in 1882, developed a small petrol motor capable of an astonishing 1,800 rpm (revolutions per minute), twice that of the Daimler. Twice the rpm meant nearly double the power. The design of their engine was to be modeled by all other manufactures, including Harley-Davidson and Indian. Motorcycles powered by De Dion type engines quickly became popular in large urban areas throughout Europe.

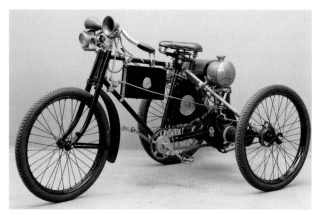

De Dion-Bouton powered tricycles were very popular at the turn of the twentieth century. The design was licensed to a number of makers in Europe as well as the United States. Pictured is a 1902 Phebus. Photo courtesy of Yesterdays Antique Motorcycles.

Not everyone supported motorized vehicles. Special interests in the U.K. pushing railroads made it difficult for those trying to promote road-going steam carriages and the newer internal combustion–powered tricycles and bicycles. The Locomotive Acts of 1865 set strict speed limits of four mph in the country, and two mph in urban areas. Someone actually had to walk ahead of cars with a red flag to warn horses and pedestrians. Fortunately, most of the restrictions were repealed by 1896. A twenty-mile-per-hour speed limit in England, however, forced those wishing to race to look elsewhere. The French, on the other hand, enjoyed much greater freedom. Napoleon had built a superb road system that welcomed motorized transportation.

Things were not the same in Japan. Jeffrey Alexander's excellent work, *Japan's Motorcycle Wars: An Industry History*, tells us that the roads were quite underdeveloped compared to Europe and the United States. They were friendlier to rickshaws than the frail motorcycles imported by foreigners. He states that records indicate the first motorcycle arrived in 1896. It was a German-made Hildebrand and

Wolfmüller. This inspired Shimazu Narazo to build Japan's first motorcycle by 1909. It featured his own 400cc two-stroke engine mounted on a Toyoda bicycle frame. Improvements to the road system began in the 1920s, greatly encouraging motorized transport of all kinds. Japan had no idea that it was destined to become the world's largest producer of motorcycles in the decades that followed.

Considered the world's first production motorcycle, the 1,500cc 2.5 hp Hildebrand and Wolfmüller inspired many to build motorcycles. The design had its issues, and several unconventional features. The most obvious was that the engine's connecting rods were attached directly to the rear wheel, the latter acting as the flywheel itself. This limited rpm to just 250. The concept was in line with Roper's steam-powered bike and the mystery machine developed by Edward Pennington of the same era. Estimates suggest that perhaps as many as 2,000 may have been built between 1894 and 1897. It was a milestone bike in motorcycle history. Photo Science Museum / Science & Society Picture Library.

Motorcycles Come to Speed

Bicycle racing was all the rage during the late nineteenth century in the Western world. Competitions held on large oval wooden racetracks called velodromes gave the large crowds their first glimpse of what a two-wheeled motorized bike looked like. These bulky machines had huge engines running at an astonishingly slow 300 rpm. They were used as pace vehicles for the racers. Bicyclists would ride within their draft, gaining greater speed.

Pictured is a typical pacer motorcycle used for bicycle racing in velodromes near the turn of the twentieth century. This photo was actually taken in 1949 of Margaret Sutcliffe at the Herne Hill Velodrome being paced by an antique Triumph. Photo Mortons Archive.

A pacer used for bicycle velodromes as displayed at the wonderful Motorcyclepedia Museum in Newburgh, NY.

Two Great American Motorcycle Companies Emerge

George M. Hendee was both a bicycle racer and manufacturer based in Springfield, Massachusetts, at the turn of the twentieth century. He was so impressed with a light pacer designed by Oscar Hedstrom

that he immediately recognized the vast potential market for motorized bicycles not just for racing, but for transportation as well. Their combined effort resulted in America's first successful motorcycle manufacturer. The Indian motorcycle was thus born in 1901 and remains an icon to this day.

George Hendee, founder of Hendee Manufacturing Company sitting atop a 1904 Indian as designed by Oscar Hedstrom. The 224cc single-cylinder engine was built by the Aurora Automatic Machinery Co. out of Illinois, and mated to an Indian bicycle in Springfield. He launched the Indian Motocycle Company in 1923, choosing to omit the 'r'.

The cost effectiveness of motorcycles over maintaining horses prompted many to make the switch, particularly police departments. Early Indian singles were elegant machines that produced 1-3/4 hp.

The very same year Indian started producing motorcycles, William S. Harley completed a technical drawing of an engine made to fit into a bicycle frame. He was only twenty-one years old. Within a couple of years, William S. Harley and Arthur Davidson sold their first motorcycle. It was a racing machine, with a 3-1/8 inch bore and 3-1/2 inch stroke.

Harley-Davidson's first factory as it stood in Milwaukee in 1903. The 10' x 15' shed was the beginning of a true American success story. The "Motor Company" has continuously produced motorcycles since that year, resulting in a company with over six billion dollars in consolidated revenue today. Photo courtesy of Harley-Davidson.

Speed Kills

Motorcycles slimmed down and developed enough power to become spectacles on the board tracks themselves. By 1910, motorcycles no larger than a heavy-duty bicycle were racing around on the boards at over ninety miles per hour. Velodromes were enlarged to become motordromes. Board track racing in the United States was a fast and furious sport that created heroes and lots of media attention during its reign between 1909 and 1913. The great number of injuries and fatalities put an end to it within a few short years. Many racers and spectators were killed. Even the New York Times ran a front page story in 1912 on

what the press referred to as "murderdromes," after a tragic episode at a track in Newark, New Jersey, killed the famous racer Eddie Hasha and five others.

Board track racing provided an exciting venue at major urban motordromes. Young men risked their lives to earn celebrity. This photo was taken at the Los Angeles Stadium Motordrome. Racing engines burnt a lot of oil back then.

Motorcycling got its first real black eye here in the United States as a result of these tragedies on the boards. The cinema quickly helped with some well-deserved damage control. Motorcycles made great props and became a staple in Max Sennett's slapstick silent films. Sennett was building his Keystone Studios right at the time Thor, Pope, Harley-Davidson, and Indian were producing truly reliable and roadworthy motorcycles.

Rebuilding the Image

The bad press resulting from board track racing fatalities encouraged manufacturers to promote the motorcycle for general transportation and recreational purposes. They encouraged their appearance in the movies.

A Harley-Davidson with sidecar made a great prop for the Keystone Cops. Photo Hulton Archive/Getty Images.

Charlie Chaplin, Buster Keaton, Mabel Normand, and the bumbling Keystone Cops used them with great effect as moving acrobatic stages for their antics. The motorcycle scene in *Mabel at the Wheel* brought smiles to many faces as Chaplin demonstrated his shaky riding skills on a single-cylinder Thor. He managed to keep the bike from falling but loses the sweet Mabel on a bumpy dirt road. Silent films introduced the idea of motorcycling to a lot of folks.

The happy young man is sitting on a typical motorcycle of 1912. These were elegant machines, requiring pedaling to get started. Lighting on early machines was provided by carbide lamps. Acetylene gas was produced by combining calcium carbide pellets with water in a small reservoir. These units were actually brighter than first generation electric lights.

Motorcycles continued to grow in popularity. People pedaling bikes wanted to go farther for both work and play. Smaller De Dion–based motors provided a solution. A number of American and European makers offered compact motor units that could easily be "clipped-on" to bicycles. Interestingly, clip-on engines were what started Honda's path to becoming a motorcycle giant in 1946.

A typical example of a small motor adapted to a standard heavy-duty bicycle. The unit shown is a 1913 Shaw. The black lever in the center of the photo tensions an idler pulley, allowing the belt to grab the crankshaft pulley and drive the rear wheel. Stanley Shaw started his business in 1911 out of a shop in Galesburg, Kansas. Motors were sold between $35 and $40.

Rural mailmen loved motorcycles for running their routes. Motorcycle combinations with box type sidecars became efficient delivery vehicles for many businesses. Motorcars and motorcycles offered another great advantage: they were cheaper to keep than horses. Prior to motorized carriages, the horse and buggy was pretty much the only way a family could get around on its own. The cost to maintain a horse was, and still is, substantial. Not only is space required for a stable, but hay and oats are costly fuels. And the beast consumed the fuel even if not providing service. Motorcycles ran on petroleum distillates like benzene and gasoline. These were available at drug stores and cheaper than buying bushels of oats.

By 1904, Indians adopted their famous red paint scheme. The humped gas tank resulted in the nickname "camel back" for machines produced between 1902 and 1909.

Motorcycles became so popular that nearly a hundred individual makers supplied the two-wheeled conveyances here in the United States, and equally as many in Europe. Interestingly enough, history has repeated itself in that the popularity of custom motorcycles today has created a similar scenario. Hundreds of small shops are putting out a handful of exciting and unique bikes. A new cottage industry has been born.

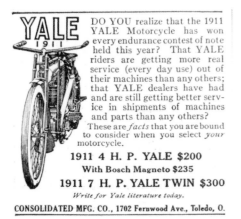

A typical motorcycle ad of the era.

The Wagner Motorcycle Company of St. Paul offered several models during its five-year run between 1909 and 1914. The designs were similar to the competition as is apparent by the period ad above. However, one model stood out. It was a bike made specifically for women. Perhaps as a publicity stunt, the owner's daughter, Clara, became the first official female motorcyclist as she rode her Wagner on long journeys.

During the salad days of motorcycling, there was always something going on that was worth a story in the papers and kept motorcycles in the public's eye. Erwin George "Cannonball" Baker was making history racing across the country in Stutz Bearcat automobiles and on Indian motorcycles. He set 143 endurance speed records, the most famous of which was his cross-country run on a 1914 Indian. He covered the 3,379 miles between San Diego and New York in eleven and a half days. Mind you, there were very few paved roads back then, and electric headlights were about as good as a candle in the wind. Day-by-day episodes of Baker's travels made great reading as he raced through small towns across the country.

"Cannonball" Baker during another one of his transcontinental runs in 1919. His remarkable ability to endure the physical demands of long distance riding under all sorts of conditions made for great stories in the papers and magazines. Indian provided the 7 hp Powerplus 61 cubic inch V-twin as Baker's sponsor.

Motorcycles Report for Duty

It took some time for the military to accept the motorcycle. Equestrian units, such as the cavalry and the messenger corps, were not keen on giving up their faithful steeds to those newfangled machines. By World War I, it was clear that the motorcycle had its place in the armies of Europe. It was less expensive to run than hay burning horses and proved quite capable of carrying messages, supplies, and guns. The latter really sold the deal. Mounting a machine gun on a horse was out of the question. Tens of thousands of units were ordered, giving the top makers a real boost in production.

World War I also gave motorcycles the opportunity to exercise their patriotic duty. Harley-Davidson, Indian, and Excelsior were the largest of the scores of motorcycle companies in the United States. These three mobilized their factories to meet the demand in 1917. Over three thousand motorcycle technicians were recruited to service these machines in the field. Despite the fact that more than 70,000 bikes were produced for the wartime effort, many of them never saw action on the European front. Of the 41,000 machines manufactured by Indian, only 10,000 made it overseas. Fully crated Indians were popping up at surplus sales for decades following the war.

Both Harley-Davidson and Indian committed much of their production to wartime machines. This 1917 Indian combination may not be the most practical war weapon, but it made for a good press photo for the Army and to sell the concept of motorcycles.

European motorcycle manufacturers answered the call as well. Noted British makes, such as Douglas, Triumph, Rudge-Multi, and Royal Enfield dedicated all their efforts to producing machines. Triumph alone supplied nearly 30,000 of its reliable three-speed Model H bikes. Germans preferred the NSU, while Belgians supplied their famous FN bikes after occupation. They were all primarily used for dispatch-

ing messages between units since wireless radios were not yet available on the combat front. Sidecar rigs were ideal for resupplying the troops in remote areas with poor roads. They also doubled to help evacuate the wounded.

A World War I–era British Rudge-Multi single-cylinder, belt drive motorcycle. It featured multiple gearing using a unique clutch as seen on the lower left of the motor. Twist grip throttles were not always employed on the early machines. Speed was adjusted via a lever on the handlebars. Rudge was like most other early motorcycle marques, having its roots in bicycle manufacturing. Dan Rudge was a bicycle builder who died in 1880—thirty years before the motorcycles bearing his name would win many races in England.

World War I also signaled the beginning of Indian's great decline, and Harley-Davidson's ascent to becoming the largest motorcycle manufacturer in the United States. Indian banked nearly all of its production on military contracts. Harley, on the other hand, only committed to 15,000 bikes. This strategy allowed it to continue to develop its domestic markets and supply dealers with new machines. Indian dealers were short-changed. They begged for much needed spare parts from the Springfield, Massachusetts, factory. New bikes were not to be had. This was the turning point in American motorcycle history. A good portion of Indian dealers changed to the Harley-Davidson, Excelsior, Emblem, and Reading-Standard brands.

The popularity of motorcycles boomed following the war. Even the Sears-Roebuck catalog featured motorcycles branded under the Sears name. That tradition was to continue on for the next fifty years, with the name Allstate replacing Sears on the tanks.

Technology was struggling to keep up with the demand for more powerful bikes. Metallurgy lagged behind engine design, unable to handle the power they produced. That did not stop development and popularity. Europeans and Americans were on the move. It was an exciting era. Racing in the U.K. became big as both the Brooklands track and the first Isle of Man TT (Tourist Trophy) opened in 1907. They allowed manufacturers to pit themselves against each other. This was not only good for publicity, but also good for testing out

new concepts. Racing, therefore, greatly encouraged development, and motorcycles in Europe were starting to show common design elements. They were clearly lighter and nimbler than American machines featuring larger and heavier engines. Americans liked the idea of more power, especially privateer racers. Several American companies already produced larger V-twins, including Indian, Thor, and Reading Standard. Harley-Davidson, who had been experimenting with racing V-twins since 1907, responded in 1909. It introduced its first twin for sale to a waiting public. Much improvement was to follow as power attracted buyers. By 1915, the 60.32 cubic inch (998cc) 11 hp Model K V-twin was introduced. It featured a three-speed gearbox and chain final drive. It proved to be a very reliable foundation for its line of large motorcycles.

Example of an original unrestored Sears motorcycle as sold through their catalog starting in 1913. Sears rebranded bikes made by other manufacturers, like Thor. This example features standard cycle parts with an Indianapolis-made Spacke V-twin engine.

Harley-Davidson's 1915 V-twin featured a three-speed gearbox and chain final drive. The company's decision to support its domestic dealer network during WWI with machines like this gave it an advantage over rival Indian after the war.

A 1919 Reading-Standard V-twin was typical of American design following the first war. These were very reliable machines made in Reading, Pennsylvania, between 1903 and 1924. Other than Harley-Davidson, Indian, and Excelsior, the Reading Standard survived the war financially. It was noted for its side-valve engines, later adopted by the other major manufacturers. The V-twin above is 1,100cc in displacement, and sold for around $300. This is an example of an unrestored original; worth more than a complete restoration among serious collectors.

The fascination with motorcycles continued as they became staples at county fairs and the circus. Horse racing tracks soon gave way to the more exciting dirt track motorcycle races. Considered safer than board track racing, dirt trackers attracted amateurs from every corner of the country. Safety gear was sorely missing though. Most racers simply wore heavy wool sweaters and leather football helmets.

From the onset, motorcycle dealers encouraged group events and riding clubs to sustain their brands. Many clubs wore uniforms of specific colors to differentiate themselves from other groups. The word "colors" today often refers to a club's identifying patches. Pictured is a gathering of club members in Bute, Montana, around a hundred years ago. Photo from US Library of Congress.

Photo courtesy of Harley Davidson.

62

Weekends saw countless county fairgrounds feature dirt track racing events. Motorcycles used for daily transportation did double-duty as racing machines. Photo from US Library of Congress.

Harley-Davidson began production of its first V-twin in 1909. Photo courtesy of Harley-Davidson.

More powerful machines created other venues. Hill climbing became popular as racers outfitted their bikes with chains and raced up steep slopes to reach the top. Many officially sanctioned hill climbs attracted professional racers. Carnivals also featured bikes built for a unique form of entertainment, riding on the vertical walls of barrel-shaped motordromes. These "Wall of Death" exhibits still draw crowds today.

"Wall of Death" attractions have endured eighty years as they still attract crowds at amusement parks and motorcycle events.

Tough Times Ahead

Things were going pretty well for motorcycles for a while until the Great Depression hit in 1929. Demand for bikes was simply not there. The Model T had already been around for much over a decade and was available used for under $100. If a family had money, they would rather buy a cheap old Ford than a bike during those days. Famous makes such as Pope, Pierce, Merkel, and Thor had already succumbed to the manufacturing dominance of Indian and Harley-Davidson. They closed shop long before the collapse of the stock market. Others, like Emblem of Angola, NY, hung in a bit longer, shifting its sales to Europe. Even the mighty Excelsior closed its doors to manufacturing the famous brand in 1924. Its spin-off brand, the Super-X, kept producing superb

large capacity V-twins into 1931, but could not match the lower production cost of the Harley-Davidson factory. The same scenario played out across the ocean. Manufacturers in France, Belgium, Czechoslovakia, Sweden, and Switzerland had a difficult time competing with the big manufacturers in Germany, Italy, and Britain. Some were still struggling with rebuilding their factories after the war. BMW's strength as an airplane engine maker gave it a clear advantage to enter motorcycle manufacturing in Germany.

Norton, a company that started producing motorcycles in England in 1902, hit a home run with its 500cc overhead valve large singe-cylinder bikes during the 1920s and 1930s. This Model 20 was a performance version with two exhaust ports. These machines established the marque as a highly reliable brand and racing leader. The European tradition of making good handling smaller displacement bikes, compared to the large American V-twins, would win them the US market in the 1950s. Photo courtesy of Yesterdays Antique Motorcycles.

Things were not good for motorcycle sales until the mid-1930s. The era did bring many new design concepts. British and Italian designers were on a hot streak. Crocker, Harley-Davidson, and Vincent introduced new production overhead valve engines that took street bike performance to the next level. Advances in engineering also reduced the mechanical maintenance associated with ownership. Speed records were being broken on both sides of the ocean as manufacturers clamored for market share. Fast bikes always sold better than slow ones.

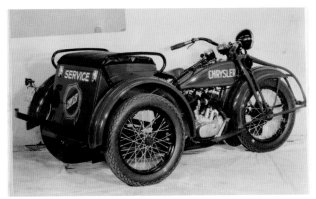

Introduced in 1937, the sturdy and reliable WL 45 flathead was Harley's first model with recirculating lubrication, and was produced until 1973 to power the company's practical three-wheelers used for delivery and service calls. Ease of maintenance and reliability kept the simple side-valve around despite the company's introduction of overhead valve motors in 1936. Photo courtesy of Harley-Davidson.

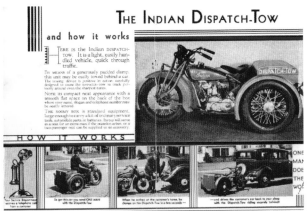

This interesting phenomenon that evolved out of both Indian and Harley-Davidson during the Depression years would be enviable today—the Indian Dispatch-Tow (1931) and the Harley-Davidson Servi-Car (1932). These three-wheelers started replacing large sidecar delivery outfits, and became very popular among auto service shops and car dealers. The service person would make a housecall to pick up the car. He'd attach his trike to the rear bumper of the car to be serviced with a special hitch, drive it back to the shop, and return it after repairs. The first problem preventing this kind of great service today would be the cheap plastic disposable bumpers on modern cars. Pictured is an original Indian dealer ad courtesy of the Antique Motorcycle Club of America.

Even though motorcycle sales suffered during the Depression era, they did offer an affordable alternative to more expensive delivery vans. Large sidecar outfits like this 1930 Indian 402 four-cylinder could haul both personnel and cargo.

War Calls Again

The 1930s also brought bad blood between brands. The Harley-Indian wars were at their peak as rider loyalty created rifts between friends. Dealers didn't do much to discourage it. A new war looming across the ocean, however, focused everyone on more serious matters. Indian by this time had lost its edge as a manufacturer and was hoping to regain profits from war contracts. Once again an automobile put a damper on things. The Willy's Jeep nearly eliminated the need for motorcycles on the front. Two-way radios further reduced reliance on dispatch riders. It was a disappointing turn of events for the American motorcycle manufacturers.

The small four-wheel drive utility vehicle made by Willys-Overland Motors known as the Jeep had a great effect on wartime motorcycle production. The inexpensive and light Piper Cub L-4 aircraft had a similar effect on the more costly reconnaissance airplane makers. Photo from the Rudy Arnold Photo Collection, Smithsonian National Air and Space Museum (NASM XRA-1075).

Indian converted its 45 cubic inch, 750cc Scout model for military specifications for WWII. Full valance fenders were replaced by simple mudguards to deal with combat conditions. Indian also offered an underpowered 500cc version; the 741.

Harley-Davidson produced tens of thousands of its W model 750cc side-valve toward the war effort dubbed the WLA. The L stood for higher compression, while the A stood for Army. Many were sold to other countries, like Russia. The large number of surplus WLAs available to civilians after the war inspired many owners to chop and bob them for street use.

Indian responded to a military bid for desert warfare motorcycles with the 1941 Model 841 90 degree 45 cubic inch V-twin. This bike featured a transversely mounted engine, shaft drive, foot shift, and hand clutch—advanced features for Indians of the day. One thousand of these were delivered to the Army. Harley-Davidson's "XA" entry emulated BMW's opposing twin design. Neither model was adopted by the Army in volume. Instead, flathead V-twins were preferred.

This highly restored and customized example of an Indian 841 has been "civilianized" with fully skirted fenders.

The British motorcycle industry had flourished prior to the Depression. Scores of manufacturers had established loyal followings among customers and race enthusiasts. Ariel, AJS, Matchless, BSA, Norton, Brough, Velocette, Triumph, Douglas, Royal Enfield, Excelsior (unrelated to United States maker), Panther, Sunbeam, and Vincent became household names as their machines became fixtures on the international race circuits. Orders for war bikes allowed several marques to regain their strength. The largest manufacturer leading into WWII was BSA. Birmingham Small Arms Company was founded in 1854 as a gun manufacturing consortium. Its overwhelming production capability made it a major motorcycle manufacturer in England between 1905 and 1973. BSA alone supplied over one hundred thousand motorcycles to the Allied forces. Unlike Indian and Harley-Davidson, British motorcycle manufacturers gained from the war. Their smaller, lighter machines were more useful over rough terrain than the heavier American models. An astonishing total of 425,000 British wartime motorcycles were made.

Japanese wartime motorcycle production was significantly less compared to the Allies. Several manufacturers, including Miyata, Meguro, Showa, and Maruyama made light machines for dispatch duty. The military spec Type-97 motorcycle, built by several manufacturers, was the heavyweight, available with a powered sidecar. A young automobile service station worker, Soichiro Honda, did not engage in motorcycle manufacture at this time but found opportunity in mastering the difficult art of manufacturing piston rings. He supplied them to the Japanese aircraft industry for its fighters. His skill in advanced manufacturing practices was to change the motorcycle industry.

BSA supported its country's war effort with a low cost, easy to maintain side-valve single-cylinder bike like this 496cc M20. Over 126,300 were made. Side-valve engines simplify maintenance by having fewer moving parts associated with opening and closing the valves. The cast iron head saved on precious aluminum needed for aircraft manufacture.

Familiar to all WWII movie buffs is the BMW with sidecar. It is shown here with a model R12 motorcycle, made between 1935 and 1942. The opposing twin displaced 745cc put out about 20 hp at 4,000 rpm and had a top speed of 66 mph. Photo courtesy of Mike Dunn.

Triumph's Coventry factory was demolished by the German Blitz on November 14, 1940. The company set up temporary shop in Warwick to meet its commitment to wartime production. A brand new factory was built in Meriden. Fully operational by 1942, it continued to produce Triumphs until 1983. Photo shows some of the thousands of bikes awaiting shipment in 1943. Many surplus bikes became bargain purchases for postwar riders. Photo: Morton's Archives.

The end of World War II signaled a new era for motorcycles. Returning GIs on both continents were looking to escape the horrors of war and enjoy the freedom of the open roads. This was particularly true here in the United States. The motorcycle was an inexpensive means to achieve this.

World War II German sidecar combinations are alive and well among a special group of vintage bike enthusiasts devoted to their restoration and use. Pictured is a pair of 750cc Zündapps outfitted with extra fuel cans, ammo storage, and machine gun turret. Photo courtesy of Mike Dunn.

Two-Strokes to the Rescue

British manufacturers were under a government directive to "export or die," having to sell the majority of their production overseas in order to rebuild the nation's economy. BSA repaired its bombed factories to continue its leadership role, supplying small, inexpensive two-stroke bikes for the people of England. Its larger bikes were shipped to more lucrative markets abroad. Petrol rationing was a reality. It was based on working status and need. The average motorist was only allowed a few gallons a month. It lasted until 1950. Small motorcycles offered an immediate solution to the masses of commuters needing transportation. Their thrifty two-strokes could go farther with less gas.

The very same scenario was playing out in Japan. Industrious Japanese, like Honda, took to the challenge of mobilizing the people. Simple, inexpensive transportation drives emerging economies. He began by installing war-surplus 50cc Tohatsu two-stroke generator engines onto bicycles. He only had 500 units available to produce the popular add-on that drove the rear wheel with a belt. By November of 1946, Honda built his own 50cc Type-A 1/2-hp motor. Demand was high as others adapted the motor to bikes. Honda saw the opportunity and built his first complete motorcycle in 1949. It was a 98cc 2.3 hp two-stroke called the Type-D. Honda called the machine "Dream" based on his dream to build motorcycles. Other manufacturers were doing the same, including Miyata, Sanyo, and Showa. Suzuki, an automobile manufacturer, followed Honda's footsteps by introducing its own 36cc clip-on motor to power bicycles in 1952. Soichiro Honda could not have imagined that by 2014 his company would have produced its 300 millionth motorcycle.

The Germans Give Back

The Allies deemed the German designs as patent-free as part of their war reparations. Harley-Davidson took advantage of that to introduce the S125, its own faithful reproduction of the great little RT125 commuter bike made by Germany's DKW. Britain's BSA also introduced a DKW clone called the Bantam. Yamaha®, a company rooted in musical instrument manufacture, did the same by introducing a 125cc in 1954, following a visit to Germany. Named the YA-1, it was remarkably similar to the DKW design. The small two-stroke with its Teutonic heritage brought transportation to a lot of people that otherwise may never have been able to afford it. There is no doubt that it was during the postwar reconstruction era that the seeds for Japan's dominance as a motorcycle manufacturer were being sown. Occupying US forces saw a country of dedicated and disciplined people capable of rebuilding itself. America supplied aid. An underlying reason was the threat that a floundering Japanese economy could render it to communism. It was in everyone's interest to see Japan succeed as an industrial nation.

The BSA Bantam engine was only different from Harley's version in the placement of the foot controls. As was traditional before the 1970s, British bikes had the transmission foot shift lever on the right side. The Bantam survived an illustrious twenty-three-year run, with numerous model improvements, including a 175cc engine with 7.5 hp and a top speed of 60 mph.

Not all small utilitarian two-strokes were founded on German designs. New Orleans–based Simplex produced the lightweight Servi-Cycle between 1935 and 1960. The later models were offered as variable-speed automatics. The Simplex brand name was used by several manufacturers, including British, Italian, and Dutch makers. Photo courtesy of Division of Work & Industry, National Museum of American History, Smithsonian Institution.

Imagine telling your buddies that you got a new vintage Harley® and then showing up on this 1949 S125. Despite its modest size, and 4.5 hp, it's a reliable performer and is quite collectible.

Even Indian Motorcycles tried its hand at small, entry-level two-stroke bikes after the war by importing Czechoslovakian-made 125cc CZ motorcycles. This nice example, restored by William Becker, is a 1948. Indian advertised it as, "Now you can buy an Indian for only $381." Photo by Roman Torres.

Made in Japan

Japan became well known for its great reverse engineering skills. It imported motorcycles from all over the world to copy—the same as it did with German cameras to launch its optical industry. Nearly sixty motorcycle makers emerged, producing small, light machines for the population. Larger machines were also available from companies like Cabton. The company was Japan's largest motorcycle manufacturer prior to 1940. They made bikes with 250–600cc displacements. Cabton's RTS 600 model of 1953 was a 28 hp vertical twin capable of 80 mph.

German designs clearly influenced and propelled Japan's postwar motorcycle industry. It is evident in this DKW. The German company would provide a two-stroke engine foundation for many companies, including British, American, Russian, and Japanese makers. Photo courtesy of Mike Dunn.

Tohatsu was another big player in Japan, making a 60cc bike called the Puppy. It dominated motorcycle production in 1955, producing a remarkable 72,000 units. Stale designs could not keep the company in the market as Honda dominated in the years to follow.

Another great brand entering the postwar motorcycle arena in 1949 was Kawasaki. The company had an advantage over other manufacturers with its strong foundation in engine design and manufacture. Its entrée was a 148cc four-stroke powered bike. Even though Kawasaki was the last of the "big-four" Japanese motorcycle manufacturers (Honda, Yamaha, Suzuki, Kawasaki) to enter the market, it has endured as a major player.

Rikuo continued to make the Harley-Davidson reproduction, but under their own badge. Seeing success, Subaru (Fuji) jumped on board with its Rabbit model, and Mitsubishi with its Silver Pigeon. Meguro Manufacturing Company was a large maker of motorcycles that produced a broad variety of OHV singles and twins after the war. Meguro was ultimately absorbed by Kawasaki in 1964 after several years of partnership.

Miyata also jumped into consumer production immediately after the war in 1946 with its 200cc models. The company had a long history of bicycle production. As BSA, it had its roots in gun manufacturing. Import competition drove it to repurpose its barrels for bicycle frames early in the twentieth century. Their interest in motorcycles was kindled after a Triumph was imported for evaluation in 1914.

This rare 1956 Yamaguchi represented the classic Japanese postwar motorcycle. The bikes resembled European models with their DKW-like two-strokes, plunger frames, and elegant styling. Photo courtesy of Bonhams.

Despite the growing domestic market in Japan during the late 1940s, Japanese manufacturers struggled to expand abroad. Their machines were considered unrefined and dated in comparison to the newer European bikes. The words Made in Japan were not flattering. Unbeknownst to the British, who enjoyed dominance in the motorcycle industry, their fate was being determined by a handful of industrious Japanese motorcycle makers as early as 1950. Soichiro Honda had great dreams.

German maker DKW continued building motorcycles and mopeds after the war. Their Victoria and Express brands were combined under the Zweirad Union banner in 1958 to produce some interesting looking bikes through 1974. Photo by Stephen Covell.

Made in Russia

Much of the discussion on motorcycle history revolves around American, British, and Japanese makes. Motorcycle production in Russia and members of the former Soviet Union was just as significant. It rivaled world production and developed many noted brands: CZ, Dnepr, IMZ Ural®, IZH, Jawa®, Minsk, MZ, NATI, PMZ, TIZ, TMZ, Vostok, Volk, and more. Many of the machines were reverse-engineered from popular European models—something that helped Japan launch its motorcycle enterprise as well. The popularity of the Ural brand has brought awareness of Russian-made bikes to most Western enthusiasts over the past thirty years. Russian bikes have a good following in the United States with many forums, the most popular being russianiron.com/forums/.

Russia's largest postwar motorcycle maker, IZH, a division of arms manufacturer Kalashnikov Concern, was also heavily influenced by DKW and Adler designs. Pictured is the very popular Planeta-2, built between 1965 and 1971. Its sister, the Jupiter, was a two-cylinder two-stroke of the same 350cc displacement. IZH was founded in 1928 and became one of the largest motorcycle manufacturers in the world. Photo courtesy of Kalashnikov Concern Press-Service.

Postwar Russian motorcycle production boomed. Companies used the available German designs to build millions of practical motorcycles for commuters. Most were two-strokes because of the inherent simplicity of that type of motor. Pictured is the IZH assembly line during the 1950s. Photo courtesy of Kalashnikov Concern Press-Service.

IZH continued to develop its designs to meet the high demand for motorcycles throughout Eastern Europe and Asia. The IZH Planeta-5 was a two-cylinder water-cooled two-stroke made from 1987 and 2008. It is unfortunate that they are not common in the United States, as they would make great conversation pieces at any bike gathering. Photo courtesy of Kalashnikov Concern Press-Service.

This 1956 Russian-made M72 is a copy of the 1938 BMW R71. It was produced by several manufacturers from 1942 to 1960. The 750cc R71 was BMW's last side-valve model. The R71 was also copied by Harley-Davidson as the XA for possible use in the desert during WWII. Photo courtesy of James De Besse.

Postwar Motorcycle Clubs

While Honda was still building his clip-on engines in 1948, American GIs turned to the bikes they learned to ride overseas, including Harley-Davidson, Indian, BSA, and Triumph. There were plenty of war surplus machines available for cheap. As jobs were scarce, many young men took to cruising the country on their bikes. Combat veterans who saw the horrors of war in particular sought escape on the road and within a close circle of trusted friends. They had enough of regimentation. The motorcycle was the means to forgetting the past and to being free. This was the era that launched a number of motorcycle clubs, including one called the Boozefighters Motorcycle Club. It was established in 1946 in Los Angeles. The AMA (American Motorcycle Association, now known as American Motorcyclist Association) expanded rapidly as well, offering racing venues for these new bikers. Their gatherings were more wholesome—offering racing, rallies, picnics, and group rides. The association would routinely award the best dressed clubs with patches to be worn on their uniforms. These events were called Gypsy Tours. Biker clubs, such as the Boozefighters, found little satisfaction in these fashion shows and the structured AMA regulations. They clearly preferred to remain independent.

As a Vietnam combat veteran, I can relate to WWII and Korean War veterans taking to bikes after coming home from war. My first priority was to get a Triumph and hit the road. The freedom and reflection offered by my motorcycle during that time will always be cherished.

Mayhem in Hollister

A big black eye for motorcycling resulted from one particular gathering of motorcyclists in July of 1947. The California town of Hollister hosted an AMA–sanctioned Gypsy Tour. It had done so since the 1930s without any issues. It was big business for the town. Lots of young visitors brought lots of money for food and drinks. After all, there were over twenty-one bars in Hollister. More than 4,000 bikers poured into town starting on the evening of July 3rd, including the Boozefighters and numerous other clubs. Beer was flowing and bikers became a bit rowdy. The locals fully expected it. There were a lot of arrests, basically to lock up the drunken bikers for their own safety. A number of them ended up in the hospital as beer and bikes don't mix too well. It was for the most part harmless fun, with no murders, rapes, or major crime. That all changed with the click of the shutter. A photojournalist named Barney Peterson was sent there to cover the event. Clearly giving into an opportunity, he staged a photo with a chubby biker sitting on a motorcycle, surrounded by mounds of beer bottles.

This photo of a drunken biker taken in Hollister, California, in July of 1947 only encouraged the notion among non-motorcyclists that all bikers were undesirables. The young man in the back is Gus Deserpa, a local resident that witnessed the staging of the photo. Interestingly, the shot just before this one showed a pleasant and smiling biker. Photo © 1947 Barney Peterson/San Francisco Chronicle/San Francisco Chronicle/Corbis.

The Hollister biker photo made it to a number of major papers, including the *San Francisco Chronicle*, the *Chicago Daily Tribune*, and even the *New York Times*. It was not until *Life* magazine ran a full-page photo of the seemingly drunk biker, tagged "Cyclist's Holiday," that the nation's perception of the "biker" was born. The less-than-flattering subhead read, "He and friends terrorize a town." The rest of the brief article painted a horrific story of drunken disorder and mayhem. This made for great press and contrasted well to an angelic couple posing in lederhosen on the front cover.

Things could not have been that bad. The town, as well as the AMA, continued to support the annual event. The publicity, however, was fodder for the press and Hollywood. The AMA is said to have made a comment stating that only 1 percent of motorcyclists are outlaws and that the rest are good citizens. Whether the AMA made this statement or not, the number stuck as outlaw motorcycle clubs today are labeled as "one-percenters." Outlaw bikers feel that this is a good badge. It supports the biker credo of individuality and freedom.

The term "outlaw" has to be defined carefully in this context. Outlaw motorcycle clubs were those not sanctioned by the AMA. They operated outside the laws of the AMA. This included clubs that may not have wanted association with the AMA and its regulations or did not fit the organization's guidelines. Today, outlaw clubs are mostly those purported by the authorities to have gang-related activities. The four dominant ones in the United States are the Hells Angels, the Pagans, the Outlaws, and the Bandidos (in no particular order). These organizations are quite territorial and demand high levels of commitment from their members. Veterans from more recent wars, such as the Vietnam "conflict," are represented well among many of the major, minor, and subsidiary biker clubs.

Wearing of the Colors

The wearing of a three-piece motorcycle club patch on the back of the jacket symbolizes a strong commitment to the brotherhood of a club's membership. It is said that this tradition was born out of defiance by the early outlaw clubs against the AMA. Standard club patches were torn into three pieces to define independence. The commitment to a true motorcycle club is quite different than what is expected of motorcycle manufacturers' clubs. True motorcycle clubs (MC) go beyond just riding. They have a strong social community among their members. Riding club members, sometimes called "roamers" in the post–WWII years, came together simply to share the joy of riding and picnicking together. Dealerships sponsored these groups. They led the way for motorcyclists to support charities through special runs. It was a good excuse to ride and do something for the community. Even the most hard core outlaw clubs today will sponsor or participate in fund drives. The purpose is often more for public relations benefit.

The coveted three-piece club patch symbolizing Motorcycle Clubs is well represented in the hit television show *Sons of Anarchy*. The patch has to be earned by the member. The three components represent the club name, its logo or crest, and chapter location. Three-piece patches are often referred to as a club's "colors." Photo © 2012 London Entertainment/Splash/Splash news/Corbis.

The Biker Defined

The events at Hollister inspired the 1953 hit movie *The Wild One*, starring Marlon Brando. The movie is a great example of film creating unprecedented brand awareness. Brando played the leader of an outlaw gang called the Black Rebels Motorcycle Club. He rode on a not so scary looking 650cc Triumph Thunderbird. Every bike enthusiast must study the variety of 1940s and 1950s era bikes in the film, observing the stark contrast between Brando's nimble Triumph and the big American V-twins like Lee Marvin was riding. The film clearly contributed to the British bike invasion. It catapulted sales of Triumphs as consumers quickly learned that they were more affordable, lighter, reliable, and faster off the line than the domestic bikes of the day. It was a smash hit for Triumph but painted motorcyclists as rude and crude ruffians for years to come.

Marlon Brando's character, Johnny, poses with a Triumph Thunderbird 6T motorcycle on the movie set of *The Wild One*. His costume and attitude continue to set a benchmark for motorcycle style today. Photo Eric Ryan/Getty Images.

Brando's character, Johnny, undoubtedly supported the image of the American biker *Life* magazine portrayed six years earlier. He was defiant to authority and challenged many social norms. He sought independence on the road and enjoyed the support of his followers. His motorcycle was the only thing he trusted. This negative "biker" image followed motorcyclists for decades after the release of *The Wild One*. Less flattering cheap motorcycle gang movies perpetuated the public's fascination with the outlaw biker subculture. Dic-

tionary definitions were also less than flattering during this time. This has changed today. The high numbers of respectable Americans dressing up as Johnnys and riding their loud bikes has redefined the term "biker." This will be addressed at the end of this chapter.

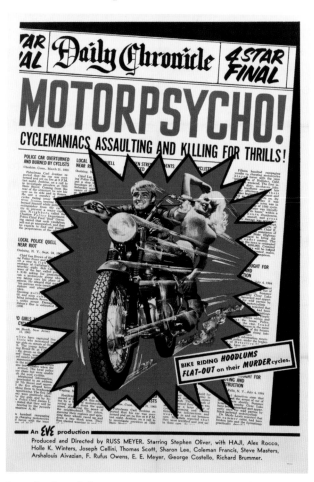

Low-budget biker gang movies were popular during the 1960s and 1970s. They surely defined the biker subculture as social misfits. Pictured is a poster for Russ Meyer's 1965 action film *Motorpsycho!* starring Steve Oliver and Holle K. Winters. Movie Poster Image Art/Getty Images.

Rockers and Mods

Things weren't much better in England. Young hooligans started taking to the streets on British-made bikes in the 1950s. They would modify the machines for speed and race them between coffee shops and truck stops, giving rise to the café racer genre. These bikers emulated the British rock musicians wearing leathers and pompadour hairstyles. They called themselves "Rockers." High-speed runs through the streets of London soon created a negative public view. Interestingly, there was another subculture that was called the Mods. These people focused on fashion and music that was more in line with soul, and rhythm and blues. They rode around in scooters, wearing polyester leisure suits and caps. Clashes between Rockers and Mods were reported. The most notable was in Brighton, a seaside town in southern England. As was the case with the Hollister event, the media took full advantage to paint motorcyclists as undesirables. Regardless of public opinion, young men and women on both sides of the ocean found refuge in the motorcycle as a vehicle to rebel against restrictions placed upon them by society.

In order to help guide troubled youngsters, the Church of England founded the 59 Club in 1959. Motorcyclists Father Bill Shergold (front center) and Father Graham Hulle started the motorcycle chapter of the 59 Club in 1962. Café racing hooligans soon joined in well-publicized charity runs. The club is very much alive today. Many of its original members have become respectable citizens that still ride. Photo Mortons Archive.

The American Daredevil

Hollywood loved to exploit the bad biker image for years following *The Wild One*. Low budget B class movies abounded, showing reckless and immoral bikers run rampant. Many a young star began their careers in these films. While Tinseltown was trashing bikers, one bad boy turned motorcycle evangelist became a household name. Evel Knievel, born in 1938 as Robert Craig Knievel in Montana, devoted most of his adult life to daredevil extravaganzas of motorcycle showmanship. He made hundreds of jumps over automobiles and trucks placed side-by-side. He also broke nearly every bone in his body. Knievel's stunts brought millions of viewers to the television as everyone held their breath to see if he would make it. His most famous jump took place at Caesar's Palace, Las Vegas, on December 31, 1967.

The iconic Evel Knievel shown on his preferred bike prior to a jump in 1971—a Harley-Davidson XR-750. Photo Ralph Crane/Getty Images.

The jump over the fountain resulted in a horrible televised crash. He crushed his pelvis and femur, fractured his hip, wrist, both ankles, and got a concussion. That did not daunt this American hero. As soon as he was partially healed, he prepared for the next jump. His most publicized stunt resulted in a poorly executed attempt at jumping the Snake River Canyon on a rocket-propelled bike. Knievel's life is well represented in the excellent movie starring George Hamilton and is a must-see for any motorcyclist. It reflects well on his early years and stunts on Triumph motorcycles.

Knievel's record attempts have not been lost to history. On August 6, 2015, daredevil Doug Danger broke Evel Knievel's record by jumping over twenty-two cars at the Sturgis Buffalo Chip amphitheater. This in itself would be a most courageous but not impossible stunt given the new extreme motocross bikes available today. What made this jump remarkable was that Doug Danger did it on Knievel's own 1972 Harley-Davidson XR750!

The British Invasion

While Americans were busy worrying about biker gangs in the 1950s, the British launched their invasion. The US market was ripe for their fast, light motorcycles. Triumph 650cc twins had a better power-to-weight ratio than the massive American V-twins. They also featured something quite common in Europe but relatively new to the United States: foot shifting and hand-operated clutches. America responded with open arms. Movies like *The Wild One* showed domestic bikers what these machines were all about. GIs stationed in England brought them home as well. Meanwhile, Italian makers like Gilera, MV Agusta, and Moto Guzzi were building motorcycles with advanced engine designs that would become the models for Japanese superbikes to come. Few of these exotic machines were seen on American roads at that time.

Triumphs of the 1950s were affordable and fast alternatives to the traditional American V-twins. The United States became a huge market for British bikes, absorbing over 70 percent of their production for many years. Twin models were available in 350cc, 500cc, and 650cc engine sizes. The 1970s produced 750cc engines in two and three cylinders.

Harley-Davidson was still producing flathead (side-valve) engined bikes like this 750cc K series in the 1950s despite the fact that it offered larger bikes with overhead valves since 1936. Introduced in 1952, the K featured unit construction (engine and transmission in same housing), foot shifting and hand-operated clutch to compete against the early British imports. This basic V-twin engine in KR racing configuration dominated flat track racing through the 1960s. K bikes are the ancestors to the Sportster, as is evident in this nice custom. They were eventually enlarged to 883cc. Harley® ended the K's run of non-racing bikes in 1956.

One Last Stand

Indian, under Ralph B. Rogers, made a valiant attempt at building its own light parallel twins to compete against the British. Emulating British design, the product was put to market prematurely. They also cost more than comparable BSA, Triumph, and Matchless bikes. They failed miserably. Indian produced its last Chief in 1953 and devoted the next few years to simply importing British bikes, such as Royal Enfield and Velocette. Select models were badged as Indians. They even attempted a joint venture with Vincent. The "Vindian" prototype features a Vincent V-twin in a Chief frame. High cost precluded success.

Indian's attempt to copy the advanced sporty British designs resulted in several potentially nice bikes like this 1949 218cc Arrow, featuring a four-speed foot-shift transmission and telescopic front forks. Other models introduced were the 436cc two-cylinder Scout and expensive 500cc Warrior.

Honda Prepares for Domination

While the American motorcycle industry was being torn apart by the British, the Japanese were preparing to deal the British a blow of their own. In August of 1958, Honda introduced a phenomenon: the Super Cub. This step-through design went on to dominate markets worldwide. Honda's decision to power the bike with a four-stroke version of his 50cc motor paid off. It was quieter and cleaner than the popular two-strokes produced by other makers and, therefore, more appealing to the average consumer.

The bike that changed America's thinking about motorcycles. The 50cc Super Cub C100 launched Honda's dynamic growth with its introduction in 1958. Unlike similar machines of the era sporting two-stroke engines, the Super Cub featured a four-stroke overhead valve design that propelled it to world dominance. The Super Cub lives on in a variety of configurations up to 109cc and is the VW Beetle of motorcycles. Over 70 million units have been produced between 1958 and 2008. Photo courtesy of American Honda Motor Co., Inc.

This small and unobtrusive storefront opened in 1959 on Pico Boulevard in Los Angeles was Honda's launch point into the vast American motorcycle market. At that time, as seen in the back of the pickup truck, Honda offered the Super Cub and 125cc twin-cylinder C90 Benly. In addition, Honda imported the larger 250cc and 305cc Dream bikes. Photo courtesy of American Honda Motor Co., Inc.

Honda's big challenge was to get Americans out of the mindset that motorcycles were for rough guys only. The company's ad campaign launched in 1963 was simply bril-

liant. While Harley-Davidson and BSA advertised in motorcycle magazines, showing tough and sexy images designed to attract men, Honda presented its products in consumer magazines like *Life*. Their slogan "You Meet the Nicest People on a Honda" underscored the images of happy young couples in tennis shorts riding around on a Super Cub. It was a home run. The bike's easy to use configuration and low cost attracted those who may have never thought of owning a motorcycle. The larger machines available at that time required mechanical skill to maintain and strength to operate. The Super Cub not only brought motorcycling to the masses but prepared them for larger Japanese bikes yet to come.

A milestone in motorcycling and advertising: the Honda ads of the 1960s. The campaign created by Grey Advertising introduced a "civilized" view of motorcycling to the masses. Photo courtesy of American Honda Motor Co., Inc.

Period photo of a Bronx, NY, biker that typifies the image many people had of motorcyclists during the time Honda was introducing a whole new perspective on the sport.

Soichiro Honda was known to be a tough boss and certainly a perfectionist; especially when it came to quality manufacturing. He was a hands-on executive who expected a lot from his employees. The results spoke for themselves. Photo courtesy American Honda Motor Co., Inc.

Soichiro Honda did not view the British dominance of the huge US market as a threat. Ironically, even though Edward Turner was impressed with Honda's automated manufacturing upon a visit to Japan, he felt that the American market was already saturated enough with bikes. He could not see interest in smaller displacement products from the island country as affecting British market dominance. He was wrong. While the British motorcycle manufacturers continued to stay focused on larger displacement machines with traditional and dated engine designs, Honda invested heavily in research, development, and assembly line automation. This allowed it to produce more advanced quality products at a lower price point. The company studied everyone and anyone making motorcycles.

Italian motorcycle engineering produced remarkable examples of high-performance engine designs during the 1950s and 1960s like this 175cc high-cam Parilla 175 Turismo Speciale. Spanish-born Giovanni Parrilla was inspired by Norton's great racing success, as is evident in the Manx-like appearance of his racing machines, and started building his own in 1946. Parrilla continued to produce some very nice bikes under Moto Parilla through 1967, after which he focused on go-kart engines. Unfortunately, the most advanced designs by many of the Italian makers did not make it to the US consumer market for another decade. However, Honda was dissecting them in its R&D department. Italian engine designs inspired many of their racers and street bikes. Photo courtesy of Carollo Moto Classiche.

Honda saw the gap left for under 500cc bikes as a real opportunity. After all, the rest of the world appreciated the value of small displacement motorcycles. Honda and other Japanese makers imported British and Italian bikes on a regular basis to study their engineering. The Japanese Ministry of Trade sent investigators to Europe to examine in great detail the industry and markets. This followed the Japanese tradition of kengaku, the studying abroad to gain knowledge. The Brits did not take Honda and other Japanese bike manufacturers as serious contenders in the large displacement market until it was too late. We'll see later how the 1969 Honda 750 pretty much ended the British motorcycle industry.

Honda's first motorcycle was introduced in 1949. The Dream D-Type was powered by a 98cc 2.3 hp two-stroke. Design elements were borrowed from a number of makers to expedite the development process. Compare this bike with the white CZ Sport below. Photo courtesy of American Honda Motor Co., Inc.

This beautifully restored 1938 CZ 250 Sport was powered by the company's noted two-stroke engine. The marque survived German occupation and was co-branded with Jawa for a while. It continued producing motorcycles until 1997. CZ saw some success at the Isle of Man TT, and at the International Six Day Trials with Sammy Miller in the saddle.

Honda's next machine was the four-stroke Dream E-Type, introduced in 1951. The stylish art-deco motorcycle came with a 146cc overhead valve engine and 3-speed transmission. It was only sold in Japan. Production increased to two thousand units per month by 1952. The 1954 Dream E-Type featured a larger 220cc engine and plunger rear suspension. Familiar engineering features from European models are evident, particularly NSU. This bike represented Honda's initiative to develop motorcycles that could compete in the large American market.

German motorcycle manufacturer NSU provided much of the inspiration for Honda's early bikes. NSU started building motorized bicycles in 1901 by clipping Swiss-made Zedel engines onto their bicycles. The company became a leading motorcycle producer through both World Wars. Pictured is a 1942 overhead valve single. The company survived through 1965. Photo courtesy Mike Dunn.

Honda's successful C90 Benly 125cc parallel twin introduced in 1958 offered affordable options for the fertile American market. Photo courtesy of American Honda Motor Co., Inc.

A lovely example of the Dutch Nimbus four-cylinder motorcycle. It produced 22 hp at 4500 rpm. The elegantly engineered engine featured an overhead cam design that actuated the valves from the top. Final drive was by shaft. Earlier models feature fuel-in-frame chassis and rear suspension.

Casualties of the Motorcycle Wars

The 1950s were make-it-or-break-it years for all motorcycle manufacturers. It saw the death of many great British marques, like the immortal Vincent, that simply could not compete against the less expensive high-volume bikes produced by BSA, Triumph, and Norton. One such casualty was an obscure Danish company making the Nimbus motorcycle pictured on this page. Started in 1919, the company specialized in four-cylinder air-cooled motorcycles. Predating many other makers, they featured telescopic forks to suspend the front wheel. Production was limited to just under thirteen thousand units, and ceased in 1959.

Motorcycles Go to the Movies

While motorcycle companies were fighting for market share, movies and their stars kept them in the public eye. We are certainly influenced by those who shape our culture. Celebrities have always been good marketers of bikes. Some rode for the image, while others actually enjoyed it as an escape. Full helmets today camouflage stars as they race through the canyons of California or idle through Rodeo Drive in Beverly Hills.

Elvis typically rode a Harley, but in the 1964 film *Roustabout*, he gave Barbara Stanwyck a ride on a highly modern, technologically advanced 305cc Honda CB77. It signaled the coming of the Japanese invasion that would bring the British motorcycle industry to its knees. Photo © 1964 Sunset Boulevard/Corbis.

There were countless heroes of the silver screen that presented a respectable view of motorcycling, including Clark Gable, who turned heads as he rode his 1934 Harley-Davidson® RL in the Hollywood Hills. One of the most popular was Elvis Presley. Elvis made a dozen movies with motorcycles in them during the 1960s; including *Roustabout, Stay Away Joe, It Happened at the World's Fair, Clambake,* and many more.

84

The Real Deal

Steve McQueen was the most glamorous Hollywood sportsman of them all. He actually raced motorcycles in the desert and on the track, providing a heartthrob image that young men needed to emulate in order to win over their star-struck girlfriends.

McQueen on the set of *The Great Escape*, attempting to outrun the Germans. Despite the fact that it was supposed to be a German bike he commandeered for his escape, McQueen actually rode a Triumph TR6 Trophy 650cc motorcycle, a personal favorite of his. Photo Silver Screen Collection/Getty Images.

Everyone wanted to get on a bike after the famous jump scene in the 1963 hit movie *The Great Escape*. McQueen was a capable rider, but the studio could not afford to lose the high-grossing actor to an accident. They opted to have his riding pal and stuntman, Bud Ekins, do the jump over the barbed wire made out of rubber bands.

The jump was a remarkable feat in itself considering the weight of the Triumph. Modern motocross bikes would make light of a jump like that, but to do it with a 360 pound bike is another story.

A Self-Promoting Machine

Motorcycles sell themselves. The more there are on the road, the more people see them and want one. That's why there is little motorcycle advertising on TV. If you miss them on the street because you live in a cave, the popular magazines you subscribe to will surely direct your attention to the latest hot bikes. Each publication features machines to support its special interest. Motorcycle magazines like *Cycle World* report on the latest machines. Their reviews on handling and technology offer great insight into any featured bike. *Popular Mechanics'* followers enjoy reading about the mechanical specifications, while the cover of *Men's Health* may feature a sporty Moto Guzzi V7 café racer. Well-heeled enthusiasts may be drawn to the skillfully lit photo of an exotic dual-cam, 45-degree, aluminum alloy billet 2,150cc V-twin Ecosse on the cover of *Robb Report*. Others may fantasize about owning the remarkable new Brough-Superior SS100 or a modern-day Horex while thumbing through a copy of the *duPont Registry* while waiting at the dentist's office. Whatever the publication, the motorcycle will surely make its presence. Even the *Wall Street Journal* writes about bikes. Harley-Davidson's healthy revenue is surely something to talk about.

The revival of famous marques is always big news in motorcycling, especially when they come out with exciting new high-tech designs. Horex is such an example. Its roots go back to 1920s Germany. It survived WWII to produce some nice standards. Tough times saw the company fade, but a loyal following and a recent acquisition has brought the brand into the limelight with its exotic six-cylinder machines. Photo courtesy of Horex.

Movies Love Motorcycles

Action movies thrive on motorcycles, and the makers eagerly compete to get a part in the script. This form of exposure surely reaches the right target demographic and offers great opportunity to attract potential customers. An example is Arnold Schwarzenegger as the iconic biker in *Terminator 2* on his Harley-Davidson Fat Boy®. He was hero, villain, and sportsman all in one shot. If that didn't sell motorcycles, I don't know what would. Nothing on two wheels sounds as good as a well-tuned Harley® revving up through the gears. The film got the soundtrack just right on that. It was an excellent combination to inspire baby boomers to buy a bike. Fat Boy sales skyrocketed.

Terminator 2 featured Arnold Schwarzenegger on a Harley-Davidson Fat Boy as the quintessential American biker. Photo © 1984 Cinema Photo/ Corbis.

Television shows like *American Chopper* are eye candy for anyone looking to get on two wheels. The boys at Orange County Chopper did a fantastic, albeit over-dramatic, job of entertaining and educating the enthusiast, clearly demonstrating the creative side of motorcycle building. Even Discovery Channel gets in on the act with its features on Café Racers and motorcycle history.

Easy Rider

Inasmuch as *The Wild One* painted a negative picture of the American motorcyclist, the all-time classic *Easy Rider* showed a different side. Peter Fonda and Dennis Hopper, as unlikely a pair as one can imagine, had different reasons to ride, but shared the dream of freedom on the open road. Fonda's character was searching for his own meaning of life, and not to trash bars or chase good girls down the street as depicted in *The Wild One*. Hopper, on the other hand, was more visceral, and a bike was just a means to get there.

The 1969 movie highlighted all the social prejudices happening within this country at that time. It tried to deal with issues that reflected our nation's confusion with the war, racism, and its youth culture, all from the saddle of a motorcycle. In addition to giving Jack Nicholson his big break on the screen, the film made another impact. It created the stylistic definition of the American custom chopper.

Easy Rider brought motorcycles to the self-actualizing youth of the Vietnam era. Motorcycles faced the same prejudice as long hair and the search for individuality. Both bikes featured Harley-Davidson "Panhead" engines, sitting in hardtail frames. Photo Silver Screen Collection/ Getty Images.

A true reflection of cultural recognition of the motorcycle today was seen on Madison Avenue in Manhattan. Bonhams was displaying reproductions of the *Easy Rider* bikes that were up for auction. The original bikes were crafted by Cliff Vaughs and Ben Hardy with Peter Fonda's input. Two *Captain America* bikes were built, of which one was crashed and restored, and the other stolen after the filming. One "original" copy has resurfaced and was sold at auction for $1.3 million in 2014. Questions about its authenticity prompted the buyer to back out. Regardless, both bikes remain the ultimate in pure chopper form and design.

Despite *Easy Rider's* great success, few films portrayed a positive image of motorcyclists. *Then Came Bronson, On Any Sunday,* and *Evel Knievel* were the exception. The box office was full of degenerate biker movies such as *Angel Unchained, Hell's Bloody Devils,* and *The Peace Killers.* Things have changed today. Nearly every action film has a motorcycle chase scene in it. Other films use the motorcycle as the vehicle for dealing with the curve balls life throws at you. A good one is the 2008 movie *One Week,* starring Joshua Jackson. The main character leaves all behind as he sets out traversing Canada on an 850cc Norton Commando after discovering he has cancer. Time alone in the saddle allows for reflection, even for mundane reasons such as not liking one's job.

For sportbike enthusiasts, the scenes of Angelina Jolie burning up the tires of her customized Yamaha in *Tomb Raider* and a Triumph Street Triple in *Salt* were hot enough to melt the butter on the popcorn. And, how about that Trinity in *Matrix Reloaded* on that screaming 996 Ducati? Carrie-Anne Moss's enigmatic character defying all the laws of physics was actually the work of stunt double and AMA Hall of Famer Debbie Evans, a true legend on two wheels. Interest in Ducati soared after that remarkable adrenaline rush on the screen. Ducati jumped on the opportunity and released two models with the Matrix moniker.

Tom Cruise had that same affect in the 1986 hit film *Top Gun.* Anyone with a pulse had to love that bit on the runway when he opened up his Kawasaki GPz900R Ninja. That was the golden era of Japanese superbikes, and we all had to have one. Cruise continues to promote the thrills of motorcycling in his *Mission Impossible* movies.

Years after his screen ride on a Ninja, actor Tom Cruise brings actress Katie Holmes to the Los Angeles fan screening of *War of the Worlds* at the Grauman's Chinese Theatre on Honda's futuristic, limited run six-cylinder NRX1800 Valkyrie® Rune®. This bike weighs over 800 pounds and costs $26,000. Cruise is an avid motorcyclist who uses bikes with great effect for his entrances. He follows in the footsteps of other noted Hollywood celebrities in popularizing a positive image of motorcycling. Photo Kevin Winter/Getty Images.

One of my favorites is the 2004 Spanish film *Motorcycle Diaries.* It's the story of twenty-three-year-old Ernesto (Che) Guevara and his buddy's 1952 voyage throughout South America. The bike scenes will be especially valued by vintage enthusiasts as the boys struggle to keep their 1939 Norton 500cc single alive. The story goes far beyond motorcycles, chronicling the young medical student's discovery of the social injustices that drove him to Marxism.

Immortalizing a Land Speed Racer

Another biographical film, *The World's Fastest Indian,* embodies an equally reflective story about one man's passion to overcome the challenges of age, money, time, and distance. It features Anthony Hopkins as New Zealander Burt Munro fulfilling his dream of taking his customized 1920 Indian Scout to the Bonneville Salt Flats to set a speed record. Burt certainly did that.

He was in his late sixties as he rode his streamlined (enclosed) Indian to 183.58 mph, setting a record in the category of "streamlined motorcycles under 1,000cc." His official qualification run of 190.07 mph in 1967 made his bike the fastest Indian motorcycle on record. He did manage to exceed 200 mph at one point, but unofficially. The 950cc V-twin Scout was highly modified with overhead valves and hand-cast pistons.

The film introduces the viewer to two other motorcycling greats, Rollie Free and Marty Dickerson. Both set numerous speed records on the Bonneville, Utah, Salt Flats as well. Free's historic run is featured in the Racing chapter of this book.

If one truly thinks about it, there are scores of movies that show our heroes on bikes. Prince rode a Hondamatic 400 in *Purple Rain,* and Richard Gere rode a venerable Triumph Bonneville in *An Officer and a Gentleman,* while the *Mad Max* bad boys favored high-performance Japanese fours. Nearly every action movie made today, from *007* to *X-Men,* contains exciting motorcycle chase scenes.

The Ultimate Motorcycle Documentary

There are many movies about motorcycling itself, but none as classic as *On Any Sunday.* This 1971 documentary was produced jointly by Bruce Brown and Steve McQueen. It is a wonderful glimpse into the world of motorcycling as it was in the 1960s and 1970s. The film introduces the viewer to all that motorcycling has to offer—from road races to off-road desert racing. It features many of the greats of the time, including AMA Hall of Famers Mal-

Burt Munro with his *Munro Special* on the Salt Flats in 1962. Photo by Chuck Nerpel/ The Enthusiast Network /Getty Images.

colm Smith, Mert Lawwill, and Cal Rayborn. The 2014 release of *On Any Sunday - The Next Chapter* brings viewers up to date with even more exciting footage. *Why We Ride* is another recent documentary introduced in 2013. It not only discusses the reasons we love to ride, but also those who inspire us to do so.

The Billionaire and the Movie Star

Hollywood was not the only one to put bikes into the limelight. Perhaps the most influential individual to shower credibility upon motorcyclists in the eyes of a suspicious and fearful public was millionaire publisher Malcolm Forbes. During the 1970s and 1980s Forbes publicized motorcycling by engaging celebrities to join him on his rides. He even had a giant Harley-Davidson hot air balloon built to fly on his estate in New Jersey. He named his motorcycle club the Capitalist Tools. Forbes was inducted into the AMA Hall of Fame in 1999 for not just those reasons, but also for his great work in getting legislators to loosen the restrictions that kept motorcycles off certain highways in New Jersey.

Malcolm Forbes gifted a Harley-Davidson Sportster named Passion to his riding pal, Elizabeth Taylor. This combination of celebrity power legitimatized motorcycling in the eyes of many who scorned the sport. Harley-Davidson certainly benefited from the publicity. Photo © 1987 Ricki Rosen/CORBIS SABA.

Bikers Come Together

The popularity of motorcycles on the screen and on the street has certainly brought them into the mainstream. Most motorcyclists are far from the outlaws portrayed in the B movies of the past. Hard core bikers belonging to certain motorcycle clubs may be the exception. Television shows like Sons of Anarchy sensationalize the American outlaw biker image. Many motorcyclists riding big V-twins may wish to be seen in this vein but would find it difficult to commit to. So, they dress up, mount up, and take to the streets. Bearded, burly, tattooed, and hard-riding, these folks crowd the streets of Daytona Beach, Leesburg, Sturgis, and Laconia during their annual pilgrimages. John Travolta's movie *The Wild Hogs* does a great job reflecting on these biker stereotypes. Much bravado is a put on and costumed by apparel merchants. But one cannot judge a book by its cover. After all, one-percenter biker clubs frequent these events as well. It pays to behave. Typically, everyone gets along just fine. It really is all about the freedom we share on two wheels and a celebration of unity.

90

Daytona Beach, Florida, offers two major motorcycle gatherings every year. Bike Week typically happens in March, while Biketoberfest takes place in October. The sound of hundreds of thousands of V-twins fills the air with music. The Daytona International Speedway is nearby and hosts many racing events and custom builder exhibits during the ten-day soirée.

Of all the large motorcycle gatherings, Sturgis is considered to be the most prolific. The Sturgis® Motorcycle Rally™ happens annually in late summer in Sturgis, South Dakota. This two-week rally has its roots in a small annual motorcycle club gathering that started in 1938. The event draws over a half-million bikes, bringing hundreds of millions in revenue to the state. It is an R-rated environment best left to adults. Getting there on a bike may take a week of long hours in the saddle, offering bragging rights to many who made the pilgrimage. Photo David McNew/Getty Images.

Biker events are all about bikes, babes, and booze. There is a lot of partying that goes on for a week or two. Even though the majority of motorcycles frequenting these events are Harley-Davidsons, sportbike enthusiasts have joined in on the fun.

The connection between war veterans and motorcycles is stronger than ever today. The annual Run For The Wall brings hundreds of thousands of riders from all over the country to Washington, DC, on Memorial Day weekend to honor those lost or missing in Vietnam and other wars. The Rolling Thunder event, started in 1988, gathers these and other riders in the Pentagon parking lot in preparation for a run to the Vietnam Memorial. It shows the resolve of countless Americans to support veterans that felt abandoned by their country, and honor those lost. Photo courtesy of John Loehr.

Patriotism runs high among bikers, particularly those riding American-made machines. Photo by Elvert Barnes.

The Need to Belong

Motorcycling invites socialization. Even a lone biker loves the praise he may receive from others admiring his machine. Friends will spend as much time talking about their motorcycles as they do riding them. Riding in groups has its own reward—the opportunity to talk about the ride afterward. These rituals happen every weekend throughout the United States. For others, the motorcycle is an easy chair from which to view the wonders of this country. They are connected with mobile communications devices, speaking to each other as they rack up the miles on roads carpeting our country's vast and glorious landscape. And then there is the sporting crowd, riding like swarms of bees through traffic. They gather at the track to race and exchange tips on exhilarating maneuvers. The need to share and the need to belong have made motorcycling the new social club for men and women today.

There are many reasons to join a club, or even an online forum such as the Brit Iron Rebels Worldwide (britironrebels.com). Much expertise is available in technical information, equipment, riding routes, and events. Every conceivable interest, diversity, ethnicity, gender, and other social preference is represented in some sort of a motorcycle group. The Blue Knights®, for example, is a club made up of active and retired law-enforcement officers, whereas the Motor Maids and Women on Wheels (WOW) are clubs strictly for female riders.

The Blue Knights motorcycle club has been in existence since 1974. It is composed of police officers who enjoy riding and who take an active role in community affairs. Photo by Elvert Barnes.

There are hundreds of groups, clubs, and forums, each with a specific interest. The Antique Motorcycle Club of America (AMCA) has been a home to antique and vintage bike enthusiasts since 1954. The Vincent HRD Owners Club is a most-exclusive group representing thousands of privileged owners of the well-known marque throughout the world. The Vintage Japanese Motorcycle Club is full of experts to help you get any old Japanese bike running (vjmc.org). There are countless owners groups that support specific makes like the Vintage BMW Owners Group (vintagebmw.org). And, nearly every maker offers a club specific to its bikes. Harley-Davidson has its well-established Harley Owners Group® (HOG), Triumph has its RAT, Moto Guzzi has its MGNOC, Kawasaki has its Riders of Kawasaki (ROK), and the list goes on. Other clubs focus on styles of riding—from sport to off-road. Spiritual-based clubs are common throughout the country. Riders are either affiliated with a specific church or faith. The largest is the Christian Motorcyclist Association. Age-specific and special interest clubs exist as well. There is a club for anyone and everyone. A simple Internet search will open the doors to this vast world.

The Biker Today

The term "biker" traditionally implied a tough guy with lots of tattoos and most likely a member of a hard-core motorcycle club. That definition has changed in recent decades as more and more regular folks are taking to motorcycling. Some of these people may look like hard-core bikers, but that doesn't necessarily mean they are. Motorcyclists love to dress the image that tickles their alter egos. Sportbike riders, for example, will often wear full race leathers and armor to look the part of a GP racer.

A biker today may be best defined as someone who has a passion for motorcycling and rides his or her machine as frequently as possible, regardless of the weather. Motorcyclists straddling their low-slung American V-twins consider themselves a reflection of the American cowboy. Artist Dave Mann exemplified this in his paintings of biker lifestyle back in the 1970s. His centerfolds in *Easyriders* magazine created a model of the American biker for many to follow. However, even this lone biker thrives to be with his trusted friends. We are social beings.

The "American Biker" can be defined by brand loyalty toward American-made machines, particularly Harley-Davidson motorcycles. This by no means limits his or her interest in other makes and types of motorcycles. Most bikers appreciate a good machine no matter where it is from. The bike in front is a rare 1986 Harley-Davidson "Liberty Edition" FXRS, commemorating the bicentennial. Less than 750 were made. The durability of its Evolution engine has served the biker in the picture well for many years and many miles.

The spectrum of motorcyclists is quite broad, and not all motorcyclists are bikers. The scale ranges between those who simply own a motorcycle to those that practically live on one and can be called true bikers. Among these bikers are those die-hard enthusiasts who spend countless hours repairing and restoring old machines just to enjoy a few long minutes riding them on the road before they break down again. They feel great satisfaction in their handicraft. There are bikers who are sportbike riders who simply cannot satiate their thirst and passion for speed and control, while off-road bikers enjoy unrestrained command to traverse any terrain. Touring bikers enjoy endless hours and miles in the saddle. Others simply ride for transportation. A bike may be the only vehicle they own. These motorcyclists may also be defined as true bikers. The moniker of biker does require a level of commitment, where the motorcycle becomes part of that person's lifestyle. It is always there, available, and a preferred or necessary method of transportation. Real bikers don't just dress the part; they live the part. Bikers also know enough to do some basic maintenance

on their machine. And above all, true bikers appreciate all other motorcyclists, regardless of the make or style of bike they ride.

Black leather jackets with lots of patches play a big role in motorcycling culture. These are costumes that dress and protect our alter egos— be it hard-core biker or 1950s rocker.

Love It or Leave It

Our society's love-hate relationship with motorcycles is an ongoing tug-of-war. While we wave at veterans riding their bikes in a parade, bad-boy biker movies like the 2003 film *Biker Boyz* remind us of the crazies that take to two wheels. Riding a wheelie at 80 miles per hour on a superbike is an amazing feat, but creates a negative image when done on public streets.

Stunt riding is a skilled sport, but best kept off the highways. Non-motorcyclists find stunt riding on the street as offensive as a group of hard-core bikers waking up the neighborhood on a Sunday morning.

Baby boomers have taken motorcycling to the next level. Respectable citizens park their Harleys and Ducatis in pristine Mc-Mansion garages, only to be seen on early Sunday mornings as they savor a few minutes of reckless freedom before soccer practice. Major motorcycle brands have created a presence that goes beyond their machines. Apparel sales have become big income streams for all makers. Harley-Da-

vidson has even entered the restaurant business with its Harley-Davidson Cafe. Motorcycle sales are watched carefully by investors. The industry represents billions of dollars in revenue and offers many jobs to those building them.

The past hundred years have truly benefited from the invention and development of the motorcycle. They continue to contribute to our society and define a subculture. Motorcycles, and their little brother, the scooter, offer enormous potential to help reduce emissions while offering affordable transportation. This is particularly true with the superb electric models being introduced. Motorcycle engine development has always been highly advanced in creating small power plants with high output and efficiency. These designs trickle down to our automobiles, creating more powerful engines with greater fuel economy. The future of motorcycles in our lives remains bright.

For those who wish they had a motorcycle but either can't ride one, or just can't afford one, a U.K.–based company offers life-size plastic model kits for around $800. Several makes are available, including a Bonneville, Norton, and a chopper. Assembly can take between 20 and 30 hours. These bikes look great in any man-cave, restaurant, or bar. Photo courtesy of fullsizekits.com.

Chapter 3

A HISTORY OF THE ENGINE

This chapter is a historical overview of the mechanical evolution that has lead to the modern motorcycle engine. The four-hundred-year journey began with steam. These noble machines ruled our railways and even saw their way onto a few motorcycles. They have become a distant memory to the internal combustion engines that replaced them. The motors that move our motorcycles today are marvels of engineering and efficiency, but the future is clear: it is electric.

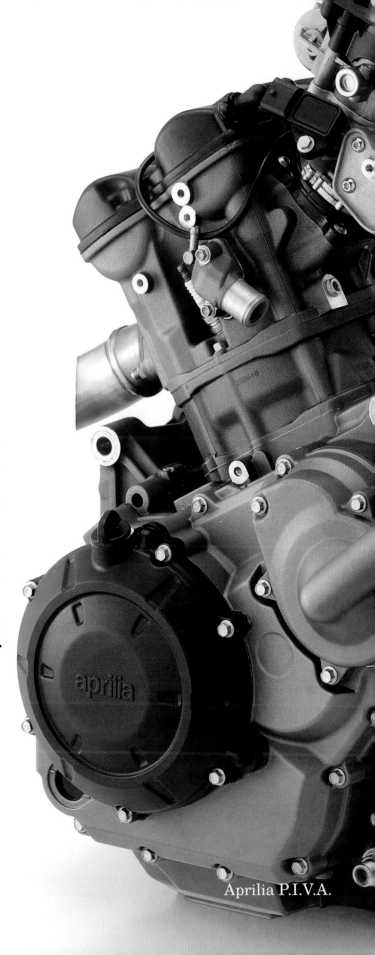

Aprilia P.I.V.A.

THE ENGINE

The Basic Components of an Internal-Combustion Engine

Photo courtesy of American Honda Motor Co., Inc.

Camshaft – a steel shaft that is used to activate the valves in a four-stroke cycle internal combustion engine. Egg shaped lobes are specially ground to determine the amount of lift and duration. Each intake and exhaust valve typically has its own cam lobe. The camshaft rotates once for every two rotations of the crankshaft. It is rotated by gears, chains, or cogged belts driven off the crankshaft. Camshafts may be housed near the crankshaft or within the cylinder head.

Spark Plug – a metal and ceramic device that threads into the cylinder head. High voltage current from the ignition coil leads to it and results in a spark at the tip of the spark plug inside the combustion chamber. This spark ignites the compressed air/fuel mixture.

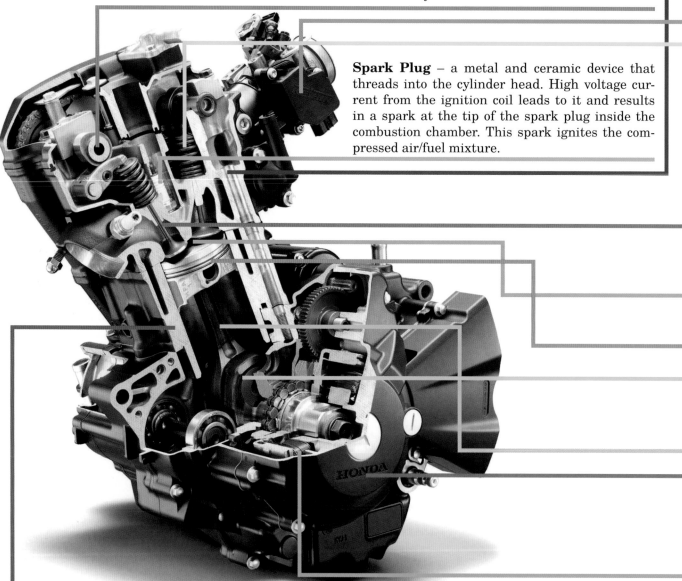

Cylinder – a perfectly round tube that guides the piston during its reciprocating motion. It is liberally lubricated with splashing oil from the crankshaft. Cylinders are typically made of iron. Most come with wear resistant coatings today. Cylinders absorb much of the heat created during the combustion process and are therefore cooled by aluminum fins (air-cooled engine), or surrounded by a water jacket (liquid-cooled engine) to dissipate the heat. Cylinders are typically bolted on to the crankcase.

Cylinder head – a complex casting that is secured to the top of the cylinder. The cylinder head in most modern four-stroke engines houses the valves, camshaft(s), and spark plug. Antique engines used cast iron heads that did not dissipate heat as well as those made of aluminum alloy.

Carburetor or Throttle Body – mixing chamber for the air and fuel that is being drawn into the engine via the intake manifold. Throttle bodies are associated with Electronic Fuel Injection systems.

Valve Springs – coil springs that close the valves shut when the cam is not acting on them, such as during the compression and power strokes..

Valves – mushroom shaped "poppet" valves that open and close to allow the air/fuel mixture in (intake) and hot exhaust gases out (exhaust).

Combustion Chamber – the area between the bottom of the cylinder head and the top of the cylinder. This is where the air/fuel mixture is compressed during the top of the piston's compression stroke in preparation for ignition to create the power stroke.

Piston – a round shaped aluminum alloy casting that rides up and down within the engine's cylinder. The piston has grooves that hold the piston rings. These create a seal against the cylinder wall to prevent explosive gases from escaping and oil from entering the combustion chamber. The piston has two holes cast into its walls to hold a piston pin (also called a wrist pin) that connects the piston to the top of the connecting rod. Antique engines used cast iron pistons. Modern high-performance engines use forged alloy pistons.

Connecting Rod – an alloy rod with a small upper bearing and a larger lower bearing. The top holds the piston pin, while the bottom is secured around the crank journal. Bearings may be made of soft metal shells or steel roller bearings.

Crankcase – alloy castings that when combined act as the foundation for an engine's components. It secures the bearings that hold the rotating shafts within the engine. It may also act as a stressed member of the motorcycle's frame.

Crankshaft – a shaft that is held in place by bearings on either end. It has an offset crank journal that connects to the connecting rod. This offset allows it to convert the reciprocating motion of the piston into rotational motion. The crankshaft may have counterweights attached to it or integrally forged to help balance the rotation created by the reciprocating piston. Crankshafts are typically drilled with passageways to lubricate the connecting rod bearings with pressurized oil.

Alternator – attached to the crankshaft to generate electricity.

The Engine That Powers Our Cycles

In this chapter we'll look at the evolution of the four-stroke cycle internal combustion engine that powers most of our bikes today. It is remarkable to consider that the hundreds of millions of people who use an internal combustion engine to get around don't know who invented it. After all, everyone knows who invented the light bulb. As with anything motorized, the names Ford, Harley-Davidson, Indian, and even Briggs & Stratton are mentioned as the possible founders. The story is actually much richer than that. Those fortunate enough to find a copy of the book *Internal Fire*, written by C. Lyle Cummins Jr., will have an opportunity to learn about the internal combustion engine's development in great detail. A current scholarly book, titled *Flame Ignition* by Wayne S. Grenning, builds further on this history with an unprecedented number of color photographs of rare engines. It is also recommended that readers interested in early engines take a look at the Coolspring Power Museum in Coolspring, Pennsylvania, coolspringpowermuseum.org.

The Power of Movement

Ever since the discovery of the wheel, man has tried to put power to it. For thousands of years one could travel no faster than a horse could pull a carriage. From the days of Da Vinci, engineers and inventors attempted to create self-propelled vehicles. The motor that powers our cycles today has a direct line to this ancestry.

A lot of progress has been made in motorcycle engineering and technology in the seventy-eight years that separate these bikes. That is a short span of time considering the 350 years' development that led to today's motorcycle engines. The 1926 Indian Big Chief was a state-of-the-art consumer product in its day, relying on magneto ignition, manual oil pump, and kick starting to operate. The Ducati sport touring bike in the back is a modern rocket ship equipped with electronically controlled fuel injection and engine performance management systems.

The dynamic struggle and competition between creative minds racing to build and market a reliable power plant played out like an Italian opera: full of intrigue, betrayal, and mystery. Patents would be challenged and ideas stolen as engineers from France, Britain, Germany, and Italy worked on hundreds of designs to create the first practical engine.

Boiling Water

The search began with a boiling kettle of water. Steam was recognized to be a source of power by the early Greeks. Hero of Alexandria conceived of several steam-powered devices two thousand years ago. Even Sir Isaac Newton envisioned a powered vehicle propelled by a jet of steam.

Hero's steam-powered aeolipile predicted the power of steam-driven machines. Illustration by Fouad A. Saad / Shutterstock.com

The availability of gunpowder since the ninth century inspired the idea of generating power with an exploding charge. Harnessing it was another problem. Christiaan Huygens attempted to create an engine using the explosive in 1673. Difficulties arose in how repetitive power cycles could be generated using a crude feeding mechanism combined with a means to ignite the charges safely. Hopeless, it was back to steam for most inventors, including a preacher from England.

The Power of Harnessing Condensation

Thomas Newcomen, born in 1664 in Dartmouth, had great interest in the works of those seeking to create a machine to generate power. He found Huygens's ideas intriguing but impractical. It was Thomas Savery's work that truly inspired him. Savery built a simple pistonless steam engine in 1700 to solve a major problem for miners in England: the removal of water that filled the shafts deep below ground. It used the principle of condensation. When hot steam inside

a cylinder cools, it creates a vacuum. A one-way valve allowed water from below to be sucked up into this low pressure chamber. Newcomen succeeded in expanding on this concept with his brilliant piston-based steam engine of 1712; capable of raising ten gallons of water 150 feet with each stroke. His reliable steam engine started a revolution in design and application.

Engraving drawn by Henry Beighton of Newcastle in 1717, showing what is believed to be his own modified version of Newcomen's engine for pumping water from mines. Beighton had invented a safety valve that year which prevented boiler failure, improving upon the original atmospheric engine designed by Thomas Newcomen in 1712. Illustration shows the huge scale of these original engines. The steam cylinder containing the piston sits directly above the coal-fired boiler. Illustration Science Museum / Science & Society Picture Library.

It's Thermodynamic

Newcomen's engine relied heavily on the ongoing study of thermodynamics (the study of energy conversion from heat to mechanical work). It was based on the concept that heat could be used to develop

101

mechanical motion. The idea was simple. It was heat that created the expansion of air or water vapor in a cylinder that could therefore be used to push a piston upward. It was the subsequent cooling of the air in the cylinder that resulted in lowering the pressure in the cylinder, allowing the piston to be pushed back down by atmospheric pressure. Atmospheric pressure is the weight of the air bearing down on us from our atmosphere. It was not the steam pressure that created the power stroke in these early engines, it was the returning piston pushed by atmospheric pressure. This was the concept employed by most pioneers of steam and gas engines until the development of the four-stroke cycle motor 150 years later.

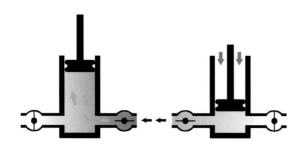

Basic principle of an atmospheric steam engine. (left) Hot steam enters the cylinder, causing the air to expand and drive the piston slowly upward. (right) As the cylinder cools, the air pressure in the cylinder becomes lower than that of the atmosphere, resulting in the piston being pushed down. This produces the power stroke. Valves mechanically linked to the piston rod control the flow. Illustration by Daniel Ensanian.

Our atmosphere is an ocean of air that has a force of 14.7 pounds per square inch at sea level. Atmospheric engines of all sorts, from simple hot air to steam engines, relied on the weight of the air to return the piston to its starting position. Their design was limited to the 14.7 lb/in.2 The cylinder of an atmospheric engine does not need to be vertical, as was the case of Newcomen's design. It did, however, help to have gravity assist to pull down manhole cover–sized pistons.

A Perfectly Round Hole

A great challenge in engine development was the lack of precision boring machines capable of making a smooth, round hole. This was critical for providing a proper seal for the piston. Leather had to be used to seal the piston tight against the uneven surface of the cylinder bore in early steam engines. We are spoiled today with our precision machines, capable of boring perfectly round holes within a few thousands of an inch. Snug fitting pistons within smooth round bores minimize the loss of gas pressure, thus creating greater efficiency.

The Power of Watt

It was Scotsman James Watt that took things to the next level, bringing us closer to the motorcycle. His improvements on Newcomen's engine resulted in reliable, powerful steam engines. Part of Watt's success was based on iron worker John Wilkinson's work. Wilkinson had developed a process to make perfectly round holes for the large diameter bores Watt's engines required. These ranged from two to four feet in diameter. Watt's innovations inspired others in the region. French engineer and mechanic, Nicolas Joseph Cugnot, began work on what is considered to be the very first viable self-propelled vehicle in 1769. It was cumbersome and even crashed into a wall on its maiden voyage. But it proved the concept.

The 1771 Cugnot steam tractor as exhibited in the Musée des Arts et Métiers, Paris. Photo Science Museum / Science & Society Picture Library.

Watt and his partner, Boulton, built as many as five hundred engines. The addition of an external cooling condenser further increased efficiency. It permitted the engine's steam to go through its expansion-cooling cycle faster. This innovation allowed their later engines to employ double-acting power strokes, where steam acted on the piston in both directions. This created more pressure than just atmospheric pressure to return the piston to its first position. A heavy flywheel would maintain rotational momentum to help the engine through its cycle. Double-action was key to the locomotives of the nineteenth and twentieth centuries. To put the timeline into perspective, this was happening during our Revolutionary War.

An advanced double-acting rotative Boulton & Watt steam engine of 1797. Some of these engines were over twenty feet tall. Watt's earlier engines had cylinders as large as fifty inches in diameter. Illustration Science Museum / Science & Society Picture Library.

Selling the Concept

Watt's biggest challenge was convincing potential customers that his engines could be economical replacements for the horse. At first it was his word against theirs. Horses had to eat, and steam generation required coal. In a stroke of marketing brilliance, Watt set off to quantify the work a horse actually produces so that he could offer a comparison to his engines.

Observing and measuring horses at work gave James Watt the data he needed to develop the formula for horsepower. Honoring his discovery, the unit Watt has been applied to a measure of electrical power. One horsepower equals 746 watts.

Pure Horsepower

Studying the work of horses as they turned wheels to power textile mills and pumps, Watt concluded that, conservatively, a horse could lift 33,000 pounds one foot in one minute. He referred to this as a unit of "horsepower." Horsepower became the standard in evaluating the performance and power of motors.

Horsepower (hp) is the stuff we boast of when showing off a new bike. Brake horsepower (bhp) refers to the power put out at the crankshaft directly. That will be a bit different than power at the rear wheel because some is lost through the transmission. The term "brake" refers to the instrument used to measure this value. A brake provides resistance against the engine in order to measure its ability to overcome it. Brakes today are called dynamometers. Serious speed buffs get their motors tuned on a "dyno" to quantify and improve horsepower and torque values. Watt was content with just being able to say that his engines put out the equivalent of three or four horses.

Steam engines, and some early gas engines, used a "flyball" governor to maintain consistent revolutions per minute. This optimized the engine's performance and prevented overrunning. The heavy spinning steel balls would spread outward from centrifugal force as the engine sped up. This outward motion acted on linkages that would reduce steam pressure, or gas intake. The term "balls to the wall" describes an engine at high speed when the steel balls are facing toward the walls of the engine room.

Leading the Way to Internal Combustion

Watt's workshop produced several other innovations that would lead to the modern four-stroke cycle internal combustion engine. One of his assistants, William Murdock, invented the slide valve. It was used to regulate steam in double-acting engines, and later in early gas engines. He also pioneered the production of coal gas used for illuminating lamps. It was a critical fuel for early gas-powered motors. When we refer to early engines as "gas engines," we are referring to a gas, not gasoline.

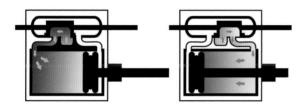

Illustration showing a double-acting steam engine with a slide valve. Note how the valve redirects the steam to produce power strokes in either direction. The valve's shaft is typically connected to a linkage on the piston rod. A few drops of oil are introduced into the cylinder on each stroke to help lubricate the piston. Slide valves were also used on early gas engines. Illustration by Daniel Ensanian.

External combustion engines, like the steam engine, were not the only game in town as Watt's engines chugged happily away. The term "external combustion" refers to the way steam is generated, external to the inside of the cylinder driving the piston. A boiler is required to heat water to generate steam. Inventors since the days of Huygens recognized the real value of internal combustion, where an explosion inside a cylinder is used to power the piston. The piston would simply need to push a connect-ing rod linked by a crank to a wheel. The problem was how to create regular pulses of exploding power inside a cylinder.

Getting Closer

Along comes Swiss engineer Isaac de Rivaz. He played with gunpowder and steam at first, but quickly realized that internal combustion using a gas was the way to go. A true visionary in the eyes of "green" people today, he focused on a mixture of hydrogen and oxygen as his fuel to power a carriage. He used a clever new device invented by Allesandro Volta to ignite the mixture inside the tall cylinder. Volta had developed a spark-generating condenser. Since De Rivaz's engine was of the atmospheric type, the explosion of the hydrogen gas simply raised the piston. A ratchet and chain mechanism drove the wheel as the piston dropped with the aid of gravity and atmospheric pressure.

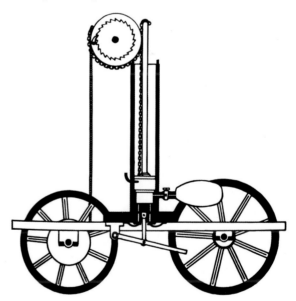

A drawing of Isaac De Rivaz's self-propelled carriage of 1805, featuring a hydrogen gas–driven internal combustion engine of the atmospheric type. Hydrogen gas is contained in the bladder. Ratchet mechanism on top engages with downward motion of the piston to drive the wheels.

De Rivaz's vehicle is considered the first internal combustion engine–powered vehicle. Despite the short-lived success of his 1807 patented design, technical complications precluded practical application. Lack of a pressurized hydrogen fuel cell was the biggest obstacle. Without it, the vehicle had a very limited range.

While internal combustion development was going on, steam continued to dominate propulsion. The bicycle was evolving from the simple hobbyhorse to a serious mode of transportation. Pedals were added to the front wheel, and steering allowed great mobility in crowded urban areas. The 1885 Rover bicycle featured the now-standard diamond frame and a chain-driven rear wheel. Smaller and smaller steam engines began to appear as machining and foundry work matured. It was just a matter of time before the marriage of motor and bicycle. The first workable examples of steam-powered bicycles appeared nearly simultaneously in 1869 on both sides of the Atlantic Ocean. I consider these to be the first "real" motorcycles.

Roper's Velocipede

Sylvester H. Roper, of Roxbury, Massachusetts, was an avid experimenter of steam-driven vehicles. The efforts of Roper, along with Michaux and Copeland, would signal the beginning of motorcycling. They all fitted an engine to a bicycle. Many would contend that a motorcycle must have a gasoline-powered engine rather than a steam engine. It is, however, the opinion of the author that a bicycle powered by any engine can be called a motorcycle, be it steam, internal combustion gas engine, turbine, or electric motor.

Roper started on his bike in 1867. By 1869, he was demonstrating his amazing steam-powered velocipede at fairs and circuses. The bike was purpose-built, with a strong, forged iron backbone acting as the frame. Suspended beneath the seat was a vertical, spring mounted, charcoal burning fire-tube boiler.

The Roper steam velocipede as it remains today in the care of the Smithsonian. It was a gift to the museum from John H. Bacon. The throttle and "spoon" brake were both actuated by twisting the handlebars. Roper's small twin-cylinder steam engine had 2-1/4-inch bores. Its cranks acted directly upon the rear axle. The rear wheel served as the flywheel. Photo courtesy of Division of Work & Industry, National Museum of American History, Smithsonian Institution.

Roper's steam bike had a large chimney pipe sticking out from the top of the boiler housing that could be rotated to modify the draft running through the firebox. Water for the boiler was supplied from a tank within the seat. This was a real motorcycle, being self-propelled with an engine in a cycle frame.

As Roper made his rounds in Massachusetts to the jeers of pedestrians, the French bicycle manufacturer Michaux had adapted a small steam engine made by fellow countryman Louis-Guillaume Perreaux to one of their "bone-shaker" cycles around the same time, perhaps even a year earlier. The result was elegant and efficient. But, like Roper and other experimenters, Michaux was not to see profits from this enterprise.

Undaunted, Roper continued to refine his steam bikes. His last iteration housed a steam engine within a metal-framed safe-ty bicycle. He raced it on a track on June 1, 1896, in Cambridge, only to suffer a heart attack. Some believe it was from excitement. He had successfully achieved 30 mph. Roper was a true pioneer biker.

Alternate Fuels

Numerous engineers and designers continued down the path of steam-powered bikes, but the limitations were obvious. Steam engines required boiling water. That took time. They also required water, as well as a source of fuel to be stored on board, be it charcoal, alcohol, or kerosene. The Humber bicycle makers in England took a fresh new approach in 1897. They built a battery-powered tandem electric bike. Unfortunately, batteries were not up to the task. They were large and heavy, and drained quickly. It would take another hundred years for the

The Michaux-Perreaux steam velocipede with belt-driven rear wheel. The boiler was fired with alcohol instead of charcoal. As with Roper's design, the fundamental layout of the motorcycle was evolving. Photo Science Museum / Science & Society Picture Library.

dream of an efficient electric bike to be realized. Humber, like most, accepted the fact that the best solution for mobility was the internal combustion engine.

Photo of prototype steam bike fitted with a small 1.5 hp steam engine built in 1889 by the brothers Heinrich and Wilhelm Hildebrand of Munich, Germany. The water is carried in the curved tank above the rear wheel. In the early 1890s, the Hildebrand brothers abandoned steam propulsion and switched to petrol engines for their motorcycles. Photo Science Museum / Science & Society Picture Library.

Development in steam-powered motorcycles continued long after gasoline-powered internal combustion engine bikes replaced them. This Pearson and Cox used kerosene to fire its tube boiler to produce a respectable 3 hp in 1912. Three horsepower was in line with petrol engines of the time. Photo Science Museum / Science & Society Picture Library.

Lenoir Brings Us Closer

Work to create an internal combustion engine accelerated at a feverish rate on both sides of the Atlantic. Coal gas was found to be a new and exciting fuel to ignite within the cylinder. It was rich in hydrogen and methane, and quite common in that it was used to illuminate streets and homes. Mixing it with sufficient oxygen from the air made it quite volatile once ignited. Italian inventors Eugenio Barsanti and Felice Matteucci took things to the next level in 1854, incorporating electric sparkplugs in their atmospheric internal combustion engines fueled by this illuminating gas. By 1859, the Belgian-born scientist Jean Joseph Étienne Lenoir built a working single-cylinder double-acting engine running on a mix of coal gas and air in his French workshop. It borrowed the sparkplug concept from Barsanti-Metucci. The engine resembled a double-acting steam engine in appearance and function. Combustion occurred on both sides of the piston, alternating power strokes as slide valves controlled intake of the illuminating gas/air mixture, as well as exhaust. Ignition occurred soon after intake began. The intake valve would close at approximately one-third of the piston's rearward stroke to allow ignition. There was no compression of the fuel mixture as the mixture was at atmospheric pressure at ignition. It was basically a two-cycle process: intake-explosion and exhaust. Lenoir's engine was the first real production internal combustion engine, with nearly 500 units made. Horsepower ranged between 4 and 6, at about 100 rpm. Lenoir's success, however, would soon be overshadowed by the efforts of a pair of Germans—Otto and Langen.

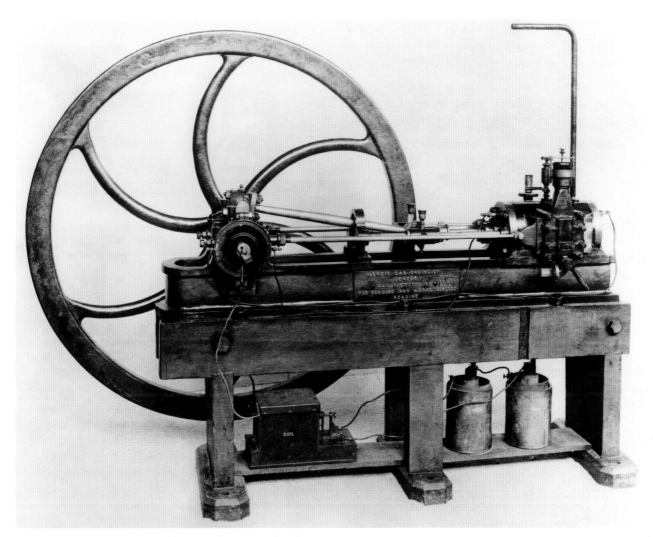

The Lenoir Gas Engine of 1860. This was the first practical internal combustion engine. Jean Lenoir (1822–1900) was a Belgian who moved to Paris to work as a metal enameller at the age of 26. Due to the availability in the mid-19th century of piped supplies of coal gas, he developed a compact engine using coal gas and electric spark to ignite. Note the batteries and ignition coil underneath the engine. This engine was seen as an improvement on the steam engine, which needed a boiler, bulky fuel, and a large water supply. Coal gas was mixed with the air at a ratio of 1:7 by weight. A large flywheel was needed to keep rotational momentum on the slow-revolving engine to get it through its cycle. The marketing buzz around gas engines promised great advantages over steam. However, this euphoria quickly declined as high fuel consumption questioned the efficiency of these machines. Major improvements were to come as others took the gas engine to the next step in its evolution. Photo Science Museum / Science & Society Picture Library.

The Four-Stroke Concept

Before we get to Otto and Langen, it is noteworthy to mention that the French engineer Alphonse Beau de Rochas conceived of the idea of the four-stroke cycle internal combustion engine while others were continuing development of underpowered non-compression types. His unpublished patent of January 16, 1862, identified four specific strokes of the piston. Induction admitted the gas/air mixture, compression of the mixture follows, ignition to create the power stroke, and finally the exhaust stroke to expel the burnt gasses. The key to Rochas's approach was the compression of the gas/air mixture prior to ignition.

This compression allows much more rapid incineration of the volatile mixture inside the cylinder. The resulting explosion creates higher temperature gasses that produce greater amounts of pressure to push the piston than if the mixture were not compressed at all. Engine designs prior to his relied on fuel/air mixtures that were nearly at atmospheric pressure inside the cylinder. It's like comparing the power of a small firecracker exploding out in the open versus one jammed into a small tin. The latter creates much more pressure and blows the can apart. This is a major concept used to extract horsepower from engines today. The higher the compression, the more power. Modern motorcycle engines may achieve greater than 13:1 compression ratios, but must heed the side effects of doing so.

De Rochas never officially filed his papers, but his concepts were well documented and showed up twenty-three years later in legal disputes with Nikolaus Otto, claimed founder of the four-stroke cycle engine. Ironically, an Austrian named Christian Reithmann was granted a German patent for a very similar four-stroke engine design a year later, but failed to capitalize on it as Otto did.

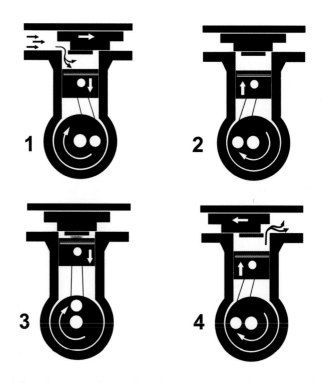

The four strokes of a four-stroke cycle internal combustion engine as illustrated with a highly simplified representation of a slide valve system. The slide valve is actuated by levers attached to the crankshaft. 1) Intake stroke draws in air and fuel vapor. In reality the air is pushed in by atmospheric pressure as the downward motion of the piston creates lower air pressure in the cylinder. The illustration does not show a carburetor, which mixes the liquid fuel with air. Coal gas could easily have been used and would have been fed by a small tube. 2) Compression stroke compresses the gas/air mixture after the slide valve creates a tight seal. Modern engines use mushroom-shaped valves for better sealing. 3) Ignition to ignite the compressed fuel/air mixture creates the power stroke. Ignition may have been by a small tube entering the combustion chamber and exposing the compressed mixture to a flame, or an electric spark as we have today. 4) Exhaust stroke occurs when the slide valve opens an exhaust port for the hot spent gasses to exit. The cycle then repeats. The momentum of a heavy flywheel maintains rotation. An engine's size, or displacement, represents the total volume of the cylinder and head when the piston is at the very bottom of its stroke. This is called bottom-dead-center, or BDC. Displacement may be given in cubic centimeters (cc) or cubic inches (ci).

Otto Starts a Revolution

Nikolaus August Otto was born in 1832 in Holzhausen, Germany. His family's financial state did not allow him to pursue his dream of going to technical school. He became a sugar and houseware merchant traveling the countryside. Despite his lack of formal training, Otto became enamored with the internal combustion engine. He recognized the limitations of Lenoir's engine: its lack of mobility. Mobility, however, would be possible if the engine could run off a liquid fuel that could be carried on board a vehicle. He designed an air carburetor that could meter the proper amount of alcohol to the engine and mix it with air. Despite this innovation, the engines were still far too heavy and cumbersome for adaptation to a small carriage.

Together with Eugen Langen (1833–1895), Otto pioneered the four-stroke internal combustion engine in 1876. However, Otto's patent was invalidated in 1886 when it was discovered that another inventor, the Frenchman Alphonse Beau de Rochas (1815–1845), had described the four-stroke cycle principle in an earlier published paper. Photo Science Museum / Science & Society Picture Library.

Otto ordered a Lenoir engine to experiment with. He recognized its limitation in design. The power stroke occurred soon after the intake stroke without any compression of the gas/air mixture. It dawned on him to have the ignition occur after the piston compressed the gas/air mixture; perhaps inspired by Beau de Rochas. This created an amazing increase in power. He even experimented with a four-cylinder design; dedicating every "taller" he had to the cause.

His partner to be, Eugene Langen, lived in Cologne, Germany. Unlike Otto, he studied at a technical school. Ironically, Langen was a partner in a sugar refining company. It was only a matter of time before the two would meet based on Otto's trade. Their common passion for engines would prompt them to start the world's first, and oldest, company making internal combustion engines. The N.A. Otto & Company exists today under its direct descendant, Deutz, AG.

Show Time

Otto and Langen were determined to create new engine designs surpassing those of Lenoir and others. Technical problems with compression engines shifted their focus on developing a more efficient non-compression atmospheric engine. The opportunity to showcase their machine came in 1867 at the Paris Exposition. The odds were stacked against them as well-known designers shared the stage; each claiming their ideas to be superior. As luck would have it, one of the judges stressed the importance of efficiency over power. The Otto & Langen engine clearly won on that front. Orders came pouring in, and the company became the first commercially successful engine manufacturer in history, with licensees worldwide. Numerous agreements were made to allow manufacture in other countries. British engine manufacturer Crossley was the most notable.

Wayne S. Grenning, engineer and engine historian, shown with the very Otto & Langen engine that won a Gold Medal at the Paris Exposition in 1867. Engine S/N #1 runs on illuminating gas (coal gas) and is ignited by a small carrier flame that explodes the gas/air mixture via a timed slide valve. Electric ignition was not quite reliable enough for Otto. The motor produces only 1/2-hp, but weighs a massive 1,600 pounds. It is on private exhibition only at the Deutz, AG Technikum Museum in Germany. It is fired up for special occasions. Photo courtesy of Wayne S. Grenning.

Otto and Langen incorporated a new company in 1872 called Gasmotoren-Fabrik Deutz AG. They hired an engineering talent named Gottlieb Daimler to run production. Daimler brought a bright young engineer along to head the design department. The name may seem equally familiar: Wilhelm Maybach. Daimler and Maybach greatly improved on the Otto and Langen design. But all was not peachy. Daimler was demanding and butted heads with his bosses. After ten years he set off to start his own firm. In the interim, Otto was faced with the reality that his engine was too massive and could produce only 3 hp. He set off to design an engine that would ultimately change the world.

Eureka

Otto went against all current wisdom in designing his new motor. Unlike popular belief that every other stroke of the piston should produce work, Otto focused on creating as much power as possible from a single power stroke as speculated by de Rochas years earlier. That power stroke would have the energy to bring the engine through its working cycles in time for the next power stroke. A heavy flywheel was used to help the process. This all required separate intake, compression, ignition, and exhaust strokes over two complete rotations of the crankshaft. Otto and his assistant, Franz Rings, built a prototype during the first six months of 1876.

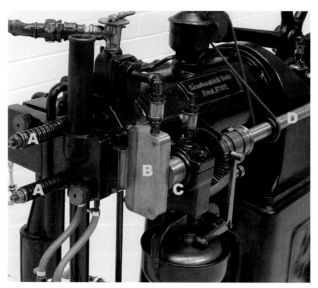

Detailed view of a slide valve mechanism shows camshaft D rotating cam C to slide the slide valve plate B back and forth. Springs A apply pressure on the lubricated slide valve mechanism to prevent gas pressure from escaping. Photo of this Deutz engine courtesy of Wayne S. Grenning.

This compact 1876 Otto prototype engine fits on a workbench and is the DNA from which all four-stroke cycle automobile and motorcycles engines were derived. It survived the World Wars in Germany as its protectors hid it from harm's way. The camshaft that activates the valves is seen up front and features the same gearing as all modern engines—rotating once for every two revolutions of the flywheel. The Gasmotorenfabrik Deutz production motor pictured in the chapter introduction weighed 2,200 pounds and produced 2 hp at 180 rpm. Photo courtesy of Wayne S. Grenning.

The engine used a slide valve to control the air/gas mixture entering the cylinder. An open flame was used to ignite the compressed mixture as a small valve opened just enough to expose the pressurized gas in the cylinder to the flame. Timing was precise, as the external flame had to be "carried" into the cylinder via channels in the valve without extinguishing it. This set a clear limitation of about 200 rpm as it became increasingly difficult to carry the flame at higher speeds. Exhaust was accomplished by a rocker arm activating a poppet valve, just like it remains to this day. The engine ran so quietly as opposed to the clanking and clacking of

atmospheric models that it was given the name "Silent Otto." Maybach improved on the basic design by incorporating a better compression release to aid in starting, something quite common on large single-cylinder motorcycle engines to come.

The Humble Piston

It is noteworthy at this point to mention one component of the internal combustion engine that takes the most abuse. It is the piston that is found in engines used to power our automobiles and motorcycles. Most of these engines are of the four-stroke cycle type as developed by Nikolaus

Otto in 1876, but with mushroom shaped overhead valves instead of slide valves. The engine's process to produce power involves the four specific strokes of its reciprocating piston.

It all begins with a round piston riding within a perfectly round cylinder. Early pistons were made of cast iron. They were heavy and retained heat. Their heavy mass limited higher engine speeds. By the 1930s most pistons were being made out of aluminum alloy. Aluminum dissipates heat better than iron. During the height of combustion, temperatures can reach over 4,500 degrees Fahrenheit. Fortunately this is for only a few microseconds. The heat-conducting characteristics of aluminum transfer the heat immediately to the cooler cylinder walls. Oil splashing underneath the pistons on a four-stroke engine helps cool it further. The rush of fresh, cool air from the next intake stroke also aids significantly to cool the piston for its next combustion stroke.

Pistons come in all sizes and shapes. Most modern pistons are actually slightly oval in shape, rounding out as they expand from heat. The right front piston is off a two-stroke engine. It shows two transfer port holes that match up with ports in the cylinder. During the combustion stroke pressures can easily approach one thousand pounds per square inch. An average large bore piston experiences over ten thousand pounds of pressure during the peak of combustion.

Cylinders and fins may reach a temperature of 300 degrees Fahrenheit or more. Liquid-cooled engines help remove this heat

more efficiently. The hot water surrounding a cylinder is pumped to a radiator that dissipates the heat into the open air. A moving motorcycle allows cool ambient air to flow over the radiator fins. A stationary motorcycle may activate an electric fan behind the radiator to create cooling air flow. Regardless, pistons still retain more than 600 degrees Fahrenheit in heat.

Pistons have sealing rings, called piston rings. They expand around the piston and push against the cylinder walls to seal against gas pressure losses. They also prevent oil from getting past the piston and entering the combustion chamber above. Oil splashing inside the engine is critical for lubricating the piston. A smoking engine may indicate worn cylinder walls or bad piston rings.

Pistons endure the most inconceivable punishment via extremes in temperature and friction. This two-stroke piston shows significant wear from years of use. The scuff marks may also have been the result of insufficient oil mixed with the gas. Note the melted and eroded upper edge of the piston facing the exhaust port. This was most likely caused by a lean mixture and high rpms. The upper piston ring deteriorated enough to be broken into pieces and blown out of the engine.

The piston is joined to the crankshaft by a connecting rod. The lower end of this rod is attached to a crank pin that is off-center from the crankshaft's axis. This provides the leverage to rotate the crankshaft. Holes drilled in the crankshaft supply oil to the soft metal shell bearings protecting the crank journals from wear. Crankshafts may have heavy steel or iron weights attached to them to maintain rotational momentum as the engine goes through its strokes. After all, only one of the four strokes produces power on a four-stroke engine. These "flywheels" may be part of the crankshaft or may be external to the engine, as on the Moto Guzzi Falcone shown elsewhere in this book.

Photo shows a single piston joined to a crankshaft via aluminum alloy connecting rod pivoting on a crank-pin (also called crank-journal) on a mid-1970's British parallel twin. The lower end of this rod can be split by removing the two bolts visible. This permits the use of shell bearings. The longer the connecting rod, the greater the torque, or pushing force. This is because the crank-pin has to be off-set further from the crankshaft's axis to allow rotation. The further from the axis, the more leverage. The concept is similar to having a longer handle on a shovel or a hammer. The downside to long stroke engines is lower rpms. There is just too much mass to move up and down quickly. Short stroke multi-cylinder engines, and two-stroke engines, make up for this by being able to rev much higher. A large ball bearing on the end of the crankshaft fits into one side of the crankcase. Another bearing on the other side serves the same function. The large flywheel helps the engine rotate through the non-power-producing strokes. The heavy flywheel also has counterweights on the bottom to balance the rotation.

Daimler Moves In

There was no love lost between Otto and Daimler. He left Otto's company and took Maybach with him. The assumption is that Daimler took many of Otto's ideas as well. He did continue his own development with several notable achievements. The first was the incorporation of a small carbure-tor that could evaporate liquid fuels and efficiently mix them with air. The ratios of fuel to air varies with the type of fuel used, but modern day engines use approximate-ly 15 parts air to 1 part of fuel by weight to achieve efficient combustion. The carbu-retor allowed the mobility Daimler needed to power his vision of an automobile. Appendix C provides more detail on air-fuel ratio and the function of a carburetor.

Daimler patented his engine in December of 1883. Meanwhile, inventor Karl Benz had already received a patent for a liquid-fueled engine in October of 1882. Daimler's 1883 engine, however, utilized an atmospheric inlet valve instead of a slide valve. The valve opened during the intake stroke to admit the gas/air mixture and created a better seal during the compression stroke. Some would say atmospheric valves are opened by suction as the piston moves downward, but in reality it is the atmospheric pressure of the earth that pushes it open and forces the gas/air mixture into the low pressure chamber.

The Internal-Combustion Vehicle Hits the Road

By 1885, Daimler and Maybach succeeded in demonstrating the viability of internal combustion–powered mobility. Their two-speed "bone shaker" motorcycle served as a test bed for a flame ignited 1/2-hp engine running at 750 revolutions per minute. The bike had a twist-grip throttle; a tradition maintained by motorcycles today. Daimler and Maybach continued to innovate. They even developed the first V-twin internal combustion engine for more power.

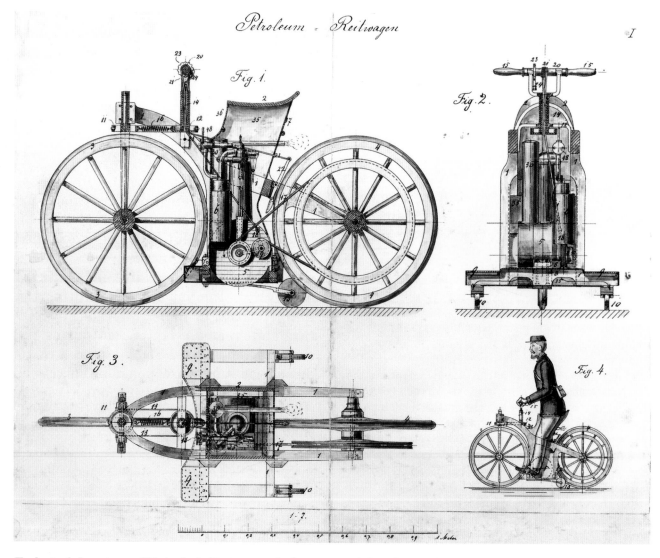

Technical drawings of Daimler's Reitwagen (riding wagon) dated 1884 features a 264cc (16.1 cu. in.). Otto engine resting on rubber blocks. Illustration courtesy of Mercedes-Benz Museum.

Who Was Really First?

Several other inventors working independently developed prototypes for internal combustion–powered vehicles. Italian inventor Enrico Bernardi may have actually been the first to create a working petrol-fueled engine. His "Motrice Pia" was revealed to the public in Turin on August 5, 1882. The engine was named after his daughter. He adapted the 122.5cc single horizontal cylinder, flame-ignited Otto cycle engine, with a cast iron double-wall cylinder with a cooling water jacket to his son's tricycle shortly thereafter.

Englishman Edward Butler displayed a three-wheeled prototype ahead of Daimler's, as well in 1884. But it was Karl Benz who used a similar engine to Daimler's that actually patented the first automobile in 1886. Benz's rich history in engine development and practical thinking created a highly successful design. He had perfected a two-stroke engine that was to set a standard for the breed. He was also a pioneer in the efficient use of electrical ignition, the adaptation of a clutch, water-cooling, and an advanced evaporative carburetor.

It is interesting to note that Austrian inventor Siegfried Marcus is said to have fitted a gasoline-powered engine to a small wagon ten years earlier but never applied for a patent. He did advance his design to present the world with a viable automobile in 1888, but the distinction as the first successful petrol-powered motor vehicle still goes to Daimler and Maybach's bone shaker.

The Daimler engine of 1885 distinctly featuring its large brass carburetor. This type of carburetor employed a float and valve system to maintain a consistent level of the highly volatile petroleum distillates used in the early days as fuel. The fuel's vapor is mixed with the air to provide the explosive stuff for combustion. Modern carburetors using less volatile gasoline require a fine spray of the fuel to be mixed with the incoming air to provide sufficient fuel for ignition. The latter is more effective with higher revving, faster breathing engines appearing in the first decade of the twentieth century. Modern fuel injection takes things to the next level, forcing a spray of fuel directly into the cylinder. Intake and exhaust valves were of the poppet type. Intake valve opened by suction, exhaust by cam. Photo courtesy of Daimler AG.

Another replica of the 1885 Daimler Reitwagen as photographed at the Barber Vintage Motorsports Museum. The original machine, which was destroyed, can be considered to be the first practical internal combustion engine-powered motorcycle, training wheels and all. Its 1/2-hp engine could propel it down the street at a respectable 7 miles per hour.

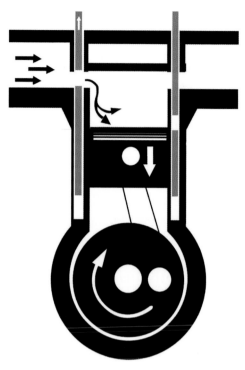

Daimler experimented with an intake and exhaust valve system utilizing a sliding cylinder (gray) that fits snug around the outside of the combustion cylinder. This "sleeve valve" was actuated by gears, levers, and cams to move up and down in proper timing. Openings in the sleeve allowed intake and exhaust as they passed by their respective ports in the combustion cylinder's wall. Variations of this system included a design that moved the combustion cylinder up and down in concert with the sleeve. This style appeared on automobile and tractor engines through the 1920s. As engines developed higher compression, sleeve and slide valve systems became inadequate as they leaked. The poppet valve was, and still is, superior in sealing the combustion chamber. The engine in this drawing is shown in the intake stroke. The sleeve cylinder is moving upwards as the engine is turning at this point.

Enter the Count

Automobile engines were large and bulky, not ideal for motorcycles. They were typically made of cast iron with huge flywheels to help the engine get through its cycles. A major advancement in engine design was made in 1884 by Count De Dion and his engineer, Georges Bouton, in France. It offered

Daimler and Maybach developed the first V-twin engine in 1889. It produced 1.5 hp at 600 rpm. Ignition was by hot-tube. Photo courtesy of Daimler AG.

a better solution and would kick-start the installation of motors to cycle frames. They felt that smaller, lighter, and higher revving engines could make better power. They were correct. Their 211cc singles of 1897 were able to generate as much power at 1,800 rpm as engines three times their size rotating at 600 rpm. Combined with aluminum crankcases, electrical ignition via spark plug, poppet valves instead of slide valves, and a surface evaporative carburetor, the De Dion design became the standard for most major motorcycle builders to follow.

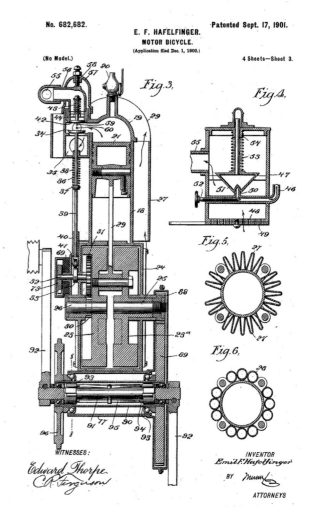

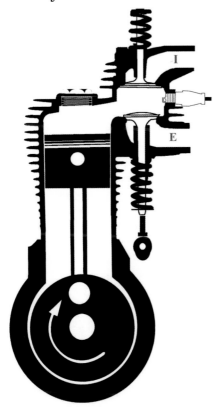

The basic layout of a De Dion-Bouton engine includes an atmospheric inlet (also called intake) valve (on top) and a cam actuated exhaust valve (below). The intake port (I) leads to a carburetor that mixes air with fuel vapor. The exhaust cam is rotated via a gear driven off the crankshaft. Engine in this example is shown in the compression stroke, with both valves closed. Early models varied. Some had the mushroom-shaped "poppet" intake valve facing down, while others had it on the opposite side of the exhaust valve. Poppet valves seal better than slide valves. Illustration by Christian Bangert.

Drawing for a US patent issued to Emil Hafelfinger in September of 1901 for his derivation of a De Dion–based engine design. He had built his first "motor-bicycle" a year earlier. Emil was also a partner in the Royal Motor Works, maker of the highly prized Royal Pioneer motorcycle. The drawing illustrates an atmospheric intake valve and a cam actuated exhaust valve. The bulb-like valve on top is used as both a compression release and primer. Illustration on right is of a simple float-regulated surface (evaporative) carburetor. The triangular float made of brass meters the proper amount of fuel into the bowl. Highly volatile fuel vapors mixed with air get drawn into the engine during the intake stroke.

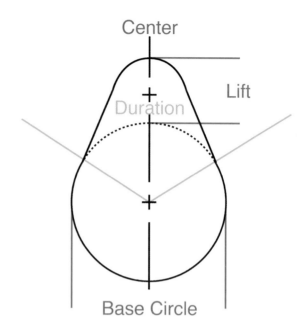

Photo of a pre-1900 De Dion motorcycle engine. The exhaust valve is operated off a single camshaft. Fins served to cool the engine. Note the atmospheric intake valve (also referred to as a suction valve) to the left of the exhaust valve.

Cam design can be extremely complicated. Lift determines how much a valve is opened. The duration controls how long a valve stays open. Many other factors on a cam lobe influence an engine's performance, including ramp angles, the shape of a cam's nose (tip), and its overall timing in relation to piston position.

Motorcycle engines use a broad variety of camshaft designs depending on the engine configuration and number of cylinders. The camshaft on the bottom is for a two-cylinder, two-valves-per-cylinder engine. It has four cam lobes. Two tappets are shown. These ride on the cam lobes directly to act upon the valve stem, or via a pushrod on later overhead valve engines. The smaller cam, with gear attached, is more similar to what is found on a De Dion–type single-cylinder engine; albeit with a single cam lobe instead of two.

This working example of an 1898 De Dion tri-cycle features an evaporative fuel carburetor (copper tank under seat) and electric ignition powered by a battery contained within the black box under the frame. De Dion–powered trikes were all the rage in Europe at the turn of the twentieth century. Licenses for manufacture were granted all over the world.

Details of this popular cycle show the ignition coil strapped to the right side of the cross member. Engine oil was held in a small glass (green) reservoir. Early motors did not use oil pumps and relied on internal splashing of the oil for lubrication. The poor machining tolerances allowed some of the oil to sneak past the pistons to be burnt up. This type of lubrication is thus called "total loss."

The applications of the internal combustion engine seemed endless as inventors began attaching them to pumps, grinders, conveyors, and pretty much anything on wheels. The basic De Dion design was copied by many builders who began adapting them to bicycles. Constant development kept up with limitations. Robert Bosh's self-generating magneto developed in the 1890s eliminated the need for batteries to power the sparking system. John Boyd Dunlop's advancement of the pneumatic tire in 1894 offered a more comfortable ride.

Alternative Ignition

Igniting the compressed fuel/air mixture within the cylinder at the right time is critical for achieving efficiency. This "ignition timing" changes with the speed at which the motor operates. The higher the rpms, the earlier the ignition must occur. It takes time for an explosion to obtain its maximum pressure within the cylinder. If the mixture is ignited too late, such as after the piston passes top-dead-center, valuable power will be lost. The ignition timing on most engines is, therefore, set at several degrees before-top-dead-center (BTDC). Many bikes up to the 1960s required the rider to adjust the ignition timing manually. It would have to be "retarded" to make starting easier. Modern ignition systems "advance" the timing automatically as the engine speeds up. High-performance engines can easily have their spark occur 30 degree BTDC at higher rpms.

Flame ignition had clear limits on engine rpm. This was not so much a problem with very early atmospheric gas engines as they operated slowly. Variations to flame ignition systems incorporated a primary external flame that re-ignited the carrier flame between engine cycles utilizing

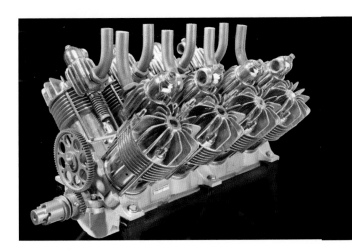

De Dion–type engines were not limited to single-cylinders. V-twins were very common. American aircraft designer Glen Curtiss built V-8 versions of the atmospheric intake engine to power his aircraft. It produced as much as 40 hp. He used this engine in 1907 to set a land speed record on a motorcycle at over 136 mph. The large gear in the center rotates a single eight-lobe camshaft to actuate the eight exhaust valves. Like Otto's original four-stroke cycle engine, it rotates once for every two crankshaft rotations. Holes help reduce weight. Photo courtesy of Smithsonian National Air and Space Museum (NASM 2002-13919).

a rotating igniter chamber. This became necessary for engines that compressed the gas/air mixture within the cylinder. The igniter chamber prevented the engine's compression stroke from blowing out the primary flame.

Electrical ignition via a spark could be timed more precisely with an electrical contact breaker actuated by a cam linked to the crankshaft. High-voltage created in an ignition coil generated the spark within the cylinder to ignite the mixture. Early spark systems were not always reliable. Alternative ignition systems were tried during the latter nineteenth century. One such system was hot-tube ignition. This method incorporates a metal or ceramic tube extending out of the cylinder head by six to ten inches. This tube is heated with an open flame from an alcohol or gasoline burner. As the piston compresses the fuel/air mixture, some of it enters the small orifice leading into the tube. Ignition will occur once the fuel/air mixture reaches the red-hot portion of the tube. Ignition timing can be fine-tuned by moving the flame so that the hot spot is either closer or farther from the cylinder.

Limits in rpm and keeping a flame burning were problems that pushed engineers toward electrical ignition systems. These included both the battery-ignition coil type as well as the self-generating magneto type. The latter consists of an armature with coils of wire rotating within a magnetic field. This field is generated by permanent magnets fixed to the inside of the aluminum magneto housing. Contact breakers built within the magneto unit time the release of the high-voltage electric current used to create a spark at the tip of the spark plug.

Photo shows a magneto armature and its housing. Permanent magnets are mounted within the aluminum housing. The large gear is attached to the end of the armature. It meshes with smaller gears that are connected to the crankshaft.

This 1949 Matchless engine's magneto is rotated by a chain driven off the crankshaft. The chain is located behind the aluminum cover with the logo.

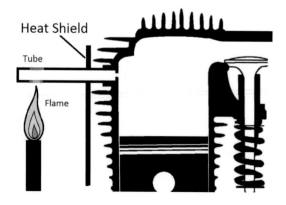

Drawing of a simple hot-tube ignition system. These could be found on multi-cylinder automobile engines as well. Keeping flames lit was always a challenge for the motorist.

Out Come the Opportunists

Exciting development is typically followed by opportunists. Edward J. Pennington's patent for a two-cylinder "Motor-Vehicle" was issued on December 29, 1896. He was quite the charismatic entrepreneur. He developed a barely functioning motorized bike that folks would see only glimpses of during his short demo runs. The two cylinders attached to the rear of the bike overheated quickly and would seize if the demonstration lingered. He was quick to ask for investors, and got them. Unfortunately Pennington was more interested in the money than advancing his design. It all went nowhere.

(No Model.)

E. J. PENNINGTON.
MOTOR VEHICLE.

No. 574,262.   Patented Dec. 29, 1896.

3 Sheets—Sheet 1.

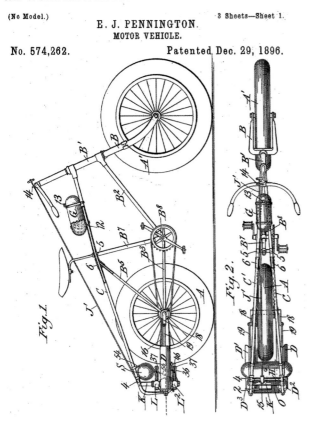

Pennington's US patent drawing of 1896 shows details of his two-cylinder motorbike featuring large, fat pneumatic tires.

(No Model.)

E. J. PENNINGTON.
MOTOR VEHICLE.

No. 574,262.   Patented Dec. 29, 1896.

3 Sheets—Sheet 3.

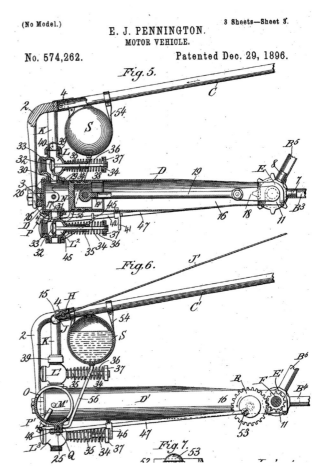

A close-up view of Pennington's engine drawing shows a clever exhaust valve mechanism. The lower image indicates that a reciprocating shaft, driven off a gear (F), has a tang attached to it that pushes the exhaust valve open. The tang (46) can be adjusted for proper timing. The top view shows the intake valve is fed with the fuel/air mixture through the frame tube itself. Intake was atmospheric. The small tank supplies oil to the two engines. Overheating, however, was the design's downfall.

The Motorcycle Takes Shape

The shape of the motorcycles was not standardized until the Werner design of 1901. It placed its 2.75 hp 262cc engine low between wheels and made the crankcase a stressed member of the diamond frame. Harley-Davidson and Indian used the same configuration; a De Dion–style engine set in a diamond-shaped bicycle frame.

The biggest challenge in engine development was not coming up with innovative configurations but dealing with the limitations of metallurgy of the times. It simply could not keep up with the demands of new designs for quite a while. Iron pistons and cast iron cylinders could not tolerate the heat at higher compression ratios and speeds. Cylinders and pistons would crack at high revolutions. Aluminum became the solution after manufacturing methods were refined. Heat-treating advances were also an important requirement to maintain the strength of rapidly rotating parts bearing stressful loads. All of this would eventually be solved over the decades that followed.

William Harley and Arthur Davidson also used the De Dion/Werner configuration when they launched their motorcycles in 1903. Note the beefy leather belt drive and idler pulley. Belt drive is now standard on Harley's, albeit with high-tech cogged Kevlar ones. The small lever mounted to the front of the gas tank adjusts ignition timing.

An example of the Werner design style as used by an early 1900s Yale motorcycle.

Indian designer Oscar Hedstrom adapted his own De Dion–style engine to be part of the rear down-tube on his 1901 Indian. His initial 224cc engine was very much like that exhibited by Emil Hafelfinger that same year. Engine design was such a dynamic endeavor that everyone "borrowed" ideas from each other. Indian used a chain final drive from the onset. Starting required holding the exhaust valve open while pedaling. There was no clutch. One had to kill the electric ignition to bring the bike to a stop. Note the ignition contact breaker at the front of the crankcase with a wire leading to the ignition coil

More Revs for More Power

The next big step in engine design was to increase revolutions per minute to obtain more power. Atmospheric, or suction-activated poppet valve, intake engines had their limitations. As an engine speeds up, the valve could not open and close fast enough to supply a sufficient supply of fuel and air. It was self-limiting. Activating the intake valve mechanically via a cam, like the exhaust valve, allowed the engine to control intake volume. The faster an engine rotated, the faster the intake valve opened and closed.

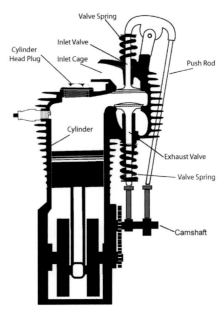

Basic layout of an Inlet-Over-Exhaust (IOE) engine. A gear at the end of the crankshaft engages the cam gear(s). Some engines have a separate geared cam for both the intake and exhaust valves, while others have a single camshaft with multiple lobes (as shown). The intake valve is operated via a cam acting on a pushrod and rocker lever. Tappets are situated between the cam and the valve stem or pushrod. Proper clearance is required at these points for efficient running. Both intake and exhaust valves are lifted by a cam once every other crankshaft revolution. These types of engines are often referred to as "F" heads. Illustration by Christian Bangert.

This 1913 Harley-Davidson Model 9A features a 560cc IOE single-cylinder engine capable of 5 hp. Note the diagonal gear train cover that houses the intake cam and gears that drive the magneto behind the engine. The exhaust cam is driven directly off a gear engaging the crankshaft. Lubrication is of the total loss type.

More Cylinders for More Power

It didn't take long for motorcyclists to want more power. The manufacturers gave it to them with bigger engines. These include two- and four-cylinder models. The V-twin configuration was ideal. It added a cylinder without requiring a larger crankcase. Harley-Davidson introduced its first V-twin in 1907. The problem with narrow angle V-twins is the same as with single-cylinder bikes: vibration. At higher rpms it can get quite annoying. Early engines were limited in their speed, and

riders were much more Spartan in accepting a lot of inconvenience. Today, editors of bike magazines grumble if their hands go numb after twenty minutes road testing a new bike. Rightfully so, we expect comfort when paying big bucks for a machine.

The Merkel IOE V-twin demonstrates just how compact the two-cylinder V design was—requiring no larger crankcase than a big single. Starting the bike required pedaling.

Many big V-twins today are rubber mounted to the frame to quell the vibes. Some models have counterbalancers built into them to do this even more effectively. L-twins, where the engine's cylinders are at 90 degrees to each other, have much less vibration. So why don't the makers like Harley-Davidson, Indian, or Victory go to the L? Simple . . . the sound. The uneven firing pulses of V-twin with a 45- to 50-degree angle between the cylinders have a nice cadence that is hard to replicate in other configurations. The other reason makers stick with the V shape is space. The engines just fit neater into the frame. Regardless, L-twins are V-twins.

V-twins typically offer a lot of torque: the cranking force that throws you back in your seat as you accelerate. This is because of their long connecting rods. Again, think of them as levers. The longer the lever, the more torque. It's the torque we feel in a motor, not the horsepower. Horsepower comes into play for when we want to go faster and faster. Big single-cylinder engines, like the traditional British 500cc "thumper," produce a lot of torque at low rpms.

This 1915 Harley-Davidson "Dodge City" 8-valve racer was a 61 cubic inch V-twin factory bike with four valves per cylinder. The extra valves allowed the engine to "breathe" better. It produced an amazing 53 hp. Racing engine modifications by most manufacturers find themselves on production bikes later down the road, as was the case with overhead valve Harley engines.

Multi-cylinder bikes were not exempt from all the different valve configurations. The beautiful Ace motorcycle, later to become the Indian 4, used both IOE and EOI (exhaust over inlet) configurations during its evolution. Ace roots lead back to the Henderson brothers, who developed the famous four-cylinder bike of the same name. This pristine 1927 example originally sold for $325.

Two-Stroke Engines— A Lesson in Simplicity

The two-stroke cycle engine was evolving parallel to the four-stroke. Many of the very early illuminating gas engines were two-stroke in principle. As the name implies, these engines complete their power cycle in just two strokes: one stroke up and another one down. Being internal combustion engines, they still require induction, compression, ignition, and exhaust phases. In a two-stroke, these are shared between the two strokes. The result is that a power pulse is produced during each rotation of the crankshaft, whereas a four-stroke creates one every other rotation. Two-strokes, therefore, produce a lot of power for a small package. This is why they became a favorite of Grand Prix racers between the mid-1970s and the millennium.

The most notable early motorcycle using a two-stroke motor appeared in 1910. The Scott was powered by a two-cylinder liquid-cooled two-stroke engine. It featured several other innovations in later models that other makers would not offer until decades later. These included a telescoping-type front fork, a kick-starter, and chain final drive. Most bikes of the early days used a leather belt final drive, something not very reliable when it got wet.

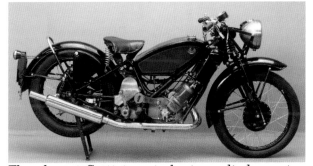

The elegant Scott two-stroke two-cylinder motorcycle endured a long, but often shaky, run between the 1930s and 1950s. Their Squirrel line was the most popular. Pictured is a 1930 Flying Squirrel 596cc two-cylinder water-cooled model. Photo courtesy of Yesterdays Antique Motorcycles.

Two-strokes have less moving parts than four-strokes. Missing are camshafts, mushroom-type valves, rockers, and pushrods. This, combined with a power stroke every revolution, allows for higher revolutions per minute. Various two-stroke designs evolved over the years. The most basic involves a transfer port cast parallel to the cylinder wall. It allows the fuel mixture to be transferred from the crankcase to the cylinder so that the piston can compress it in preparation for ignition. Since the fuel mixture enters the combustion chamber through the crankcase, the engine cannot have a separate oiling system to lubricate the bearings. Oil is mixed into the gasoline or injected into the intake port with a pump. The latter is often referred to as auto-lube. Ratios typically range from 32 to 50 parts of gas to 1 part of oil, depending on need.

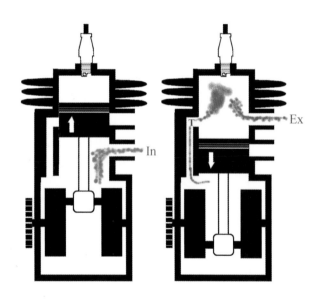

A highly simplified illustration of the two strokes of a two-stroke cycle engine. The left image shows the induction of the air/gas/oil mixture into the crankcase. This is quite unlike a four-stroke, where the gas/air mix is inducted directly into the combustion chamber above the piston. As the piston moves upward to compress the previous charge, it creates low pressure in the crankcase. Atmospheric pressure pushes the fuel mixture through the intake port via the carburetor to fill this low pressure area. As the piston reaches the top of its stroke, it blocks the transfer port and exhaust port. The

power stroke occurs after the spark plug fires and ignites the compressed fuel mixture. The image on the right shows the fuel mixture in the crankcase being pressurized and pushed up above the piston via a transfer port (T) to bring a fresh charge into the combustion chamber. At the same time, hot exhaust gasses are pushed out through the exhaust port (Ex). This overlapping, or scavenging, is where a two-stroke motor loses efficiency. Note that the intake port is blocked at this point.

This cutaway of a basic single-cylinder water-cooled two-stroke shows the brilliant simplicity of this type of engine. This engine has reed-valves (orange) just behind the carburetor. These reeds allow the fuel/mixture in but not out when the crankcase becomes pressurized. Other designs may use a rotating disc to keep the mixture from escaping.

A tremendous amount of engineering has been done over the past fifty years on two-strokes to obtain a very high power-to-weight ratio. Engines have featured multiport designs, reed-valves, disc valves, variable exhaust porting, and countless exhaust expansion chamber designs. The primary challenge was to get the optimum torque at the broadest rpm range possible. Two-strokes generally have a narrower "power-band," making most of their power near the upper half of the rpm range. Those familiar with two-stroke bikes, like the Yamaha RD-350, or Kawasaki H1, can tell you how different they are when launching from a standstill. Two-strokes require a lot of revving to get enough power to get started. This results in quite a few unplanned wheelies.

Two-strokes were highly popular in the 1960s and 1970s for both street and off-road bikes. Their downfall was the oil that was mixed with the gasoline in order to lubricate the crank journal, bearings, and cylinder walls. This resulted in smoky exhaust. This eventually made two-stroke road bikes obsolete as stringent EPA environmental laws prevailed.

German makers like Adler and DKW refined two-stroke engines to a high level of efficiency. These designs were copied by the Japanese extensively after WWII.

The Reliable Side-Valve

The popularity of motorcycles created over a hundred American manufacturers of bikes and bike-related parts before the stock market crash of 1929. Production costs had to be kept in line with competitive pricing. The less expensive four-stroke side-valve engine configuration, therefore, dominated. Initially, a single iron casting incorporated both the cylinder and head. Later models had a removable aluminum alloy head to help cool the motor. Cam actuated valves were situated vertically below the head. This "flathead" engine de-

sign was used by Harley-Davidson and Indian into the 1950s on both single-cylinder and V-twin engine configurations.

Side-valve engines have their valves facing upward and are actuated by cam followers riding on a gear-driven camshaft just below. The followers push up on the tappets as the crankshaft rotates to open and close the valves at the appropriate time. Valve timing is critical to engine performance. The gas/air mixture entering from the left has to make a sharp turn to get into the combustion chamber. This slows flow and therefore robs power.

129

The most endearing of all side-valves is found on Indian motorcycles as shown on this 1940s-era Chief. Note the d ly finned removable aluminum alloy cylinder heads. The big twin was reliable and looked good. Indian kept the de until its demise in 1953. Engine lubrication was by a geared pump located between the exhaust pipes. A section of right gas tank was devoted to holding the circulating oil. Ignition was via coil and distributor, sitting atop the oil pum

Four-cylinder engines used side-valves (or L-heads) as well. Most upgraded to IOE (F-head) or OHV designs for improved air flow. Note the screw caps on top for access to the valves. This cast iron engine ran a bit hot due to poor airflow to the rear cylinders.

View of a 1926 Indian Chief V-twin side-valve engine showing the single casting comprising each cylinder and cylinder head. Large access plugs on top of the cylinder head allowed periodic de-carbonizing of engines and removal of valves. Note the brass oil pump on the side of the engine behind the brake lever. This pump did not circulate oil throughout the engine. It was still a total-loss lubrication system. The oil pump simply introduced a few drops of precious lubrication to the rear of the front cylinder. The rear cylinder didn't need that feature. It received plenty of oil splash from the flywheel. A manual pump on the gas tank allowed the rider to squirt in more oil as the engine needed it. How did he know when he needed it? Well, the manual said when the engine starts slowing down.

The low cost of manufacturing side-valve engines kept them alive well into the 1950s. This unit-construction Harley-Davidson KH engine featured large finned aluminum alloy heads for better cooling. This allowed the use of higher compression pistons.

Close-up of a 1912 554cc four-cylinder T-head Pierce engine. T-heads are side-valve engines that place their valves on opposite sides of the cylinder. View is of the intake side. The tube going to each cylinder is the intake manifold. It feeds fuel/air from the carburetor mounted to the rear (right) of the engine. T-head engines were more costly to manufacture.

Side-valve engine configurations included horizontally opposed twins, also known as flat twins. Cylinders are placed 180 degrees apart. BMW, Zündapp, ABC, and Douglas used this popular aircraft engine format for their bikes.

131

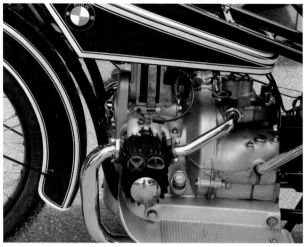

This well restored 1923 BMW R32 features an opposing twin cylinder side-valve engine. Note the single casting comprising the cylinder and cylinder head. Chrome intake manifolds unite at a common carburetor above the gearbox. The "boxer" engine became a popular BMW trait for years to come. They vibrate less than V-twins and are easy to maintain. The term boxer implied the action of a boxer's gloves as it relates to the movement of the pistons.

This 1936 K500 Zündapp engine shows how compact and neat side-valve flat twin engines are. The aluminum covers above each cylinder allow access to the valve springs and tappets for adjustment. Note that the cylinders are not directly opposite each other. They are offset slightly because of the separate crankpins used on the crankshaft in boxer engines. Photo courtesy of Mike Dunn.

Overhead valve engines like this Zündapp KS600 have a wider stance than their side-valve counterparts. This model employs a single carburetor to feed both cylinders. It can be seen behind the ignition coil mounted on top of the engine. Manifolds go to each intake port. Photo courtesy of Mike Dunn.

Moving Upward

Side-valves had their limitations. They would retain heat and thus limit the compression ratio of the engine. Higher compression of the fuel/air mixture was the real source of power. Compression ratios of 8:1 would often pre-ignite the gas/air mixture in these motors due to some red-hot component or carbon stuck to the cylinder head. Most side-valve engines ran at relatively mild compression ratios between 4:1 and 6:1. Another weakness of side-valves is the indirect path the fuel/air mixture has to take to get inside the cylinder. It is usually a sharp upright turn, and the reverse upon exiting as exhaust. As a result, flatheads have "breathing" problems, limiting optimal output in relation to displacement. The answer to both problems was well known— put the valves on top of the head for better cooling and more direct porting and flow. Overhead valve (OHV) engines came initially with open valve rockers and springs. This made a mess on top of the bike as oil mixed with dirt. Enclosing the valve train was an obvious next step. It allowed constant lubrication, as well as protection.

An example of an early overhead valve engine with exposed valve train. The rockers would have to be lubricated manually. Rust and dirt was always an issue with these exposed systems. The addition of rocker boxes, also known as valve covers, on most post-1930s engines enclosed the mechanism. This kept dirt out and allowed for pressure-fed lubrication.

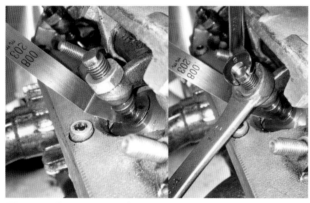

The gap between rocker arm and valve stem is critical to an engine's performance. Some rockers have adjusting screws. A feeler gauge (left) is used to check the specified value when an engine is cold. The photo on right shows how two wrenches are used to prevent unwanted rotation of the adjusting screw once the proper gap has been set. The feeler gauge should be able to move with a slight bit of resistance. Some overhead valve systems have the adjusting screw at the top of the cam followers (also called lifters or tappets) just below the pushrods. Most pushrod actuated overhead valve motorcycle engines today use hydraulic cam followers. Oil pressure maintains just the right setting and eliminates the need for adjustment.

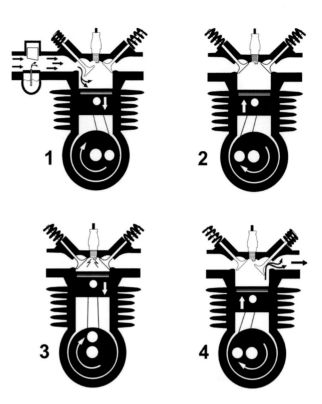

Illustration of the four strokes of an overhead valve engine. 1) Intake valve opens to admit gas/air mixture created by a carburetor. 2) The momentum of the flywheel rotates the crankshaft to raise the piston for compression. 3) Just prior to the piston coming to top-dead-center (TDC) the spark fires to ignite the mixture. This creates the power stroke. 4) Spent exhaust gasses are evacuated via an open exhaust valve. Valve actuation may be by pushrods and rockers, or by the lobes of a camshaft acting directly on the valve stems to push them open. Illustration by Christian Bangert.

Large British singles like this 1934 BSA W34/8 500cc OHV single were the norm in Europe during the 1930s through the 1950s. Their simplicity offered reliability at a good price. Photo courtesy Yesterdays Antique Motorcycles.

Even BMW saw the value of offering light OHV single-cylinder bikes for urban and entry-level riders since 1925. This beautiful restoration is a 250cc shaft-drive R27, offered between model years 1960 and 1966. The bike's low power combined with higher cost, as compared to British and Japanese bikes, brought it limited success. The R27 ended the BMW single-cylinder line. For a little bit more, people were buying the superb BMW R50S twin. Courtesy of William Becker.

This engine cutaway of a 1960s-era British BSA single shows the basic layout of a typical overhead valve engine. Pushrods are on the other side. Visible is the single-row chain that connects the crankshaft to the clutch. It is just behind the alternator. Photo taken at the AMA Hall of Fame Motorcycle Museum.

The 1933 499cc Rudge TT Replica engine featured the company's four-valve radial cylinder head. Two exhaust pipes help the big single exhale its exhaust gasses.

Looking much like an overhead cam engine, this Parilla single-cylinder is actually of the high-cam design. The camshaft is situated high on the side of the engine. A chain running off the crankshaft rotates it. Short pushrods act upon the rocker arms. The pushrods, hidden behind rubber tubes, are at steep angles to the cam. This design eliminates the flexing associated with longer pushrods. Velocette and Vincent also employed high-cam engines, albeit not as high as this example. Photo courtesy of Carollo Moto Classiche.

The Glorious OHV V-Twin

Harley-Davidson introduced its "Knucklehead" OHV V-twin in 1936. The nickname was coined from the shape of its rocker box covers. Later year OHV Harleys would include the "Panhead" and "Shovelhead." These large V-twins had long engine strokes, limiting their ability to rev safely much beyond 5,000 rpm. Higher rpm translates into power. Large V-twin manufacturers made up for that by making the engines bigger. While 61 and 74 cubic inch engines were the norm decades ago, V-twins now are readily available with 110 cubic inch engines. Large bores with long strokes do provide a tremendous benefit: torque. Nothing has the pulling ability of a large V-twin. Each power stroke is like a jackhammer doing its work. It's a pleasant sensation, and the sound is even more appealing.

Knucklehead Harleys were the company's first production overhead valve bikes. The name was derived from the shape of the overhead valve rocker-box covers.

This Indian V-twin racer featured four overhead valves per cylinder; something quite common on sportbikes today, but hardly the case a hundred years ago. Note the single carburetor and manifold feeding both intakes. Also note the manual engine oiler attached to oil tank under the seat.

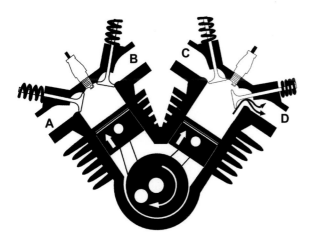

V-twin engines typically share a common crankpin for both connecting rods. Some are side-by-side; others are forked. The design allows a compact engine for a lot of extra power. Vibration is an issue. L-twins, as used by Ducati and Aprilia, have a 90-degree angle between cylinders and are much better balanced than V-twins in the 45- to 50-degree range. Many V-twins share a common carburetor between the intake ports B and C. Others, like the Vincent and early Ducati L-twins, would have a separate carburetor at intake ports A and C.

One of the most magnificent OHV V-twins is the 998cc Vincent, also introduced in 1936. This third-generation design is found on a 1954 Vincent Rapide. The 50-degree V-twin engine is hung from a strong backbone to become part of the bike's frame, much like Ducatis today. The two camshafts reside relatively high within the timing side cases on this pushrod engine. It was also designed as a unit construction machine, meaning that the engine and transmission are contained in one big case. It produced 45 hp and was capable of over 110 mph. Its sister bike, the Black Shadow, added 10 hp and 15 mph, making it the fastest production bike for decades.

A Vincent V-twin engine is being readied to have its transmission gears fitted at the factory in 1952. Series B, C, and D Vincent V-twins were of unit construction, incorporating the transmission with the crankcase. Photo Mortons Archive.

A rare and beautiful 1915 Iver Johnson has an unusual V-twin engine configuration. The US maker wanted the bike to sound more like a parallel twin, with even firing pulses. It therefore built the side-valve motor with two offset crankpins; one for each piston.

Yale V-twins, like this 1913 model, were unique in that the cooling fins were kept horizontal for better airflow.

V-twins have been around as long as motorcycles themselves. Nearly every major manufacturer of motorcycle engines over the past 100 years has offered a V-twin. This rare 1936 BSA Y-13 750cc shares a remarkable likeness in overhead valve layout with an original 1936 Harley "Knuckle-head." Valve gear is only partially enclosed, leaving the springs exposed to the air. Only 1600 of these remarkable machines were made between 1936 and 1938. They featured dry-sump lubrication, using a separate oil tank to store the circulating oil.

Some overhead valve V-twins lay transversely across the frame as with this Moto Guzzi. The 90-degree V aids in a smooth running motor. The Buel in the background features a more traditional inline V-twin configuration.

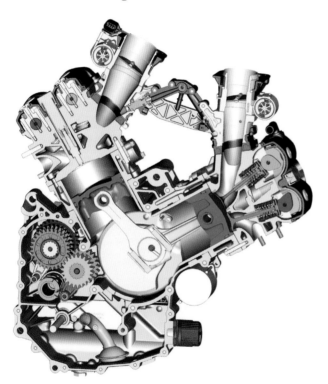

Contemporary twins, such as this 90-degree L-twin design by Italian maker Aprilia, are marvels of engineering. The compact power unit houses both the engine and transmission. Illustration thanks to Aprilia, Piaggio & C SpA.

Running Parallel

V-twins were getting very popular in the United States from the mid-teens on. They have become synonymous with the American motorcycle. But back in 1937, something was happening in England that would have a great impact on American V-twins; the Triumph Speed Twin. Triumph motorcycle engineer and designer Edward Turner created a revolution in 1937 by introducing this parallel twin–powered motorcycle. Parallel twins were nothing new, but Turner's efficient design made them legendary.

The Speed Twin had the same impact on the motorcycling world as the Honda CB750 had in 1969. Its lightweight parallel overhead valve twin-cylinder engine displaced 498cc, but yet produced significantly more power than the all-too-common large British singles of the time. At 6,000 rpm it reached nearly 29 hp. A shorter stroke allowed the engine to rev freely and take advantage of a four-speed gearbox. So significant was this design that it launched Britain as the leader in motorcycle sales worldwide. Every major maker, including Norton, BSA, Matchless, and Royal Enfield offered parallel twins.

The 1937 Triumph Speed Twin 498cc motorcycle shaped a generation of bikes to come. BSA followed Triumph's lead with parallel twin bikes with the 500cc A7 and 650cc A10 series. Colorful names such as Golden Flash, Road Rocket, and Lightning described these beloved machines. Original factory pre-production photo, Mortons Archive.

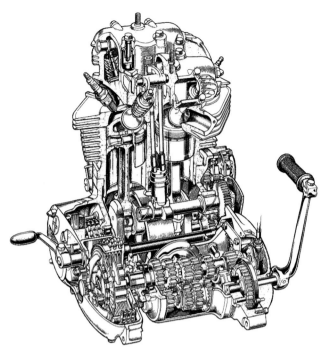

Turner's immortal parallel twin endured for forty-five years. It evolved to unit construction in 1963, housing the crankcase and transmission in one compact package. This illustration of a 1970s-era T140 (750cc) reveals the classic gear-driven high camshafts (intake side shown) with pushrods and rocker arms leading to the overhead valves. Also clearly illustrated is the transmission gear cluster and clutch mechanism. Mortons Archive.

Mid-1950s-era British twins evolved to the popular 650cc engine displacement. They were beating out American V-twins on the street and on the track. Highly tuned parallel twins were putting out nearly as much power as the heavier V-twins. Power was typically between 40 and 45 horses for the parallel twins. This narrow margin motivated Harley-Davidson to get competitive in its engineering. It began working on a lighter machine that resulted in the 883cc OHV Sportster. The initial version had only 40 hp, but its light weight compensated for that shortcoming. Later models would bring the machines up over 50 hp. Larger overhead valve 1,200cc Harleys produced between 50 and 55 hp, but their heavy weight limited their speed off the line. The Sportster was of "unit construction," where the engine and transmission are housed within the same case. Unit-construction motorcycle engines had appeared on and off since 1908, when Scott featured it in their two-strokes. Meanwhile, Indians, with their dated side-valves, were starting to fade out and were left in the dust in this battle. They resorted to copying British designs and importing British Royal Enfield and Velocette motorcycles.

Timing side view of a late-1960s Triumph engine showing the index marks (yellow) used to properly synchronize the crankshaft with each of the two camshafts. An idler gear is used in the center to rotate both camshaft gears. The brass device running off the intake cam gear is the oil pump.

This 1954 T110 "pre-unit" Triumph Tiger's engine and gearbox are not contained in the same housing but are connected via a separate primary chain case on the left side of the engine. Its light weight and powerful 649cc engine surprised many V-twin bike owners when racing on the street or around the track.

in this case). Hondas had the chain run between the cylinders, while most British twins had the gears or chain on the side of the engine. The side of the engine that houses the precisely aligned gears that drive the cam(s) is called the timing side. This engine has only one camshaft that manages the opening and closing of both the intake and exhaust valves. The author was installing this engine within the frame, and blue masking tape and foam was used to protect the paint.

A Norton 750cc engine, with cylinder head removed, is typical of most British parallel twins. Pistons travel up and down together; however, combustion alternates between 360-degree rotations. Vibration is common. Modern 360-degree twins use a counterbalance shaft to minimize it. Some makers used crankshafts with crankpins set 180 degrees to each other, where pistons moved opposite to each other. This reduced primary vibration, but produced high-frequency secondary vibration instead. The early Honda 450s used a 180-degree crank. The camshaft on parallel twins is driven off the crankshaft via gears or a chain (as

Triumph's venerable parallel twin survived with little changes over the decades. Pictured is a 1968 TR6R single carburetor 650cc model.

Some bikes, like the Sunbeam or this mid-1930s Matchless Silver Hawk, had two parallel cylinders positioned front to back. Cooling the rear cylinder was usually the only real concern with these smooth engines.

Edward Turner's creative mind came up with an unconventional four-cylinder engine design in the 1930s. It basically combined two parallel twin engines joined by large gears in one crankcase. The smooth running 1,000cc Square Four was built and marketed by Ariel through 1959. Pictured is a 1956 4G Mark II. Note the distributor that supplies ignition to the four-cylinders. The large oil tank behind the engine was helpful in cooling the motor. A single SU carburetor fed the four cylinders with a central manifold. The engine and transmission were not of unit construction. The gearbox can be seen as a separate unit behind the motor.

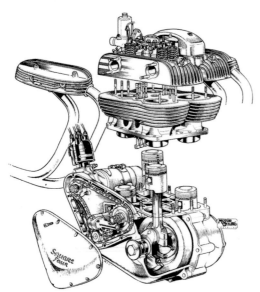

Exploded view of the Ariel Square Four, showing one of the two tandem crankshafts. Pistons travel perfectly parallel to each other in a four-barreled cylinder casting. Illustrated is the aluminum alloy Mark II made from 1953 through 1959. It offered significantly better cooling than the previous models. Note the automotive-type distributor mounted near the rear of the engine. Illustration by Motor Cycling, Mortons Archive.

Overhead Cams

Engine development continued on a feverish scale. One design was to set the standard for most four-stroke motorcycle engines today. Overhead cam (OHC) engines place the camshaft above the valves in the cylinder head. They started to appear as early as 1902. Europeans, in particular the Italians and French, favored overhead cam designs. The concept was simple. Placing the cam on top eliminated the power-robbing pushrods. It also offered more precise valve actuation. American makers stuck to cheaper flatheads and pushrod operated overhead valve engines. A few experimented with the design.

The American-made Cyclone racer's 996cc 45-degree V-twin engine used bevel-gear-driven single overhead cams to actuate the valves, something that Ducati would be famous for decades later. Designed by Andrew Strand, the engine could produce 45 hp, propelling the light bike up to 115 mph on the board tracks. The cost to manufacture these types of engines was prohibitive and best left for racing efforts. Reliability was also an issue, primarily due to metal failure. Drive on these types of racers was directly off the crankshaft, meaning there was no transmission. Photo courtesy of Mid-American Auctions.

Overhead pushrod type valve trains have their limitations. Foremost is the reciprocating mass that pushrods and tappets create. This puts additional stress on the engine. OHC systems have less reciprocating components. Pushrod engines also have slop and flex to deal with. This reduces an engine's efficiency as it achieves higher rpm.

Overhead cam systems offer another benefit. They allow improved air and exhaust flow through the engine. The valves are more vertical than on a pushrod-actuated overhead valve engine. This creates the room for more direct porting. Overhead cam engines can thus breathe better and create higher rpm. This translates to more power for equivalent engine displacement.

SOHC

OHC engines come in two varieties: single overhead cam (SOHC) and dual overhead cam (DOHC). In a SOHC system, the single cam has lobes for opening both the intake and exhaust valves. SOHC valve trains typically require rocker arms to actuate the valves. The cam cannot be over both intake and exhaust valves. It sits between the two. In a SOHC V-twin, a single cam resides in each cylinder head, sitting between the intake and exhaust valves.

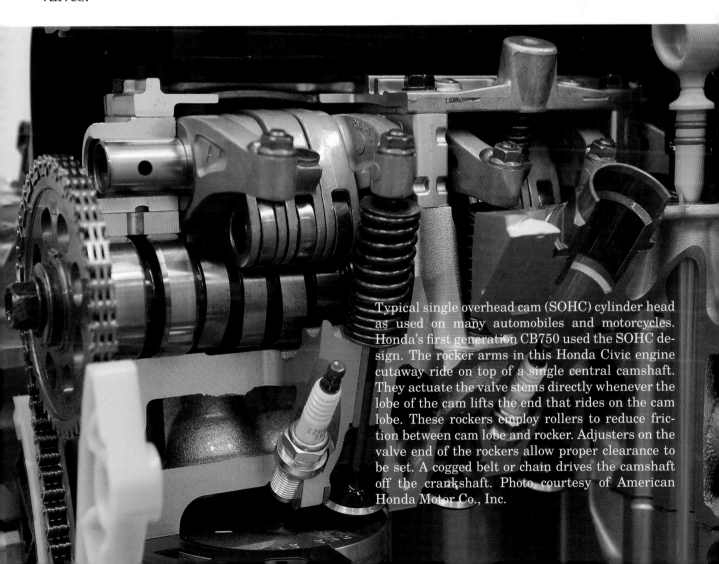

Typical single overhead cam (SOHC) cylinder head as used on many automobiles and motorcycles. Honda's first generation CB750 used the SOHC design. The rocker arms in this Honda Civic engine cutaway ride on top of a single central camshaft. They actuate the valve stems directly whenever the lobe of the cam lifts the end that rides on the cam lobe. These rockers employ rollers to reduce friction between cam lobe and rocker. Adjusters on the valve end of the rockers allow proper clearance to be set. A cogged belt or chain drives the camshaft off the crankshaft. Photo courtesy of American Honda Motor Co., Inc.

Honda motorcycles were quick to take advantage of the overhead cam layout. Their short-stroke single overhead cam small singles and twins introduced in the 1960s allowed them to rev up to 10,000 rpm. The cam chain ran up a channel between the two cylinders.

Engine cutaway of a Victory V-twin cylinder head with a central single overhead cam. The very end of the cam is visible above the spark plug cap. Four rockers are used since the head uses two valves for intake and two for exhaust. This is for better flow.

DOHC

In a DOHC setup, there is one camshaft for intake and one for the exhaust. In most modern DOHC engines, each cam lobe acts directly on the valves, pushing down on a tappet bucket covering the top of the valve stem. Rockers are not necessary. DOHC valve trains, therefore, act faster on the valves, allowing higher rpm.

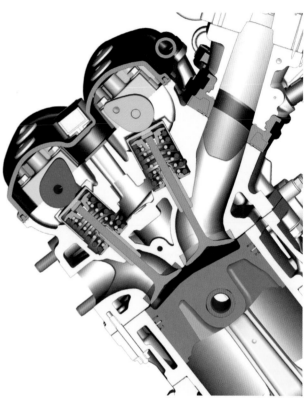

Illustration showing a double overhead cam engine design. The cams (red and light blue) act directly on the valve tappets (buckets) to minimize delays caused by pushrod or rocker components. This allows for even higher rpm. Shims placed inside the tappet buckets adjust for proper valve clearance. Illustration thanks to Aprilia, Piaggio & C SpA.

Cutaway view of a Honda Gold Wing overhead cam with tappets and valves. The design is compact and efficient. Photo courtesy of American Honda Motor Co., Inc.

The single-cylinder four-valve Honda CBR®250R engine uses a DOHC arrangement that incorporates rockers. The design allows for valve stems in a radial pattern. Photo courtesy of American Honda Motor Co., Inc.

Learning from the Italians

The Japanese, especially Honda, studied the European OHC engines with great interest. Of special significance were those made by Gilera. The company's GP wins certainly proved their capability. The Italian maker offered double overhead cam designs that generated more power from small 125cc, 250cc, 350cc, and 500cc engines than singles or twins of the time. MV Agusta carried on Gilera's legacy.

This dual overhead cam (DOHC) 1974 MV Agusta America 750cc is a prime example of Italian engine design. It uses separate cams for the intake and exhaust valves. The round cam housings are visible on top of the engine. This design, initiated by Italian motorcycle maker Gilera, strongly influenced Japanese motorcycle maker Honda.

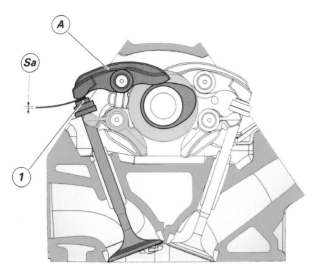

Ducati's famous desmodromic valve system was developed by Fabio Taglioni in 1956 for the company's 125cc Grand Prix bike. It set the stage for today's current line of performance engines by the Italian marque. "Desmo" valve actuation is direct and does not rely on springs to close the valves. Cams both open and close the valves with precise timing regardless of rpm. This eliminates "valve float," a condition where the valves open and close so quickly that they do not have a chance to seat. The blue rocker in the illustration opens the valve, while the yellow one closes it. Small helper springs aid the valves seat in the event that clearances (Sa) have not been adjusted properly. Illustration thanks to Ducati Motor Holding S.p.A.

Overhead Cam Drive Mechanisms

Overhead camshafts can be connected to the crankshaft for rotation in a variety of ways. The first is by a series of gears starting at the crankshaft and working themselves up to the camshaft in the cylinder head. This tends to create a bit of slop and robs power. The second is via a shaft fitted with bevel gears on each end. This shaft runs parallel to the cylinder. Bevel drives allow the rotation of shafts 90 degrees to each other. The lower bevel is made up of two gears cut at 45-degree angles to each other. This allows vertical rotation of the

shaft heading toward the cylinder head. A second set of bevel gears on top allows this rotation to act directly on the horizontal camshaft. Norton used this design for its famous International and Manx models, while Ducati employed it on its early L-twins. The third method is the most efficient. It uses a chain running between the crankshaft and the camshaft. Chains have been replaced by cogged (toothed) Kevlar belts on many modern engines.

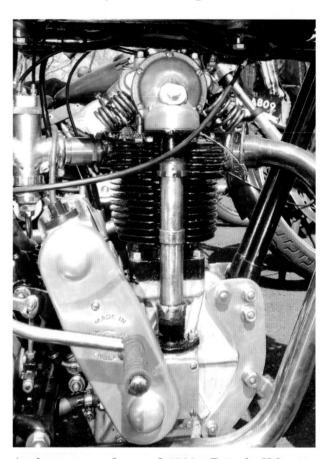

A close view of a mid-1920s British Velocette "K" engine shows a bevel-driven single overhead cam. Valve springs are of the exposed "hairspring" type. The company was an early adopter of production overhead cam engines for their 350cc and 500cc bikes. Norton used a similar arrangement on its International and Manx bikes.

144

Italian motorcycle maker Ducati gained recognition in the United States from the early 1960s through the mid-1970s with its bevel-drive overhead cam singles, ranging in size from 250cc to 450cc. Pictured is a 1967 350 Mark 3 D. It was the first Ducati with Desmodromic valve actuation on a production model. Mark 3 Ds were also offered in 250cc.

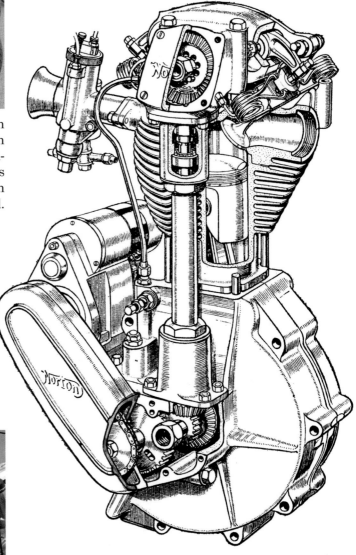

Ducati gained even greater recognition in 1971 for its first twin: the 750GT. The company would keep this "L-twin" configuration going forward. The two cylinders were set 90 degrees apart and utilized beveled gears to drive an overhead camshaft on each cylinder. Valve actuation was by rocker and springs.

Cutaway illustration of the famous Norton Manx engine showing its bevel gear–driven single overhead camshaft. These engines were available in 350cc and 500cc displacements. Note the use of hairsprings instead of the more conventional coil springs to close the valves. Factory racing engines were of the dual overhead cam variety. Illustration Mortons Archive.

This particular Ducati proudly displays its bevel drive through a sight glass atop the cylinder head.

The camshafts on most modern engines are rotated via a sprocket and chain arrangement driven off the crankshaft. This modern Indian Scout engine uses double overhead cams on each of its two cylinders. The sprocket on the right operates the intake cam, while the left one operates the exhaust cam. The cam chain tensioner adjuster is visible in the center of the photo. The large bolt has a spring in it to maintain proper pressure on the black plastic guide.

Some overhead cam engines use a cogged Kevlar belt instead of a chain to drive the camshaft. This Ducati engine on a Bimota® motorcycle would normally have protective covers over the belts. Belt tension adjustment is critical and is accomplished by moving the idler pulley.

Multi-Cylinder Bikes

Honda's single overhead cam CB750 started the Japanese four-cylinder superbike race in 1969. Kawasaki followed with a counter punch in 1972 with its larger 903cc Z1 engine that featured two overhead cams. It took Suzuki a few patient years to follow with its superb 1976 GS750. Multi-cylinder engines are most popular today, with three-, four-, and six-cylinder configurations.

The legendary SOHC Honda CB750 brought overhead cam four-cylinder technology to the masses in 1969. A central camshaft actuated both intake and exhaust valves using rockers.

One can appreciate the technical development in four-cylinder engines when comparing this 1920s-era Henderson engine with Honda's 1969 CB750 motor.

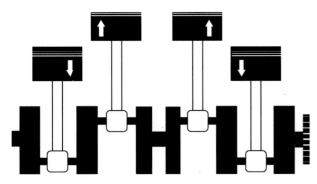

Pistons on conventional four-cylinder engines typically travel in pairs. Adjacent crankpins are 180 degrees apart. Since all crankpins reside on the same plane, this type of crankshaft is called flat-plane.

Kawasaki's fabulous DOHC 903cc Z1 four-cylinder engine used two cams to actuate the valves directly. Valve adjustment was by shims instead of screws, greatly lightening the valve train. The author took this picture while attending the Kawasaki service school in 1972. This engine set a new standard for all Japanese bikes. The chain that drives the cams can be seen on the top between the two middle cylinders.

Smoothing Out a Multi

The torque we feel as we roll-on the throttle is a result of two forces. The first is the torque created by the piston acting on the crankpin of the crankshaft during the com-

bustion/power stroke. This is called combustion torque. The second is the torque created by the rotating mass of the crankshaft combined with the upward and downward movement of the piston. This is called inertial torque. In both cases, this torque is not even. Pistons come to a complete stop at the top and bottom of their strokes, while the heavy counterweights on a crankshaft exert their own uneven rotational forces. The more cylinders, the less noticeable is the effect of both types of torque, also known as composite torque. A single-cylinder engine reveals torque quite distinctly; therefore, the notion that they are "torquey." They also vibrate the most. So will parallel twin engines that have their pistons travel up and down together if not fitted with a counterbalancer.

Cross-plane crankshaft technology is designed not only to smooth vibration by distributing the inertial torque factor more evenly, but also to deliver better torque response overall when throttling up. The concept has been used on many V-8s for years, as well as V-4 engines on motorcycles. The idea is to have each crankpin at 90 degrees to the other in pairs. In the motorcycle world, Yamaha took the lead on cross-plane engine designs with its four-cylinder R1. Their success with their race bikes has brought cross-plane technology to the showroom.

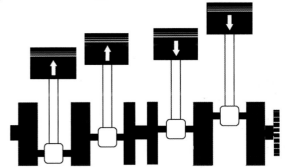

Cross-plane crankshaft design on four-cylinder engines have crankpins set at 90 degrees from each other in pairs. The two in the center are at 180 degrees to each other; as one piston goes up, the other goes down.

Cutaway of a Honda CB750K four-cylinder double overhead cam engine as displayed at the AMA Hall of Fame details all the major components of a high-performance motorcycle engine. Camshafts are driven by a chain running between the two inner cylinders. The clutch (round unit by footpeg) connects the engine's crankshaft to the transmission. It is inside the same case and shares the same lubrication, therefore, termed "wet clutch." It is driven by primary gears off the crankshaft. Item 2 is the alternator. This cutaway illustrates nicely how large the cylinder head really is on a DOHC engine. Photo courtesy American Motorcyclists Association.

Honda's inline six-cylinder, twenty-four-valve, CBX was produced from 1978 and 1982 in a demonstration of engineering achievement. The 1,047cc engine produced 105 hp. Needless to say, valve and carburetor adjustment was not for the faint of heart backyard mechanic.

Honda's innovative R&D department did not stop at anything. Its 1,000cc water-cooled flat four-cylinder Gold Wing was introduced in 1974. It set new standards for smoothness and long-distance riding comfort. It also borrowed a concept from the flat twin BMWs: shaft drive. The Gold Wing in its various forms is Honda's longest running production model to date.

The solid design of the Gold Wing engine evolved into a stunning flat six reaching 1,832cc by 2001. Banks of three cylinders oppose each other. Smooth, even power with lots of torque make these engines perfect for cross-country trips. Photo courtesy of American Honda Motor Co., Inc.

Four-cylinder engines run very smoothly without any major vibration. Pistons go up and down in pairs, balancing each other's force. Three-cylinder engines can be almost as smooth by staggering the crankpins evenly at 120 degrees. Combustion happens every 240 degrees of crankshaft rotation. In a last-ditch effort to compete against high-tech Japanese bikes, Triumph and BSA introduced an excellent air-cooled overhead valve triple in 1968. Unfortunately for the British motorcycle industry, the CB750 Honda was less expensive and far above in technical attributes. Remarkably, triples live strong in the superb modern Hinckley-made Triumphs and feature modern overhead cam designs.

Triples have a variety of crankshaft designs. Laverda 180-degree triples had the outer two pistons move in concert with each other while the center piston was 180 degrees in the opposite position. This cutaway view of a modern Yamaha three-cylinder engine shows the company's "cross-plane concept" crankshaft. It employs an interesting crankshaft layout where the outer two crank pins are at 180 degrees to each other and the center one 90 degrees to them. The left-most piston is hidden but is at bottom-dead-center. A balance shaft is typically required to eliminate the rocking vibration created by the crankshaft with this type of a design. Each crank configuration creates its own exhaust note, prompting many makers to use a specific design and modify any idiosyncrasies by other means.

Following in the tradition of "bigger is better," Triumph's Rocket III engine is about as big as they get. This massive 2,300cc three-cylinder engine was introduced in 2004 and is larger than those found in most compact cars. It is the largest engine as of this writing on any production bike. Remarkably, once rolling, this 870 pound bike handles quite nicely. Photo courtesy of Triumph Motorcycles.

Today's new Horex VR6 motorcycles use an innovative and unusual six-cylinder configuration. Photo courtesy of Horex.

Multi-cylinder engines come in all sorts of crazy designs. Noted custom bike builder Arlen Ness joined two Harley-Davidson Sportster engines to create this four-cylinder, supercharged monster.

Staying the Course

While European and Japanese motorcycle makers evolved the multi-cylinder overhead cam engine, Harley-Davidson stayed with its conventional pushrod design, banking on its loyal following and American image. Sales were impacted significantly in the 1990s when the Japanese started introducing V-twin cruisers of their own at significantly lower prices. Most were water-cooled. Yamaha decided to appeal to the American V-twin market by building a very large air-

cooled motor. Its Star® line currently offers bikes with a massive 113 cubic inch (1,854cc) air-cooled V-twin OHV motors with four valves per cylinder. Advances in materials and alloys extract more power from these air-cooled V-twins.

Harley-Davidson's next generation of big twin motor is the 4-valve per head Milwaukee-Eight™ in 107 and 114 cubic inches. It features an internal single counter-balancer, liquid cooling around the exhaust ports, and two sparkplugs per head. This all allows for higher compression and a good boost in torque. Photo courtesy of Harley-Davidson.

This Hyosung cruiser has a water-cooled engine for optimum power. This permits higher compression ratios. Smaller displacement water-cooled engines can produce more power per cubic inch. The radiator is clearly visible behind the front wheel. Harley-Davidson has introduced water-cooled heads for some of its touring bikes. Cooling just the heads (where most of the heat is) does not require them to re-engineer their reliable engine. Otherwise, new cylinders with water passages would have to be designed. Photo courtesy of Hyosung Motors USA.

The Rotary Engine

Not to be forgotten, the practical rotary engine was developed in the early 1950s by German engineer Felix Wankel working for NSU. He had been developing the concept independently for decades earlier. This type of internal combustion engine uses the eccentric motion of a triangular-shaped rotor to replace the four strokes of a conventional piston-driven Otto-cycle engine. Norton, Suzuki, Hercules, and Mazda exploited the excellent power-to-weight ratio of this nearly vibration-free engine. They come in one- and two-rotor formats.

View of a rotary engine rotor within its epitrochoid combustion chamber. The large space on top of the rotor (I) intakes the fuel/air mixture. As the rotor rotates, it compresses the mixture ready for combustion (C). The rotor expels the exhaust gasses as it passes the exhaust port (E). It is a continuous process that causes the engine to hum rather than "putt." The gear inside the rotor rotates the crankshaft. Challenges facing the Wankel include effective rotor sealing at each apex of the triangular rotor, high heat, fuel economy, and emissions—all things that automaker Mazda has been able to overcome with its superb engineering. Photo courtesy of Mazda North American Operations.

The Wankel rotary engine did find its way onto several motorcycles, albeit without much success. The German motorcycle maker Hercules (a division of Sachs) was the first. It produced air-cooled 294cc rotary-powered bikes between 1974 and 1977. Sachs had experience in making rotary-powered watercraft and snowmobiles in the 1960s. Pictured is a magnificent example of a very rare oil-injected W-2000 Hercules in factory red. Only a handful were made in red out of the 199 oil-injected bikes introduced in 1976. Oil in the gas helped lubricate the rotor and seals. It was typically mixed in the tank prior to automatic injection. The higher cost of the bike, combined with only about 30 hp, limited its success. The round structure on the front of the engine contains a cooling fan. The W-2000 was also sold under the DKW brand for some exports for around $1,900. Photo courtesy of Jess Stockwell.

Suzuki's RE5 water-cooled rotary engine bike was a noble attempt at using the Wankel for a practical motorcycle. Technically complex compared to the Hercules, and not so great fuel economy, limited production for the years 1974 through 1976. Pictured is a European model with lower handlebars. Photo courtesy of Glenn Jenkins.

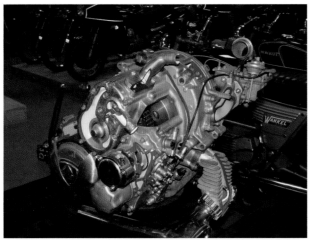

Suzuki's single-rotor water-cooled Wankel-type engine was a complex marvel of engineering. Its 497cc combustion chamber did produce a reasonable 62 hp. Oil was used to cool the rotor from the inside. A slight amount of oil was injected into the fuel mixture to further aid apex seal lubrication. High exhaust heat from rotary engines required a special exhaust manifold. Suzuki used a finned cast aluminum piece that splayed into two exhaust pipes. Photo courtesy of Jess Stockwell.

A Suzuki RE5 rotor with one of the engine side cases. The black spiral pattern in the side housing is the molybdenum disulfide coating. This acts as a hard surface so the aluminum housing isn't worn away by the rotor rubbing against it. Combined with a little bit of oil in the petrol mix, it stays lubricated with little wear after high mileage. Photo courtesy of Andy Summers.

Norton experimented with the Wankel rotary engine as well. Norton hoped that a rotary-powered motorcycle would bring it back as a viable manufacturer after its demise in 1978. The roots of the Norton rotary, however, go back to a new engine program established by BSA back in 1969. By 1974, a prototype two-rotor air-cooled engine was being displayed to the press. Hopes were high, but it was not until 1987 that the Norton Classic rotary (pictured) came to market. Only 100 were produced. Norton continued to develop water-cooled two-rotor 588cc models. The 85 hp Commander was a fully faired motorcycle. It was well received and saw some duty as a police bike between 1988 and 1992. Norton's NRS588 rotary-powered racers put on a good show on the tracks. Photo Mortons Archive.

Works photo of twin-rotor Norton Classic engine being assembled. Note the deep finning to help cool the hot-running Wankel. A special air-induction system was employed to bring cool air within the motor. The simplicity of the Wankel design is easily recognized by the absence of valves, rockers, cams, and pushrods. Photo Mortons Archive.

The Quest Continues

No doubt, liquid-fueled internal combustion engine development will continue and be adapted to other technologies like CNG (compressed natural gas) and hydrogen engines. For now, real advances are being made in electronic fuel injection, electronic engine control, and even variable-valve timing—all squeezing more and more power out of each drop of fuel. Honda's experiments in the late 1970s with oval pistons went far beyond what Nicolas Otto could have dreamed of. Regarding diesel engine–powered bikes, they do exist. Unfortunately they have proven to be impractical for now. The engines weigh considerably more than comparably powered gasoline engines.

(left) One of the four oval pistons from a Honda NR (New Racing) V-4 500cc engine introduced for Grand Prix racing in 1979. The cutting edge technology was designed to increase flow via eight valves per cylinder while maintaining four-cylinders as required by GP rules. The complex motor had its troubles but was capable of producing 130 bhp at over 20,000 rpm! Photos courtesy of Honda Motor Co.

The fate of the liquid fuel motor, however, seems a bit uncertain as remarkable electric motorcycles are brought to market. Vintage bike enthusiasts already struggle with ethanol blended gasoline as it ruins plastic components in the carburetor and washes away valuable lubrication from the cylinder walls. What will the future hold for vintage internal combustion bike owners? If the steam engine is an example, fundamental technology will always be revered by the mechanically devoted. The legacy of its rich history will endure, at least among the die-hards that love the smell of petrol and the popping and spitting of an old machine. Let's hope that gasoline will still be available.

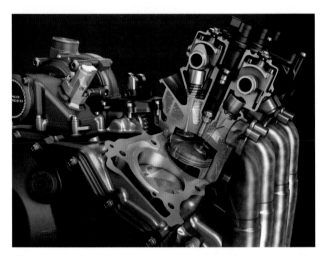

The pinnacle of the four-stroke cycle engine for the modern motorcycle is Kawasaki's 998cc inline four-cylinder engine for their H2TM series of superbikes. The supercharged motor is capable of 14,000 rpm and 300 hp. The supercharger (red) forces air at higher pressures into the engine. Materials, metallurgy, and electronics make this a very highly advanced engine. Photo courtesy of Kawasaki Motors Corp., U.S.A.

Things Can Go Wrong

Those of us who know the internal workings of an engine can't help but wonder how they do what they do so well. The average piston in an engine goes up and down six thousand times a minute. That translates to millions of strokes on any day trip. Adding valves, gears, and ignition systems, results in scores of components needing to function properly in order to propel us down the road.

Older engines have the disadvantage of less

advanced metallurgy in their components. They therefore wear out faster, or are prone to breaking under extreme stress. Many vintage bike enthusiasts will replace their engine's internals with modern components. Another key factor is to use the best lubricants possible. High zinc oils provide good protection between components. Their use as automobile lubrication has declined due to issues with catalytic converters and the EPA. They are however available in racing formulations.

The author pushed the limits on this 650cc Triumph engine back in the 1970s. The cast iron flywheel exploded, blowing out the crankcase.

An inexpensive valve spring collar caused major damage to the author's prized BSA Gold Star engine. The aluminum piece (shown by red lines) broke in half at high rpms. Without this retainer, the valve dropped into the cylinder and was smashed by the piston. Damage to the head, piston, and connecting rod resulted in a very expensive repair.

A faulty oil pump caused the shell bearing on this connecting rod to melt and disintegrate.

The crank journal associated with the above connecting rod was deeply scored. Note how the soft shell bearing metal clogged the oil hole in the journal. Fortunately, the damage was not extensive and the journal was reground. Oversized shell bearings had to be fitted to obtain the proper clearance.

Respecting a vintage engine's limitations will allow years of uninterrupted use. Pushing them hard will result in serious issues. That's why most have a tachometer. The good news is that there are plenty of used and new spare parts around for all but the very rare or esoteric bikes. There are also numerous good shop manuals and websites that can educate the reader on the proper care of an engine. One of the best private websites is dansmc.com.

The Drivetrain

Most motorcycles have a similar layout in the placement of their power and drive components. As with the original Werner design, motorcycles today cradle the power unit low and in the middle of the chassis. Controlling the power requires a means of disengaging it from the rear wheel. This calls for a clutch mechanism. Not all bikes had this luxury in the pioneering days. The rider would have to either kill the engine, or release the tension on the leather drive belt to coast to a stop. Most pioneer bikes drove the rear wheel directly off the crankshaft pulley via the leather belt. Mechanical clutch mechanisms were added to help the rider control the bike's movement. Most early American models used a hand lever by the gas tank to disengage the engine from the rear wheel. By the 1920s most had migrated to a more convenient foot pedal to disengage and engage the clutch. Europeans favored a hand lever on the handlebar.

In order to maximize an engine's limited power band, transmissions were adapted on most bikes by the 1920s. They initially had only two or three gear ratios. The additional gears permitted the bike to go faster at any given rpm. Without transmission gearing, a bike could only go as fast as its engine permitted. This greatly limited the machine's speed. Additional gear ratios easily doubled and tripled the revolution of the rear wheel at a given rpm. Bikes today typically have six speeds. Once the power has been transmitted through the gears, it exits via a drive sprocket. A chain or cogged belt engages the rear wheel sprocket to finally create movement. Some bikes use shaft drive, like in an automobile, to power the rear wheel.

Photo shows the foot-actuated clutch release mechanism found on popular large American V-twins up until the early 1950s. Foot clutches went in tandem with hand shifting. Indian kept this design on the Chief until its end in 1953. Harley-Davidson switched over to foot shifting and hand clutch operation in 1952. Contrary to what most believe, these mechanisms were not the "suicide clutches" people speak of. Foot clutches do require that one be mindful of the fact that the clutch should be disengaged when coming to a halt. The foot will then be available to hold up the bike. Foot clutch mechanisms, like the one pictured on this 1926 Chief, had a friction disk so that once disengaged, the clutch remained there with the foot removed. A true suicide clutch would offer no such option and would require the bike to be put into neutral before coming to a stop. No doubt, hand clutch levers and foot shifting greatly improved maneuvering a motorcycle. Note the small silver priming valves protruding out of the side of each cylinder head. These were unscrewed just enough to inject gasoline into the cylinder for cold weather starting. The gas also diluted the thick engine oil inside the cylinder for easier starting. A gasoline-injector pump was built into the gas cap on these early bikes. These looked like large brass syringes and were used to force the gas into the small hole.

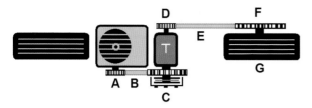

This illustration of a motorcycle drive train as seen from above is representative of most bikes made in the last ninety years. (A) engine crankshaft sprocket, (B) primary chain or belt, (C) clutch mechanism, (T) transmission, (D) drive sprocket, (E) final drive chain or belt, (F) rear wheel sprocket, (G) rear wheel.

As motorcycle engines evolved, it became clear that a transmission would be useful for taking proper advantage of their extra power. A sprocket on the crankshaft connects the engine to the clutch (being pointed to) by a chain. A clutch allows the rider to disengage the engine from the transmission when he either wants to stand still or shift into another gear. The clutch consists of alternating plain and friction plates. The friction plates have fibrous material glued to metal base plates. A spring-loaded cover presses all of these plates together, connecting the engine with the transmission. Clutch springs are placed on the four bolts within the clutch hub on this model. Note the protruding clutch release shaft in the center of the hub. A lever on the handlebar is connected to this shaft by a cable. It pushes the clutch cover plate away from the internal clutch plates to separate them. This allows the engine to spin without transmitting power to the transmission. Also note the shock absorber mounted to the crankshaft. This device uses a large spring to smooth out the sudden pulses of the power stroke, also preventing wear on the chain and clutch sprocket. This entire system is called the primary drive.

The transmission, located behind the engine, offers several gears that can be used to maintain the best engine rpm for the desired speed traveled. It is a separate unit on this mid-1960s Norton Atlas. The foot-operated gear selector can be seen below the engine. Triumphs and BSAs of the era started integrating the transmission within the crankcase. That is called "unit" construction.

An example of a chain-driven primary drive that has been converted to a cogged belt. The belt on this Norton Commando runs from the crankshaft sprocket to the clutch sprocket. Alternating plates inside the clutch can be separated or engaged to control power to the inner clutch hub. This hub is an extension of the transmission's main shaft. The tabs on alternating friction plates in this clutch engage with this hub, while tabs on the plain plates engage with the clutch housing. The clutch plates alternate between friction plates and smooth metal plates (the one in my hand). Wet plate systems using primary drive chains can operate in an oil bath to lubricate the chain. Belt-driven systems run dry. The large, round object on the left in front of the crankshaft sprocket is the alternator.

Custom motorcycle builders often replace the primary chain with a large cogged belt. The advantages, other than looking impressive, are that they run quieter and have no need for oil. Many, like this one, are exposed and beg caution with loose pant legs. Six heavy-duty clutch springs reside underneath the bolt heads on the outer clutch cover. A long rod going through the transmission shaft pushes against this cover to separate the plates to disengage drive. Photo by Dino Petrocelli.

Cutaway view of a modern Indian Chief's primary side. Note the use of large gears rather than a chain or belt to drive the clutch. The large, round device in front of the crankshaft gear is a shock absorber.

Marking the Spot

Those of us familiar with old bikes laugh at the notion that these soulful machines intentionally leave their mark wherever they go with a few drops of oil. I have ruined a few driveways in my day with oil puddles. It is also not uncommon to see cookie trays under old British and American bikes displayed at museums.

Old machines leaked oil because the machining and casting tolerances between engine cases and covers were not as precise as those made in recent decades. Gasket materials and sealers were also not as advanced as the synthetic non-hardening stuff used today. As a result of time and vibration the seals loosened on these old engines enough to let some oil drip out.

Modern gasket sealants will eliminate this bike's engine and transmission from leaking after a rebuild.

People immediately recognized that Hondas of the 1960s did not have oil leaking problems when parked for a long time. It was puzzling until one looked at the engine design itself. Hondas, and many Italian and Japanese multi-cylinder bikes, had horizontally split engine cases. Most American and British engines had vertically split cases. Horizontally split cases don't have any joints subject to oil leaking when the engine is at rest. Oil is contained in the neat lower section of the crankcase.

Oil leaking on modern bikes is virtually unheard of. Precise tolerances, assembly techniques, and modern sealing materials all conspire to deprive new bikes from leaving their mark. The only chance they have is to make a hole on a warm driveway with the side stand.

Photo shows a Honda 350 parallel twin engine's horizontally split crankcase halves. The lower half is on the right. The upper half is upside down in the photo to show the transmission gear cluster and the crankshaft. This engine has a wet sump system. Oil stays in the lower crankcase half. Some is circulated by a pump to critical engine components. Dry sump systems continuously pump the oil out of the crankcase and return it to an oil tank. Most vintage British bikes used dry sump systems. Harley-Davidson has been using dry sump lubrication on its big bikes since 1937. Photo by Paul Ensanian.

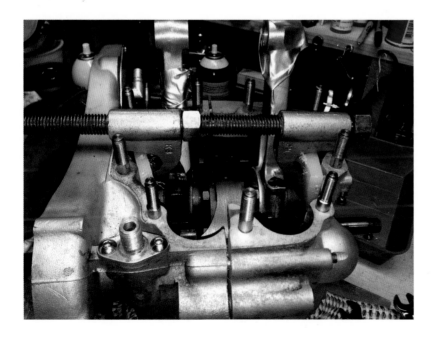

This photo shows a typical British parallel twin's engine cases being split by the author using a tool to gently separate the halves. Modern gasket sealers will pretty much eliminate leaking after reassembly.

Triumph Motorcycles

Robert Watson

Chapter 4

THE RELIABLE STANDARD

Standard motorcycles provide the most utility. They are capable of serving us fairly well for most of our riding needs—be it a quick jaunt across town or a weekend trip across two states. They seat both rider and passenger comfortably. Standards were getting lost among the myriad of highly specialized machines serving the sport, touring, and off-road segments. A recent revival in retro models, however, has brought the good old standard back.

Moto Guzzi V9, Piaggio & C SpA.

The General-Purpose Motorcycle

Motorcycles have evolved into highly specialized purpose-built vehicles, ranging from near race-ready sportbikes to high-flying extreme off-road machines. This is quite a departure from motorcycling's humble beginnings. Prior to the 1950s, bikes were pretty much built for general purpose riding. Some of the larger makers offered both performance models for the private racer and factory options to the otherwise standard bike for special applications. These were mostly suspension and frame mods for improved off-road capabilities.

Conventional motorcycles, often referred to as standards, provided basic transportation while doubling as sporting or touring machines. Depending on the era, standards may have also been referred to as roadsters or street bikes. The common denominator was that they strived for reliability and everyday utility, given the constraints of the technology available.

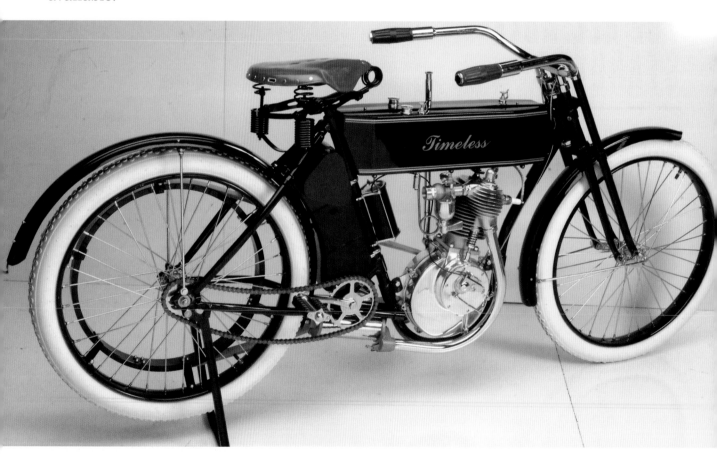

Standard motorcycles made over 100 years ago were basically motorized heavy-duty bicycles compared to today's hefty machines. The key to a brand's success was reliability. The example in the photo is a high-quality modern reproduction of a Model 6 Harley-Davidson, originally made in 1910 with a 494cc single-cylinder engine. The Motor Company survived, while so many others failed, due to the reliability of its machines. Enthusiasts looking for a pristine and reliable reproduction can order one from Timeless Classics at a fraction of the cost of an original. These bikes are for collectors and are not street-ready. The Model 6 sold for $210 back in 1910. timelessmotorcompany.com

Engines on standards were, and still are, typically in a slightly lower state of tune compared to their racing cousins. This results in more reliable and longer lasting motors. Due to the absence of specialized machines available in the first decades of the twentieth century, standards were liberally modified by enthusiasts. Removing fenders, cutting and welding frames, modifying engines, exhaust, and fitting different tires created the specialized bikes that challenged competitors on the board tracks, fairground ovals, endurance circuits, or up a muddy hill to see who makes it to the top. Factory teams enjoyed the benefits of being able to create one-off racing machines. Most started off as stripped and modified standards.

An example of how stock motorcycles were heavily modified for specialized racing purposes as shown in this 1927 Indian hill climber.

Defining the Breed

Categorizing bikes as standards can get to be a bit tricky. Many machines are equally adept at daily commuting as well as sport riding. The line gets fuzzy as modern standard bikes roll off the assembly lines with engines and suspensions found only on exotic sporting machines decades earlier. The basic layout of a standard motorcycle, however, has remained pretty much the same since the turn of the twentieth century. The design was refined by the Werner brothers in Paris, and set the standard

for other makers for decades to come. The foundation was a bicycle-style frame that cradled a power unit (engine) low and to the center, with a gas tank mounted directly above. The low center of gravity created by the low hanging motor greatly improved the stability of the bike. Handlebars held the controls, including throttle, spark advance, and possibly a brake and clutch lever. Some earlier models also had throttle levers mounted to the frame above the gas tank. As engines became more powerful, sturdier frames evolved to handle the stresses. It was not a coincidence that many early motorcycle builders came from the bicycle industry.

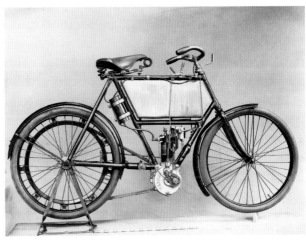

The shape of things to come was created in France by expatriate Russian brothers Michel and Eugene Werner in the late 1800s. It was their "New" Werner design of 1901 that set the standard in modern motorcycle design. Gone are the cumbersome handlebar mounted motors and hot tube ignitions, replaced by a low fitting engine that becomes part of the frame itself. Improved carburetion and electric spark ignition offered a level of reliability far above the competition. The Werners continued innovating motorcycle designs until their financial demise in 1905; an unfortunate turn of events in that they actually built a parallel twin engine motorcycle far ahead of other makers. Photo Science Museum / Science & Society Picture Library.

This 1910 Chicago-made Excelsior is highly prized due to its original unrestored condition. It clearly demonstrated the Werner design concept of using the engine's crankcase as a stressed member of the frame. Excelsior was one of the "big three" motorcycle manufacturers to survive, joining Harley-Davidson and Indian. Most used inlet-over-exhaust "F" head engine designs using atmospheric induction. Excelsiors were very reliable standards. Long rubber handgrip extensions were used to minimize road vibration on the hands.

Final drive on early bikes was primarily via leather belt or chain, the former making life tough for the motorcyclist whenever it rained. They had a tendency to slip. The addition of a transmission allowed multiple gears to offer a variety of motoring speeds without stressing the low-revving motors. That unit sat directly behind the engine and was usually connected by a chain running from the engine's crankshaft sprocket to a larger clutch sprocket.

Marsh bikes, like dozens of other American makes, had a short life. They were made by the Motor Cycle Manufacturing Company of Brockton, Massachusetts, between 1900 and 1906. The 1904 model pictured here represented its peak. Lighting was by igniting acetylene gas that was created in the lamp's lower chamber by calcium carbide pellets dropped into water.

Flanders was another short-lived American motorcycle company out of Michigan. They built several single-cylinder models and one V-twin between 1910 and 1915. The number 4 on this unrestored bike represents the machine's maximum horsepower. The vertical levers control drive belt tension and clutch engagement with the crankshaft. Note the loop frame that was becoming popular with American motorcycle designers. This model retailed for $165.

A pristine example of a Toledo, Ohio–made Yale as photographed at the Barber Vintage Motorsports Museum. Yale made bikes between 1902 and 1915. Their high-quality and state-of-the-art bikes included singles and 5 and 7 hp V-twin models. Ignition is provided by the advanced Bosh magneto mounted in front of the engine. Note the distinctive engine fins and the absence of a front brake on this 1912 model. As with many bikes of the period, one would start by pedaling and then engaging the motor.

Not for the Meek

Standards made between 1900 and the 1930s were Spartan affairs to ride. There were a lot of levers and pedals to manage.

The addition of a clutch mechanism to disengage drive from the engine during a stop or when shifting if a transmission was fitted added another control to manage. American makers started off with tank-mounted clutch levers but evolved to prefer the foot clutch, while Europeans migrated toward hand levers on the handlebars. Part of this was due to the smaller clutches and weaker clutch springs on the European bikes.

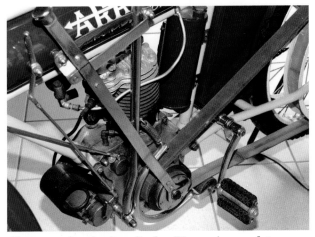

Close-up of a single-cylinder Pierce Arrow drive system. The vertical lever in the center of the photo is used to tension the drive belt. The forward lever acts as the clutch, engaging the crankshaft pulley. This allowed one to stop a bike with engine running.

Most bikes with transmissions had the gear change lever located tank side. Gear selection was a matter of sliding the cogs together gently with no distinct stop to locate the proper position in early transmissions. Foot pedal shifting was desired to free the hands but not available for decades. It was not until 1928 when the British marquee Velocette developed a reliable positive-stop foot shifting mechanism that allowed the rider to flick the pedal with his toes without worrying about skipping or missing gears. Much like today's bikes, the lever simply selected the next or previous gear depending on if it was flicked up or down.

Getting a Brake

Front brakes were curiously missing from the pioneer bikes until the 1920s, making starting the bike on a hill a difficult task. But motorcyclists were rugged individuals who endured a bit of hardship for the exhilaration of life on two wheels. The rationale in the United States was that since most of the riding was done on dirt and gravel roads, a front brake would only lead to locking the wheel and therefore sliding. Indian finally offered up a front brake in 1928, meeting the needs of stopping the newer and faster bikes traveling on better roads. The brakes on very early motorcycles employing pedals were of the coaster (back-pedal) brake type found on bicycles today. That became ineffective as motorcycles became heavier and faster. A variety of braking systems evolved, including rim brakes, band brakes, drum brakes, and disc brakes. Mechanically activated disc brakes started to appear on motorcycles during the 1920s. Douglas was the first to put mechanical disc brakes on their production machines. Pulling on the brake lever pushed a cast aluminum shoe against a Fibrax-lined disk. Braking action using this system was not progressive—meaning that the harder one pulls on a brake, the more braking is applied. The aluminum shoe tended to grab the disc and lock the wheel. Douglas went back to drum brakes for most of its line.

This British BSA motorcycle of 1924 featured a hand-shift multi-speed transmission, kick starting, and a hand clutch. Note the sprung passenger seat over the rear fender. An auxiliary rim on each wheel acted as a brake. A rubber friction block would bear against it to slow the bike down. This was a major step ahead of the "spoon" brakes found on some bikes twenty years earlier. Spoon brakes consisted of a large metal spoon pushing down on the tire itself.

Some early bikes used a band brake on the rear wheel well into the 1920s. The unit consisted of a metal band lined with friction material that was wrapped around the outside of a cast iron brake drum. A lever simply pulled one side of the band to apply pressure against the rotating drum. There were two problems. One was their tendency to smoke with prolonged braking, and the other was that they slipped when wet.

By the 1930s, nearly everyone was using the expanding-shoe type brake that resides within the brake drum. This offered some weather protection. Friction material was either riveted or glued onto the aluminum shoes. The brake lever (black) rotated a cam that expanded the shoes within the iron drum. That lever was connected to a hand lever by a cable for the front brake, or by a foot lever for the rear brake. Drum brakes were barely adequate as bikes became faster. Hydraulic disc brakes took things to a much higher level in years to follow and are the norm today.

Hydraulically activated disc brakes started becoming popular in the 1960s. A master cylinder mounted on the handlebar pumps fluid to a caliper unit mounted on the front fork(s). The pistons within the caliper housing push the brake pads against the disc rotor. This clamping action provides tremendous stopping force with little effort from the handlebar-mounted brake lever or rear brake foot pedal. Sportbikes, or very heavy bikes requiring extra braking power, often use dual-discs up front.

Providing a Vehicle for Transportation

Standards served a significant role in mobilizing the workforce while permitting the average family a means of inexpensive transportation. Unlike motorized bicycles using clip-on engines, standards were real motorcycles capable of moving quickly and handling the weight of strapped-on cargo or a passenger.

Riding position was, and still is, equally standard on a standard. One sits rather erect, with feet resting comfortably on footpegs or footboards in line with the knees, or a bit further back. Handlebars are comfortably set back avoiding the wrist and back pain associated with low race-style bars. A solo saddle graced earlier models, evolving to larger double seats, or sprouting a passenger's pillion seat over the rear fender. Standards also accommodated three or four via the addition of the popular sidecar. As stated earlier in the book, Henry Ford's Model T all but replaced the motorcycle-sidecar combination as an affordable family vehicle.

Standard motorcycles typically offer a comfortable riding position as demonstrated by the rider on this early 1970s Norton Commando. This "sit-up-and-beg" stance results in less back, neck, and wrist pain than a bike with low racing-style handlebars. Lower bars do put more weight on the front end for quicker steering, and reduce wind drag as well, but at a price.

This remarkable X-ray by artist Nick Veasey shows how proper the riding position was on standard motorcycles a hundred years ago. The spine on the rider of this Indian shows excellent posture. Photo courtesy Nick Veasey, nickveasey.com

Smoothing the Bumps

Form followed function on the pioneer bikes, and comfort was limited clearly by technology. Most had some rudimentary type of sprung front suspension to soak up the bumps from the rough cobblestone and dirt roads of the era. It would take another thirty years before sprung rear suspensions started replacing the "hard tail" bicycle-style frames on nearly all bikes. Exceptions did exist, including American-built Pope motorcycles that had a sprung rear wheel as early as 1912. Indian also offered sprung rear frames beginning with its 1913 models. The rear wheel was mounted on a "swingarm" that pivoted at the rear section of the frame. Swinging arm frames evolved over the decades to follow. Matchless was one of the first to offer it on their bikes after World War I. Velocette's swingarm racing bike of 1936 set the standard of using two coil spring shock units on bikes for the next forty years. "Twin-shock" suspension would give away to the "mono-shock" popular today. Yamaha was one of the first to employ them on their bikes in the 1970s.

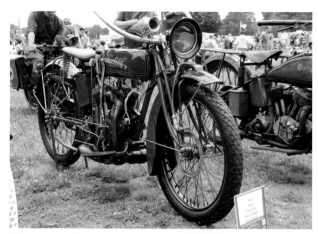

The rear leaf springs and swingarm are clearly visible on this chain drive 1918 Indian Powerplus. Note the overwhelming number of control levers. Absent is a front brake. The large gear on the front wheel is the speedometer drive. Indian introduced the "Hendee Special" version of the Powerplus in 1914 as the first electric start motorcycle. Poor battery life ended this innovative model quickly. However, all Indians from that point on featured electric lighting.

Sidecars provided an opportunity to take the family on a ride or haul cargo. This pristine combination features a 1912 Zenith "Gradua" 6 hp 770cc V-twin, using a JAP engine. The company made bikes in London between 1904 and 1950. The Gradua featured a variable pulley belt drive that allowed gear ratio changes to accommodate a variety of driving conditions, acting in essence like a transmission. Photo courtesy of Yesterdays Antique Motorcycles yesterdays.nl

As always, the sidecar offered civility with its spring suspension. The missus and kids could enjoy a ride in the country while dad bounced merrily on the coil spring–mounted saddle.

On the Bright Side

Prior to electric lighting, motorcyclists had to use carbide lamps, also know as acetylene lamps. These were devices that produced a bright light from the burning of acetylene gas. The gas was created by the interaction of water and calcium carbide crystals. Carbide lamps were very common among miners and cave explorers due to their simplicity and inherent bright light.

A 1914 FN features a handlebar-mounted acetylene gas generator to feed the large auxiliary headlamp on top and a taillight. The standard headlight has its own generation chamber. Red tubing goes to the taillight. This pristine restoration of the company's single-cylinder bike was offered for sale at $65,000 in 2015. Photo by Stephen Covell.

An original example made by the British company Lucas of a carbide lamp as used on motorcycles a hundred years ago. Lamps feature a double chamber that allows water to be mixed with the crystals at a regulated rate. The flame is ignited with a match. Note the chimney on top of the reflector housing.

Even though electric lighting was available in the 1920s, many motorcycle manufacturers still offered gas lamps. They did not require an electric generator and were brighter than incandescent bulbs of the times. This 1929 British-made Sunbeam S9 has a single acetylene generator located below the seat. Red rubber tubing splits to feed both head and tail lamps with gas. Photo by Stephen Covell.

Designs Diverge

American and European motorcycle manufacturers paralleled their designs during the first decade and a half of the twentieth century. World War I changed that. The popularity of the motorcycle on the battlefield carried forward to the postwar era. Europe fully embraced the low cost transportation solution offered by motorcycles. As scores of American marques disappeared due to competitive pressures and the Model T, European makers expanded to over one hundred. Britain, Germany, Italy, France, Belgium, Sweden, Switzerland, and Czechoslovakia all boasted popular brands. Benefiting from wartime aircraft manufacture and development, innovative designs and engineering advanced motorcycling tremendously. Multi-cylinder bikes appeared in two- and four-cylinder configurations. The benefit of having more than one cylinder was clear—they smoothed out the powerful thumping pulses associated with single-cylinder engines.

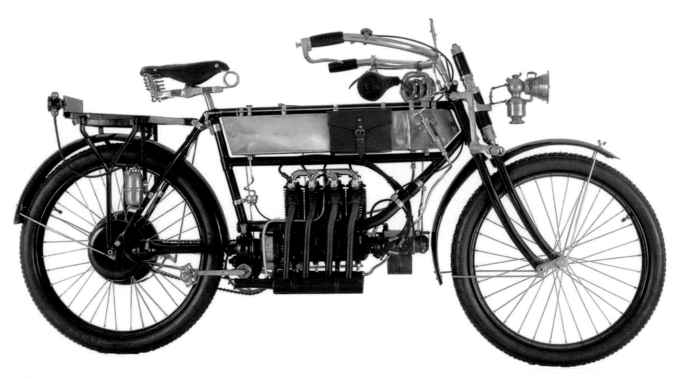

Belgium's FN motorcycle company also had its roots in arms manufacture. Its production spanned from 1901 to 1962, resulting in machines with notable innovations. The 1910 shown above is just one example. It features a 363cc four-cylinder engine with a clutch, internal rear brake, and shaft drive in an era when most other makers were still using belt drives. The four won the 1908 Multi-Cylinder TT in 1908. Later versions enlarged the motor to 750cc, and included a clutch, gearbox, and leading-link forks. Photo: Solvang Vintage Motorcycle Museum, motosolvang.com

Taking some cues from the FN, the Pierce Cycle Company of Buffalo, New York, built its own high-quality and high priced four in 1912. Pierce Cycle was a division of the famous Pierce Arrow Motor Car Company. Like their cars, products were targeted at a wealthier customer. The four's frame was made of huge four-inch tubing, holding the 554cc engine as a stressed component. Final drive, like the FN, was via shaft. Note the extended all-rubber handgrip extensions. They were used on many early American bikes to help minimize vibration coming through the handlebars. Photo courtesy of Bonhams.

The Ner-a-Car was an interesting concept developed in 1918 by Carl Neracher. It was made in Syracuse, NY, and in England between 1921 and 1927. Despite its seemingly unusual configuration, the 221cc two-stroke powered bike was remarkably stable and easy to handle. It originally sold for $225. Only a hundred of the nearly sixteen thousand made are said to exist. Photo Science Museum / Science & Society Picture Library.

From Guns to Bikes

Germany and Britain had strong military supply manufacturers that quickly shifted to provide affordable transportation by introducing reliable standard motorcycles right after the war. Examples include U.K.'s Birmingham Small Arms (BSA), Douglas, Royal Enfield, and ABC companies. The former made guns and cannons, the latter was known for its affiliation with the Sopwith Aircraft Company. BSA evolved to become the world's largest motorcycle manufacturer within a few decades. The Czechoslovakian firm of CZ (Ceska Zbrojovka) is another arms manufacturer that started building motorcycles in 1930, as was Russian maker IZH, a division of Kalashnikov Concern, the maker of the famous AK-47.

This charming and high-quality 1926 ABC (All British Cycles) motorcycle proudly displayed at the Barber Vintage Motorsports Museum. The flat horizontally opposed twin is only 398cc in size, but features a multi-plate clutch, drum brakes, four-speed gearbox, and front and rear leaf spring suspension. All that innovation was not cheap. ABCs cost nearly three times the price of more popular single-cylinder makes. Despite licensing to a reputable French concern, production ceased in 1925.

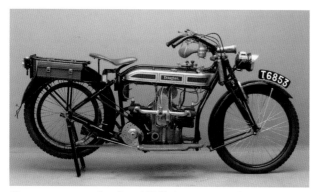

Competing with the ABC twin was the Douglas. It also featured a horizontally opposed air-cooled twin. Sizes ranged from 350cc to 600cc. Output initially was just under 3 hp for the smaller engine. Douglas had great success racing its bikes. The company also produced many popular standards in transverse twin-cylinder configuration, featuring shaft drive. Their 350cc Dragonfly introduced in 1954 had much in common with the BMWs of the time. Pictured is a 1919 4 hp 600cc side-valve twin. Photo courtesy of Yesterdays Antique Motorcycles.

Airplanes Engines and BMW

BMW clearly benefited from its experience in aircraft engine production during WWI. The Bavarian company produced motorcycle engines for others after the Treaty of Versailles banned production of aircraft motors in Germany. The original engine was similar to the British Douglas flat twin. The motor's success in Victoria motorcycles encouraged BMW to build its own bikes in 1923. This resulted in the successful 494cc "boxer" flat twin shaft-drive R32. BMW continued to evolve its flat twins for the next eighty years.

Only 3,000 of the side-valve 8.5 hp R32 machines were built by BMW between 1923 and 1926.

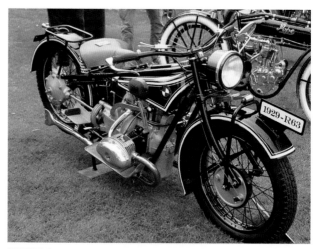

BMW kept innovating to produce more powerful bikes. By 1929, they were offering a 750cc twin that when supercharged would see a top speed of 133.8 mph. The exclusive overhead valve R63 was only offered for 1928 and 1929. Photo by Stephen Covell.

The Stylish Moto Guzzi

Perhaps one of the most romantic stories relating to pioneering motorcycle manufacturers that produced great standards comes from . . . where else . . . Italy. World War I flying corps buddies Carlo Gucci, Giovanni Ravelli, and Giorgio Parodi brought their dreams of starting a motorcycle company after the war to reality. Unfortunately, Ravelli lost his life just prior to the end of the conflict. That did not deter his ideas to be realized by his partners.

Production of the first Moto Guzzi bikes started in 1921 and featured an interesting horizontal single-cylinder machine of 498cc, with an external flywheel. Called a "bacon slicer" by enthusiasts, this feature lasted for decades on their singles.

The Moto Guzzi Normale (meaning "standard") was built from 1921 through 1924. It was the first production model manufactured by the ex-WWI Italian flyers. It featured an 8 hp horizontal engine with an overhead exhaust valve, a side intake valve, and the renowned external flywheel. The machine was capable of 50 mph. Unlike most bikes of the day, it had a centerstand. Photo by Moto Guzzi, supplied by Seth Dorfler.

Moto Guzzi continued to produce its remarkable line of 250cc and 500cc singles into the 1960s. This mid-1950s 500cc Falcone is as desirable today as it was back then.

Americans Like 'Em Big

By the 1920s the trend was clear: Americans liked bigger standard bikes powered by large displacement V-twins and four-cylinder engines. Indian, Excelsior, Henderson, ACE, and Harley-Davidson kept building bigger bikes in engine size and weight as reserved Europeans put more focus on smaller, lither, and more economical machines. Some of that was a reaction to the roads themselves. Americans had more room with ever-evolving highways to ride on. Europeans had narrower roads to work with, especially in the cities. Smaller bikes are easier to handle under those conditions. Other considerations included the high cost of gasoline in postwar Europe. Large V-twins and four-cylinder bikes are best classified as cruisers today. In their day, however, they served as standards.

America's love affair with large, powerful bikes resulted in a number of four-cylinder models, such as this 1929 Cleveland, capable of 100 mph speeds in its Tornado version. Interestingly, Cleveland started in 1915 building small 221cc two-cycle motorcycles. Sales of the small bikes were predictably better in Europe than in the United States. Unfortunately, the stock market crash of 1929 took its toll on the company, and production ceased after nearly 40,000 bikes made under the Cleveland name. Indian, Ace, and Henderson continued the production of four-cylinder motorcycles into the 1930s. These roadsters would be classified as cruisers today.

A good comparison between bikes that sold well in Europe and the United States. The nimble 1933 BSA model B33-2 249cc single on the left and the 1934 Harley-Davidson Model V 1207cc side-valve behind it were both hand-shift machines with hard-tail frames. There was, however, over 100 pounds difference in weight between them.

World's Fastest Standard Motorcycle

Not everyone was worried about the high price of petrol. A young man in Stevenage, England, was sowing the seeds of his dream to create the world's best and fastest standard motorcycle.

Vincent HRD had its beginnings with Philip C. Vincent (PCV) leaving his studies at Cambridge at the age of twenty to build motorcycles. He asked his father to loan him the money to buy the closed HRD company. HRD formerly belonged to Howard R. Davies, well known as the 1921 Senior TT winner on a 350cc AJS. Davies was a hero to the young Vincent, but as fate would have it, Davies was not able to survive a tough and competitive market for building motorcycles. Philip wanted to follow in Davies's footsteps and bought the brand based on a promise to his dad that he would honor the loan of money with a patent of his own design. He achieved this with a clever design for a rear suspension.

Vincent built his first bikes in 1928. Most of the

work was done with hand tools. They featured his patented triangulated spring frame. Most bikes of the era had solid frames with only a front suspension. Vincent's design sprung the rear section without compromising rigidity. He got great reviews for the bike's handling. Remarkably, many of today's bikes feature a similar design.

Philip Vincent's patented triangulated swinging arm frame as seen on the left. The rear section pivots on bearings just behind the transmission. Coil springs are housed in the two units below the seat. Vincent's fundamental sprung frame design continues to be used today in modern "mono-shock" suspensions as shown on the Kawasaki on the right.

Vincent used JAP (J. A. Prestwich), Rudge, and other proprietary engines made in England and Switzerland. He was disappointed by their unreliability at the famous Isle of Man TT races—an important venue to gain the recognition of the motorcycling press. He sought the help of Phil Irving, an Australian engineer, to design a 500cc single with a unique high-cam in 1934. This resulted in the standard Meteor and the sporting Comet of 1935.

By 1936, they doubled the cylinders to produce the famous V-twin Rapide. The fabled story goes that a translucent drawing of one single-cylinder engine inadvertently landed on top of another to give them the idea. The symmetry allowed another cylinder to be added to the cases without much modification.

Vincent's revolutionary 998cc Series A Rapide is totally unattainable today by all but the wealthiest collectors. It sold for 142 GBP back then;

nearly twice the cost of other less sophisticated standards. There were only around eighty built and are selling for far over $400,000 today. The bike blew the doors off the industry with its 110 mph out of the crate performance. It was marketed as "The World's Fastest Standard Motorcycle." The only criticism it received from the motorcycling press was the name "plumber's nightmare" because of all the external oil lines—something that Phil Vincent thought demonstrated care in proper lubrication.

This rare and superb example of a Vincent Series A Rapide still provides reliable transportation for its proud owner. Its introduction in 1936 took motorcycles to another level, much as the Honda CB750 would thirty-three years later. Photo courtesy of Arthur Farrow, Vincent HRD Club.

Not quite as costly and complex as a Vincent Rapide, Harley-Davidson offered its first overhead valve big twin in 1936 as well. Dubbed the EL "Knucklehead," this 61 cubic inch machine is revered by collectors as a milestone bike. Pictured is a 1947 model FL (74 cubic inch), the last year of production for the iconic Knucklehead.

Vincent HRD had a seven-year hiatus on motorcycle manufacturing during World War II just as they were gaining momentum. Unlike the bigger manufacturers, like BSA and Triumph, they did not make motorcycles for the military, but parts for aircraft and other weapons in their modest workshop. All during that time Philip Vincent and his brilliant engineer, Phil Irving, plotted their strategy for building the ultimate high-speed standard. In 1946 the Series B Rapide was launched with a much more refined engine layout (less external plumbing). The cylinder angle was increased from 47 to 50 degrees. Compression remained low at 6.45:1 in order to handle to low octane postwar "pool" gas. A unit (in same case as the engine) transmission replaced the prior model's weak Burman unit. It used the same Brampton-made girder forks. Refinements continued as the motorcycling press raved about this 110 mph vibration-free V-twin monster. Unfortunately for the British enthusiast, the government dictated an "export or die" rule requiring most machines to head overseas to help restore its economy. Those that failed to comply were cut off from precious and limited postwar resources, including aluminum and steel. Many Rapides ended up in Argentina. Philip's father had a cattle ranch there that helped fund the factory. The shortage of supplies inspired great engineering by the team. Series B, C, and Ds featured a strong spine frame that suspended the engine without the use of traditional cradle tubes. This reduced the need for precious steel.

Close-up of a Vincent Series B Rapide showing the oil passages cast within the cases. The B models used girder Brampton-type front forks as was used on the Series A. Vincent dropped the HRD logo after Philip's visit to the United States in 1949 when he realized that many Americans thought the initials stood for Harley R. Davidson.

This 1954 Series C Rapide will easily fetch between $50,000–$60,000 today—about half of what a Shadow goes for. Only 2,759 Series C Rapides were made. Many were shipped to Argentina where PCV's father lived. The differences between the bikes are minor. Besides the blackened engine, some internal component polishing, ribbed brake drums, and larger carburetors, the Shadow is nearly identical to the Rapide. These bikes had dual brake drums front and rear. The new super strong Girdraulic front fork was made of aluminum. Separate spring tubes suspended the wheel, and a single damper mounted by the steering head absorbed the shock.

The Black Shadow

Vincent's manufacturing team was made up of motorcycle lovers. PCV clearly advertised for help by stating that salary should be secondary to enthusiasm for building fast bikes. The need for speed quickly intoxicated the engineers. Vincent himself suffered serious injuries in a bad high-speed fall testing one of his bikes. Everyone saw the unlimited potential of the robust Rapide engine. A few minor technical modifications would make it immortal among motorcycles. So was born the Black Shadow, capable of a whopping 55 hp and 125-mph+ speed out of the crate. Featured in the chapter on sporting machines, the Black Shadow held its title as the world's fastest standard motorcycle for decades, right into the 1970s.

No other name in motorcycling evokes such a mystique as the Vincent Black Shadow. The huge 150-mph speedometer tells the whole story. Photo by Stephen Covell.

A Gentleman's Bike

Other refinements abounded on this "gentleman's" motorcycle. Vincent's featured dual brakes with a balance arm on each wheel, totally adjustable foot controls, under the seat toolbox drawer, large knurled knobs for toolless chain adjustment, no-tool wheel removal, left and right side stands that can jointly be used as a front stand for fork removal, dual rear sprocket option, and last, but hardly least, the ability to separate the front and rear halves of the bike for easy access to the engine and frame. Series C Vincents appeared in 1949 and featured other innovations, including a super strong "Girdraulic" front fork of their own design.

Tommy bars on each axle allowed easy wheel removal without the use of tools.

What other motorcycle offers such a convenient tool drawer under the seat? Also visible are the two enclosed coil spring units and a damper for the triangulated rear swinging section.

Foot controls and pegs are highly adjustable on Vincents. This allows riders with varying shoe sizes to set shift and brake levers to their liking.

Vincent continued to improve the Black Shadow to create the record-making and -breaking Black Lightning, covered in the chapter on racing. Other innovations abounded until the company's demise in 1956. Vincent was ahead of his time in offering a partially enclosed standard motorcycle. The public just wasn't ready for an enclosed machine. That is a different story today. Look at a modern Harley-Davidson Ultra Classic® as an example.

Today, the Vincent HRD Owners Club is the most prolific of all the vintage owners' clubs. Vincents are only overshadowed by the even more exclusive British-made Brough Superior. The Brough Superior was the brainchild of another young British enthusiast, George Brough (pronounced "bruff"). The marque is covered in the chapter on cruisers.

The Unapproachable Norton

No marque was more famous to the average British bike enthusiast than the "unapproachable" Norton. Starting in 1902, James Lansdowne Norton built his first complete motorcycle. It was powered by a 147cc French-built Clement motor. Norton was ambitious and built a number of bikes using Peugeot and Clement engines. By 1907, he had developed his own 475cc side-valve motor. The year 1909 saw the famous 633cc "Big 4" rolling out of the factory. Dan Bradbury broke the 70 mph mark in the U.K. on that monster single. Nortons were winning races and continued to do so for decades.

Norton's rise to fame was based on a strange twist of fate. Norton was too small of a company and, therefore, not invited to bid on

WWI military orders. Initially disappointed, Norton engineers spent their time well on development at the Birmingham factory. This paid off. The postwar boom in motorcycle orders allowed Norton to prosper as it offered chain-driven big singles with three-speed transmissions and nimble handling. Its 1922 Model 18 featured a 490cc overhead valve engine capable of nearly 18 hp. Its reliability and durability kept it in the company's catalog until 1954.

The Great Depression put a major damper on motorcycle production but hardly its popularity. Perhaps as an escape from reality, public interest in road racing grew. Nortons were the ones to beat on and off the track, winning over 250 major titles in the years to come. Their reliable overhead valve singles defined the British standard motorbike in the 1930s. World War II allowed the company to finally contribute to its nation's need. Norton produced over 100,000 motorcycles toward the war effort. Of course, this resulted in a loyal postwar following by veterans. By 1946, Norton was offering a civilian line-up that included the original Big 4 633cc single, 16H, Model 18, ES2, and 350cc, and 500cc International sporting models.

By the mid-1930s, the Norton Model 18 500cc single represented the quintessential British standard motorcycle. Its elegant lines and well-proportioned profile was the foundation for models offered by other marques of the day.

Norton continued to develop and set new benchmarks. In 1949, in cooperation with frame builder Rex McCandless, Norton introduced its "featherbed" framed machines featuring a sprung rear swingarm suspension. The term was coined by racer Harold Daniell after his first ride. Norton also improved on the front suspension with its famous "Roadholder" telescopic forks. The combination is still revered by classic motorcycle enthusiasts today.

A gleaming example of a 1962 Norton ES2 500cc single, featuring a featherbed frame and Roadholder telescopic forks. The ES2 saw numerous frame changes prior to the featherbed, including a plunger rear end and a more conventional pivoted fork. The frame performed so well that many enthusiasts swapped out the Norton motors for other more powerful engines. Triumph twins fitted within Norton frames are referred to as Tritons.

A Decade of Innovation

Many advanced technical designs were born between 1930 and 1940 in Europe. Great new engine concepts were introduced by Edward Turner and Valentine Page, working for Britain's famous Ariel and Triumph companies. Turner's ideas would define the standard in standard motorcycles for years to come, and he would eventually become the head of Triumph.

Ariel was one of the oldest motorcycle manufacturers around. The company started by building penny-farthing bicycles using their patented wire spoke wheels. Their first powered venture was to build three- and four-wheeled cycles powered by the popular De Dion engine in 1898. Their first motorcycle was designed and built by Charles Sangster in 1902. Ariel developed many models and supplied bikes to the British Army during WWI.

Following in his father's footsteps, Jack Sangster brought some of the best talent to Ariel by hiring brilliant young engineers. Val Page designed the superb Ariel 500cc overhead valve singles that were offered in a variety of configurations. Single-cylinder engines offered the benefits of simplicity and good engine cooling.

Ariel attracted much of the days engineering talent and continued to prosper with its reliable standards.

One of the more notable designs by a young Edward Turner started off as a sketch on a napkin. His idea was realized by 1930 as the Ariel Square 4 model 4G. The machine's unique four-cylinder configuration consisted basically of two parallel twin engines joined by gears in a common crankcase. The original design was a 500cc overhead cam design. Reliability of the complex valve mechanism was shaky at best, and a conventional pushrod overhead valve design was employed by

1937. The engine evolved in 601cc and 997cc formats, lasting until 1959. The large displacement Square 4 was considered a contender to the Vincent of the day, but lacked the punch of the snarling V-twins from Stevenage. These bikes, built in Selly Oak, were better suited for comfortable highway riding and sidecar work.

An Ariel Square 4 with telescopic forks introduced in mid-1946. Also featured is a plunger-type rear suspension, introduced a year earlier. This version of the 4G still had cast iron cylinder heads and constrained exhaust porting. The engines were prone to some overheating at slow speeds due to the limited air that could reach the rear pair of cylinders.

By 1949, an aluminum cylinder head replaced the cast iron one on the Square 4. Further cooling was achieved in 1953 with the addition of art deco–styled separate aluminum exhaust manifolds. A single carburetor behind the engine fed the fuel/air mixture via an integral manifold.

Perhaps the ultimate example of sidecar comfort is this 1958 Ariel Square 4–powered combination exhibited at the Barber Vintage Motorsports Museum. The Square 4's good power band and torque made it an ideal sidecar bike.

Ariel continued valiantly to produce singles, twins, and fours in a highly competitive British manufacturing market. Motorcycle giant BSA purchased the marque and shared many of its parallel twin engines with Ariel. Attempting to stay ahead of the competition, Val Page looked at the two-stroke technology advanced by companies such as Adler out of Germany, and Suzuki and Yamaha from Japan. In 1958, the company introduced the unique 250cc Leader. Unfortunately, it was not enough to save the company.

Other famous British marques shared a similar swan song. AJS (A. J. Stevens & Co) out of Wolverhampton introduced its first motorcycle in 1910 as a 292cc single. By 1914, the company was winning Isle of Man races. A notable win was by rider Howard R. Davies in the Senior TT of 1921—the only senior win on a 350cc bike. Despite an extensive range of singles, V-twins and exotic racers, AJS suffered from a lack of funds and was purchased by Matchless. Production shifted to Plumstead. Later, AJS and Matchless motorcycles shared near identical features. It is

the pre-Matchless bikes that are sought after by collectors.

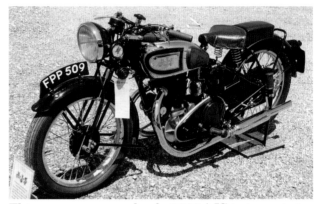

This gorgeous example of a 1939 AJS twin-port single represents the company's superb contribution to standard motorcycles prior to WWII. It features a single-cylinder engine with two exhaust pipes.

Standard motorcycles are certainly not limited to big four-stroke engines. Alfred Scott started producing reliable two-stroke powered bikes for sale as early as 1908. His 333cc twin cylinder engine featured water cooling. Scott motorcycles placed well at the races and therefore survived in various forms until 1972. Photo shows a late 1920s model of the famous Squirrel line of Scotts offered in 500cc and 600cc displacements. Scotts also featured a three-speed gearbox actuated by foot using Velocette's gear-change mechanism. They were "sporting" standards in that they were quite fast and nimble.

Inspired by Racing Brothers

Matchless was founded in 1901 by the Collier family. Young Harry and his brother Charlie were avid motorcycle racers.

It was in 1929 that the company finally achieved recognition from the motorcycle press with its 400cc Silver Arrow and 593cc Silver Hawk V-twins. Unfortunately, sales did not reflect the media's enthusiasm. Its acquisition of AJS helped tremendously, as well as the purchase of another well-known British marque, Sunbeam. The combined brands were joined as a new entity, called AMC (Associated Motor Cycles). Military purchases of over 70,000 bikes for WWII gained the brand considerable recognition primarily with its reliable G3 347cc singles, offered with the optional new hydraulically dampened Teledraulic front forks. AJS and Matchless built a strong following and contributed to the British invasion on American motorcycling. It built numerous parallel twins, ranging from 498cc to 750cc under the AMC umbrella. The larger twins were Norton engines during a period of joint ownership between the companies. The AJS/Matchless brand produced its last four-stroke singles in 1966 and Norton-powered twins until 1969.

A nice, clean customized Matchless twin from the late 1960s powered by a 750cc Norton Atlas engine. Forks, hubs, and brakes were also provided by Norton as Matchless ceased to build these components on its own. The Atlas engine was prone to significant vibration at higher rpms.

The Matchless brand was revived briefly in 1987 by Les Williams in a modern frame powered by a 494cc Rotax engine.

An International Affair

Other parts of the world were also busy designing and building innovative motorcycles. Sweden's Husqvarna®, better known today for its off-road bikes, also had its roots in arms manufacture. The company started building motorcycles using small FN-made single-cylinder motors in

The classic Matchless 500cc single as it appeared in 1949 as the G80. The bike's engine still used hairspring valve springs, but had other advances that would make it a favorite standard. The most notable of these was the sprung rear suspension using "candlestick" hydraulic dampers. Larger dampers called jampots were used on future models. Matchless preferred to mount its magneto behind the cylinder, as shown in the photo, while AJS mounted it in front.

1903, the same year Harley-Davidson began. The company never enjoyed high volume production. As a result, manufacturing costs were high, and it was forced to source its engines from other makers, like the English-made JAP. Husqvarna's success in motocross shifted its focus to off-road machines in 1960, an arena in which it still thrives today under the KTM umbrella.

This rare 1927 Husqvarna model 180, 550cc V-twin motorcycle used a side-valve engine of its own design and manufacture. Similar to the Indian Scout, it even shared an American-made Schebler carburetor. Photo courtesy of Yesterdays Antique Motorcycles.

Italy's Gilera had a similar history to the British marques. It started its production in 1909 after learning the business from another well-known maker, Bianchi. World War II gave the company a boost. Single-cylinder models in 499cc powered military tricycles and sidecar bikes. As with the British, postwar sales of the company's 499cc overhead valve singles kept the firm viable. Its Saturno was a favorite among commuters and anyone looking for a reliable standard. Gilera is best known for its highly advanced four-cylinder race engines raced in the 1950s. The marque survives under the umbrella of Italy's Piaggio Group.

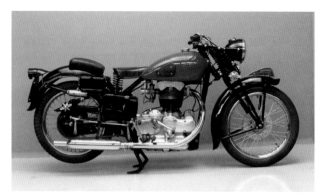

Gilera's popular and reliable standard, the 500cc Saturno, took some of its styling cues from British-made singles, including the girder front forks with friction dampers. Photo courtesy of Yesterdays Antique Motorcycles.

Japan's Miyata was started in 1909. It produced small displacement motorcycles for Japan's limited prewar market. It was, however, after WWII that the country needed an inexpensive means of transportation. Miyata complied with its 500cc parallel twins and 125cc two-stroke singles.

A Triumph for Triumph

Hundreds of large and small companies built motorcycles before and after World War II. Many are the dreams of collectors today. None, however, was, and is, as famous as the British-made Triumph. Triumphs mobilized an entire generation of young British and American enthusiasts in the 1950s and 1960s. So popular was the brand that examples abound in the market today along with an unparalleled supply of spare parts and accessories available.

Triumph was started by an educated German named Siegfried Bettman. He emigrated to England in 1883 to engage in the import and export trade of bicycles and sewing machines. By 1887, the Triumph Cycle Company was registered and started building its bicycles at a small factory in Coventry. Keen on innovation, Bettman and his engineer, Mauritz Schulte, began studying motorized bikes of the times. One model in particular stood out: the Hildebrand and Wolfmüller 1,488cc water-cooled twin cylinder motorcycle. The team purchased one for evaluation. The bike's unusual layout prompted Schulte to favor the De Dion–style engine configuration for its own development.

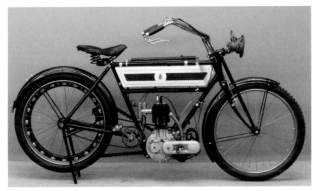

The 1907 Triumph with its 3-1/2 hp side-valve engine was quite conventional and followed the Werner design. Clean examples such as this can easily bring $16,000. Photo courtesy of Yesterdays Antique Motorcycles.

The company's introduced its own 363cc single-cylinder engine in 1904. Much like its competitors, Triumph evolved in innovation and notoriety. Its ball bearing–supported crankshaft engines proved to be durable. Winning races and good showings at impressive endurance runs generated good publicity for the brand. Val Page joined Triumph early in the 1930s to build the company's well-loved singles in 250cc, 350cc, and 500cc versions. Edward Turner joined the firm a few years later and gave the bikes a cosmetic makeover. The result was an attractive lineup of motorcycles recognized the world over.

Triumph's handsome T90, shown in its 1938 version, was the company's reliable 500cc single. Its frame and girder front end would serve as the foundation for Ed Turner's revolutionary Speed Twin.

Turner was a tough boss but in tune with what the market needed. Unlike Vincent, he was frugal and considered the cost of production seriously as he designed his masterpiece: the Speed Twin. Introduced at the London show in 1937, the bike featured Turner's near perfect 498cc parallel twin engine. Parallel twins had been around in some form or another for decades, but it was the compact high camshaft pushrod-activated overhead valve engine capable of 28 hp at 6,000 rpm that turned the tide. Paired with a four-speed transmission, the Speed Twin launched a whole new era in motorcycling.

The immortal 1938 Triumph 5T Speed Twin with its Amaranth red and chrome tank panels draws immediate attention at the Barber Vintage museum today. The engine's light-alloy connecting rods, good cooling profile, and excellent power-to-weight ratio provided notable performance.

By 1939, Triumph upped the ante by introducing a high-performance version of the 498cc Speed Twin dubbed the Tiger 100. Increased compression and internal engine refinements made it an instant hit with the sporting crowd with its thirty-three horses.

War and Postwar Years

World War II called Triumph to duty as it did for all large European motorcycle manufacturers. The war was not kind—the Coventry factory was demolished by the Germans in a bombing raid. Turner left Triumph for a while to join BSA but returned to help launch reliable standard motorcycles for the redevelopment of a war-torn country. Production shifted to a new plant in Meriden. The demand for motorcycles in the United States urged Triumph to take a good look at that seemingly endless market. Returning GIs were ready to hit the road. American-built machines were limited to Harleys and Indians. Triumph saw great opportunity as GIs stationed in England and Europe were already introduced to the British makes. Even though BMWs and Zündapps were a consideration for those introduced to them in Germany, German-made bikes were not popular in the United States immediately after the war.

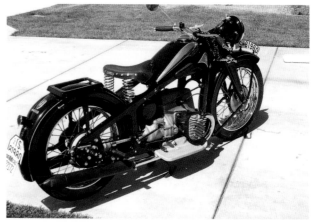

BMW was certainly not the only German company making horizontally opposed twins. Zündapp started producing motorcycles in 1917. This elegant 1934 K500 was still popular on the streets of Germany after the Allies arrived. More than 15,000 were made between 1933 and 1939. The 498cc twin produced a modest 16 hp at 4,800 rpm. In addition to the Zündapp, the Swiss company of Condor offered a similar flat twin after WWII. Photo courtesy of Mike Dunn.

Understanding the American consumers' need for size and speed, Triumph increased the bore and stroke of the Speed Twin to 71mm x 82mm, resulting in its legendary 649cc parallel twin. Launched in 1950 as the 6T Thunderbird, it was an instant success. The movie *The Wild One* skyrocketed its sales and let the American makers know in no uncertain terms that the British invasion was in full force. Triumph's venerable T120 649cc Bonneville appeared in 1959. It featured twin carburetors, a new one-piece forged crankshaft, and 8.5:1 compression.

Setting the standard in standard motorcycles worldwide was the 1950s 650cc Triumph Thunderbird. Faster off the line and more maneuverable than most, it gave the large American V-twins a serious run for the money. It is said that the name was inspired by a South Carolina motel that Edward Turner stayed at on his way to Daytona. The 6T was made until 1966. Most British and European bikes used narrow large diameter 18-inch or 19-inch wheels compared to the wide 16-inch wheels fitted to the big Harleys and Indians of the time. This made for lighter and more tactile handling.

While the British were dominating the motorcycle spotlight, German maker BMW was quietly making its quality flat twins. This 1954 594cc R68 BMW is an example of what was rarely seen on the US roads compared to Harleys, Indians, and Triumphs. BMW's hallmark was its supreme reliability. The simple overhead valve engine, combined with an automotive style dry clutch and shaft drive, had little to break. Note the plunger rear suspension.

BSA joined aggressively in developing bikes for the US market in 500cc and 650cc parallel twin configuration. Pictured is a 1951 A10 Golden Flash 650cc. Introduced in 1950, the engine had cast iron cylinder heads. It was based on BSA's A7 series 500cc twins. The plunger-style rear end was less stable at high speed cornering than swingarm models introduced in 1954. The Golden Flash was available in gold or black. Higher performance variants of the A10 included the Road Rocket and Super Rocket. Photo courtesy of Yesterdays Antique Motorcycles

Germany's Victoria brand goes way back to 1899. It produced popular bikes through 1966—the latter years under a merger with DKW and Express called Zweirad Union. Hardly any were ever seen in the United States. This neat little 1956 V35 features a 350cc transverse four-stroke V-twin with shaft drive.

Triumph, BSA, and Norton were hardly the only British makes to be exported. Matchless, AJS, Sunbeam, and Velocette were a few others that sought sales opportunities abroad—albeit in much smaller numbers.

Two-Strokes for the Masses

Meanwhile, serving the postwar U.K. and European markets, British engine maker Villiers offered motorcycle builders a low cost power plant modeled after DKW's two-strokes. This allowed countless commuters to afford efficient and reliable transportation. Villiers specialized in two-stroke engines of various sizes, ranging from 99cc singles all the way to 324cc twins. Numerous British makers utilized these engines by offering alternatives to the popular BSA Bantam. Well-known marques included Cotton, Francis-Barnett, James, and Panther. The British marque Excelsior (unrelated to the US maker) also offered economical two-strokes. Operating between 1896 and 1964, it was the very first large scale British motorcycle manufacturer. The company's best-known model, the Talisman, introduced twin cylinder two-strokes to the market. It evolved from its original 243cc configuration in 1949 to 328cc by 1957. These motors were well known for their smoothness. Two-strokes continue to provide affordable transportation to millions of people in emerging countries.

Harley-Davidson's most basic bike was the Hummer, named after one of their dealers who specialized in two-strokes. The 125cc machine was available from 1955 to 1959.

Commuter and utility bikes with high gas mileage were much in demand in the postwar 1950s. BSA's 123cc D1 Bantam offered over 90 mpg. The GPO model was used by the British Post Office. Photo by Stephen Covell.

Clamoring for Market Share

Many motorcycle manufacturers flourished after the war. One example is Veloce Ltd. It was founded by German immigrant Johannes Gutgemann in 1904. Brother Percy soon joined to help designed several well-received bikes badged Velocette. This included two-stroke 206cc ultralights and four-stroke overhead cam singles identified as K machines. The "K" stood for camshaft in German. Racing victories created strong brand recognition for the company.

In addition to its reliable standard singles, Velocette is best known for having developed the first practical positive-stop foot actuated gearshift mechanism in 1928. It was the engineering feat of racer Harold Willis. This feature greatly enhanced handling capabilities as it freed a hand while shifting.

Phil Irving, of Vincent fame, joined Velocette for a while to design the high camshaft pushrod singles we see at vintage shows today. A market favorite was the 350cc MAC model, available in a sprung frame version in 1953. The Hall Green factory bumped up its displacement to 500cc to create the MSS series of bikes. The MSS had a long run. Built primarily as a standard roadster, it was often configured as a clubman racer. Some models even left the factory as off-road bikes.

Photo shows a 1963 MSS Clubman Velocette featuring the high camshaft, pushrod-actuated, overhead valve engine. This pristine example was offered for sale at a vintage event for $19,000.

Phil Irving, designer of the Vincent engine, worked for Velocette for a while. That influenced him to design a high-cam single-cylinder engine for Philip Vincent. That engine was doubled to produce the famous Series A Rapide. The postwar 500cc single-cylinder Comet (right) was an upgraded engine that was actually derived from the new twin cylinder Rapide design (front). Comets are therefore referred to as "half a Vincent." Comets were quite expensive compared to other British 500cc singles. Thanks to Arthur Farrow for this great shot of a pair of Royal Canadian Mounties trying on Vincents.

The magic words when speaking Velocette are Venom and Thruxton—both fast variants of their durable 500cc singles. The Venom was brought to market in 1955 to compete with other makers' fast singles and twins. Less than 6,000 were made before production ended in 1970. The popular 350cc Viper was also introduced in 1955. The model enjoyed a reasonably long run until 1969 because of its lower cost and ease of operation. Big singles were not easy to start. The 350cc bikes, however, required less effort to kick over than the massive 500s.

The British motorcycle industry of the 1960s was often accused of lacking innovation. It was less an issue with innovation than it was in innovating practical products within their core competency and market. Nearly every marque dabbled in scooters, as an example. Nearly all failed miserably. In 1948, Velocette experimented with an unusual configuration consisting of a water-cooled, shaft-drive, three-speed 149cc side-valve transverse flat twin. This rather unique combination may have been better received by the consumer if it were not for the unconventional pressed steel frame. The LE (little engine) survived in various models only because of its utility as a police service vehicle. The Velocette marque held strong until it met its demise in 1971. Many of its best designs remained on the drawing board.

The LE Mark II was introduced in 1950 with an enlarged 192cc transverse engine. These bikes were ideal for commuters. They were prone to cylinder head leaking but were easily repaired roadside.

Despite some hiccups, British bike manufacturers were making hay in the glorious sunshine of the 1950s and early 1960s. Their standards became a common sight on American roads. Harley-Davidson and Indian were far too late in reacting to the market-savvy designs coming across the Atlantic. They felt the pain as sales declined. Ironically, the British would feel the same way about Japanese bikes a decade later.

Indian's Arrow was a hasty but noble effort to produce an inexpensive British-like single-cylinder standard. Pictured is an attractive 1949 model with a 218cc engine. Photo by Stephen Covell.

Harley Meets the Challenge

Harley-Davidson needed to defend its turf in the United States. The company scrambled to create a sporty standard using an aging engine design from the W series flatheads. The K model Harley was introduced in 1952. It was powered by a 45 cubic inch engine (750cc) that did little to bring chills down Brit bike owners' spines. The engine did, however, offer hidden potential in the hands of the right tuner. The bike brought something new to Harley, a unit construction transmission, a swingarm rear suspension, and telescoping front forks. Introduction of a longer stroke 883cc engine resulted in the faster KH model in 1954. Despite its modest 38 hp performance, it did set the stage for the Sportster to come. The K series also found its niche on the dirt tracks, dominating dirt ovals nationwide.

The newly designed 1957 overhead valve 40 hp Sportster finally gave the Brit 500cc bikes a run for their money. Model variations improved on cam designs to create more powerful versions that could easily compete with the larger 650cc imports. The XLCH model of 1958 was the best consumer Sportster of them all, offering a "competition hot" engine package accentuated by a small "peanut" gas tank and superb styling. With 45 hp on tap, it could outrun most British bikes on the top end.

The Sportster continues to be a good seller for Harley today. It is offered in 1,200cc and 883cc versions; the latter aimed at the entry level and female market. Despite its long history, the Sportster has seen little major improvement in its basic architecture. Recent rubber-mounting of the engine has reduced vibration a bit without taking away the charm of the machine's old-school feel.

Harley-Davidson's response to the British invasion was their sporty 1952 742cc K Model. It featured many innovations for Harley-Davidson, including a unit construction engine-transmission, and a four-speed foot-operated gearbox. Even though the side-valve V-twin could not hang with the faster 650 Triumphs, it had great success on the track as racers modified the willing engine. It competed easily against British 500cc twins in AMA races. In 1954, the engine was bumped up to 883cc as the KH model.

In 1957 Harley-Davidson updated the flathead KH series bike to an OHV V-twin named the Sportster to compete against the Brit bikes. The XL Sportster had cast iron heads, unit construction engine/transmission, and displaced 883cc. 1958 introduced the competition model XLCH. The popularity of converting the "competition hot" XLCH for road use prompted Harley to offer the pictured street version in 1959. The 1960 XLH model offered a more civil configuration with a large dual seat and saddlebags. By 1972 the Sportster grew to 1,000cc (61 cubic inches) for added power.

Parallel Twins Dominate

Norton jumped on the opportunity to export to the vast American market soon after WWII. Its original entry for the big-bike oriented US market included the 487cc Model 7 Dominator. It was developed by Bert Hopwood in 1947 and put to market for 1949. The engine featured cast iron heads with overhead valves fitted to a conventional frame. Its similarity to Triumph's Speed Twin was no coincidence. Bert had worked with Edward Turner on the original Speed Twin design. Placing the same engine in a featherbed frame produced the Model 88 Dominator of 1953. It had a good ten-year run. The 88 was enlarged to 596cc in 1956 and was offered as the 99 Dominator. A faster 650cc version was launched in 1960. The 650SS could easily beat T6 Triumphs and BSA A10 Road Rockets. Dominator models that came in SS versions sported twin carbs.

Eye candy for the motorcycle lover. This 1953 88 Dominator has a 500cc vertical twin engine mounted in Norton's famous featherbed frame. Note the strong loop construction that provided stable handling in the turns that made this frame famous. Frames made prior to 1960 are referred to as "wideline"; being nearly a foot wide at the loop. Rider comfort prompted the "slimline" version to be developed.

The "Domi" was enlarged once more in the early 1960s to become the 58 hp 750cc Atlas, making it the largest displacement parallel twin of its day. Variations of the Atlas included the P11 and Ranger models. The Atlas laid the foundation for the company's famous 750cc Commando line.

Both Norton and Triumph experimented with stylish enclosed rear sections on their bikes. Part of the thinking was that these less intimidating bikes may attract buyers who were considering scooters. Triumph's Twenty-One model was dubbed the "bathtub" Triumph by enthusiasts. Norton named theirs the DeLuxe. Pictured is a 1960 88 Dominator DeLuxe. The 596cc 99 Dominators were also available as DeLuxe versions between 1960 and 1962. Smaller versions were made as the 250cc Jubilee and the 350cc Navigator.

BSA sales grew tremendously between 1964 and 1966 as early baby boomers enamored by the fast sporting standards advertised in the magazines earned enough to afford them. Pictured is a 1970 BSA 650cc Lightning. It was designed to go head-to-head with Triumph's Bonneville. It also featured twin carbs. Boomers continued to be the primary source of new motorcycle sales through the 1970s, and later in the new millennium, as their desire to recapture the thrill of the open road caught up with their income. Harley-Davidson benefited from this greatly. Photo courtesy of Andrea Young.

Indian rebadged several brands of British-made bikes during the late 1950s in an effort to maintain its brand. Pictured is a 700cc parallel twin Royal Enfield Meteor with Indian tank badges. These were sold under the Indian Sales Corporation through 1959. That entity was later purchased by Associated Motorcycles Limited, marketers of Norton, AJS, and Matchless motorcycles. They continued to sell British-made Indians through 1961. The brand had a serious identity crisis during this era. This Meteor was displayed at the Antique Automobile Club of America Museum.

American motorcycle legend, author, and original owner of *Cycle* magazine, Floyd Clymer, devised several creative ways to help keep the Indian brand alive. He acquired the rights to the name in 1967 to produce several remarkable and rare standard motorcycles for the US market. Among them were a 500cc Velocette and the larger 736cc Royal-Enfield Interceptor Mk. II displayed at the Barber Motorsports Museum. Both had Italian design and suspension components. Unfortunately, Clymer passed away before gaining sufficient momentum to keep the idea going.

This early-1960s deluxe version of an AJS model 31 was powered by a 646cc ohv twin. Built under the AMC umbrella, a matching Matchless was also available as the G12. Both bikes were well received in America because of their high speed capability. The AJS 31 was produced between 1958 and 1966.

The best Indian could do to stem the incoming tide of UK made bikes was an eleventh hour effort to build its own British-style bikes. The 1949 Super Scout 249 had an overhead valve 436cc vertical twin engine. Rush to market produced an underpowered machine that could not compete with the Brits. The pictured 500cc Warrior produced a bit more power. Unfortunately for Indian, the British Pound experienced a devaluation that priced the Warrior out of the market. It was bad timing for Indian. The Warrior TT fared much better. It was a racer well suited for the dirt tracks. Both Warrior models were made between 1950 and 1952. The company resorted to importing Royal Enfield motorcycles starting in the spring of 1955.

British Singles to the End

Despite the popularity of British parallel twins, Triumph and BSA continued to produce singles. The idea was to offer entry-level bikes at an affordable price. Triumph's Tiger Cub and BSA's 250cc and 441cc singles started many off on motorcycles. The Royal Enfield continues this legacy today.

The easy to handle 199cc four-stroke Triumph Tiger Cub standard started many off on the road to motorcycling. It came onto the scene in 1954 as an evolution to the 149cc Terrier. The Cub was initially introduced with a plunger rear suspension frame. It eventually ended up with a BSA Bantam frame, as shown in the early 1960s scrambler version above. The last Cub, dubbed the Super Cub, came off the BSA assembly line in 1969 as the ailing British marques merged production to survive. Ironically, Honda's 50cc "Super Cub" was dominating the market.

BSA produced many attractive-looking singles like this 1968 441cc Shooting Star. It used basically the same engine as its off-road capable brother, the 441 Victor, seen in the back with the yellow aluminum tank. These singles are easy to work on and are still attainable for the newcomer to vintage motorcycling. Just a word of caution: it takes a certain knack to starting these one-lunged beasts. But, once you have it, you are good to go. Unfortunately, modern-day ethanol-laced gasoline will wreak havoc with the bike's fiberglass tank. It will require a good coating inside with tank sealer to keep the alcohol from dissolving the resin.

The Sun Sets on the British Empire

The fate of the British dominance of the motorcycle market was already sealed by the early 1960s. The big four Japanese makers began to export their machines in volume. Honda's success was not taken lightly by other Japanese producers. Yamaha enjoyed recognition in 1963 with its 73cc YG-1 lightweight motorcycle, capable of a whopping 125 miles per gallon. It performed better than the Honda Super Cub and looked like a real bike.

Yamaha capitalized on bringing low-cost entry fee bikes for beginning riders. This small 100cc twin followed Honda's basic philosophy: to get customers going on small bikes, knowing that they will work themselves up to bigger ones. The slightly larger Yamaha AS-1 was another successful example. The small 125cc 15 hp two-stroke twin was quite fast—often raising eyebrows for those left at the stop light with bigger bikes. Low cost and speed was a good combination to attract young riders.

Kawasaki offered up more powerful 125cc bikes in high numbers as well. Their plan was based on the assumption that consumers wanted something larger than 100cc machines. As a result it produced the Pet model that looked remarkably like a Super Cub on steroids. Its partnership with Meguro in 1960, Japan's longest running motorcycle manufacturer up to that point, gave Kawasaki great momentum. Meguro had obtained licensing to produce a copy of the BSA 500cc A7 known as the K1. Kawasaki soon enlarged the motor to 625cc to produce the W1 parallel twin. The bike evolved over the next eight years as a reliable alternative to British-made motorcycles.

Kawasaki's W series parallel twin maintains all the traditional British styling cues and looks remarkably similar to a pre-unit BSA A10. It had a good run between 1967 and 1975. An updated version of the bike was introduced in 1999 as the W650.

Current interest in retro standards has revived the W series once again, this time as the W800. Designed to compete with the retro Bonneville, it has a fuel-injected 800cc motor. At the time of publishing, the bike was not available in the United States. Photo courtesy of Kawasaki Motors.

Harley-Davidson Responds

The folks at Harley-Davidson recognized the impact made on the American motorcycle market by Honda and the other Japanese makers with their small displacement bikes. Harley had already been in the small bike game with its DKW derivatives, the 125S and Hummer two-strokes. This wasn't enough. They needed more savvy designs in both two- and four-stroke configurations. In 1960, Harley-Davidson bought fifty percent of Italian maker Aeronautica Macchi. Aermacchi, as it was to be called, had a great racing history with its single-cylinder engines. The company produced a variety of small bikes for Harley over the next eighteen years. The impact of the Japanese invasion did put a lot of stress on Harley-Davidson. In 1969, American Machine and Foundry (AMF) acquired interest in Harley-Davidson. Under AMF's management, severe cuts in production and labor were implemented. The quality of the bikes suffered in that they did not meet the traditional value associated with Harley-Davidson. The acquisition, however, did allow the company to regain its footing in a new and turbulent motorcycle market. By 1981, a group of investors regained the company, and it has flourished since.

Harley-Davidson's relationship with Aermacchi resulted in the Sprint line of standards starting in 1961 with the 18 hp 250cc model. By 1969, it had evolved to a very competent 350. An enduro version was offered in 1973 as the SX 350. Pictured is a 1967 250 SS. Sprints had a lukewarm reception in their day but are highly sought after today. Photo courtesy of Jamie Goodson.

Motorcycle swap-meet visitors may walk right by this unassuming little 1966 Harley-Davidson M-50 without much thought. It does have tremendous history associated with it. Made by Aermacchi for Harley-Davidson, the small two-stroke was designed to compete directly against Honda's Super Cub. Other two-strokes included the M65 S and the ML-125 S Rapido.

Understanding the American Market

Honda recognized American's "bigger is better" philosophy back in its salad days.

Bikes evolved in 90cc, 125cc, 160cc, 250cc, 300cc, and 305cc displacement to take their place on American roads. Honda Super Cub owners were eager to move up. Precision engineering allowed for overwhelming performance out of small displacements—considered toys by many American and British bike owners. They were soon to be embarrassed as 10,000 rpm 305cc machines left their 500cc bikes in the dust.

The single-cylinder overhead valve Honda 90 was a great move up from the Super Cub. It looked more like a motorcycle than a scooter. Photo by Stephen Covell.

These machines utilized engine designs previously limited to racing bikes. Honda studied the best of the Italian overhead cam engines to come up with its own chain-driven single overhead cam parallel twins. Combined with styling from British and German designs, the results were appealing. The Japanese invasion of the prime US motorcycle market was not only realized by producing these clean-looking quality machines that challenged the larger British bikes on speed, but by offering something neither American nor British bikes had: electric start. This was a major factor in differentiation from other brands and opened up motorcycling to a whole new segment.

The 24 hp 250cc Honda C72 Dream 250, made between 1960 and 1967, clearly signaled Honda's direction in providing American consumers with larger bikes. The bike pictured is a CA72, replacing pressed steel handlebars with tubular ones.

A sportier version of Honda's strong single overhead cam Dream 250 came to market soon after as the CB72. Gone was the pressed steel frame. The new tube construction frame used the engine as a stressed member. A CL72 250 Scrambler was also available, adding higher pipes and a skid plate.

The reliable pressed steel frame Hondas continued their presence with the larger 305cc engine through the 1960s. This 1962 CA77 Honda Dream features a linking-arm "cushion" front suspension that is best used for casual riding and commuting. The use of telescopic forks on the Super Hawk took advantage of the engine's 23 hp for a sportier ride.

Honda's CB77 Super Hawk 305 was finally the "big" bike Super Cub fans were hoping for. It was fast and stylish, but most of all it made believers out of those who never would have thought that a small engine like that could last tens of thousands of miles without problems. Produced between 1961 and 1967, the 28 hp Super Hawk put Honda on the map as a real contender in the US motorcycle market. Photo courtesy of American Honda Motor Co., Inc.

Motorcycles using Honda's innovative engine designs of the 1960s continue to provide inexpensive transportation for millions in emerging economies. There are countless standard bikes offered that are below 250cc. Fuel economy is a high priority. Hero MotoCorp Ltd. in India is the world's largest manufacturer of two-wheeled vehicles. The company was formerly known as Hero Honda Motors Ltd., a joint venture between Hero and Honda started in 1984. The joint venture ended in 2010. Hero continues to be a major producer of two-wheeled vehicles in Asia. Pictured is a 97cc Hero standard. Photo by Tamara Hayden.

Yamaha, Suzuki, and Kawasaki focused much of their early effort on two-stroke bikes. Many advances were made in two-stroke technology, including multi-port cylinders with up to seven ports, reed valve induction, and power valve exhaust designs. Yamaha's YD series of 250cc two-strokes were capable of impressive 90-mph speeds. A major hurdle in market acceptance was overcome by the introduction of automatic lubrication systems. This eliminated the need to pre-mix gas and oil. Decades later, EPA rulings on clean air pretty much killed two-strokes on public roads.

By 1962, only fifteen motorcycle manufacturers remained in Japan. One of them was tire manufacturer Bridgestone. It started by producing mopeds in 1952. Known for their quality-built two-strokes, displacing from 50cc to 350cc, the bikes became a favorite in Europe. Many employed their unique rotary valve induction system. Their famous 175cc Hurricane Scrambler produced 20 hp—enough to get noticed on the street. The large covers on the sides of the engines housed the carburetors, feeding a rotary valve system to admit the fuel/air in a proper timed sequence. The company sold through a variety of channels, including the Sears Roebuck catalog. Bridgestone ceased production by 1972. Fable has it that pressure from the big four forced them to consider the consequences of losing their lucrative motorcycle tire business. A more likely scenario is that the looming stringent emissions regulations foretold the demise of the street two-stroke.

While Honda was focusing on four-stroke engines, Suzuki made its mark with its hot two-stroke standards. Its 29 hp 250cc T20 Super Six, known in the United States as the X-6, offered superb handling and great looks during the late 60s.

There are few baby boomers who don't say, "I wanted one like that when I was in high-school." Kawasaki produced many wonderful two-strokes that were affordable and reliable, like this elegant 250cc triple.

While the Japanese big four competed for US market share in the early 60s, an Austrian company named Puch was supplying Sears Roebuck with a 250cc two-stroke to sell through its catalog. The understated Allstate "250" sold for $499.99, and featured a unique split-single design. A Y-shaped connecting rod on a single crankshaft operated two pistons.

Spanish maker Bultaco, best known for its fantastic off-road bikes in the 1960s, also offered a great little 244cc single-cylinder two-stroke standard street bike named the Metralla for European and US markets.

Despite the very large number of Russian standard motorcycles produced, few found themselves in the United States during the Cold War–era. This beautifully restored 1975 IZH Planeta Sport 350cc single-cylinder two-stroke shows its diverse German, Spanish, and Japanese styling cues. Photo courtesy of Alex Neumann.

The British Fight Back

If there were any doubts by the British manufacturers that the Japanese could make larger bikes, the 1965 444cc double overhead cam parallel twin Honda CB450 K0 proved it in no uncertain terms. The British motorcycle industry needed a quick lift that would give it a fresh start. Engineers at both Triumph and BSA suggested several advanced designs to their bosses as early as 1963. Strong sales of British bikes clouded good business sense. The feeling in the boardroom was that Americans liked the products being shipped and would remain loyal to the brands and designs. Triumph engineer Doug Hele didn't buy that. He proposed adapting a third cylinder to the basic 500cc Triumph twin to make a 750. The project finally launched after Edward Turner's retirement in 1964. Two triples, one for BSA and one for

Triumph, were to be readied for the 1969 model year. For whatever reason, perhaps an attempt to reach a more modern audience, a design company was engaged. More familiar with designing household appliances than bikes, the results were a bit strange. Both bikes had angular gas tanks, referred to as a "bread bin." The BSA had strange "ray-gun" mufflers, making the bike look like something out of Buck Rogers. Ironically, the original prototypes placed in standard Bonneville frames looked a whole lot better.

Honda's CB450 saw some minor changes for 1968 as the K1. The "Black Bomber" as it was called, was not quite up to the task of beating British 650s, but certainly gave them a run. Its introduction was instrumental in getting the British makers to consider newer designs. The engine was unique in that torsion bars replaced conventional valve springs.

Honda's 450 was also offered as a scrambler in 1968. High pipes, stubby front fender, sleeker tank, and braced handlebars differentiated it from the CB. Scramblers allowed very limited off-road capabilities. Pictured is the author on a CL450 scrambler in 1970 while on military R&R in Hawaii.

The T150 Triumph and BSA Rocket 3 were launched in the United States in 1968 with great fanfare. BSA arranged a showing at Daytona, which proved the bikes could keep up with anything out there with 130-mph performance. Meanwhile, Norton-Villiers was scrambling to design an exciting new model that would represent Britain's best twin. In 1968, it released the 750 Commando, a bike that looked fast and carried a name well known for its racing heritage.

The BSA Rocket 3 was a noble effort by BSA/Triumph to fight for US market share. Introduced in 1968, it, along with the Norton Commando, was quickly overshadowed by the Honda CB750. Even though the 740cc triple made good power with its 58 horses, it lacked the Honda's electric start and disc brake. It also cost more than the Honda. Despite the futuristic looks, technology was dated. Development funds were short, and engineers stayed with a traditional pushrod valve configuration. The more conservatively styled Triumph Tridents used most of the same components and sold better due to the ergonomics of the bike and improved frame construction and geometry.

Norton Commando to the Rescue

Norton initially considered a new 800cc double overhead cam engine for the Commando, but time and resources did not allow it. This is something that in hindsight may have been well worth the wait. A modified Atlas engine was used instead— slightly canted forward to add speedy styling cues. The bike was the best of the British, but still quite archaic compared to what Honda was working on thousands of miles away. What made the Commando unique was a rubber mounted engine and drivetrain cradle that helped reduce the traditional parallel twin vibration. Dubbed the "Isolastic" frame, it retained the handling Norton was famous for.

The Norton Commando is without a doubt one of the best-looking bikes ever made. The original 1968 750cc version had drum brakes and a fiberglass fastback rear section. Subsequent models added a front disc and more traditional styling. The engine was increased to 830cc in 1973. But 1975 saw both the addition of an electric starter and the end of the line. The bike on the left is an 850 Mk III electric start Commando.

Enter the CB750

The 1968 750 Commando was fast for its time, capable of beating any stock Harley-Davidson Sportster with its high-13 second quarter mile acceleration. It lacked electric start and a disc brake—items that would be added later. Things seemed optimistic for 1968. That was to be short-lived. Honda changed the rules once again in 1969 by introducing its CB750. This is considered to be the first true production superbike. It sent a shock wave throughout the industry. A smooth 67 hp single overhead cam four-cylinder engine sat transversely in an elegant frame capable of 120-mph speeds. Honda's unprecedented R&D program gave it a tremendous advantage in putting a bike like that to market at a low price.

The CB750 was a dream come true for the bike enthusiast. At $1,495, it featured a state-of-the art engine, electric start, and a reliable disc brake, while most comparable European bikes cost twice that much. Its introduction in 1969 changed motorcycling forever.

Honda tested the market in 1976 with a two-speed automatic transmission version of the CB750 with the CB750A. It only lasted two years as the market showed little interest. The standard 5-speed CB750 raised the bar far above anyone's expectations, and people liked shifting through the gears to experience the broad power band of the engine. Moto Guzzi experienced similar results in offering automatics during this innovative era. Honda's recent attempts at an automatic have proven successful with several models, including the VFR®1200F and the CTX®700N. Both feature a smooth dual-clutch transmission with automatic and manual modes. Shifting in manual mode is a fingertip kind of affair.

It has been nearly fifty years since the Honda CB750 rocked the motorcycling world. One thing remains the same; bikes still have two wheels and a motor. The difference is in the hidden technology. This includes electronic engine management and automatic transmission options as is available on the CTX700N. Combined with anti-lock brakes, this makes for a secure mount for daily use. Riding position is more cruiser than standard. Photo courtesy of American Honda Motor Co., Inc.

Overhead cam fours like the CB750 were nothing new. Italian makers Gilera and MV were racing those decades earlier. Honda's own race program was based on such engine configurations. Unlike the Italians, Honda knew how to make them inexpensively and reliably. The original CB750 design lasted until 1978, with nearly 400,000 made. Double overhead cam models kept the moniker alive until 2007. No doubt, the CB750 rocked the motorcycle world and was to start the next phase of the Japanese invasion marked by large displacement fast standards.

Considered the best bike made by Triumph's Meriden plant, the 1969 T120 650cc Bonneville was rooted in dated technology with its pushrod engine and drum brakes. Handling, however, was still considered better than the Japanese bikes of the period.

A Bad Decision by Norton

In an effort to compete with the CB750, Norton bumped up the compression on its 750 Commando for 1972 by shaving the cylinder heads down and adding a hotter cam. The results were disastrous. Thousands of Combat Commandos disintegrated within a few months of use. The stock crankshaft bearings could not handle the 65 hp load. It was a blow the company could ill afford. Norton engineers devised an innovative barrel-shaped bearing called the "Superblend" to correct the flaw. The subsequent 850 Commando model was intentionally detuned to avoid further problems.

One of Britain's best efforts was the 736cc 1970 Royal Enfield Interceptor Mark II. The Mark II was considered very fast for its day. Its predecessors, the 692cc Meteor, Super Meteor, and higher output Constellation, were introduced twelve years earlier. They were the largest displacements British parallel twins offered at that time.

Italy's Laverda was well rooted in agricultural machinery manufacture when it decided to try its hand at motorcycles in 1948. Their 750cc parallel twins set a very high standard in durability. The first to hit our shores was the American Eagle model in 1968. The 750SF pictured was introduced a couple of years later and is highly collectible today. Laverda continued to impress with a great line of triples, including the famous 140-mph Jota. The company could not compete against the overwhelming Japanese marketing and development budgets, and ceased productions in 1985.

As the Japanese and British manufacturers faced off, Moto Guzzi quietly introduced its 704cc V7 transverse V-twin in 1967—a configuration well recognized today. Despite its subdued marketing effort in the United States, the V7 was ideally suited to American highways. The V7 750cc Special came next in 1969, capable of 110 mph: a speed the Vincent Rapide achieved back in 1936. Moto Guzzi evolved the shaft-drive bike to the highly prized 850cc LeMans sportbike series.

Forty years after its introduction, Moto Guzzi released a thoroughly modern version of the well-loved V7. It is offered today in a few configurations, including the Classic (pictured), sport, and café racer. The 744cc air-cooled fuel-injected engine combined with a stable frame makes for an excellent all-around standard motorcycle. Photo courtesy of Moto Guzzi, Piaggio Group Americas, Inc.tourer, and an exciting turbo for the 1982 model year. Photo courtesy of American Honda Motor Co., Inc.

Honda experimented with transversely mounted V-twins with shaft drive back in 1978 with the innovative liquid-cooled 500cc CX500. Honda offered several variants, including the CX650C cruiser, GL500 Silver Wing® tourer, and an exciting turbo for the 1982 model year. Photo courtesy of American Honda Motor Co., Inc.

The End of an Era

While the Japanese were clearly dominating the American market, primarily led by Honda, the British were still manufacturing technologically dated motorcycles virtually by hand. The Commando and triples were not contemporary in engine design. Edward Turner awoke to this reality far too late. In a mad last-minute effort, he attempted to design an overhead cam 350cc twin in the early 1970s named the BSA Fury or Triumph Bandit. Hasty engineering and poor metallurgy resulted in short-lived engines that never saw production. Triumph even experimented with the new Wankel-design rotary engine. There was just not enough time and money to reverse the course. The noble Norton Commando and new triples by BSA and Triumph were left to bear the burden of competing with the Japanese high-performance bikes.

Yamaha introduced its 53 hp XS 650cc overhead cam parallel twin for 1970. It is a perfect example of how technologically advanced Japanese motorcycles were over comparable British models. The 1972 model pictured shows a typical Japanese unit construction power plant (engine and gearbox in one case) with a horizontally split crankcase. Horizontally split cases prevented oil leaking when the bike sat for a long time—something the vertical seam engines used in most British bikes were known for. It was the first year for electric start and front disc brake. The XS650 was produced in world markets until 1985, with a half-million made.

By 1978, Yamaha started to offer the XS650 in "Special" models. The styling differences from the standard XS were aimed to appeal to a new market of buyers—Americans interested in Japanese custom cruisers. Pictured is a 650 Special II.

BSA closed its doors in 1973 after its attempts to counter the Honda 750 with its three-cylinder Rocket 3 failed. A new conglomerate funded by the government, Norton-Villiers-Triumph (NVT), was formed in 1972 to tackle the challenges of reviving a declining national industry. Labor conflicts further handicapped British production. The worst was a takeover by Triumph workers in 1973 of the Meriden factory that resulted in a lockout. This created a stop in exports of the well-loved Bonneville for eighteen months. By 1974, only three models remained after the dust had settled: the Norton Commando, the Triumph Bonneville, and the Triumph Trident. Commando production at the Wolverhampton factory officially ended in 1976, although 1,500 partially assembled machines were completed by NVT elsewhere through 1977. The last of these, primarily electric start 850 Mark 3 Interstates, were delivered by 1978.

Despite the overwhelming success of the CB750, Honda recognized the need for lower-priced options in the four-cylinder bracket. A range of smaller fours was introduced in 1971, starting with a 500cc midweight. As expected, sales were phenomenal as the smaller, lighter bikes offered remarkable performance at an affordable price. Subsequent models were introduced in 400cc and 350cc versions. By 1974, Honda boosted the capacity of their 500cc bike to 550cc to achieve 50 hp at 9,000 rpm. The 550 Four pictured makes an excellent standard capable of meeting any demand twenty-first century traffic can throw at it.

The Trident had a small chance of keeping the British in the high-performance motorcycle business by appealing to those who were loyal to the brand. Unfortunately, it had to wait until 1975 to be fitted with electric start, front and back disc brakes, and a five-speed gearbox. The Honda CB750 had become a household name by 1975, and consumers expected no less in technology. The electric start T160 Trident only saw one year of production before ending its line in 1976. It listed for $2,870. Note that the engine is canted forward on this model, and that by this time the foot gear change was placed on the left as a means of standardization with European and Japanese bikes. The T160 was, and remains, an impressive bike. With 58 hp and modern brakes, it makes an excellent daily rider. Photo courtesy of Reed Taussig.

Kawasaki recognized America's thirst for speed and decided to go all out with the neck-snapping H1 Mach III 500cc three-cylinder two-stroke. Introduced in 1969, the bike was an instant smash with its under-thirteen-seconds quarter-mile acceleration. Owners grinned as they ignored slurs about the bike's scary handling and poor gas mileage. Photo of my buddy RG rolling one out to test at Kawasaki's service school.

Speed-crazed street racers rejoiced when the company introduced the faster H2 Mach IV 750cc 74 hp three-cylinder two-stroke. It sold from 1972 through 1975. These bikes represented a grand exit for two-stroke street bikes as environmental regulations strangled the breed before the decade was over. Remarkably, Kawasaki is up to its old tricks once again with the revival of the H2 name with its unimaginable 300 hp H2R superbike.

While the British and Japanese were battling it out, Germany's BMW kept building upon its flat twin design with newer models. The opposing pistons canceled vibration to very comfortable levels. Considered highly reliable and long lasting, their popularity was limited by their higher cost. BMW riders of the 1960s and 1970s were considered an elite, intelligent, and discerning breed, capable of spending long hours in the saddle. Remarkably, because they were not Japanese, they were not chastised by British- or American-made bike owners. New for 1972 was a radical and short-lived change for the R75/5 750cc model. Chrome tank panels were a love-it-or-hate-it affair designed to give the bike a more modern look. Dubbed the "Toaster tank," the bike had another issue: a twitchy, short wheelbase. Later models added 50mm to the swingarm to add stability. They also dispensed with the chrome panels. Simplicity, good engineering, and reliability make these bikes models for a good standard motorcycle. The author's own R75/5 starts and runs as well as it did over forty years ago and will carry a passenger in style.

Who's on First?

Leadership position in the motorcycle industry is a fickle thing. The next best thing seems to draw all the attention quickly. Soon after Honda shook the world with its CB750, Kawasaki turned heads later in 1969 with its insanely fast H1 two-stroke triple. In 1972, the honor was clearly theirs again as it unleashed its 903cc double overhead cam Z1 superbike standard. This let the world know that Honda was not the only game in town when it came to R&D. It also let the British know that they were terminally far behind and had no chance of catching up. The Z1 concept was actually conceived a few years ahead of Honda's introduction of the CB750 as an upgrade to the 650 line. Once the Kawasaki team saw that Honda's bike was a 750, it decided wisely to boost the displacement to over 900cc.

Kawasaki's 82 hp 903cc Z1 created an instant "wow" factor in 1972. Capable of 133 mph, the bike overshadowed all the sizzle the two-stroke H-1 triple had created. Ironically, the code name for the development project was "New York Steak." The Z1 remained basically the same through 1975, but spawned the evolution toward even more exciting models that launched the superbike wars among the big four Japanese makers.

Kawasaki's recognition as a high-tech four-stroke four-cylinder engine producer carried over to smaller displacement machines after its Z1 success. Introduced in 1976, the Z650 offered buyers plenty of power at 64 horses and was perhaps Kawasaki's first great handling bike. The model continued in various forms through 1983. Pictured is a 1977 KZ650.

This young man is posing proudly with his 1979 KZ750. This 745cc overhead cam parallel twin by Kawasaki was an interesting bike in that it was made between 1976 and 1983, during an era where the company was promoting its high-performance four-cylinder machines. The thinking may have been to offer buyers of traditional British parallel twins a technologically advanced option without compromising the feel of a twin. Its rugged simplicity has endured the test of time and makes an affordable vintage bike for the millennial generation of enthusiasts. Later KZ750s were fours. Photo by Ali Lorenzi.

While the trend to four-stroke overhead cam engines was clear among Japanese manufacturers, Yamaha, like Kawasaki, continued to refine its two-strokes. Introduced in 1973, the RD350 was affectionately called "the giant killer," referring to its ability to out-accelerate Harleys, Nortons, and Triumphs. Not as quick as the H1 and H2, the RD series did produce much better handling bikes. Yamaha and Suzuki designed and sold water-cooled two-strokes to meet the ever-stringent US emissions regulations, but ultimately opted to focus on four-strokes instead. In its last hurrah, Yamaha introduced the RD400F in 1979 to celebrate its race-winning two-strokes. Its elegant white-painted sister, the 1980 RD400G, was the last two-stroke street bike brought to the US market.

Suzuki was late getting into the four-cylinder four-stroke game. It had built its reputation on solid two-strokes, the last of which was the water-cooled GT750 triple introduced in 1971. It had to make a change. Honda and Kawasaki fours were selling like hotcakes. Its engineers went to work studying their competitors' fours, and introduced a refined blend in 1976. The double overhead cam GS750 sold well, even at the higher price of $2,200. It would see upgrades to four valves per cylinder in 1980 while giving birth to larger varieties such as the GS1000. The GS series was recognized as having superior high-speed handling over its rivals.

Factories Close, Others Open

Norton-Villiers-Triumph closed its doors in 1978, marking the end of a great chapter in motorcycle history. Its principal owner, Dennis Poore, experimented with a Wankel-based Norton, but met with the same short-lived fate as many others who had dabbled in the rotary engine. Triumph's workers cooperative factory in Meriden also struggled, as it lacked the resources to compete.

Triumph's Meriden plant chief engineer, Brian Jones, could not handle the inevi-

tability of failure and made one last glorious effort. Based on a custom design by Triumph's American unit, modifications to a stock Bonneville resulted in the mildly chopper-styled TSX. The bike offered items most Americans should have considered ideal for their tastes. These included a slightly lowered seat with a higher passenger rear section. Not quite a typical "King and Queen" chopper seat, it did cater to colonialist style. Higher handlebars, shorter mufflers, cast wheels, and a beefy sixteen-inch rear tire gave this electric start 750 twin standard a nice customized look.

A very rare Triumph TSX in Gypsy Red paint. The bike was designed to appeal to American buyers favoring hints of custom cruiser styling. The Japanese makers were much more successful with their lower cost offerings. Photo courtesy of Morgan Rue.

Reviews following the bike's 1982 launch were mixed. Triumph should have opted for more traditional paint schemes. Most models came with a burgundy, orange, and yellow-striped design. Sales suffered as Japanese bikes set new levels of quality and performance. A high price of over $3,600 also did not help. The TSX only lasted through August 1983—the year Triumph ceased all production at Meriden. It is estimated that only 371 of these rare bikes were made, of which a bit over half were shipped to the United States. Speculation and hindsight suggests that had Triumph offered its more powerful TSS with its eight-valve engine from the onset, things may have turned out different. The company even had an advanced model on the boards for 1984—the TSS-AV. This bike featured anti-vibration rubber engine mountings. The Japanese fours had spoiled the buying public to expect smooth running engines.

A valiant effort to rekindle the ailing British motorcycle industry was made by Lord Alexander Hesketh in the early 1980s. The V1000 was designed by Formula 1 engine builders, Weslake Engineering, but launched prematurely. Resulting problems combined with poor financial backing ended the marque by 1984.

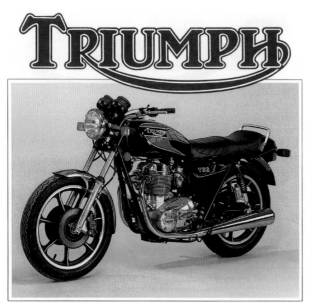

The last of the Meriden Triumphs was the 1983 T140W electric start 750cc TSS. It should have appealed to the buyer preferring American- or British-made bikes over Japanese. It offered plenty of power and good brakes. Only 112 are said to have made it to the United States. Photo Mortons Archive.

British bike enthusiasts were saddened as the home of the immortal Bonneville closed its doors. The large abundance of dealers and spare parts in the United States kept Triumph alive for a while until the inventory of new bikes was depleted. The brand's spirit was, however, still strong. It would see a rebirth in seven short years.

Nearly every major maker considered the innovative Wankel rotary engine to power its standard bikes. The only Japanese rotary effectively brought to market was the water-cooled Suzuki RE-5 introduced in 1974. High cost, some concerns about higher fuel consumption during America's oil crisis, and resulting slow sales limited its production life to 1976. Pictured is a pristine 1975 RE5M with its distinctive cylindrical instrument cluster and taillight. The engine was a 497cc water-cooled single rotor Wankel-type engine producing 62 hp at 6,500 rpm. Photo courtesy of Wayne Waddington.

The 1976 Suzuki rotary was labeled the RE5A. It featured a more conventional instrument cluster and taillight. Photo courtesy of Wayne Waddington.

Ducati had a pretty diverse lineup of motorcycles in the 1970s like this short-lived 1978 500GTV parallel twin. Limited advertising combined with a fit and finish that was not quite up to the quality of the Japanese bikes kept them under the radar for most consumers. The marque's claim to fame would come with its exciting L-twin sportbikes. Ducati's naked L-twin Monster series, introduced in the 1990s, is considered by many to be a standard despite its raw sporting attitude. It remains the company's best seller.

Italian maker Benelli, under the ownership of Argentinian De Tomaso, went against the mainstream in introducing a two-stroke 250cc model in 1977, long after the Japanese had shifted their efforts to four-strokes. This by no means meant the company was going backwards. It challenged the Japanese with an exciting six-cylinder overhead cam 750cc four-stroke called the Sei in 1974. A 900cc version came soon after in 1978.

The UJM

Japanese bikes became fairly standardized in how they looked by the 1970s. This resulted in the term *Universal Japanese Motorcycle*. But, things started to change quickly as high-performance engines inspired sporting inclinations. Before one knew it, by the late 1980s it was hard to find a good old naked standard. Bikes sprouted plastic sport fairings and sleek low profiles. Motocross bikes also evolved. Little choice was left for those looking for a basic naked standard. Harley-Davidson's Sportster was still selling in modest numbers, as were the more expensive BMWs. The former, however, didn't offer the technology and maintenance-free reliability of the UJMs, while the later cost much more.

Japanese manufacturers responded to consumer demand for good old standards by building exciting new models. Yamaha introduced the remarkable XS750 in 1976 as an upgrade to its sturdy XS650 twin. It utilized an overhead cam to feed a three-cylinder engine, laid out much like the BSA and Triumph triples. Final drive was by shaft. Development of double overhead cam four-cylinder sporting standards by the big four Japanese makers during the 1980s resulted in superb machines at prices far below US and European models. Yamaha's YX600 Radian was such an example. It is a well-balanced bike that had a good run between 1986 and 1990.

Subsequent models offered over the next fifteen years, like the Kawasaki Zephyr, looked as if they were made a decade earlier. Styling and simplicity became the new keywords as manufacturers introduced many new naked bikes to meet consumer demand. Notable was the Honda Nighthawk® 750. It proved that the Japanese understood the concept of a standard better than anyone. Suzuki followed with its Bandit series and wonderful SV650 line of standards.

Kawasaki produced the Zephyr line of bikes in the late 1980s and through the 1990s to meet the demand for naked standards. They were air-cooled inline four-cylinder motorcycles in 400cc, 550cc 750cc and 1,100cc displacements. Pictured is a 1989 ZR400. Photo courtesy of **Kawasaki Motors Corporation, U.S.A.**

Honda's hot R&D team kept putting out new engine configurations—some before they were thoroughly tested for endurance. In 1982, it introduced the V45 Sabre® with a rubber-mounted 90-degree-V four-cylinder, DOHC engine, putting out an impressive 82 hp. The V45's water-cooled 750cc mill suffered from early development issues and a less-than-assuring frame. The same engine served the Magna® cruiser and Interceptor® sportbike. Two years later they offered the 121 hp V65 1100cc V-4; a much-improved and very fast super standard. Problems with the engine were resolved to create an impressive new platform for bikes to come. Photo of author by Jo Ensanian.

Japanese motorcycle makers, like Honda, were a major thorn in the side of American bike manufacturer Harley-Davidson during the early 1980s. The Motor Company's profits dropped as American riders were buying the much more advanced and reliable Japanese bikes at a lower cost. Congressional pressure got the US International Trade Commission to enact a huge tariff on all imported bikes larger than 700cc. The Japanese responded with sub-700cc machines that were more powerful and advanced than many previous 750cc models. The CB700SC Nighthawk 700S is a perfect example of that. The 696cc air-cooled, inline, four-cylinder standard was strictly sold in the United States. It was low maintenance with hydraulic valve lifters and shaft drive. It produced an impressive 80 hp and lasted for two years before model changes were made. Even though it may look like a sportbike, riding position is pure standard.

The big four produced bikes for all levels of experience and interest. The 1984 Honda VT500 Ascot on the left is a 491cc liquid-cooled V-twin powered midweight standard with great manners. The engine would be enlarged over the following years to power the VT series of cruisers. Suzuki was just as busy making high-performance half-liter bikes. The GS450E on the right is a parallel twin with dual overhead cams.

Despite its initial poor sales experience with automatic transmission motorcycles, Honda introduced 400cc and 450cc automatic models in the early 1980s. This CM450A Hondamatic Hawk was offered in 1982. It was based on the 450 parallel twin SOHC engine. The bike was actually semi-automatic. It lacked a clutch lever because a torque converter would engage the engine to the transmission at a certain rpm. It did require shifting between low and high range. The model lasted only a couple of years as motorcyclists felt the power robbed by the torque converter wasn't worth the automation. Most felt that shifting is half the fun of riding. Prince featured a 400cc automatic in his movie *Purple Rain*. The bike pictured is displayed at the fabulous Antique Auto Museum in Hershey, PA. Motorcycle manufacturers, like Honda, Yamaha, and Aprilia keep introducing automatics to test the market's reaction.

Nothing is Forever

Japanese dominance could not last forever. Due to the great interest in cruisers, Harley-Davidson became a major producer in the new millennium. The coals of the British motorcycle industry were not cold either. They were starting to glow as the Triumph marque was to emerge yet again. John Bloor, a real estate tycoon, bought the rights to the marque in 1984. A brief revival brought some hope in 1985. With the help of Les Harris, a well-known and respected parts distributor, Bloor managed to build original Bonnevilles from an inventory of engines, frames, and other parts for sale in Europe. Forks, silencers, and brakes were Italian. By 1990, he had assembled a

211

team of engineers to produce thoroughly modern Triumphs in a new factory at Hinckley, Leicestershire, England. Triumph prospers today as it offers a variety of motorcycles that challenge the best Japanese and Italian makers. Its Bonneville still remains the hallmark standard.

Triumph's new generation of bikes introduced for 1991 started off as water-cooled triples and fours, in sizes ranging from 750cc to 1,200cc. Pictured is a Hinckley-made 900cc triple aptly named the Thunderbird®.

Triumph's Street Twin has taken over the role of being Triumph's smaller parallel twin–powered standard and retains the basic engine of the previous generation Bonneville, but with a good boost in torque. It is designed to allow extensive customization via accessories, offering riders a high degree of personalization. Hidden behind the traditional styling is a host of electronic features, including ride-by-wire throttle, ABS, and traction control. The bike pictured is fitted with the high-pipe option. Photo courtesy of Triumph Motorcycles.

Triumph's Hinckley-generation Bonneville is faithful to the original, and represents the ideal modern standard. It offers enough comfort for 400-mile daytrips and excellent handling for spirited rides through the twisties. The original line featured a smooth 865cc parallel twin engine.

The popularity of Triumph in the United States today is exceeding the post-*Wild One* era. For 2016, the Bonneville T120 and Thruxton lines are fitted with 1,199cc water-cooled engines to greatly boost torque. Additional contemporary features, like ABS, switchable traction control, ride-by-wire throttle, several adjustable ride modes, and a slip-assist clutch are included. Keeping up the current trend in blacked-out bikes, the Bonneville is also offered in this stealthy scheme. Photo courtesy of Triumph Motorcycles.

The three-wheeled Can-Am® Spyder deserves recognition in that it has brought motorcycling to a segment of people that may have never considered it. This three-wheeler was introduced in 2007 by Canadian motorsport company Bombardier Recreational Products, the same company that make the wonderful Sea-Doo watercraft and Ski-Doo snowmobiles. Unlike trikes, the motorcycle (as it is classified) has a single rear drive wheel and two wheels up front used for steering. It is powered by a Rotax 990 V-twin engine capable of producing an impressive 106 hp. Stability and comfort are keys with these three-wheelers. New models employ an advanced Vehicle Stability System that provides great confidence when cornering briskly. They may look a bit strange heading toward you on the highway, but deep down inside most motorcyclists want to try one. It is a great way to allay the fears of a passenger reluctant to get on a two-wheeler. The Can-Am is also a great open cockpit vehicle for shorter folks who find it difficult to manage tall two-wheelers. Models are available that are configured as standards, touring bikes, or as radically styled cruisers. Photo courtesy of Bombardier Recreational Products Inc.

Still Going Strong

The standard is still alive and well today. A number of manufacturers make standard bikes reminiscent of what the term embodies: utility and reliability. Some are called retro in that they look like the bikes from the 1960s, while others look remarkably like sportbikes with exotic bodywork. New interest in adventure bikes has blurred the lines between a standard and a dual sport. What would have been categorized as a standard is now seeing itself in this popular new category. In all cases, a standard will get you farther on the road than most other configurations due to its neutral seating position and easy to reach handlebars. Just ask anyone riding a sportbike after a couple of hours on the highway. Standards are clearly a good choice for a daily rider.

Due to its upright seating ergonomics and a relatively flat seat, the standard allows the ideal platform for riding two-up. Riding double is a dance, where the rider signals with subtlety, and the passenger responds with no intrusion. The pair learns to be one with the machine and one with each other, moving effortlessly with it. The passenger should not give in to instincts to counter a lean or to disturb the balance. Sport touring machines are next on the list of bikes that make two-up riding more intimate. Photo by Lori Weiniger.

New Standards

Moto Guzzi improved on its successful V7 line with their larger V9 models. Improvements include a redesigned combustion chamber that yields greater torque. Pictured is the attractive V9 Roamer. Photo courtesy of Piaggo & C SpA.

In order to attract entry-level and urban riders, Harley-Davidson introduced the Street® 750 and 500 V-twins for 2014. These bikes offer the comfortable ergonomics of a standard while mixing in a bit of traditional Harley cruiser styling. They also feature water-cooled engines and strong cast wheels to deal with rough city streets. These motorcycles are affordable starting at under $7,000. They make perfect bikes for any couple looking to get into motorcycling or a touring cruiser owner looking for a nimble about-town machine. Pictured is the 750cc model. Photo courtesy of Harley-Davidson.

Suzuki still has the classification of "standard" in its catalog. The Bandit GFS series was a highly popular line of bikes made between 1995 and 2010 in sizes ranging from 600cc to 1250cc. Its elegant styling underscores the term sport standard. It was replaced with the sportier GSX1250FA, but the famous GSX® bikes should really be where they belong—in the sport category.

Kawasaki does not have the classification of "standard" in its catalog as of this writing, but it does produce a bike that satisfies the definition well. The highly versatile Versys® is a 649cc liquid-cooled, DOHC, parallel twin that seems to be capable of doing it all. It finds itself in both the sportbike and adventure bike segments. Note the upright seating and high handlebars for comfort. Photo courtesy Kawasaki Motors Corp.

Not all standards need to be huge. The retro-styled standard TU250X® 250cc single from Suzuki makes an excellent entry-level machine or local runabout. It has a surprisingly large and comfortable passenger seat.

Yamaha continues the retro-standard revival with its 2015 SR400. This single-cylinder bike takes retro to another level: it is kick-start only. It has already become a favorite for customizers and café racers. Photo courtesy of Yamaha Motor Corp.

Many retro singles are modeled after the British single, such as the Royal-Enfield. It remains one of the most respected standard bikes all over the world. The sturdy machines replace pack animals in the high altitudes of the Himalayas. Photo by Tamara Hayden.

As it is in the fashion industry, something old can become something new again. This is the case with Honda's superb new CB1100 standard. Its style reflects the classic 1969 CB750, but with larger motor, fuel injection, six speeds, and an anti-lock braking system. Photo American Honda Motor Co., Inc.

Mash is a relatively new retro line of bikes offered in Europe. Designed in France and manufactured in China, these bikes are good representations of vintage British and Japanese motorcycles. They are available in a standard, flat track, and café racer configurations. Pictured is the 398cc Roadstar twin standard. Photo courtesy of David Angel, F2 Motorcycles Ltd.

There are many motorcycle brands out there that have been around for a very long time. None, however, has endured the test of time as well as Royal Enfield. The Enfield brand has been associated with motorcycles since 1898. It started by using the revolutionary new De Dion engine design developed a few years earlier in France. The word "Royal" was added after the company started producing parts for Royal Small Arms in Enfield, Middlesex, England. Perhaps that's what inspired their ad line, "Built like a gun." By 1901, they were building motorized bicycles in Redditch. The company was actually quite innovative, offering dry-sump lubrication via a geared oil pump and a three-speed countershaft-type gearbox by 1914. It would be decades later that American motorcycle engines standardized those technical elements.

The De Dion-Bouton engine design revolutionized motoring at the turn of the twentieth century. Its small displacement allowed higher revolutions per minute (rpm) and thus created more power for its size. Its design was copied by nearly all early motorcycle builders, including Royal Enfield, Harley-Davidson, and Indian. The engine was easily adapted to bicycle frames.

The famous Royal Enfield *Bullet* model line began its life in 1928 and featured single-cylinder

engines in a variety of sizes. By 1933, the Bullet series evolved to include 250cc, 350cc, and 500cc overhead valve "sporting" singles. Enfield singles saw many periodic improvements. Telescopic forks and rear sprung suspensions were introduced in 1948 for 350cc and 500cc Bullets. Bullets are still being made and are used for daily riding, touring, hauling, and racing.

This 1948 Royal Enfield Model G 350cc single was an affordable and reliable means of fast transportation right after WWII. The Crusader model became their most popular U.K.–made single thereafter. Purist collectors prefer the U.K.–made Enfields over those made in India after 1957, despite their generally solid construction. Minor issues in metal quality and finish initially created some concern among vintage bike enthusiasts. Any pre-1970s Royal Enfield makes a nice vintage ride, while new ones offer that minimalist vintage feel.

Royal Enfield offered its Z Cycar in 1936. The bike was powered by a 148cc two-stroke motor. It featured leg protection and was, therefore, often referred to as the "Ladies Model." Note the hand shifter by the tank. The bike originally sold for nineteen guineas. Photo by Stephen Covell.

Royal Enfield singles provide reliable transportation and utility for hundreds of thousands around the world. Photo by Tamara Hayden.

Enfield singles, particularly the Bullet, started being produced in India in the 1950s. The Indian government felt that this basic single would be a good bike to meet the demands of their rough roads. After all, there were plenty of them there because of England's colonial history with India. At first, parts were shipped in from the U.K. and assembled there. Slow business in the U.K. prompted Enfield to sell

the machine tooling for its Bullet 346cc model to Madras Motorcycle Company, an Indian concern, in 1957. Enfield of India was thus born. Bikes were manufactured locally in Madras to supply the Indian Army and police forces. Cultural industrial integration between two countries 5,000 miles apart kept the brand alive.

The same basic platform is used for their sporting models, like this sleek 535cc fuel-injected, electric-start Continental GT café racer.

The Royal Enfield marque continued to offer a variety of other singles and twins until it sold its Redditch, England–based factory in 1967. Enfield models, such as its Interceptor 750cc parallel twin, were made until 1970 in the U.K. by the Norton-Villiers group. The sturdy Interceptor saw several badges on its tanks, including Rickman and Indian, as Norton struggled and sold the rights to the bike whenever it could. It was, however, the humble Enfield Bullet that proved to be the survivor. By 1990, the large Indian manufacturer, Eicher Motors, purchased Enfield India to continue to manufacture and develop the single. Not only did this basic "thumper" gain popularity on the roads of Bombay and Chennai (Madras), but it satisfied the longings of British bike enthusiasts remiss of the simple and affordable classic single by offering no less than six quality variations.

Harley-Davidson, Inc.

Indian Motorcycle International, LLC

Chapter 5

THE CRUISER CRAZE

Cruisers have become the largest segment of motorcycles in the United States today. Their style harks back to motorcycles designed during our country's Great Depression. This chapter takes a look at how the genre developed, where it is heading, and the many options available to buyers today.

Yamaha Motor Corporation, U.S.A.

Made for America

The cruiser has clearly become the most popular motorcycle segment in the United States today. It is an American concept made for American roads. Harley-Davidson dominates this market with over 260,000 bikes sold a year. Harley's popularity, however, has spawned a tremendous amount of look-alike bikes from Japanese makers over the past thirty years. This has worked in favor of the motorcyclist by offering lots of lower cost choices in a variety of exciting styles.

As American as it gets—the author's Harley-Davidson Fat Boy® cruiser in front of a small town general store selling apple pie and waving the stars and stripes.

Indian and Harley-Davidson defined the design for the cruiser with their bikes from the 1930s and 1940s. This nice mid-1930s Indian Chief is an example of the enduring style emulated by many makers today.

Husband and wife enjoy a day on their own cruisers, riding side by side. The smile on her face tells the whole story. It doesn't matter to either of them that one is American made and the other Japanese.

Cruisers may be loosely defined as bikes with a relaxed riding position, feet forward of the knees, handlebars a bit higher, wider, and pulled back. They have their ancestry firmly rooted in the American V-twins of the 1930s and 1940s when the basic design guidelines for the genre were developed. What we call a cruiser today may have been referred to as a roadster back then.

The average cruiser is not exclusively designed with long distance touring in mind, but more for just cruising around or taking weekend rides. Cruising may be a 30-mph roll down Main Street on a Saturday night, or a brisk 60-mph run with riding buddies through the back roads on a Sunday morning. However, the broad term used to classify bikes as cruisers includes many highly capable long distance tourers. Many cruisers are offered in variations specifically designed for long distance riding. Differentiation is evident in the use of some additional creature comforts like footboards instead of forward controls, windscreens with radios, saddlebags, cup holders, and a host of other features. The term "bagger" refers to a cruiser with saddlebags, be they hard or soft.

Big cruisers make longer distance riding more enjoyable than sportbikes. This good-looking 2009 Suzuki Boulevard® M109R is typical of large, modern, and stylistic cruisers in that it is powered by a huge V-twin engine that makes its power down low (rpm) for a relaxed ride. In this case, it's a 1,783cc (108.8 cubic inch) engine. Photo courtesy of American Suzuki Motor Corporation.

The cruiser category is seeing more and more women riders because of the breed's inherent low seat height. Cruisers from Japan, like this Yamaha Star Bolt®, have greatly expanded the options. Photo courtesy of Yamaha Motor Corporation, U.S.A.

Big and Powerful

By the 1930s, the standard American motorcycle cradled a V-twin engine 750cc to 1,200cc in size. Those who could afford the power and luxury of four-cylinder cruisers had several choices. These included Ace, Cleveland, Henderson, and Indian. Hand-shifting and foot-clutching was the norm to work the hardy three-speed transmissions of the day. Most came with a large sprung saddle that offered hours of comfort on long hauls on the emerging highway system. In general, Americans rode solo unless a sidecar was used. Many Europeans added a small padded "pillion" seat to accommodate a passenger. Most were bolted directly onto the fender, while some were sprung. The latter offered modest comfort as both driver and passenger bounced up and down independently of each other.

This 1929 Indian 4 shows its direct lineage to the Ace. Indian acquired Ace's assets in 1927 and initially labeled the bikes as Indian Ace. The four-cylinder machine rounded out Indian's portfolio. Its power and speed made it very popular with police departments.

Power, reliability, and the general recreational nature of large American cruisers greatly encouraged passengers to ride along. Unfortunately, most were to be confined far back on top of the large rear fender. Some models even sported a small set of handlebars for the passenger to hold on to.

Cruisers of the past, like this well-built 1922 Ace, were not limited to two cylinders. The Ace, designed by William Henderson, had a 1,229cc four-cylinder engine that was to become the fastest bike on the road during the era. Ergonomics are pure cruiser in today's standard.

Sidecars were much more popular in the early days of motorcycling than they are today. They allowed families to travel and cargo to be carried. This 1,200cc mid-1930s Harley-Davidson VLD put out 36 hp and has been customized with a dual seat. Note the spare tire mounted to the back of the sidecar.

This 1940 Indian Sport Scout (750cc) had a luggage rack on the back of the fender that would occasionally see a passenger atop of it. A thick pillow would be an asset, as the bike had not yet acquired a sprung rear suspension.

Taking on a Buddy

By the 1940s, both big manufacturers offered dual seats. Harley-Davidson introduced a large saddle for two-up riding aptly named the "Buddy" seat. Indian followed suit with its "Chum-me" seat. The large double seats were sprung independently of the frame since rear suspensions were still absent.

The Harley-Davidson WL still lacked a rear suspension but sported a large, softly sprung "Buddy" seat with rear grab rail and auxiliary springs to accommodate a passenger. Long leather fringes absent from this bike were often attached to the sides to dress it up.

Softening the Ride

Harley-Davidson offered the well-known, large 5.00 x 16" tires on its big twins in 1941 to help soften the ride a bit. This came as a reaction to Indian's introduction of a sprung rear suspension. The new frames were offered on the Chief and four-cylinder models. Rear suspension units were of the plunger type as seen on European machines years earlier. Nothing stellar for absorbing pothole jolts, but a step in the right direction toward improving the ride.

Indians featured skirted fenders by 1940—something that would become their hallmark to this day. The 1946 Indian Chief pictured in "Jade Green" factory color would not have been called a cruiser in its day, but rather a roadster. Note the soft tail rear suspension behind the rear crash bar. Indian followed the British and German practice of a plunger rear end as used by BMW, Norton, BSA, and Ariel.

Several attempts were made to revive the iconic Indian badge since its demise in 1953. One was by a group of British investors that made new Indians in Kings Mountain, NC. The Chief Vintage above was put together with a variety of third-party components that left many reviewers a bit short. A weak economy in 2009 resulted in low sales volume and eventual closure.

Indian Chief's new 1,811cc overhead valve engine maintains much of the character of its side-valve original. The rocker covers are finned to give the engine that classic flathead look. Pushrod tubes remain pure Indian. Photo Indian Motorcycles International, LLC.

The Indian name is finally secure under American motorsports manufacturer Polaris since its purchase of the brand in 2011. Backed by their experience with the Victory brand, and deep pockets, Polaris' Indian team did the impossible. It created a superb new motorcycle, with its own new 111 cubic inch 49-degree balanced V-twin engine in only two years. The Chief line offers six models, including the basic Classic, the pictured Vintage with windshield and saddlebags, the versatile Springfield™ with easily removable bags and windshield, and the fully equipped Roadmaster® touring bike. Pricing is competitive with the other American cruisers. Reviews have been very positive. Photo courtesy of Indian Motorcycle International, LLC.

William and Thomas Henderson brough four-cylinder motorcycles to the mainstream with their advanced designs over a hundred years ago. They sold their brand to Ignatz Schwinn in 1918. Schwinn branded the bikes under his Excelsior line. Bill and Tom had a falling out with Schwinn and started the Ace brand two years later. This Excelsior Henderson "Streamliner" model was popular as a police cruiser in that it was capable of exceeding 85 mph. It was produced between 1929 and 1931.

Made for Comfort

Despite their powerful engines, cruisers are less sporty and less sportbike-like in their handling due to their focus on comfort. High speed cornering tends to be a bit restrictive on many models since most cruisers are low to the ground and may have floorboards that can drag. Forward foot controls will also change the handling characteristics of a cruiser compared to a sportbike. The further forward the foot controls, the less weight is exerted on the front forks by the rider's arms and torso. This softens steering response. Sport cruisers have more conventionally placed footpegs.

This highly revealing and technically brilliant X-ray of a cruiser and rider is by artist Nick Veasey. Photo courtesy of Nick Veasey.

227

Triumph makes a variety of comfortable parallel twin cruisers ranging from 865cc to 1,699cc. The liquid-cooled Thunderbird line is represented by a series of large displacement machines with huge 1,597cc and 1,699cc engines. With great looks and plenty of power with 96 horses, the Storm and Commander models offer cruiser buyers non-V-twin options.

Most manufacturers today offer cruisers in classic V-twin format emulating the quintessential cruiser, the Harley-Davidson. New models by Moto Guzzi and Triumph are designed to compete directly in the cruiser market using different engine configurations.

The Magnificent Crocker

No one can deny that the supermodel of all cruisers is the highly prized Crocker.

The Crocker was the brainchild of American motorcycle racer, Indian dealer, and engine designer Albert Crocker. His life was a colorful kaleidoscope of motorcycling in the first half of the twentieth century. As a successful racer with an aptitude for

The perfect lines of the Crocker V-twin as shown below characterize the cruiser genre. Photo of this modern reproduction is courtesy of The Crocker Motorcycle Company, crockermotorcycleco.com

engineering, he designed and built his own overhead valve single-cylinder engines in the 1930s to compete in speedway competition (referred to as short track racing in the United States on quarter-mile cinder tracks). About fifty "Speedway" Crockers were built.

Seeing a need for a more contemporary motorcycle design than the side-valve Indians and Harleys of the day, Crocker built what is considered today to be one of the three most coveted bikes among elite motorcycle connoisseurs, the 61 cubic inch (1,000cc) overhead valve Crocker V-twin. The rarity of original models compelled Michael Schacht of the Crocker Motorcycle Company to maintain a registry. At this time, he says, at least seventy Crockers have been registered that still exist. Al Crocker built around 100 Crocker "Twins" between 1936 and 1942.

The immortal Crocker, introduced in 1936, continues to set the style for cruisers today. The originals had exposed valve springs on the cylinder heads. Gas tanks are cast aluminum. Photo by Lori Weiniger at the Wheels Through Time museum.

Introduced early in 1936, this motorcycle put out an astonishing 50 hp at 5,800 rpm at a weight of less than 480 pounds. The hemispherical "Hemi" head model beat all comers with sixty horses capable of accelerating the bike to 60 mph in first gear. It featured overhead valves, something that neither Harley-Davidson nor Indian had put into mass production prior to Crocker's

V-twin. Albert's familiarity with Indians is clearly visible in the engine's design. The primary side borrowed a lot from the Chief and the Scout. The bike, however, had its own innovations, including a transmission housing that was integral with the frame, cast aluminum gas tank, and a "California Bobber" style rear fender. No expense was spared to make it the finest American motorcycle of the time.

The Crocker Reborn

The Crocker Motorcycle Company today offers enough quality reproduction parts to build a complete new bike. They manufacture both the Big and Small Tank Crockers, with options for Parallel Valve or Hemi-Head original type engines. The bikes are identical to the originals, although the new ones are made from better metals. Price for original Crockers today ranges from $300,000 to over $500,000. Creating a reproduction Crocker from new parts will cost about $135,000. This is not out of line considering some folks spend that much on custom choppers that are hardly practical as a means of transportation.

A Knockout for the Knucklehead

Unfortunately for Crocker, Harley-Davidson was well into its own overhead valve V-twin design program and rolled out its market-making "Knucklehead" a couple of months later. Despite the Crocker's performance and top speed of 110 mph, the Harley V-twin dominated sales. As with other limited run quality machines price was a big factor. Crockers were selling for around $550, while Harleys cost about $100 less—more than a couple of week's wages for the average worker. The Knucklehead also featured a four-speed transmission that made for more relaxed cruising. Crocker and Indian still had only three speeds.

The original 998cc (60.33 cubic inch) Harley-Davidson EL "Knucklehead" brought cruising to the masses at an affordable price over the Crocker. A bike like this one, with saddlebags, allowed the returning young WWII veteran an opportunity to blow off some steam and see the country before returning to the reality of the real world. Pictured is a beautifully restored 1941 Harley-Davidson FL model Knucklehead, with 74 cubic inch (1,208cc) engine capable of 48 hp at 5,000 rpm. It only cost about $460 back then, but an unmolested original will sell for over $100,000 today.

Many cruisers, like this Knucklehead, were "bobbed" by their owners. The concept came from racers lightening their bikes by cutting off sections of the rear fender and eliminating the one on front. Designers today often emulate bobbers. Further cutting and "chopping" off unnecessary weight and adding stylistic cues, such as upswept mufflers, and extended forks, resulted in the "chopper."

Harley-Davidson satisfied the postwar thirst for new bikes with its 1948 FL "Panhead." This overhead-valve engine was a bit taller than the Knucklehead, and thus required a slightly longer frame to accommodate it. The best feature on the engine was its hydraulic valve lifters, eliminating the task of adjustment. Photo by Skip Chernoff, courtesy of The Bike Works. Glenside, PA.

Harley-Davidson has always been a cruiser trendsetter. This clean early 1950s "Panhead" FL Hydra-Glide shows why. Hydra-Glide referred to the new hydraulic front forks that were introduced in 1949. The rear section of the frame remained rigid.

A wonderful period ad for the FL Hydra-Glide. Photo courtesy of Harley-Davidson.

By 1958, the Hydra-Glide was renamed as the FLH Duo-Glide as a result of a swingarm and hydraulic suspension units added to the rear.

Recognizing the need for more power, Harley improved upon its Panhead engine in 1966 with aluminum heads and a new rockerbox nicknamed the "Shovelhead." This boosted power by an impressive ten percent. Shovelheads evolved from 1,208cc to 1,338cc until their end in 1985. The motor was replaced by the "Evolution®" engine, introduced in 1984. Pictured is the unique FX Super Glide, with Shovelhead engine, as designed by William G. Davidson for 1971.This was Harley's first true factory production custom. The idea of the FX series is a lighter front end. Initial models used Sportster forks and wheels. The FX series lives today in the more traditionally styled Dyna and Softail® range. Photo courtesy of Harley-Davidson.

Despite the poor reputation AMF-era Shovelheads tend to have, they make for a great low-cost entry into vintage Harley-Davidson ownership. Often modified over the years by owners, their Spartan style is timeless.

Over sixty years since the Panhead, Harley-Davidson maintains its commitment to their enduring classic style as is evident in this current Softail Deluxe with the High Output Twin Cam 103B™ engine. A "B" designation on the engine means that it has a vibration-dampening balancer built in. The Softail suspension makes the bike look like a hardtail, but offers dampened suspension in the rear to absorb road bumps. The shock absorbers lie horizontally under the transmission. The original Softail design was purchased by Harley-Davidson from an independent engineer, Bill Davis, who developed the concept back in the mid-1970s. One of Harley-Davidson's first Softails was the 1984FXST. That year also saw the introduction of the much-improved "Evolution" engine that would replace the dated Shovelhead. Photo courtesy of Harley-Davidson.

Harley-Davidson's Wide Glide® is part of the company's Dyna® series, sporting twin shocks in the rear. Their big twins use the 103 cubic inch (1,690cc) engine format, with a 110 cubic inch option available for premium hand-assembled Custom Vehicle Operation (CVOTM) models and the more current line of "S" models. Starting with the 2017 touring lineup, a brand-new engine dubbed the Milwaukee-Eight™ is offered in 107 and 114 cubic inch displacements. The 4-valve per head engine puts out 10% more torque and features a counter-balancer to quell vibration. Photo courtesy of Harley-Davidson.

The Distinguished Brough Superior

As mentioned earlier, the Crocker is one of the three most coveted motorcycles among antique bike enthusiasts. Ironically, the other two bikes have similar history in that their creators were passionate about building high-performance motorcycles of exceptional quality. Both the Vincent Series A Rapide and the Brough Superior SS100 V-twins boasted speeds above 100 mph. Talk to any vintage bike enthusiast about Crocker, Vincent, and Brough, and they will certainly acknowledge them as the holy trinity of motorcycles.

The Brough Superior SS 100 was the ultimate British cruiser prior to World War II. Photo courtesy of Michael Schacht.

The Brough Superior SS100 had the edge on the other two in its history. It was introduced in 1924 by George Brough. This British lad was intent on building the best high-performance bike in the world. His father, a motorcycle builder himself, produced bikes simply named Brough. He was probably not thrilled about the "Superior" part of the name his son gave to his machines. He could not rightfully contest it. The Nottingham-born SS100 (Super Sport) used the proprietary British-made JAP 988cc V-twin engine built by J. A. Prestwich. Like the Crocker, it had overhead valves.

The mechanical artistry on this 1929 Brough Superior 680 invites endless exploration. Note the similarity of the sprung rear suspension to Vincent's. Valve springs are exposed on this OHV JAP engine. Photo courtesy of Scott Dell.

233

This view of a stunning 1938 Brough Superior SS100 shows the distinctive wide gas tank and comfortable seat. Photo by Stephen Covell.

Each four-speed 45 hp Brough was tested to exceed 100 mph, thus the name SS100. It was marketed as the "Rolls-Royce of Motorcycles" with the blessings of Rolls itself. Well-heeled enthusiasts, such as T. E. Lawrence (of Arabia) were among George's customers. The marque unfortunately ceased production with the onset of World War II, but is remarkably alive in Mark Upham's faithful reproductions available today. These astounding machines are indistinguishable from the originals and feature numerous "hidden" advancements. Plan on six-digit cost—a bargain considering originals are selling between $250,000 and $500,000. Exciting modern and high-tech Brough Superior models released over the past few years maintain the marques pedigree among the elite looking for an exotic sportbike.

The Price of Fame

Crocker, Vincent, and Brough faced the same problems in achieving volume production. Custom assembly, high-quality components, and high retail prices limit-

ed their sales opportunities. They simply could not become profitable enough to enter the mainstream motorcycle market by lowering their prices. The looming World War was another factor. It stopped production for all but the strongest makers. Harley-Davidson in the United States, and BSA in the U.K., engaged in large-scale wartime motorcycle manufacturing. This allowed them to be fully geared up for civilian production after the war.

Despite ceasing motorcycle production between 1939 and 1946 to support the war effort through its small factory, Vincent returned strong with an updated Rapide. High production cost and stiff competition from less expensive marques ended the line by 1956. The engine, however, was superior to any V-twin available at that time. Vincent engineer Phil Irving sought a relationship with defunct Indian to see if the 998cc Vincent engine could be fit into a Chief frame to revive both brands. That would have truly brought the Indian to the front of the American V-twin cruiser line. A lack of funds and a lack of vision ended the concept.

Perhaps the perfect cruiser would have been the marriage of a Vincent engine with an Indian Chief chassis. Australian Indian aficionado Peter Arundel took the time and trouble to re-create the elusive Vindian. Photo courtesy of Peter Arundel.

Endless Variety

Cruisers come in all shapes and sizes. The last fifty years have brought the concept to nearly every major motorcycle manufacturer.

The variety of cruisers available today is more extensive than ever. Most follow the Harley-Davidson in featuring V-twin engines, low saddles, and raked front forks, as evident in this picture of a Harley-Davidson Dyna Wide Glide and a Honda Shadow Spirit.

The Japanese bike manufacturers introduced their interpretation of the cruiser in the late 1970s by offering variations from their stock models. This 1981 Kawasaki KZ440 features a two-tier "King and Queen" chopper seat and pulled back handlebars to appeal to the American cruiser buyer. Photo thanks to Revolution Motorsports.

The trend continued with larger multi-cylinder engines until V-twins started taking over.

The Yamaha Virago was one of the first Harley-Davidson look-alike Japanese cruisers. Starting with the 1981 750cc V-twin model, it held onto the Virago name for over a quarter of a century; offering 500cc, 920cc, and 1,100cc models. This was one of the bikes that made Harley-Davidson worried about lower priced competition from Asia, especially during an era that experienced an economic recession and low bike sales. Aggressive lobbying ultimately got President Reagan to pass a tariff on bikes over 700cc in 1983. That didn't stop the Japanese bike manufacturers. They simply made smaller engines with equal or greater performance. The Virago, as an example, was reduced to 699cc. The bike in the photo is of a 1987 1,100cc Virago. Photo courtesy of Paul's Bike Shop.

Honda's Shadow continues to offer customers a lower cost option for bikes with true American cruiser styling. This VT750RS features a SOHC V-twin that is liquid-cooled and fuel injected. Photo courtesy American Honda Motor Co., Inc.

Initially branded as "The New American Motorcycle," Victory started out with its own cruisers back in 1998 under the Polaris umbrella. Their Sports Cruiser, pictured, was designed to be a hybrid that allowed better handling in an otherwise cruiser configuration. Footpegs are directly below the knee.

Increasing engine displacement and redesigning the first generation transmission resulted in bulletproof new models for Victory today. Pictured is the all-black Hammer 8-Ball®, featuring forward controls and a hefty 106 cubic inch engine that is air/oil cooled. Victory was one of the first production brands to feature huge rear tires and all-blacked-out bikes; a trend that is being followed by other makers.

Cruisers are not necessarily the exclusive domain of large displacement American V-twins. Mini-cruisers, like the highly successful 234cc Honda Rebel®, Yamaha's neat little V Star® 250, Johhny Pag's 300cc choppers, and the pictured 350cc two-stroke Russian IZH Junker bring the segment to a market that either cannot afford a big V-twin or is looking for something quite a bit lighter than an 800 pound motorcycle. IZH did a brilliant job in its "American" styling of the Junker. It was produced from 2000 to 2005. Photo courtesy of Kalashnikov Concern Press-Service.

The twin-cylinder Honda 234cc Rebel's proportions make it look deceptively like a full-sized cruiser unless one has a frame of reference, like the fellow sitting on the bike. It is an ideal entry-level machine, or perfect for the casual rider who stays close to home. There are Rebel owners that would argue the part about staying close to home.

Koreans and Chinese bike makers are entering the lucrative cruiser market. This Korean Hyosung GV650 Avitar is powered by a liquid-cooled DOHC 90 degree V-twin that puts out nearly 80 hp. It certainly turns heads in that few people recognize it. The bike is a mosaic of styling cues borrowed from Harley, Victory, BMW, and Yamaha. China's Lifan Group is trying to enter the lucrative US market with its own line of small cruisers. The idea is to offer inexpensive, cool-looking bikes. Creating an effective dealer, service, and parts network is the tricky part.

The next step up from the smaller displacement entry-level cruisers is the reliable and basic 652cc single-cylinder Suzuki Boulevard S40. Like many of the larger cruisers, it drives its rear wheel with a long-lasting, low maintenance belt. This "thumper" (large single) is a great around-the-town or commuter bike for shorter inseams. Photo courtesy of American Suzuki Motor of America, Inc.

BMW entered the cruiser segment in 1997 with their stylistic interpretation. Their attempt to gain market share met with mixed reviews from traditionalists despite its debut in a *007* movie. The bike was offered in two sizes: the R1200C and the smaller R850C. The R1200C survived through 2004.

Modern Reproductions

More cruiser models keep coming out, including true reproductions of vintage machines. Some stay true to the original design, while others add modern conveniences like disc brakes.

The Harley-Davidson XL Sportster as introduced in 1957 underscores the company's influence in retro cruiser styling today. The 55 cubic inch overhead valve V-twin featured unit construction engine and transmission. Photo courtesy of Harley-Davidson.

S&S® Cycle Inc. offered its K-Bobb, a complete vintage reproduction motorcycle under its Flathead Power™ brand of engines. The bike is modeled after a customized 1946 FL bobber but has a completely modern engine and electrical system. Photo courtesy of S&S Cycle.

This delightful 1960s-era "Panhead" clone is a brand new bike that was made by Sucker Punch Sallys custom builders using custom components.

Harley-Davidson offered the "springer" front end for its FXSTS and FLSTSB Softail bikes between 1988 and 2011. The last to feature the front end was the Cross Bones retro-bobber line. These front suspensions emulated those fitted to Harleys back in the 1930s and 1940s. They have a bit less suspension travel than telescopic forks and do require proper maintenance to keep their bushings in spec. Otherwise the linkages loosen and affect the handling. Photo thanks to 'Handcuff' Dave.

Getting Fitted for Cruising

Buying a cruiser requires a serious dose of personal reflection. The cruiser enthusiast usually has an image about him or herself on the bike. More so than sportbikes, personal expression is very important here. Magazine reviews and test rides at dealerships are extremely helpful in making a decision as to which brand and model is best suited for your needs. Options to be considered include rider ergonomics, passenger comfort, availability of accessories, clubs, and the ability to customize as time goes on. Resale value and reliability are no doubt important, but with a market saturated with good used bikes, prices have dropped considerably for all but the best Harley-Davidson models.

Brand Loyalty

The first fork in the road is typically based on brand, particularly Harley-Davidson versus all others. The Harley buyer is definitely more interested in expressing a specific image. The sound, the branding, the style, customization versatility, and acceptance by other Harley riders all contribute to the decision. Fortunately for them, Harley-Davidson offers an enormous array of configurations—ranging from full touring "baggers" to sporty street cruisers with 110 cubic inch engines. Suspension choices are also available. Softails hide the shocks under the engine, simulating the look of hard tails from the past. Dynas and Sportsters use more conventional shocks to suspend the rear on the swingarm. Newer models, like the popular Street Glide® introduced in 2006, offer great handling in a solid chassis for those looking to cruise on curvy roads.

Ergonomic Matters

Considerations for a proper fit include the handlebars. Cruisers typically have wide bars that reach back so that the rider can sit upright. Very high bars, referred to as ape-hangers, are a throwback to the 1960s. They basically say, "I'm super bad. I can ride this thing with my arms up in the air but will have a tough time in making a tight turn in the parking lot." They are not as uncomfortable as they look.

Keith Urban's custom displayed at the AMA Motorcycle Hall of Fame, with ape hangers.

Selecting a cruiser should be like getting a tailored suit. Try to overcome a bike's alluring looks if the seating ergonomics are uncomfortable. Models are offered with comfortable floorboards, conventional footpegs, or forward controls. The latter may challenge shorter riders and are not to be ignored like a tight fitting new pair of shoes. Your legs will not stretch any longer with use. Extending one's legs to reach forward controls, particularly for shorter riders, will make stop-and-go traffic a nightmare. Be practical in your decision. Of course, custom-fit forward controls are always an option. The good news for shorter riders is that there are a number of models out there that have very low seat heights. Harley-Davidson offers several lowered models that are in the twenty-five-inch seat height range.

Forward controls may not be for everyone. Make sure they fit comfortably and stay clear of hot exhaust pipes. Handlebars and hand controls are more flexible and are typically adjustable for reach and position. Be sure that you can handle the controls even at full turn. Note that this custom does not have an air filter. It would be a shame if a small pebble got sucked into that $8,000 engine. The other problem is that a loose pant leg could temporarily choke the motor.

Harley-Davidson Sportsters make great cruisers for those watching their budget or wishing a lower and lighter mount. Models range from 883cc to 1,200cc. Current models have rubber-mounted engines to smooth the vibration from the overhead valve V-twin. This attractive 883cc SuperLow® offers confidence to new riders due to its low center of gravity. Photo courtesy of Harley-Davidson.

Harley-Davidson's Sportster line keeps getting more interesting as the company encourages dealers to come up with creative ideas. The Roadster™ exudes the same raw attitude that inspired fear from the original 1958 XLCH. Photo courtesy of Harley-Davidson.

Indian's new Scout® was introduced for 2015. Its 69 cubic inch water-cooled DOHC V-twin engine puts out quite a bit of horsepower at 100 horses. It's a great bike for around $11,000. The slightly smaller engine of the Scout 60 makes the entry into a classic American cruiser highly affordable at around $9,000. Photo Indian Motorcycle International, LLC.

Competing in the same space as the Sportster and the Indian Scout is Yamaha's Star Bolt line of cruisers. The engine on these bikes is a 58 cubic inch (942cc) air-cooled four-stroke, V-twin with SOHC and four valves per cylinder. The R-Spec model pictured is a modern-day bobber. Prices start at $8,000. Photo courtesy of Yamaha Motor Corporation, U.S.A.

More Choices

If brand loyalty is not a consideration, the forks in the road will be many in searching for a cruiser that fits your style and budget. The first choice is air-cooled versus liquid (or water) cooled engines. The latter obviously allows for greater consistency in engine operating temperature, making slow crawls on a hot summer's day less stressful on the engine. Harley-Davidson recently introduced liquid-cooled heads on a couple of its touring models. Water-cooled cruisers tuck the radiator just in front of the engine. Harley-Davidson hides their radiators cleverly in the leg fairings. Some radiators are more discreet than others. A compromise is found in the Victory models, offering an air/oil cooled combination that requires a much smaller unit.

Kawasaki Vulcan® 900 Classic LT cruisers emulate the traditional American cruiser well in their styling. But looks are only skin deep. Hidden beneath the seemingly familiar façade are technical innovations that offer the buyer power, reliability, and versatility. The Vulcan series V-Twin four-stroke liquid-cooled engines sport overhead cams and four valves per cylinder, ranging in size from 900cc to 1,700cc. Comfortable floorboards make for pleasant, all day cruising. Photo courtesy of Kawasaki Motors Corp, U.S.A.

For the purist who wishes to stay air-cooled, Yamaha's Star® Motorcycle brand offers a very extensive line of cruisers with big 113 cubic inch (1,854cc) air-cooled 48-degree V-twin; pushrod OHV engines. The Star engine has four valves per cylinder compared to some that have only two, allowing more flow and thus more power. Star's success can be seen in their stylistic model lineup. Pictured is a Raider-S. Photo Yamaha Motor Corporation, U.S.A.

Yamaha offers several smaller models of exceptional cruisers that are ideal for a variety of riders. These include entry-level riders, shorter riders, or those looking for a much less expensive option in the cruiser category. Pictured is a V Star® Custom. It features a SOHC 649cc air-cooled 70-degree V-twin engine. Star also offers a 250cc V-twin for under $4,500. Photo Yamaha Motor Corporation, U.S.A.

Stylish cruisers, like this Suzuki Boulevard C90, are designed for casual riding. Their low stance provides a low center of gravity that makes them quite stable. Interestingly, bikes like this one corner very well. Floorboards designed for comfort will scrape far before the bike's grip gives out. The engine is a totally modern 1,462cc, liquid-cooled, SOHC fuel-injected V-twin. Photo courtesy of American Suzuki Motor of America, Inc.

Moto Guzzi offers several stylish big cruisers that are ahead of many of its rivals. Its 1400 lineup includes the pictured Audace, California, and Eldorado models. All feature their smooth-running transversely mounted 1,380cc V-twin. It is cooled by air and oil. Note the oil-cooler radiator near the bottom behind the front wheel. Final drive is typical Guzzi: by shaft. Electronic rider controls abound. Photo courtesy of Moto Guzzi, Piaggio Group Americas, Inc.

Ducati's XDiavel is the company's exotic and stylish interpretation of a high-end power cruiser. It has the larger 1,262cc Ducati Testastretta Desmodromic Variable Timing (DVT) L-twin engine, the latest in electronics, belt drive, and forward controls. It will certainly outrun most bikes in the cruiser category with its 156 hp. Photo courtesy of Ducati Motor Holding S.p.A .

German motorcycle maker Horex has recently re-entered the market under new ownership by 3C Carbon Group AG with its super-high-quality machines. Pictured is their new 1,218cc 167.7 hp VR6 Black Edition power cruiser. Only thirty-three of these exquisite machines will be made. Photo courtesy of Horex.

Also appearing elsewhere in this book, Yamaha's formidable V-Max power cruiser is clearly the hot-rod among the breed. Its liquid-cooled, 1,679cc, DOHC, 16-valves, 65-degree, V-4 engine puts out a tire shredding 174 hp. Photo courtesy of Yamaha Motor Corporation.

To compete in the power cruiser market and attract buyers looking for more advanced technology, Harley-Davidson teamed up with Porsche designers to introduce the VRSC V-Rod® in 2001. The engine's heritage goes back to the superb 1994 VR1000 superbike. Many air-cooled V-twin purists have some mixed feelings about the liquid-cooled 60-degree 1,250cc V-twin with the Revolution® engine, but the stylish and fast bike has carved out a nice niche for itself with a few different models, such as the V-Rod Muscle® pictured. Photo courtesy of Harley-Davidson.

Triumph entered the power cruiser market with a huge inline triple, sporting a massive 2,294cc engine that puts out a whopping 163 ft-lbs of torque. Despite weighing over 800 pounds, it is light on its feet once rolling. Photo courtesy of Triumph Motorcycles.

Polaris' success with its Indian Scout platform encouraged it to be used to create a power cruiser by its Victory Motorcycles division. New for 2017, the Victory Octane™ power cruiser is hardly a blacked out Scout. The 1,179cc V-twin engine has many performance features to give this musclebike its 104 horses. Photo courtesy of Victory Motorcycles.

There is no shortage of big power cruisers. Honda's venerable Gold Wing series offers up the striking Valkyrie with a carlike flat six-cylinder engine of 1,832cc. In a class of their own, these bikes make loyalists to other brands simply scratch their heads. Photo courtesy American Honda Motor Co., Inc.

Honda's designers went wild ten years earlier with the limited edition Valkyrie Rune cruiser. It was only available for 2004 and 2005.

As is often the case, there is always something bigger. This machine is clearly for the person who needs to have a bike in the "behemoth" class. Boss Hoss Cycles makes massive cruisers with GM V-8 engines pushing out an astonishing 445 hp. A more conservative 295 hp engine is also available. Some custom builders have even stuffed V-12 engines in a cycle frame.

Cruisers and sidecars make a great combination. Steering will be quite different than on a two-wheeler. Sidecar rigs steer more like a car. Most cruisers offer an option for either a windshield or fairing. Harley-Davidson's "Bat Wing" fairing provides ample protection from the elements.

A key advantage to trikes and sidecar combinations is their secure footing on slippery surfaces. This was certainly appreciated a hundred years ago when motorcycle sidecar rigs dominated the roads in America as an affordable means of transportation. Harley-Davidson offers a great variety of trike models, including this nice Ultra Classic, for those who like the confidence of three wheels.

The biggest trikes are made by Boss Hoss Cycles. These machines come with two-speed automatics with reverse.

The Can-Am Spyder F3-S is sure to get some attention as one exciting three-wheeler. Seating on the F3-S is pure cruiser. Its Rotax 1330 ACE in-line three-cylinder engine produces an impressive 115 hp. Photo courtesy of Bombardier Recreational Products Inc.

Kawasaki offers an exceptional motorcycle for the consumer looking for a smaller bike with cruiser ergonomics and contemporary styling. The Vulcan S has a balanced liquid-cooled DOHC 649cc parallel twin engine and a seat height of 27.8 inches. Over a dozen combinations of handlebar, seat, and footpeg positions allow pretty much anyone to feel comfortable on this modern take on the cruiser. It is also offered with ABS for under $7,400. Photo courtesy of Kawasaki Motors Corp., U.S.A.

The cruiser segment did not always exist, at least not by name. It has clearly dominated the motorcycling landscape in the United States today. Its allure has spread to Europe and Japan as well. Baby boomers still continue to lead the charge in buying them, forgoing retirement saving for living life on the road. The introduction of new contemporary cruisers using parallel twin engines has provided the buyer with many more options. It has also brought the segment to the attention of buyers who may be looking for a non-traditional cruiser. Regardless of brand or price, in an ideal world we should all have at least one cruiser in our stable.

Honda keeps innovating with leading-edge designs like its 2016 NM4 Vultus. This 670cc liquid-cooled parallel twin–powered bike is a cross between a maxi-scooter and a cruiser. It appears in this chapter because its seating is more cruiser style and offers a low 25.6-inch seat height. It also features a six-speed automatic dual-clutch transmission that can be shifted manually via handlebar controls. Photo courtesy of American Honda Motor Co., Inc.

The American lifestyle of hitting the road for adventure has made the cruiser the preferred vehicle. Photo courtesy of Harley-Davidson.

KTM Sportmotorcycle GmbH

Chapter 6

SPORTBIKES, SUPERBIKES, AND MUSCLEBIKES

Built for speed, sportbikes represent the best technology available today based on a hundred years of engine and chassis development. With superior handling, exotic frames, electronically controlled suspensions, and engines capable of over 200-mph speeds, they are not for everyone.

Aprilia P.I.V.A.

The Sportier Side of Motorcycling

The definition of the word *sport* in the dictionary references "a physical activity for enjoyment." In that case, nearly all of motorcycling is a sport. The exceptions may be the use of a motorcycle for deliveries or police work. For the rest of us, it is a sport. This would make all motorcycles sporting machines. However, when we refer to a sportbike, it truly differentiates these machines from others by their specific components and capabilities.

Sportbikes, also called sportsbikes, are clearly designed for speed and handling. A sportbike rider must accept giving up the long-distance comfort of a touring bike for high performance. Sportbikes are also best for solo riding. The high passenger seating is more for courtesy than practicality. It offsets the otherwise good balance of the machine.

Even though most motorcycles do basically the same thing, some do it better than others, given the specific type and design of the machine. A sportbike typically accelerates faster, brakes better, has significantly better cornering ability, and can achieve higher speeds than bikes of other classes. It is no coincidence that these machines are often called crotch rockets. A sportbike does nearly everything better than a large touring bike or cruiser. Some modern standards come close, but given an identical engine, the sportbike will out-handle the standard. The only price one pays is comfort. This may be a small price to pay if the use and intent truly match the rider's needs.

Showcase for Technology

Sportbikes, more often than not, are the machines that feature the latest technology. This is particularly evident in electronic systems managing a motorcycle's engine, suspension, traction, and handling. Ride-by-Wire systems are starting to replace conventional throttle cables. These systems use electronic sensors and servos to replace mechanical actuation of throttle and suspension components. Some modern sportbikes allow the rider to switch between specific ride modes—be it for track, street, or rain conditions. Traction control (TC) systems and suspension settings are automatically modified for optimum performance per selection. These technology advances are wonderful, but they are also driving many mechanically inclined enthusiasts to consider vintage motorcycles. There they can find comfort in knowing that a cable raises the slide in the carburetor, and an engine's timing can be adjusted by simply moving the position of the ignition points. This type of tinkering is good for the soul. However, modern bikes with all the bells and whistles are marvels to ride. Motorcyclists should explore all that is available to them.

A Pain in the Neck

A sportbike can be quite good around town, the track, or for quick jaunts through winding country roads. It will, however, start reminding one of its ergonomic limitations in heavy stop-and-go traffic or on long trips. Wrist, neck, and back pain are common. This is due to the inherent sportbike seating position. The rider is leaning forward to reach the low handlebars. Feet are located slightly to the rear of the machine, resting on rear-set footpegs that are also positioned higher up than on conventional bikes. This raises the legs so that knees can be tucked in by the tank. All of this puts a lot of weight on the wrists and strains the neck and back when going slow. At higher speeds the wind helps support the body.

Another one of Nick Veasey's revealing X-rays shows a rider on a vintage Matchless sportbike. Although less severe in riding position than a café racer with low handlebars, the X-ray shows clearly the unnatural curvature of the neck. This will result in fatigue as muscles compensate. Photo courtesy of Nick Veasey.

Typical high-performance sportbike seating position reduces wind resistance and puts weight up front. Pictured is Kawasaki's hot new H2 Ninja. Note the exceptional protective gear the rider is wearing. Photo courtesy of Kawasaki Motors Corp., U.S.A.

The view from the cockpit has changed somewhat over the past sixty years, but the key instruments remain the same for any sportbike. Speedometer and tachometer may now be digital compared to chronometric instruments. The low clip-on handlebars keep the body down and put weight onto the front wheel for sharper steering. Little cloth booties conceal the brake and clutch hydraulic oil reservoirs and absorb any that may leak. The red horizontal steering damper helps control sudden lateral forces acting on the front wheel, such as from rough road surfaces.

Chronometrics are clock mechanism type instruments, such as on the 1960 BSA Gold Star Clubman pictured. They cost over $1,000 each today. Tachometers, often called rev-counters, are essential on high-performance machines. They help the rider keep the rpms in their optimum range and warn against harmful over-revving. Absent on modern bikes are the choke and magneto advance levers, now handled by electronics. Note that the position of the handlebars has not change at all for true sportbikes. The big knob in the middle is the steering damper. It tightens the steering head so that it takes more resistance to turn it side to side. This can help reduce high-speed wobble.

Engineered with Purpose

Sportbikes derive their genes from racing machines. Wind resistance is a big factor in racing. The lower one can crouch down on a fast-moving bike, the less the wind resistance. Leaning forward also places more weight on to the front wheel. This greatly improves response and handling. Many sportbikes are offered with fully faired bodywork and sleek windscreens to further lower the drag coefficient. In the past decade, however, a return to the naked sportbike has seen a strong revival among most makers. Some call these machines streetfighters.

Naked sportbikes with elements of vintage and modern styling blended together are all the rage today. A perfect example is the exceptional Yamaha XSR900TM. The 847cc triple is based on the successful FZ®-09 model. It offers a host of electronic controls for traction, braking, and engine management. Footpegs are set rearward in sportbike fashion, but higher handlebars allow for greater comfort for extended riding. Photo courtesy of Yamaha Motor Corporation, U.S.A.

The joy of sport riding is clearly expressed in this picture of a rider blasting up the coast on his Aprilia Shiver 750. A naked bike like this one is more interesting to look at since all of its components are visible to the eye. Incorporating machinery into style and design is what Italian motorcycle manufacturers do best. The Shiver 750 was the first production bike ever to be equipped with a "Ride-by-Wire" electronic throttle. There are no mechanical linkages or cables controlling the fuel-injection system. Photo courtesy of Aprilia, Piaggio & C SpA.

An Athlete in Design

What makes the difference in sportbike design? The answer includes an extensive list of components that make up the motorcycle. Every part on a sportbike has a very specific purpose. There is little on these machines that is not warranted. You will not see cup holders as an option. They are designed to run hard and fast on twisting roads, responding to a rider's input with precision and assurance.

To start, the bike has to be light. This requires a very sturdy, light frame. A strong frame minimizes flexing and distortion that can upset the handling of a bike at high speeds, especially around corners. The frame can be made of steel tubing, extruded aluminum sections welded together, titanium, carbon fiber, or a variety of exotic alloys. Modern sportbikes all but eliminate the frame whenever possible by including the engine as a stressed member. Vincent used this design concept back in the 1940s. Honda used it extensively for their parallel twins back in the 1960s. Ducati made it a staple for their sportbikes, and others have followed.

The highly evolved motorcycle chassis as designed by Aprilia. Photo courtesy of Aprilia, Piaggio & C SpA.

Ducati's most successful model is the Monster. First introduced in 1993 as the M900, it is now offered in a variety of engine sizes ranging from 796cc to 1,200cc. Ducati's classic tubular steel trellis frame is clearly evident. The engine is typically attached to the frame at the cylinder head(s) and acts as a mounting point for the swingarm.

Sportbikes can vary greatly in their wheelbase: the distance between front and rear axle. This short-wheelbase Buell will respond quickly and wheelie happily for its rider. Longer wheelbases provide greater high-speed stability.

Keeping It Suspended

The suspension joins the frame to the wheels. Its job is to provide a cushion between the rough road surface and the bike. It achieves this by the use of springs and hydraulic dampers that control the impact of jolts, and the rate of rebound. Without hydraulic-filled (oil) or gas-filled (nitro-

gen) shock dampers, a bike will pogo out of control, especially at high speeds. Touring bikes have softer settings for comfort.

Suspension components aren't just for rough road surfaces. A bike entering a corner at high speed will experience compression of the front forks. Too much compression will not allow for rebound. High-performance sportbikes offer adjustable suspension settings in spring preload and damping for both compression and rebound. High-end sportbikes offer advanced electronic compression and rebound damping controlled by a computer that acts quickly to provide stability through highly variable riding conditions.

Detail of Kawasaki's high-tech H2TMR front suspension adjusters on top of each fork nut. Photo courtesy of Kawasaki Motors Corp., U.S.A.

Springs are traditionally contained within the telescoping front forks. Larger diameter front forks add rigidity. Inverting them makes them flex even less in high-speed maneuvers. This all adds up to more confident handling.

Going Single

Sportbikes have leaned more to a single rear shock unit. A coil spring surrounding the damping unit is mounted between the rear upper frame and the swingarm. Full adjustability allows the experienced sport rider to fine-tune the bike's manners in a variety of conditions. Öhlins is a name most associated with high-performance suspension units.

Detail of a single gas-dampened mono-shock rear suspension unit on a Aprilia Dorsoduro. The unit features full adjustability and a gas reservoir to control proper pressure. Photo courtesy of Aprilia, Piaggio & C SpA.

This attractive Kawasaki Ninja 650 middleweight clearly shows its single "offset lay-down" rear shock unit. The concept harks back to Philip Vincent's original design.

The Ducati Monster, as shown in this 2015 M1200, has evolved technically since 1993, while staying true to its form. It features water-cooling and higher-performance components now to make it a fantastic all-around naked sportbike. As with most sportbikes, the Monster uses a chain to drive the rear wheel. Chains are strong and can handle the sudden torque created by these powerful engines. The Monster 1200 R takes it to the next level with premium suspention and brake components. Photo courtesy of Ducati Motor Holdings S.p.A.

Tires Matter

Tires on sportbikes tend to be a bit wider than comparable standards. Sportbike tires are also softer in composition so that they grab the road better. This, of course, translates into more wear. A good sport tire can be the only thing that keeps the bike between you and the road. Compromising on tires is bad and risky practice. The contact patch that actually separates tire from road is only a couple of inches. It's scary to think about that when entering an exit ramp at 70 mph. Traction control offered on many modern sportbikes greatly improves keeping the rubber on the road. It also boosts confidence.

Keeping this Suzuki GSX-R®1000 firmly planted on the tarmac requires skill, and the right tires and suspension. The rider is seen "hanging-off" to lower the bike's center of gravity to allow as much lean-angle as possible. This rider will not be leaving "chicken strips" on his tires. Chicken strips are the unworn areas on the outside edges of a tire, indicating that the rider is afraid to lean hard on corners. Photo courtesy of Suzuki Motor of America, Inc.

High-Strung Like Thoroughbreds

Sportbike engines tend to be in a much higher state of tune compared to engines found on standards or cruisers. This involves increasing compression (for more power per explosion), hotter cams (to make the engine take deeper breaths), advanced electronic ignition control, freer flowing exhaust, and overall higher rev limits. All of this creates more power and torque in a highly responsive package. The price one pays here is longevity and tractability. These motors are highly stressed when used as intended. They cannot be expected to provide the durability of a slow churning big V-twin. However, most people won't come close to pushing these machines to a point of exhaustion unless they are tire-burning maniacs on the street or track. Modern bikes will last a long time with proper maintenance.

Tractability of high-performance engines is another factor to consider. These engines and clutches respond quickly to throttle changes. Novice riders may find it difficult to control a large displacement sportbike at very slow parking lot speeds. These are high-strung thoroughbreds that just want to go. It is best to master throttle and clutch control on a smaller bike before taking a leap to these lightspeed machines. A few machines offer the option to select power modes for better slow speed control.

The current crop of sub-700cc sportbikes have significantly more power than those built two decades ago. Advances contributing to this are not limited to metallurgy, new piston designs, better flow, and less power-robbing engineering. As with everything in the modern world lately, electronics are to thank. Guided by an array of sensors, electronic engine control software manages fuel mapping and engine timing to squeeze every ounce of power out of these motors. They also monitor knocking and pinging in the event the engine is pushed too hard. Unlike carbureted engines, these electronic control units (ECU) manage fuel injection, ignition timing, and possibly valve timing to optimize engine performance under any temperature, altitude, or speed.

Stopping Is As Important As Going

Brakes are just as important on a sportbike as the engine and suspension. All that speed needs to be controlled. High-revving four-cylinder engines have little engine braking. Engine braking is when one uses the compression of an engine to help slow down the vehicle. The use of slipper-clutches on exotic sportbikes virtually eliminates engine braking. They are designed to give the rider full control of the bike via throttle and brake by not allowing engine braking to interfere. The clutch automatically disengages the engine from the drivetrain whenever letting off the throttle. Otherwise, engine braking can come on fast and upset the delicate balance of the bike on these high-performance V- or L-twins. In extreme cases, rear wheel slip occurs—not fun when entering a fast turn.

Brakes, therefore, have to allow the rider to slow the bike down fast. Most sportbikes of larger displacement use twin-disc brakes up front. The larger the disc, the more stopping leverage can be applied. Since braking makes the bike transfer its weight to the front wheel, front brakes do most of the work. Braking with the rear wheel only on a bike at a high speed may cause it to lose traction.

Trail-braking is a technique of controlling the gentle release of the brakes as one leans deeper into a turn. This can increase traction by exerting more pressure on the front wheel. Many modern bikes offer anti-lock braking systems (ABS) that prevent the wheels from locking regardless of how hard one applies pressure to the brake lever or pedal. This can be very useful for riders who like to enter corners fast and trail-brake. ABS is also indispensable for wet weather riding. The industry's best brakes are made by Italian maker Brembo.

This computer illustration shows the complexity of a modern anti-lock braking system as installed on a BMW. The computer module (blue) monitors electrical signals from sensors on the wheel, engine, and hydraulic brake system. The pressure regulator (yellow) adjusts the proper pressure on the brake pads to keep the wheels from locking up. Illustration courtesy of BMW Motorrad USA.

Like All Good Athletes, They Come in All Sizes

Targeted at the young rider, sexy sportbikes from Japan and Britain feature high performance at a price a kid working at Burger King® can afford. For well-heeled riders, Italian machines offer an exotic option. Many are fully faired machines in a broad range of displacements. They come in four main categories: lightweights, middleweights, superbike, and musclebike (sometimes spelled muscle bike).

Lightweight bikes tend to have engines of 500cc or smaller and weigh less than 400 pounds. They are a great way for young and/or entry-level riders to learn how to handle a sportbike. Be careful though. Getting hooked on sportbikes means that you may soon want something bigger and faster.

The size of a sub-400cc lightweight sportbike is different to gauge in photos without a reference. The small profile of this single-cylinder Honda CBR250R is made obvious by its relationship to the helmet. Honda also offers a larger CBR300R and a naked CB300F using balanced single-cylinder engines. These small sportbikes make great entry points for teen riders. It allows them to develop their skills on the track so that they are better prepared for the larger, more powerful machines to come.

Larger displacement entry-level sportbikes, like this Kawasaki Ninja 300, will encourage riders to consider keeping them longer. This lightweight is a painless entry into the world of sportbikes at around $5,300. More powerful, and loaded with electronic features, it makes an ideal bike for back road fun or local commuting. The Ninja 300 is available with ABS and low seating to provide a sense of assurance to new riders. Pictured is the Special Edition model that has been upgraded with a high-performance Yoshimura exhaust. Upgrades like that are not only good for boosting performance by a few hp, but also add a lot of personalized character to the bike.

Approaching the middleweight class is Honda's parallel twin–powered CBR500R. This 471cc machine makes an excellent consideration for any young rider looking for a practical machine for the long term. It is perfect for the young woman who doesn't want to be a passenger anymore and wants a machine that can keep up with her friends. Photo courtesy of American Honda Motor Co., Inc.

A Perfect Balance

Middleweights are the real fun bikes. They are still relatively light at around 450 pounds, but have amazing power-to-weight ratios. That means that the engine's power is very high compared to the weight of the bike. Their 600cc to 750cc engines can put out over 100 hp, and sometimes way more. Those designated with an "R" emulate race models and are fitted with more advanced suspension and braking components. "RR" typically means race-replica: sharing some attributes of the real track bikes.

The great variety of middleweight sportbikes offered at reasonable prices allows easy entry into this category. This Yamaha YZF®-R6 features a 599cc liquid-cooled inline four-cylinder; DOHC, sixteen-titanium-valve engine that runs at 13:1 compression. Light weight, a state-of-the-art chassis, over 100 hp, and an $11,000 price tag make this an ideal sportbike for anyone. Photo courtesy of Yamaha Motor Corporation, U.S.A.

The Suzuki SV 650 twin cylinder is an affordable middleweight sportbike with reasonable ergonomics. They have been around since 1999, and good used ones can be found for around $2,000. They come in a sporty "S" version with low bars (as shown) and a standard configuration for greater comfort. Interestingly, the SV650 was "Big Sid" Bieberman's favorite non-Vincent bike to ride. Big Sid was a well-known Vincent motorcycle builder and tuner. The bike is very popular in amateur racing circuits based on its superb handling.

Middleweights make great track bikes and are popular on the Supersport circuits. They are, therefore, often referred to as supersports. A variation of middleweights is the supermotard class. These bikes look like off-road machines with sticky sport tires. They are represented in supermoto races where the track alternates between tarmac and dirt. Pioneers of supermotards basically took dual-sport machines and adapted sportbike wheels and tires. Anyone can get started this way by buying a used Suzuki DR650 for $1,500 and adapting some sportbike wheels obtained at a swap meet. It's not going to win races, but will be a whole lot of fun. Ducati, Aprilia, KTM, Husqvarna, Sachs, Yamaha, BMW, Honda, and Suzuki make the real deal.

Aprilia's supermotard is typical of the genre. A 750cc V-twin engine with massive torque hangs beneath a light but indestructible frame. The whole thing is held up with suspension units that have nearly twice the travel of their road-going cousins. Photo courtesy of Aprilia, Piaggio & C SpA.

The Big Boys

Superbikes are at the top. They have engines around 1,000cc or greater, mounted in high-tech frames sporting exotic suspensions. These things are fast! The typical superbike can put 140 hp to the rear wheel. That is the equivalent of a family sedan having an 800 hp engine. The modern liter-plus sportbike is a racing machine. The new buzzword "hypersport" has been given to superbikes that are very powerful and fast. Never has the gap between true race machines and sportbikes been smaller—especially when looking at marvelous examples such as Ducati's Panigale R.

Electronics Take It to the Limit

With this kind of power, it is a major benefit that most of the top makes offer rider aids such as traction control. These complex electronic systems have sensors that monitor wheel-speed, throttle position, and engine rpm to keep the rear tire from losing grip. Traction control systems vary slightly with each superbike that offers it. BMW's Dynamic Traction Control (DTC), for example, allows the rider to flip between numerous riding modes while moving to help keep the bike's tires planted. The "rain" mode is particularly useful. It does provide something anyone can appreciate: confidence. Combined with ABS, it allows one to reach limits on the track or road not imagined possible a decade ago by other than the best of racers.

The most advanced system is Bosch's Motorcycle Stability Control (MSC) system. It uses its Inertial Measurement Unit (IMU) to monitor pitch angle (the front and back motion due to acceleration/deceleration) and lean angle. This helps the computer limit braking on each wheel and control engine speed to maintain stability and traction in high speed situations—very helpful when rider skill isn't keeping up with the situation at hand.

Electronics also help with suspension settings on the fly. BMW's Dynamic Damping Control (DDC) is an electronic control unit that adjusts the suspension at intervals of 10 milliseconds to whatever condition the bike encounters, be it smooth track or rough surface around a fast turn. The DDC control unit monitors sensors for traction, banking angle, and damper feedback. This is pretty sophisticated stuff that motorheads from decades earlier would not have believed possible. All this technology makes the motorcycle seem like a bionic extension of the rider. This has created a dividing line

among some riders who feel that electronic rider aids reduce the skill level needed to manage a performance bike.

The BMW S1000R 160 hp sportbike set new standards for electronic traction control and ABS. It offers numerous settings from all-out Race Mode to Rain Mode. The latest models include Dynamic Damping Control (DDC) to continually adjust suspension compliance. The Automatic Stability Control (ASC) is a more advanced TC system that helps keep traction in a broad variety of riding conditions, particularly when accelerating out of curves. Photo courtesy of BMW Motorrad USA.

Aprilia's RSV4 supersport superbike is another example of Italian engineering at its best. Its outstanding handling and power curve offers the serious sport rider everything he or she would ever want. The 65-degree V-4 boasts 180 hp at 12,500 rpm. Its multi-map ABS can be adjusted or even disabled on the move. The RSV4RF model pictured takes it to a higher level. Lighter, more powerful, and with more technology, it is a track-ready machine. Photo courtesy of Aprilia, Piaggio & C SpA.

Ducati's remarkable 1,198cc, 205 hp L-twin Panigale R superbike is an all-out race bike made for the track. Sophisticated electronics manage the suspension, ABS, wheelies, engine braking, and traction control using a variety of sensors, including Bosch's IMU. The Öhlins suspension is managed electronically as well to complete the orchestra. The company offers a 1,285cc street-tuned version in the 1299 Panigale that begs the rider for speed and cornering. This bike's lineage goes right back to Ducati's first desmodromic four-valve per head superbike: the 916. Unlike previous desmodromic L-twins, the Panigale engine uses chains to drive the cams instead of cogged belts. Besides the longevity, Ducati owners will see a slight reduction in maintenance costs as belts would have to be changed frequently. Exhaust pipes exit under the bike for added performance. Photo courtesy of Ducati Motor Holdings S.p.A.

Ducati's new 955cc twin-cylinder 959 Panigale may be the ideal balance for those looking for a lighter package that is equally adept for the street or track. There is no compromising in technology here whatsoever. It is the first Euro 4 homologated Superquadro bike by Ducati. The electronics package includes ABS, Ducati Traction Control (DTC), Ducati Quick Shift (DQS), Engine Brake Control (EBC), and Ride-by-Wire (RbW). Ducati's riding modes change the response of each of these technologies to create the result required by the rider. Add a slipper clutch and the package is complete. Photo courtesy of Ducati Motor Holdings S.p.A.

Honda's CBR1000RR SP Repsol is what is called a race-replica. It mimics the company's winning MotoGP superbikes that dominated the circuit between 2002 and 2006, and for 2011, 2013, and 2014. MotoGP engines are significantly different than those on production bikes, but the bodywork makes them look like the real deal. As of 2015 models, Honda has held off adding rider aid electronics such as traction control. The tiny bike next to it is a pocket bike—a class of miniature bikes that is used for fun and racing by adults.

Sportbikes Love the Track

Despite the relative affordability of a superbike or track bike, over 90 percent of the people buying them will never realize their true potential. It's a shame to see so many great sportbikes spend their lives on suburban highways and not on the track. The author strongly urges those with such machines to take a look at the California Superbike School.

Established by racer Keith Code, the school offers fantastic programs to train riders on how to get the most from their machines and develop the skills needed to keep their bikes in control. Sessions are held throughout the year at nine popular racecourses. For the wanna-be racer, Keith offers special classes through his private race school, coderace.com.

Track schooling makes an ideal gift to ask for. If one can't afford that, get the *Twist of the Wrist II* DVD from Keith for around $20. It teaches the mechanics of riding, particularly managing curves, through an extraordinary combination of live footage, computer graphics, and classroom type training. It will make you a better rider.

California Superbike School offers programs for any budget and level of interest. Personal instruction by pro riders is the key to their success. California Superbike School uses the S1000RR from BMW for its students who prefer not to ride their own bikes. This liquid-cooled 999cc inline four with a claimed 199 hp was the first true modern superbike the Bavarian company built. BMW obviously studied the best engineering principles of its Japanese and Italian rivals. The results are most impressive in that the bike puts out a lot of power at a relatively light weight of just 427 pounds.

BMW's hot S1000RR takes the S1000R to a higher level, including a 199 hp engine and the advanced "Dynamic Pro" system. This computing system includes all the latest DTC, DDC, Integral Race ABS, and ASC control systems.

Pictured here is founder Keith Code (right) with his team of instructors in front of the new BMW S1000RR bikes used at the school. Photo courtesy of Keith Code, California Superbike School, super-bikeschool.com

Track days at major raceways allow sportbike riders to experience the full potential of their machines. Photo courtesy of Roberto Baldeschi-Balleani.

Power Sells

Horsepower sells bikes. Most manufacturers, however, won't state the output of their engines in terms of horsepower. That can get tricky since it can vary greatly with conditions and where it is measured. Horsepower measured at the crankshaft is higher than at the rear wheel. Power is lost as it goes through the clutch, transmission, and chain. Torque specifications are more often given, but mean little to the average power-hungry consumer.

Photo shows a factory stunt rider aboard a naked sportbike, often referred to as a streetfighter. The 1050 Speed Triple is a formidable three-cylinder sport machine fully capable of shredding tires as demonstrated. Its smaller brother, the Street Triple, is one of the best overall naked middleweight packages out there. The three-cylinder configuration gives great low-end torque compared to fours.

There is a class of large displacement bikes called musclebikes. These are all about horsepower. They first appeared as the Kawasaki 750cc H2 triple in 1972. They were brutally powerful and fast in a straight line. Handling suffered on early models. The most popular musclebike of all is the Yamaha V-Max, introduced in 1985. The 1,197cc, 113.5 hp machine survived with few changes until 2007. The popularity of power cruisers (an offshoot of musclebikes that have a more cruiser-like seating position) prompted Yamaha Star Motorcycles to introduce a bigger and faster version for 2009. Other popular musclebikes include the Harley-Davidson V-Rod Muscle®, Triumph Rocket III® Roadster, and Victory Hammer® S.

The Kawasaki H2 Mach IV is classified as a standard but can be considered the grandfather to all musclebikes. It was a 748cc three-cylinder 74 hp two-stroke offered from 1972 through 1975. The bike could easily do twelve-second quarter-mile times. Top speed was 120 mph, but its flexing frame made that something undesirable. It is receiving great interest from vintage bike enthusiasts today.

First-generation Yamaha V-Max as introduced for the 1986 model year has an intimidating hot-rod look. Air scoops on either side of the tank are decorative. The bike was fast off the line but lacked confidence in the corners.

The re-engineered second generation of the V-Max was introduced for 2009. More a power cruiser than pure sportbike, it was designed to be even fiercer with its 197 crank hp DOHC 1,679cc (102 cubic inch) V-4. Air scoops are real on the newer version. Handling was no longer a weak point, and top speed was sensibly slowed down over the original. Photo courtesy of Star Motorcycles, Yamaha Motor Corporation.

The marketing impact of speed is never forgotten as manufacturers create faster and more powerful machines. It would not take long for a bike claiming to be the fastest to lose its ranking overnight. A historical example of that is Honda's 178-mph CBR1100XX Super Blackbird, first intro-

duced in 1996. It ousted Kawasaki's ZX-11 as the fastest production bike. Within a couple of years, Suzuki introduced its GSX1300R Hayabusa. The name mocked Honda's Blackbird. The Japanese translation is "peregrine falcon," a bird of prey known to go after blackbirds. Of course Kawasaki did not stand idle. Its ZX-14 superbike took the crown from the Busa. The craziness continues.

Ducati's aggressive-looking 162 hp Diavel shouts musclebike all over, competing against the V-Rod and V-Max. The bike's power plant is based on the firm's successful 1,198cc 4-valve desmodromic liquid-cooled 90-degree twin. Photo courtesy Ducati Motor Holding S.p.A.

Honda's fast CBR1100XX Super Blackbird was named after Lockheeds' SR-71 mach 3 spy plane. Photo courtesy of American Honda Motor Co., Inc.

Suzuki's imposing Hayabusa commands attention. Its claimed top speed of 186 mph was a result of a self-imposed limit established by motorcycle manufacturers in 2000 to appease the politicians and the media. Removal of electronic limiters allow these bikes to exceed 200 mph without a problem.

Kawasaki's 1,441cc Ninja ZX-14R ABS, shown in its thirtieth anniversary colors, touts itself as the world's most powerful mass production motorcycle for 2015. At near $16,000, it offers value in engineering excellence and performance. However, its kid brother, the H2R, will bump it off its speed throne. Photo courtesy of Kawasaki Motors Corp., U.S.A.

The best place to see a broad variety of sportbikes is at regional motorcycle events or a motorcycle industry show. It's not only educational, but you'll be able to ask the owners questions if you are interested in buying a particular model. Most likely there will be an expert who knows someone who has one to sell. Local shops and clubs keep calendars on events. Many locales also have bike night someplace in town, where once a week hundreds of bikers congregate to show their bikes and meet friends.

Sportbikes Then and Now

The rest of this chapter highlights a small sampling of notable sportbikes and café racers out of the thousands that have torn up our streets and tracks over the past one hundred years.

There was a time when the riders of fast bikes, like this 1913 Model 7B Excelsior, were looked upon as daredevils, much in the same way as non-motorcyclists look at the fast sportbike riders of today. This 10 hp machine, selling for $250 back then, was made in Chicago. The company's founder was none other than Ignatz Schwinn of bicycle fame. The photo clearly shows its inlet-over-exhaust valve configuration. Orange spark plug wires originate at the magneto in front.

Through the 1930s and 1940s the British single was the sportbike of the day. Light, agile, and powerful enough, these 350cc and 500cc singles dominated the market. This 500cc 1940 Ariel VG had a dual-port exhaust, meaning that two exhaust pipes came out of the single-cylinder head.

The Norton International sportbike was introduced in 1931 to further the marque's notable racing efforts. It featured a single overhead cam 500cc engine that became a favorite of the private racer. This is a true "ride it to work during the week, and race it on the weekend" bike. This engine design would lead to Norton's famous Manx racer. As with most bikes before the 1970s, this bike had drum brakes front and rear. These were barely adequate given the 100+mph speeds these machines could achieve.

Matchless and AJS produced some innovative overhead cam singles after WWII that became popular among racers.

Italian makers kept busy after WWII making commuter bikes. However, they were not lost to just getting back and forth to work. Factories offered sport versions that became popular with private racers in the smaller displacement classes. MV Agusta's 125cc commuter was also offered in the pictured GT version popular with sportbike enthusiasts.

The Ariel Red Hunter was offered in 250cc, 350cc, and 500cc versions between 1932 and 1959. These light singles served well as both sport and standard machines. The 500 produced up to 26 hp and was capable of an impressive 82 mph.

BSA's DBD34 500cc single was, and still is, every café racer's dream bike. The machine was conceived after BSA won a gold star medal at the 1937 Brooklands circuit for doing a lap at over 100 mph (160 km/h) on a BSA Empire Star. Various models in 350cc and 500cc evolved to create the ultimate Clubman racer: the DBD34GS. The bike features a very large alloy finned cylinder head that helps cool the 42 hp high-performance hand-assembled engine. Only 6,000 DBD34's were made between 1956 and 1963. They command high dollars today.

Heeding the call from motorcyclists for a sportier bike, BMW introduced the R69S in 1960. The 600cc flat twin initially featured the endearing Earles fork (front) but changed over to the telescopic type in 1967 (rear) to provide better high-speed stability. The R69S was offered through 1969 and is most collectible today. Photo by Stephen Covell.

In 1959, British maker Veloce introduced the 105-mph Velocette Venom Clubman. It featured a close-ratio gearbox and rear-set footpegs, both indicative of sporting application to compete against the BSA Gold Star, the Norton Manx, and the Norton International sportbikes. It proved itself on the endurance track in 1961 by averaging over 100 mph for twenty-four hours at Montlhery, France. The Venom Thruxton was a step up when introduced in 1964. It became a café racer's pin-up by offering a modified head with larger valves, clip-on handlebars, rear-set foot controls, and a massive Amal GP carburetor as on the Gold Star. Pictured is a silver 1966 Thruxton showing the modified gas tank to accommodate the large carburetor. The bike behind it is a 500cc Venom that has been "Thruxton-ized" by replacing its cylinder head with one from a true Thruxton. Photo courtesy of Dick Casey.

If there is one bike that truly evokes the spirit of the sportbike, it is the Vincent Black Shadow. The mid-50s Series C pictured was capable of 125 mph right out of the crate. Its 55 hp engine runs relaxed as the rider enjoys a stable high-speed ride. The Black Shadow kept its crown as fastest production bike until the late 1960s—a remarkable feat. Braking was improved by the use of two brake drums on each wheel.

Vincent engines continue to inspire sportbike applications. Fritz Egli, a Swiss engineer, adapted leftover Vincent engines to modern frames of his design during the late 1960s and early 1970s. Frenchman Patrick Godet continues in this endeavor, as is shown in the attractive example above. The use of hydraulically actuated disc brakes offers superior braking power over traditional drum brakes.

Japan's first superbike was the Honda CB750 standard introduced in 1969. The smooth 68 hp engine brought speed and acceleration to audiences that had been unable to attain it before under $1,500. The Italian exotics were certainly capable but more expensive and less tractable. The bike pictured is one of the 4,714 original sand-cast engines to prove the concept before committing to die-casting mass production. The single-overhead cam CB750 lasted until 1978. Double overhead cam engines continued the line into the new millennium. The 1979 CB750F sportbike was the company's first AMA Superbike entry. The next step up was a 900cc engine to compete with Kawasaki's Z-1.

Despite Honda's engineering feats, their bikes still did not handle as well as the large British twins like the Triumph Bonneville or Norton Commando. Frames would need to be strengthened and suspensions improved over the years to beat out the aging Brits. Pictured is the author's 1972 Norton Commando that has been customized for modern-day use, including electronic ignition, single Mikuni carburetor, and a Brembo disc brake.

Norton is alive and well due to the efforts of Stuart Garner. Norton moved to its current home at Donington Park, England, in 2008. The first Commando 961SE (pictured) was delivered in 2010. It follows in the pure tradition of its predecessor in that it has pushrod-actuated overhead valves and a superb chassis. Updated engine components and electronics make this a reincarnation to reckon with. Norton has received government funding to help support its success. Photo courtesy of Norton Motorcycle Ltd.

Ducati's first twin was offered from 1971 to 1974. The 750GT was designed by Fabio Taglioni and featured a 90-degree twin with bevel drive overhead cams. Despite its modest 50 hp, the Ducati held its own against the more powerful Honda and Kawasaki triples due to its superb road handling. At $1,995, the bike was quite a bit more expensive than the Japanese rivals but worth the investment in today's market.

Inspired by the 1972 Imola race victory by Paul Smart on a twin-cylinder Ducati 750 with desmodromic valve action, the firm decided to offer the public a true street racer in its 750 SS (Super Sport) in 1974. Later Ducati victories would introduce a 900 SS. Ducati reintroduced a modern version of the Paul Smart bike in 2005 as the Paul Smart LE (pictured in chapter 1). The original 750 SS was far beyond the average American motorcycle buyer's radar. It belonged to those following the European race circuits, and to those capable of maintaining an exotic machine.

By 1975 Ducati introduced a bike that vintage sportbike enthusiasts dream about: the formidable 900 SS with its distinctive square cases. Photo is of a 1977.

Ducati's practical GT1000 was retro-styled after the company's sportbikes from the 1970s. They produced these only from 2007 to 2010.

A bike ahead of its time. The MV Agusta 750S America was designed to bring Italian thoroughbred sporting machines to the United States. The company's racing success was legendary. But despite its exotic double overhead cam engine and a 130 mph top speed, the market wasn't quite ready for it in 1975. The European version also looked a lot better. Marketers seemed to think Americans liked angular-shaped tanks, much like the BSA Rocket 3.

Things got serious among the Japanese rivals as they created larger and faster bikes. Honda's 1983 CB1100F hit the 100 hp mark to allow the bike a top speed of 139 mph. Honda used its Grand Prix racing success with rider "Fast" Freddie Spencer to market these superbikes. These are good-looking machines that can still hold their own today.

As its next milestone, Honda defined the sportsbike category for generations to come with its 1983 introduction of the V45 VF750F Interceptor. The bike featured a perimeter steel box section welded frame supporting the 86 hp 90-degree V4 engine as used on the Sabre. It was also the first production bike to have a slipper clutch to prevent rear wheel lock-up on fast deceleration. Final drive was by chain rather than shaft. Despite high hopes, issues relating to the chain-driven overhead cams resulted in a poor service record. The machine pictured is a second-generation Interceptor introduced in 1986. The bike, labeled VFR750F, was fitted with a re-engineered V45 engine modeled after the European VF1000R. The resulting machine was true sport, and a gift to the sportbike enthusiast. Collectors should shy away from earlier VF models. The VFR's redesigned engine with gear-driven double overhead cams, highly tuned port geometry, twinspar aluminum frame, monoshock, triple-discs, and excellent handling gave the critics something to rave about. VFRs saw good results on the racetrack as well—particularly in the AMA Superbike Championship series. The bike was branded as the Interceptor in the United States and featured impressive performance specs: 105 hp, six speeds, and a 145 mph top speed. We are talking about a bike that was officially classified as vintage in 2011. It is worth seeking one out. The Interceptor line also included a 500.

Laverda was best known in Italy for building agricultural machinery. The founder's interest in motorcycles motivated him to build his own line of bikes. Introduced in 1972, the 750 SF offered hungry European sport riders yet another great option. The single overhead engine does remind one of Honda's earlier twins. Everyone was studying the other makers' designs during this exciting era of engineering. Laverda upped the game in 1976 with the 1,000cc three-cylinder Jota, a magnificent sporting machine offering a great power-to-weight ratio with its 90 hp engine. Look for models prior to 1982. They featured the 180-degree crankpin position that gave the earlier models their signature sound and feel.

This stunning example of motorcycle design is BMW's 1975 R90S. It represents the company's victorious race bikes of the period. The R90S line was first introduced in late 1973 in smoke grey, and lasted until 1976. The pushrod-actuated overhead valve flat-twin engine was not anywhere near as technically advanced as the multi-cylinder Japanese or Italian machines, but proved to be highly reliable and capable of doing the job. The bike's sporting capabilities were not up to its sporting good looks, but no one cared. Most of the people buying these machines could afford paying twice the price of a Honda 750, and used them as great sport touring machines.

The radically styled 1981 Suzuki GSX1100S Katana drew immediate attention. Sleek bodywork and a powerful 100hp engine made it one of the fastest mass-production bikes of the day. The futuristic style was the work of Hans Muth, a former BMW designer. Pictured is a wire-wheel 1100SZ Katana. The Z model included factory performance parts. Photo courtesy of Robert Newall.

Another milestone year for motorcycling, and for Kawasaki, was 1984, with the introduction of the Ninja GPZ900R. This liquid-cooled 16-valve four-cylinder superbike was an instant hit after it appeared in *Top Gun* with Tom Cruise at the controls. The 115 hp engine was capable of 11-second quarter-mile times.

Suzuki kept evolving its sportbikes. The GSX-R1100 line ended in 1998 but was key in transitioning the company's engines during the 1980s and 1990s from air to oil, and then water-cooling. Higher compressions are attainable with cooler heads and, therefore, more power is attainable.

Yamaha's RZ350 came as a direct result of its successful RD350. The RZ is, however, liquid-cooled to produce more power. The bike came out in 1983 in commemoration of Kenny Roberts's successes on the European Grand Prix racetracks. Smog regulation soon ended the two-stroke street bike.

Race-replicas from the glory days of Grand Prix racing during the 1980s make great conversation pieces at any rally. One can imagine the Suzuki on the left going head-to-head with the Honda on the right.

The Kawasaki Ninja 500 (center) was a parallel twin available from 1987 to 2009. It was a light and nimble bike that was an ideal all-arounder because of its more upright seating position. It is a great find for entry-level vintage sportbike enthusiasts. The Honda CBX1000 six-cylinder to the right dwarfs the Ninja with three times as many cylinders.

At 600 pounds, the 1,000cc CBX was unique among other sportbikes of the day. It did promise 105 hp, making it the most powerful production bike when it was introduced. A lot of Grand Prix engineering went into the motor to manage weight and technical complexity. Camshafts, for example, were hollowed out to reduce mass. The massive engine hung from a very strong frame. The higher cost of this machine and maintenance reduced its appeal. The twenty-four small valves were a lot to adjust, and six carburetors were not easy to synchronize by a backyard mechanic. The bike was better as a sport tourer and has a strong following today. It was available only from 1978 to 1982.

BMW stayed in the sportbike game stronger than ever after the R90S. Despite its success with twin-cylinder bikes, the company explored three- and four-cylinder water-cooled technology to the fullest. Its success with the K100 prompted it to enter the superbike arena in 1989 with the four-cylinder 95 hp 987cc liquid-cooled DOHC K1. Typical of BMW, this 612 pound bike used a driveshaft. It could approach 145 mph. Only 6,921 were made during its four year run. Photo courtesy of Peter Frechie.

Few Harley-Davidson owners know about the Motor Company's remarkable 1994 VR1000 superbike designed for AMA racing. The 135 hp 60-degree liquid-cooled DOHC V-twin was the first racing bike Harley ever built from the ground up. All others were highly modified production machines. In order to race in the Superbike category, a manufacturer would have to make at least fifty production bikes. Harley did that, but sold most to Poland at $49,490 each. EPA rules made it difficult to sell in the United States. The engine was later refined by Porsche to power the V-Rod cruisers. Not quite up to the specs of a comparable Ducati, the VR1000 could have easily held its own with sportbike buyers had it been available in the United States, assuming higher volume production dropped the price to something more reasonable. The bike had an unusual paint scheme: orange-red on the right side and completely black on the other. A white stripe down the middle separated the colors. VR1000's can be found all over the world. Many have been made street-legal by fitting them with proper lights and signals. Pictured is one such example found in Japan. Harley-Davidson announced in 2015 that it intends to revive the VR1000 for World Superbike Racing, this time at the allowable 1,200cc displacement. Photo courtesy of MY Performance, classicharley.jp

There are few bikes that evoke the blue-blooded GP racing heritage of an MV Agusta F4. This exotic machine was championed by Cagiva's CEO and visionary Claudio Castiglione. Cagiva had purchased the ailing MV brand in the 1980s. For those fortunate enough to afford $19,000 for a new one when it was introduced in 1999, the remarkable 750cc F4-750S represented the highest standards in quality and engineering. Compared to liter-plus bikes, its 129 hp may be modest, but with a 13,300 redline, top speed is over 170 mph. Good used ones are well worth tracking down. Harley-Davidson bought the brand in 2009 but sold it quickly. History has proven that bike manufacturers should stick with their core products that have proven to be successful.

American sportbike builder Erik Buell started producing bikes in 1983 using highly modified Harley-Davidson Sportster engines mounted within frames of his own design. His understanding of sportbikes was derived through his successful racing career. Buell's well-deserved reputation resulted in Harley-Davidson acquiring equity in the brand ten years later. Bikes like the S1 Lightning, S3 Thunderbolt, Ulysses XB12X, and Firebolt (pictured) gave the world a unique take on high-performance sportbikes. Buell kept evolving his machines with innovative frame geometry and water-cooled Rotax-engineered engines, resulting in a glorious 2009 AMA Pro Road Racing Daytona SportBike championship win by rider Danny Eslick on an 1125R. Despite this success, Harley-Davidson closed the brand down in 2009 and purchased MV Agusta.

Most true sportbikes have a strong aftermarket product base. This tricked-out Yoshimura Suzuki GSX- R1000 is a track-day racer's dream. Its eye-catching fairings hide a ported and polished engine with a big bore kit and racing cams. This is not a kid's bike in either price or performance. Yoshimura is Suzuki's racing partner that also provides performance parts and kits for a broad array of machines on and off-road. The company was founded in 1954 and quickly gained a reputation for high-performance tuning of bikes and cars.

Erik Buell went on to start EBR Motorcycles (Erik Buell Racing), producing outstanding race bikes. Based on this success, the EBR line of street sportbikes emerged, featuring the 1190SX and RX. These machines are still powered by V-twins, albeit water-cooled advanced engines making 185 hp. EBR's flagship racer, the RS, shown in its 1190RR Superbike racing version, weighs an astonishingly light 389 pounds.—lighter than most middleweights. Note the large front brake disk, allowing greater leverage for stopping. Unfortunately, due to a lack of funding, EBR went into receivership in April of 2015. EBR's technology and design consulting business was acquired by EBR shareholder Hero MotoCorp. of India. With the aid of Liquid Asset Partners, EBR lives on. EBR Motorcycles, LLC, resumed production in 2016 of its 1190RX and 1190SX bikes. Photo courtesy of EBR Motorcycles.

The Buell Blast used a 492cc single-cylinder power plant originally derived from an 883 Harley-Davidson Sportster engine. It was a noble idea that would have introduced a lightweight entry-level sportbike to many. Unfortunately production costs killed the model in 2009.

Moto Guzzi was the first Italian marque to win an Isle of Man Senior TT. This occurred in 1935. Since then its sportbike efforts have produced some superb machines. The Le Mans line started in 1976 with the 850cc transverse mounted V-twin. The line evolved through 2004 with larger engines and better frame designs. The 1,000cc Le Mans pictured was introduced in 1984 and lasted all the way through 1993.

What at first glance seems like a typical L-twin Ducati on the left is really a bike for those with deep pockets. It is one of the ultimate superbike prizes of the new millennium. It is Ducati's $72,000 Desmosedici RR, a replica of the marques 2006 MotoGP V-4 racing machine. The bike was the closest thing to a real MotoGP racer one can drive on the street until the 2015 introduction of Honda's RC213V-S. The humble bike to the right is an Italian-built 2002 MV Agusta F4 Senna. The 750cc supersport commemorates Brazilian Formula 1 hero Ayrton Senna.

The Yamaha YZF-R1 superbike line was introduced to a speed-hungry market in 1998. Featuring a new compact gearbox design, the bike allowed the power unit to be mounted more forward in its aluminum Deltabox II frame. This distributed the weight for impressive handling, while holding the 150 hp engine secure. The latest generation of the YZF-R1 boasts 200 hp, and is loaded with MotoGP electronic gadgetry. The carbon-fiber bodied R1M takes it one step further with Öhlins Electronic Race Suspension, GPS ride data capture, and traction control presets via smartphone. Photo courtesy of Yamaha Motor Corporation.

Sitting next to a Buell is the MV Agusta Brutale. The original 910cc bike rang true to its name in more ways than one. Despite its brutal 136 horses, its handling was a bit brutal as well. Redesigned for handling in 2010, the Brutale 1090RR is a fantastic 144 hp Italian stallion. Its naked engine suspended from its red trellis frame will surely intimidate and turn heads.

Sportbike design is less fickle than the ever-changing world of high fashion. Things take a bit longer to evolve. Such is the case with the current trend in naked bikes. Gone are the cumbersome fairings on many new models, exposing a delicious view of machinery. Mechanical art is now considered in all engineering. Yamaha's exceptional FZ-07 is a perfect example of style and unabashed machine sculpture. Interestingly, this torque-laden 689cc parallel twin has found itself at home on the AMA Pro Flat Track racing circuit. Its larger brother, the FZ-09, does everything as well but with 108 horses. Both bikes could also be classified as standards since they are so very versatile. Photo courtesy of Yamaha Motor Corporation, U.S.A.

Austrian KTM is best known for its race-winning off-road machines. Its entrée into sportbikes was no less remarkable. Its 1290 Super Duke V-twin features state-of-the-art DOHC four-valve cylinder heads with twin plug ignition and advanced engine management system. A slipper clutch will keep the rear wheel of this 180 hp beast from skipping when the throttle is suddenly backed off. A single-cylinder 690 Duke is also available for those who love torque off the line.

Suzuki's GSX-S750 is classified by the company as a standard. It is, however, a nimble, bare bones four-cylinder fuel-injected sportbike with civil ergonomics. Missing are traction control and ABS. This makes it affordable and attractive to buyers looking to experience riding without electronic intervention. Pictured is the colorful Z model. Photo courtesy of Suzuki Motor of America, Inc.

The Japanese, Germans, British, and Italians are not the only ones making affordable and fun to ride middleweight sportbikes. Korean Hyosung has entered the game and is making a good impression with its GT650R. Photo courtesy of Hyosung Motors USA.

India produces many small displacement sportbikes. The largest maker is Hero MotoCorp Ltd. Its most popular sportbike is the Karizma, powered by a 223cc air-cooled, four-stroke single-cylinder, overhead cam, fuel-injected engine. The bike pictured is an Apache RTR sportbike made by TVS Motor Company. It is powered by a 177.4cc single-cylinder engine. Despite the showing of the countless testosterone-filled bikes from Japan, Germany, and Italy in these pages, there is a clear role for small displacement machines given the roads people use them on, and affordability. Bigger isn't always better. Photo courtesy of Tamara Hayden.

Chinese-made Lifan sportbikes are slowly making an appearance in the United States.

Exotic and Unusual Sportbikes

The sportbike category is all about speed, technology, and the sheer sex appeal of design. They are often the direct result of purpose-built racing machines. The Britten is a true example of that. John Britten, a New Zealander, was dissatisfied with the Italian engines used on his own race bikes. In 1986, he decided to start with a clean sheet of paper, designing a complete racing motorcycle from scratch, engine and all. Britten cast all his own engine components and fabricated radical new bodywork out of carbon fiber. The results were stunning. Two DOHC models were created: the Britten V1000 and the one-off five-valve V1100. The V1000 produced 166 hp and placed second and third in the prestigious Battle of the Twins in Daytona in 1991. This shocked the well-funded factory teams. What shocked them even more was Britten's first-place win the following year at Assen, Holland. Unfortunately, John Britten lost his life to cancer at the young age of forty-five. Only ten V1000 Brittens exist today.

The Britten has many highly innovative engineering features, including extensive use of carbon fiber. A unique feature is its cooling system. Air enters the front and is channeled through the bodywork to cool the radiator under the seat. This greatly reduces drag up front from a broad radiator. Photo courtesy of Solvang Vintage Motorcycle Museum.

Confederate makes exotic American motorcycles. They are as artistic as they are powerful. The Hellcat X132 pictured features a massive 2,163cc V-twin putting out a 121 bhp and 140 ft-lb of torque. Founder H. Matthew Chambers wanted this to be a no-expense-spared bike for people who want to be exclusive and own a very special motorcycle. Photo by Stephen Covell.

Only Italian engineers passionate about motorcycles can build a stunning technical creation such as the Vyrus. Initially collaborating with Bimota, Vyrus branched out on its own to build a leading-edge sportbike. It is distinguished by hub-center steering front suspension, and it uses Ducati engines. Photo courtesy of Vyrus. vyrus.it

The Ronin began as an appreciation of the beauty of a naked 2008 Buell® 1125 by executives from Magpul Industries, Inc. A creative design exercise resulted in the acclaimed 2010 Magpul® Ronin. Ronin Motor Works of Denver was established to build production bikes in a small shop. Photo courtesy of Ronin Motorworks LLC., the47.com

For those looking for a highly unique sportbike that can be ridden on the street, there is always the option to have one built by a quality custom shop like NYC Norton. The bike in the photo is their Seeley Norton Streetfighter. It is as custom as they come. Despite the Norton reference, little remains of an original Norton. The engine is a highly modified 1,077cc mill tuned by Steve Maney. The frame is a masterfully crafted Seeley MK2 replica racing chassis. The transmission is a five-speed magnesium gearbox by TT Industries. The front end is a racing unit from Norvil. Countless handcrafted components and an alloy tank complete the package. nycnorton.com

In the tradition of the Vincent Black Shadow, there is always a bike that claims to be the world's fastest production motorcycle. The Y2K pictured is made by Marine Turbine Technologies and has received the Guinness World Record for the world's fastest production motorcycle. For now, this may just be so, but challengers abound. The Lightning electric superbike and the 2015 Kawasaki H2R will certainly challenge the title. The Y2K jet bike was the company's first model, introduced in 2000. Subsequent models have made the machine even more formidable. The Y2K's Rolls-Royce Allison turbine produces 320 hp and a whopping 425 ft-lbs of torque. This will rocket the rider to 250 mph faster than anything else with a license plate. The only thing to watch out for on this $175,000 bike is the exhaust. It is capable of melting plastic bumpers on cars parked too close to it. Photo courtesy of Marine Turbine, marineturbine.com

Lotus, best known for its exotic sports cars, announced in 2013 that it is trying its hand at high-performance motorcycles. The C-01 is powered by a 200 hp V-twin. The frame is just as exotic as the brand's lineage. It is made of aero tech steel, titanium, and carbon fiber. Photo courtesy of Lotus Motorcycles, PMC, Daniel Simon and Herman Köpf, photographer.

Kawasaki's Ninja H2R track bike was introduced to the world late in 2014 and surely deserves recognition for engineering achievement. This remarkable 998cc supercharged rocket was designed to put Kawasaki miles ahead of the competition once again when it comes to gasoline-fueled motorcycles. It will make an even greater impact than its 750cc H2 triple did when it was introduced in 1972. The $50,000 machine is an orchestra of high-technology mechanical and electronic components, including traction and launch control to get off the line as quickly as possible without spinning the wheel. It all works flawlessly together to produce an unrivaled 326 hp sports machine. The company created its own compact 140,000-rpm supercharger, residing behind the engine, to force fuel and air into the high-revving engine at over 38 pounds of pressure. The 200 hp H2 street version will be half-the price but not one bit less exciting. Photo courtesy of Kawasaki Motors Corp., U.S.A.

Honda surprised the sportbike market in 2015 with its 999cc V-4-powered street legal MotoGP RC213V-S. It is very close to the original RC213V machine that brought Marc Márquez championships in 2013 and 2014. Changes include more real-world components, such as valve actuation by springs instead of pneumatics, and a street-friendly transmission. Special features abound to bring this hand-assembled bike's price up to a whopping $184,000. European and Australian versions boast significantly more power than the 101 hp of US imports. This limitation is designed to meet noise standards. However, what happens in the confines of a garage to bring these bikes to life is another story. A special "Sport Kit" available overseas will boost power over 212 hp. But power isn't everything. Race bikes are quick because they are light, quality built, and feature the most advanced components to date. It is Honda's first sportbike that is loaded with electronics supporting traction control, braking, and power settings. Photo courtesy of Honda Motor Co., Ltd.

Clearly the creation of gifted designers, the 2015 Feline is the work of Yacouba. This sportbike is a mélange of the latest technology, materials, and design elements. Its three-cylinder 801cc engine puts out 170 bhp. The price is even more impressive at $280,000. Photo courtesy of Yacouba.

Café Racers

Café racers make up a class of sportbikes that are based on emulating the racing machines of the 1950s and 1960s. They were popularized by British youth looking for faster machines. Just as the Americans bobbed and chopped their Harleys for added speed, the British lightened their Triumphs, Matchlesses, and BSAs to do the same. Lower handlebars or clip-ons replaced those that came with a bike, allowing a forward racer's crouch. Rear-set controls also replaced conventional foot controls and pegs. For those with money, swapping the steel gas tank for an alloy one provides the finishing touch. The combination made for quick street racers.

The term café racer was based on the fact that young groups of motorcyclists would gather at London truck stops. They played racing games after getting hyped-up on coffee. An unfortunate number of kids were killed in these dangerous street races on slick cobblestone streets. The Reverends Bill Shergold and Graham Hullet of the Church of England started the Fifty Nine Club for young motorcyclists in 1962. They effectively provided sensible leadership and guidance. The club's charity work was well received by an otherwise doubtful public.

London's Ace Café and Brighton Beach have become meccas for café racers to gather. The former is home to many café racer reunions and gatherings today. The latter hosted several clashes between the motorcycling Rockers and the trendy scooter crowd called Mods in 1964. The media took advantage and blew the conflict between the social groups far out of proportion. Rockers and Mods still meet annually to enjoy the festivities. Photo thanks to Scott Seiber.

Café racers have several clubs to keep the genre alive and well. They are great places for sharing knowledge of historical machines and technical information. The Brit Iron Rebels and the Ton Up Club have strong Internet forums and clans throughout the world. Pictured is the B.I.R. Philadelphia Clan with author's BSA Gold Star. This picture is dedicated to Cary's memory, standing second from left.

Café racers offer a remarkable connection between rider and machine. Intrinsically spartan, every vibration and engine pulse is felt through the wrists, groin, and ankles. The seating position is uncomfortable, and the bars are far too low for rides longer than a couple of hours. But, riding one makes us look cool . . . pot bellies and all. For us older folks, vintage café racers give us a sense of speed and motoring experience that can easily turn a 60-mph ride through the suburbs into an Isle of Man reincarnation. There is, however, one more trick that limits membership to this exclusive scene. Owning a café racer, especially a vintage one, requires riding skill as well as mechanical skill . . . a prerequisite to motorcycling a long time ago.

Vintage café racers are about the coolest things on two wheels today. Lori's modified 1975 Honda CB400F makes a quick and nimble machine for racing between coffee bars or on the back roads. Photo by Devon and Rina Marie Haas.

The origin of the first café racer is hard to pinpoint, but no doubt it was someone who simply stripped the unnecessary stuff of a standard and made it look like a road racer. A racer named Doug Clark was certainly one of the first to popularize the breed. He put a 650cc Triumph engine into a Norton Manx frame. This put the best of both worlds together. The Triumph parallel twin was better than anything Norton had for power, and the Norton featherbed frame with its Roadholder front forks was better than anything Triumph or BSA had. This famous combination spawned the Triton. So popular was this concept that specialists, like London-based Dresda, started producing Tritons from scratch. Dave Degens of Dresda Autos still makes them.

Café racers are hardly limited to British machinery. Converting a standard to a street racer became popular all over Europe in the 1960s. Italian Moto Guzzis, Japanese Yamahas and Kawasakis, and German BMWs were certainly up for the makeover.

This photo of young bikers admiring a Yamaha TD1B racer at an Earls Court Show in 1966 is clear evidence that Café racers derive their genes from race bikes from the 1960s. Builders today strive to replicate this look. Photo Mortons Archive.

The popularity of café racers has brought the segment to light again for both baby boomers and the young rider looking for something cooler than a stock sportbike or a loud V-twin. Any bike has become open game for a café conversion. The high cost of vintage British bikes has created countless Japanese alternatives. Small multi-cylinder Hondas from the 1970s and 1980s make ideal platforms for fast and reliable café racers. Numerous companies exist that will sell parts for the current crop of popular candidates. New Triumph Bonnevilles and Moto Guzzi V7s are ideal for conversion. Companies like BellaCorse offer an array of components to make a stock Bonneville look like a 1960s café racer.

The surge in café racer interest has prompted makers to build factory models for sale to those that don't want to trouble themselves creating one. Triumph's Thruxton, Royal Enfield's Continental GT, and Moto Guzzi's V7 racer are great current examples. Even Harley-Davidson caught the bug back in 1977 with the introduction of its all-black XLCR Café Racer.

Harley-Davidson took an innovative step in 1977 with its XLCR café racer. The 68 hp 998cc motor, combined with frame elements borrowed from the XR racer, resulted in a better handling machine than a stock Sportster. Reception by the traditional Sportster buyer was limited. Only 3,123 were made during its two-year run. They are extremely desirable today. Photo by Skip Chernoff, courtesy of The Bike Works. Glenside, PA.

Café racing is not just for the young. Seniors like Karl enjoy their high-performance vintage bikes even if it hurts a bit. He was over 70 years old when this picture was taken. The BSA Gold Star he customized has a Munch Mammut front brake.

The Triton is the quintessential British café racer. The marriage of a Triumph parallel twin engine with a Norton chassis is just perfect. Add an aluminum alloy tank, better rear shocks, and a racing seat to make it complete.

Baby boomers live to build café racers. The author (center) is flanked by two of his riding buddies that have built totally custom café racers out of their Nortons. Photo by Karen Diaz Ensanian.

Honda's CB750 SOHC engine makes for a great café racer power plant. This bike is made by award-winning Kott Motorcycles out of Newhall, CA. Kott uses copper accents on many of its quality café racers. Note the wonderful painting by Makoto Endo of the bike in the background.

Not a café racer, but built with the same philosophy for high quality, speed, and tractability, this custom street tracker is one-of-a-kind. Street trackers emulate flat-track racing bikes. William Becker spared no expense in turning a conventional Yamaha XS 650 into this eye-catching machine that blends vintage styling with contemporary technology. Nearly one hundred custom chromoly and aluminum components were made for this build. Learn more about this bike and how to design a café racer at bikeexif. com. Photo by Roman Torres.

Any motorcycle platform can be made into a café racer. This 1970s-era BMW has been stripped of anything unnecessary, including the electric starter.

Small displacement Japanese bikes, like the Honda CB400F, make ideal café racers. This four-cylinder bike was very popular with amateur racers when it was available from 1975 through 1977. A lot of work went into converting this standard into a superb example.

A stock V7 II Racer as available from Moto Guzzi dealers may have been inspired by people building café racers out of the company's reliable V7 standard. This retro-cool bike grabs attention wherever it goes, and rides as well as it looks. Photo courtesy of Moto Guzzi, Piaggio & C SpA.

A Moto Guzzi V7 standard modified brilliantly into a café racer.

Yamaha's Star line of motorcycles offers a café racer version of its sub $9,000 Bolt cruiser. This "C-Spec" air-cooled 942cc V-twin may just be the most practical production V-twin café racer out there. Photo courtesy of Yamaha Motor Corporation.

Triumph's Thruxton line for 2016 has been greatly upgraded with a 1,200cc liquid-cooled motor, and electronic engine, ride, and suspension controls. The pictured R version features race quality inverted Showa Big Piston front suspension and Öhlins shocks in the rear. Brembo calipers do the stopping up front. Photo courtesy of Triumph Motorcycles.

This stunning creation is a modern café racer designed and built by Richard Pollock in conjunction with Richard Varner of Street Master. Varner provided the paint guidelines and the drum brake specifications. Drum brakes clearly give the bike a vintage feel. The Brighton Café Racer features a modern 790cc Triumph motor that has been enhanced to produce 74 hp. Photo by David Edwards and courtesy of Mule Motorcycles mulemotorcycles.net

This vintage-powered Yamaha café racer spotted at a swap meet features an innovative custom rear suspension. Note the mono-shock mounted under the steering head with linkages going back to the swingarm under the engine.

A highly customized and beautifully crafted 1949 Indian Scout is certainly one of the most unusual café racers to appear at the shows. Photo by Stephen Covell.

Many engine and frame combinations exist to produce a unique café racer. Pictured is an Ariel Square 4 engine wedged into a Norton "featherbed" frame.

Norton's famous frame welcomes the V-twin as well. This "Norley" features a Harley-Davidson Sportster engine. Photo by Jerome Guiselin, Santiago Chopper, santiagochopper.com

Another unique and most desirable combination employing a Norton "featherbed" frame is a Norvin. Here a Vincent engine is adapted to the sturdy frame. The engine has to have its integral transmission housing machined off to make it fit. A separate transmission unit is used instead.

This superb example of a Norvin features engine and frame of the same 1955 vintage. Photos thanks to David Tompkins.

Sportbikes Are Fast – A Note of Caution

With power and speed comes risk. Most sub-700cc sportbikes today can eclipse 140 mph, with larger displacements reaching over 180 mph. Obviously, anything over the speed limit is outright dangerous on roads fraught with motorists blind to motorcycles. We all ride above it, but few of us live in open spaces where high speed riding is not consequential. Those roads may be an endless stretch in Nevada or Montana, but not where many of us ride on a daily basis.

Experienced sportbike riders recognize the risks associated with high-speed riding. Proper gear includes a reputable helmet, gloves, boots, and a riding suit with armor and spine pad.

Some of us have the skill to weave in and out of traffic at a hundred or more, but the reality is that the reaction times required to survive are beyond our capacity to synapse when someone who doesn't even know we are there jumps out in front of us. This is how most motorcycle accidents happen—an automobile cuts in front of the rider. It is therefore advisable to enjoy the full capability of a sportbike on the track, or on twisty roads where handling outweighs speed. It is also advisable to wear the proper gear, including full-face helmet, gloves, boots, leathers with armor and a spine pad. Even though many states, like Pennsylvania, Connecticut, and Florida don't enforce wearing a helmet despite enforcing the use of seatbelts, one needs to be smart about one's own life. I have fallen numerous times and can say without uncertainty that the helmet saved my life. Most serious falls end up on the head.

Even the most skilled professional rider cannot predict where and how he or she will land in a fall. In most cases, it includes the head. Photo Paul Crock/Getty Images.

Buying a Used Sportbike

Modern design sportbikes have been around for decades. Buying a used one is disconcerting for the average rider who lacks the mechanical experience to tell if they are buying a winner or loser. But with so many sportbikes made between the 1980s and 2000, with care, one can find great handling machines between $2,000 and $3,000. It pays to peruse the web forums and special interest groups to get a handle on what's what. An online site such as eBay will give one a good idea what to expect in cost. However, nothing beats having a good bike mechanic look the machine over. If you don't have one, look for used bikes at a dealership. The extra cost and warranty will be worth the aggravation if something serious breaks.

What to Look for

Don't be deceived by pretty-looking plastic. Clean fairings do not signal a mechanically sound bike. Look for any frame repairs, unusual welds, or dented metal components. Scuffed turn signals, lower frame, front forks, and mufflers indicate the bike has fallen. This is nothing alarming in itself given that we will all fall eventually, but something that signals paying attention to other areas. Check for alignment by standing behind the bike and seeing if the wheels fall on the same track. Fork tubes must be absolutely parallel. Start the engine cold. Feel it to make sure the seller didn't warm it up before. It should sound smooth, with no serious mechanical noises coming out of it. A bit of whirring is quite normal as gears and chains spin inside the cases. Clanging and slapping sounds are not good. Let the motor idle until it is good and hot to reveal any issues. A smoking exhaust is also not a good sign. Light bluish exhaust indicates a worn engine that burns oil. Check the engine oil. Dirty black oil and a dry, rusty chain say the owner didn't care about maintenance. Take a close look at the rear drive sprocket. If the teeth look worn on one side, or come to a sharp point, the bike has seen some use. If specific teeth are broken, that means the owner beat on the bike. Sprockets and chains are easily changed. Excessive corrosion on the alumi-

num engine also shows signs of neglect. Check wheels for damage. Severely dented rims usually mean excessive impact of some sort. Don't accept any unreasonable excuses for damage.

This used bike looks great at twenty feet, but closer inspection shows that it has been dumped more than once. Scuffs on the bodywork and a brand new muffler are giveaways. That all in itself should not be a problem. Most of it is cosmetic. What would be a problem is a bent frame or front forks, easily identified with careful observation.

Before you take the bike for a local spin, check front, tail, and brake lights, as well as turn signals. Don't compromise with the electrics. Anyone can charge a battery and sell a bike with a bad alternator. You must run it through all the gears to detect any brake, clutch, and transmission issues. Wear a helmet; you don't know this bike. If they don't let you ride it, walk away. If the clutch grabs abruptly or unevenly, there are issues. In all cases, check the VIN registration number on the title against the one on the bike, usually found by the steering head. If all is well and you get a sense that the owner has been forthright, make an offer far below the asking price to test a willingness to dump the bike quickly. That should raise some concerns. Don't forget to ask if there are any parts lying around in the garage, especially if aftermarket parts like exhaust pipes, mufflers, and windshields have been added.

Motorcycle Medic

Chapter 7

RIDING ON THE WILD SIDE

The world of custom motorcycles is where art meets function. Born out of necessity, and a desire for speed, custom motorcycles evolved into highly individualized vehicles for personal expression. Created by artist and mechanic, one sometimes questions their practicality but cannot deny their striking craftsmanship and beauty.

Arch Motorcycle Company

Design with a Purpose

The motorcycle has always been a good canvas for expressing one's creativity. Customization was born from necessity at first. Hill climbers needed to lengthen frames and remove absolutely anything unnecessary for tearing up a hill. Class C amateur racers stripped their street bikes of heavy front fenders, bobbed the rear one, and removed toolboxes and lights to gain a few extra miles per hour around the track. The minimalist style and clean lines of these bikes attracted much attention. Motorcyclists looking to be different emulated these sleek machines by modifying their roadsters. Creative expression, combined with bold fabrication, perpetuated this trend. Today, it has reached a point where design can easily outweigh function. There are, however, bikes that balance both. Those are the classic American bobber and chopper.

A classic Harley-Davidson Knucklehead bobber representative of Class C racing motorcycles of the 1930s and 1940s. This pristine example has been customized slightly with painted rims and a smaller rear fender.

The minimalist style of bobbed and chopped bikes started becoming a symbol for the independent biker in the 1920s. Paul D'Orléans's masterful book, *The Chopper: The Real Story*, provides great insight on how this concept unfolded in California. Harley-Davidson J models were among the first to see custom modification for street use. Upper frame tubes were cut to lower the overall appearance of the bike. These were called "cut-downs." By the late 1950s, highly customized bikes with rigid frames, low unsprung seats, extended forks, and high handlebars were being referred to as "chop-jobs." This eventually changed to the term "chopper."

Chopping Away

Light and fast British bikes encouraged further chopping of heavy American bike frame components, floorboards, and big tanks to make the big V-twins more competitive on the street and track. Customization grew quickly during the 1950s as more older Harleys and Indians were available for cheap. By the 1960s the American chopper became standardized as an art form. It was unique—ridiculed and admired by a world of motorcyclists that never really looked at machines that way before. Steering heads on frames were "raked" to exaggerate the angle of the front fork tubes. This allowed for even longer fork tubes to be installed that elevated the front end. A skinny front tire offered a light and elegant feel to the vehicle. Adding a fat rear tire balanced the whole thing out, and provided a bit of hot-rod attitude. A "sissybar" accentuated the rear, and served well as a backrest or tie-down point for a bedroll. A small "peanut" tank allowed the glorious V-twin engine to stand out. Most engines were Harley-Davidson, of course. Finishing features like high handlebars became a sign of defiance against the norm, while unmuffled upswept pipes let everyone know that a chopper was coming.

Captain America, the featured bike in *Easy Rider*, epitomizes the American custom chopper, sporting a Harley Davidson 74 cubic inch Panhead engine, so named because of the pan-shaped valve covers on top of the cylinders. Photo is of a replica at the AMA Hall of Fame Museum. The original was designed by Cliff "Soney" Vaughs and built by Ben Hardy in 1969.

Chopped Brits

British bike owners not into the Café racer scene chopped and bobbed their bikes as well. Standard Triumph frames would have their rear sections unbolted and replaced with a rigid "hardtail." Minimalism had its price. Perfectly comfortable bikes became Spartan expressions of individualism.

A classic Triumph bobber featuring a hardtail frame and sprung saddle mimics the American bobber from the 1930s. Photo courtesy of Skip Chernoff..

Not all customized Triumphs ended up as bobbers or café racers. The "street tracker" in front left the factory looking just like the stock 1979 Bonneville in the back.

This photo shows a unique take on customizing a vintage Triumph. Painting or powder coating the engine and transmission on any bike opens up a whole new world. Photo by Stephen Covell.

Custom Triumphs today can take on a very different look. Don Weimer Jr. builds one-off machines that would have had Ed Turner scratching his head. Based on a 1973 Triumph 750 Bonneville, this bike, called the Revelation, features subtle elements of a hill climber, a tribute to his father. Photo courtesy Don Weimer Jr.

Chopped Japanese

Not everyone could afford a Harley or a Triumph to chop. Others wanted to experiment with combining high-tech Japanese motors with custom chopper frames. The results produced some interesting-looking machines using Japanese engines and cycle parts. The less expensive Japanese bikes offer great opportunity for those on a budget. Today, vintage Japanese bikes are seeing a huge rebirth in the custom motorcycle segment.

It did not take long for custom bike makers to build choppers around Japanese engines. This Honda 750–powered chopper from the 1970s features a custom rigid frame, a period style coffin tank, and extended springer forks. As was often the case with choppers, there was no front brake.

A superb example of a mid-1970s Honda 350 customized into a bobber. The wide availability of small displacement Japanese bikes allows creative builders to experiment freely without significant cost. Photo courtesy of Malvina Dimeas.

The Groovy 1960s

The custom bike scene flourished during the 1960s. The style reflected the era well—creative and irreverent. Artists like Ed Roth and Kenny

Howard, more widely known as Von Dutch, led the "Kustom Kulture" movement that emerged. They presented true works of mobile art that even the non-motorcyclist could appreciate. Most of the action took place on opposite coasts. Among the best on the East Coast was New Yorker Indian Larry. A true artist and craftsman, he built motorcycles in ways few imagined. Indian Larry (DeSmedt) continued to be an icon with his bikes and with his antics. He often rode his machine standing on the seat with arms extended outward as if he was flying. His presence in film, magazines, TV, and the Discovery Channel show *Biker Build-Off* created great awareness among the average American of the chopper culture.

California artist and hot rod builder Ed Roth took full advantage of the chopper as a medium to build motorcycles reminiscent of his crazy cartoons. Ed "Big Daddy Roth" is best known for his Rat Fink character. He inspired many of the custom builders that followed.

One of Indian Larry's most stunning creations was his 2004 *Chain of Mystery* bike. It featured extensive custom engraving and casting throughout the engine and transmission. The frame and springer front forks were made of welded chain links. Indian Larry's bikes were artistic expressions of the 1950s-style customs.

The 1960s brought many great custom builders. One of the greats is Arlen Ness. His creations, like this dual Harley-Davidson Sportster–engined custom built in the 1970s, were radical to say the least. This bike, named *Two Bad*, has many highly unique engineering features, including supercharging and hub-center steering.

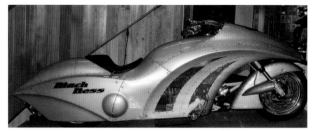

Arlen Ness continues to create the most far-reaching customs. This 2005 creation, called Mach-Ness, is powered by a helicopter jet engine. Arlen and his son Corey provide custom designs for the Victory brand.

Japanese Makers See Opportunity

The Japanese motorcycle makers were not oblivious to America's love for choppers. Models came out in the 1980s that featured V-twin engines and resembled three-quarter sized versions of custom choppers. Yamaha's Virago was the first to come to market in 1981. Honda soon followed with its Shadow line. The Virago lasted for over twenty years in various engine sizes. Honda still makes the Shadow, albeit in more traditional cruiser styling than originally introduced.

The Honda Shadow cruiser line started in 1983. Like the Yamaha Virago, they almost seemed like caricatures of the classic American chopper. Considered cool by young riders who looked at Harley-Davidsons as too expensive, these bikes sold well. Pictured is a 500cc VT500.

The biggest surprise in the cruiser world came from Honda when it introduced its 2010 custom SOHC 1,312cc liquid-cooled, shaft-driven Fury® chopper. This is quite a statement in that Honda's entry into the American market started with bikes designed to provide sporting fun for the absolute other side of the consumer bike segment: small, friendly, easy to ride machines for non-biker types. I would call this bike a "gentleman's chopper," sophisticated and technically refined.

Mass Customization

The custom bike industry flourished into the millennium. It coincided perfectly with the boom in cruiser sales. People wanted to have something different and were willing to pay big dollars for it. Custom shops sprang up all over the country. Builders would either fabricate or buy ready-made components from big manufacturers. Business was brisk. Depending on paint, engine specs, and the amount of metal fabrication that was required, a custom bike could easily cost between $40,000 and $150,000.

A close view of a one-off custom shows the extreme fabrication required that drives up cost. The single-sided swingarm alone represents a significant investment in time and material. The same applies to nearly every other detail on the bike.

Cable television shows featuring famous builders served as advertising for the industry. Demand increased, motivating the formation of several high volume production manufacturers of custom and semi-custom bikes. Semi-customs were bikes that were produced in large numbers by a manufacturer patterned after a frame of their own design. Sheet metal components were also pretty standardized. The buyer would then select options to make the bike unique. These included engines, wheels, paint, bars, and seats. Buyers could pick and choose these components and paint schemes from a catalog, saving tens of thousands of dollars compared to one-off original designs. Production semi-customs typically sold between $20,000 and 50,000. Most noted of these was Big Dog Motorcycles out of Wichita, Kansas. They made thousands of motorcycles while in business between 1994 and 2011. Their dealer network was quite extensive. The company is planning on getting back into production in 2016. American IronHorse was another noted volume builder operating out of Fort Worth, Texas, between 1995 and 2008.

Big Dog Motorcycles named its bikes along the lines of the canine theme. This 2008 K-9 with custom paint and 117 cubic inch engine is typical of the company's high-quality semi-custom choppers at prices far less than one-offs. The use of a massive rear tire was popular with custom builders. Photo courtesy of Matt Ramieri.

An award-winning American IronHorse Slammer that has been further customized with special wheels, motor detailing, paint, and LED lighting. The lights create a stunning night effect. Photo courtesy of Steve Testa.

Between the looming recession, an oversaturated custom bike market, and exotic production bikes offered by Harley-Davidson and Japanese makers, many of the large custom bike production facilities eventually closed their doors. The domain now belongs to smaller shops creating highly unique works of mechanical art. One exception is Orange County Choppers (OCC) out of Newburgh, New York. Featured on Discovery Channel's reality show *American Chopper*, the builders have enjoyed great celebrity since 2002. Paul Teutul Sr. and family continue to manufacture one-of-a-kind custom theme bikes and production choppers. Their shop and OCC Café make for a great destination.

Orange County Chopper's founder Paul Teutul Sr. with one of his one-of-a-kind custom bike creations. The level of detail and extensive fabrication can only be appreciated by thorough and careful examination. Photo courtesy of Orange County Choppers.

A decade ago this Yamaha Star Stryker® Bullet Cowl would have been the work of a creative custom shop working out of a back alley garage. It can be bought off the showroom floor for about $12,000. It sports an 80 cubic inch (1,304cc) liquid-cooled SOHC V-twin with 4 valves per cylinder. Photo courtesy of Yamaha Motor Corporation, U.S.A.

Every major manufacturer has creative designers who dream up new motorcycle concepts. Some of the innovative designs end up as production bikes, usually a bit tamed down. Pictured is one of Honda's concepts called the Zodia. Photo courtesy American Honda Motor Co., Inc.

A New Cottage Industry

Custom bike shops have sprung up all over the country over the past couple of decades. They range from an individual working out of a garage to full-blown custom shops taking advanced orders on one-off creations.

Small shop custom bike builders continue to create unique examples of the American custom bike. New Jersey–based Three Nails Motorcycle Union built this stunning bobber using premium components, including a $9,000 93 cubic inch S&S Kuncklehead motor.

Custom choppers are by no means the exclusive domain of the United States. The chopper cult is very popular overseas, especially in Japan, Germany, and Brazil. Pictured is a tasty 1973 "shovelhead"-powered custom built by the Brazilian shop Sophile Choppers. Photo courtesy of Sophile Choppers.

Most custom chopper builders will use a large air-cooled, overhead valve V-twin from Harley-Davidson, S&S Cycle, or RevTech. The engine alone can cost between $5,000 and $15,000. Add another $2,000 to $5,000 in custom paint, a $3,000 transmission, a few more thousand in wheels and controls, and one can easily see why these machines end up costing more than a luxury sedan.

Customizing a bike does not need to be expensive. Small custom shops across the country offer bolt-on accessories that can transform a stock bike into a custom in a matter of hours. The owners of a small Andover, NJ–based shop show two great examples of that. Custom handlebars, handgrips, forward controls, seat, air intake, and exhaust completely transform a machine. Add hydrographic paint and you have a unique ride without having to spend a fortune. This can all be done incrementally, making it much easier on the wallet, and solving the "what to buy me for my birthday" riddle. Photo courtesy of Full Moon Cycles.

Custom choppers have no boundaries when it comes to engines. Even the most unlikely motors can find themselves sitting in a chassis sporting flames and a raked steering head. Clearly on the opposite side of the big V-twin spectrum, this bike features a 1972 Bultaco Alpina 350cc two-stroke motor. Notice the hand shifter. Photo by Stephen Covell.

This interesting custom features 2000 Ducati 900SS L-twin motor. The powerful and light short-stroke sportbike engine is sure to launch this machine off the line quickly. Photo by Stephen Covell.

Choppers are certainly not limited to two- or four-cylinder engines. The good old V-8 has found itself here as well.

Do-it-Yourself or With a Little Help

For those with good mechanical skill, there is the option to build a bike from scratch, or assemble one from a kit. The aftermarket is thriving with makers of custom handlebars, controls, seats, frames, tanks, and wheels. Many catalogs, like J&P Cycles, Custom Chrome, and Dennis Kirk, offer engines, frames, fenders, tanks, lights, and even complete rolling frame kits that allow an enthusiastic wrench to knock out a complete bike over a winter. Local sources for powdercoating the frames and painting tanks and fenders are usually not far away. The variety of engine and frame choices may seem overwhelming, but do allow for true customization. Remarkably, most of this stuff fits without the need to weld or fabricate. Custom bike magazines are a great source for ideas and parts. For those less confident with a wrench, a small local custom bike shop can help with the technical work. These owners are typically more engaged with customers than the mechanics working at large dealerships.

Big bike events, like Sturgis and Daytona, are great places to see the latest offerings from custom bike builders, like Eddie Trotta's Thundercycle.

Art or Machine?

The rest of this chapter will feature a sampling of the endless variety of custom motorcycles out there. Every day a new design or concept rolls out of a garage, be it a ten-seat "stretch limo cruiser," or a three-wheeled rolling sculpture that looks like something out of the movie *Alien*. Enjoy the ride, and get inspired.

Cyril Huze

Cyril Huze may have been brought up in Europe but certainly creates truly extraordinary examples of custom American motorcycles. His stunning designs can easily exceed $100,000. Cyril is highly sensitive to the vision and emotion that drives his customers to commission one of his creations. Not just a motorcycle designer and builder, parts designer, and owner of Cyril Huze Custom Inc., Cyril manages one of the most informative custom motorcycle blogs around: cyrilhuzeblog.com. Photos courtesy of Cyril Huze.

The stunning "Bombshell" by Cyril Huze is a sensuous take on WWII-era Air Force aircraft.

Another Cyril Huze masterpiece, called "Fireman." It begs hours of admiration as one discovers one detail after another.

Wicked Steel

Steve Galvin is unlike any other custom builder. He is a recording musician who builds the most unusual award-winning custom bike creations right in his garage in Saint Petersburg, Florida. These bikes are so technically remarkable that anyone would think they come out of an engineering lab. Check out his website at wikkedsteel.com to see how these machines are constructed. Photos courtesy of Steve Galvin.

Steve Galvin's top show winner "Pipe Dream."

Detail of "Pipe Dream" showing that it actually has three wheels in the back. A jackshaft off the transmission is connected to a number of chains that drive the wheels. A total of five chains are used in this engineering marvel.

Another one of Steve's astonishing show-winners is his 130 hp "Area 51 Version 2.0" creation. As he says, "it is hard to stop looking at this bike." Photography by Steve Giese.

Steve describes the stunning "Dragon Bike" as having been built on a Pro-Street Frameworks frame, 45-degree rake, 6-inch stretch and stock height. Rear tire is a 330 Avon; front is a 120–70 Avon. Wheels are from Tight Customs in California. American Suspension springer front end, Ultima El Bruto 120-inch engine with a Trik-Shift six-speed gearbox. It all sounds very expensive. Photography by Steve Giese.

Kingdom Custom

Kingdom Customs Motorcycle Company is based in Waipahu, Hawaii. Dan Kokubun, president, and his team create highly luxurious performance customs. The detail work reminds one of handcrafted luxury automotive coachwork from the 1930s by Bugatti and Mercedes. Photos courtesy of Kingdom Customs Motorcycle Company LLC, kingdom-customs.com.

Detail views of the "Stiletto" showing the extensive metalworking craftsmanship that goes into custom bikes.

The "Stiletto" features S&S or Ultima engines. They are custom built for each client, and no two are the same.

Freebird Customs

Freebird Custom Trikes & Motorcycles was started by Rick Strand. His vision of highly usable bikes is well reflected in the shop's line. Rick has since left this earth, but his team, partnered with Reds Cycle in Vidor, Texas, still produces remarkable machines, including trikes for the handicapped. They also sell bike and trike kits for those looking to build their own custom. Photo courtesy of Freebird Customs, freebirdcustomtrikes.com

A signature bike for Freebird Custom Motorcycles is its gorgeous bagger named "The Purity." It was built with 14k gold, white buffalo hide leather seat, high chrome, and gold-painted artwork.

Another Freebird signature product is this quality built trike, named "Purgatory." It's the closest a trike can possibly get to looking like a real chopper.

Matt Risley Innovation

Matt Risley Innovation is based in Phoenix, Arizona. Its founder, Matt, may have started his education off pursuing a teaching degree, but he ended up instead with an advanced technical degree that is well reflected in his custom bikes and trikes. Photo courtesy Matt Risley Innovation LLC.

One of the most eye-catching and elegant trikes around is MRI's 2006 creation for customer Barbara. Over 2,500 hours of labor went into this machine. It is powered by a huge 124 cubic inch S&S motor. It also has two TVs, two amplifiers, and two cameras.

SS Trike

While we are talking about trikes, it is imperative to mention the amazing custom trike creations coming out of Rudolph, Wisconsin. SS Trike builds machines that bring out the kid in us. Looking like an adult version of the notorious "Big Wheel" low-riding tricycle, these machines are certain to bring out the same kind of joy reminiscent of carefree years. Many custom styles and options are available. The price for this unique machine is about $40,000. Photo courtesy of SS Trike LLC, sstrikes.com.

The technical specifications on this SS Trike offer insight into the unique nature of the machine. The 117 cubic inch fuel-injected S&S X-Wedge engine powers the wheels through a two-speed automatic transmission with lockup torque converter. Final drive is a maintenance-free shaft. Seat height is available between thirteen and sixteen inches.

Motorcycle Medic

Motorcycle Medic out of Pittsfield, Massachusetts, produces custom bikes than can only be described as pure "eye candy," especially the pink and lime-green bagger below. Kevin Boyle's creations are totally original. Photos courtesy of Kevin Boyle, vtwinmedic.com.

A careful look reveals technical details that defy convention. One example is found in this red Buell–powered bike. The engine becomes a stressed member of the frame, quite unusual for a custom V-twin chopper.

The graceful curve of the backbone frame is perfectly followed by the custom crafted gas tank.

There is no doubt that this lovely "Shovelhead" Electra Glide® bagger will be the envy of many, particularly the lady riders.

The diversity of Kevin Boyle's designs is evident on this bike. This classic chopper is all about raw power and speed. Lean and mean, it makes for a great daily rider.

FAT300 Custom Cycles

Custom bikes can be found in every segment of motorcycling. In the sports category, there are café racers, and then there are creations such as those produced by George Hatziyiantis out of Cape Coral, Florida. FAT300 Custom Cycles derives its name from the 300mm wide rear tire so often used in extreme custom bikes. George and his team certainly are not limited to 300mm. Photos courtesy of George Hatziyiantis, fat300customcycles.com.

The extended swingarm on this hot Kawasaki ZX14 will keep the front end from flipping too high as the nitrous oxide boosted engine launches this rocket off the line.

Arch Motorcycles

Movie stars like being seen on motorcycles. It adds to the charisma. However, very few are true motorcyclists. Keanu Reeves, co-founder of Arch Motorcycle Company, is definitely the real deal. He has spent tens of thousands of miles in the saddle, on all sorts of bikes. His love of bikes, and a desire to create something true to his own vision of the motorcycle, brought him to designer and builder Gard Hollinger. Together they produced the KRGT-1, an ultra high-quality custom motorcycle that hides a wealth of technology beneath its gleaming exterior. Photos courtesy of Arch Motorcycle Company, archmotorcycle.com.

Co-founders Keanu Reeves and Gard Hollinger with the radiant KRGT-1.

At a distance, the KRGT-1 may look like a café racer to some, a custom cruiser to others, and certainly a sport-bike to most. But walking up to it reveals remarkable design elements surrounding its 124 cubic inch S&S V-twin engine. Foremost is the gas tank. It is machined from 534 pounds of billet aluminum. The process takes sixty-six hours and yields two nine-pound fuel cells that are then custom finished and joined. The right cell interior was designed and reinforced to act as a structural chassis member. Co-developed with S&S Cycle, an innovative "Arch Down Draft Induction System" is contained between the two fuel-cell chambers and frame.

Roquechop Design

Philip Roquebrune, out of Quebec, says that he builds "hardcore handmade bikes." One look will verify that this is an accurate description. The beefy and powerful style is reminiscent of custom chop-jobs from the 1970s built by small back-alley urban shops. There is, however, a difference: quality of components and design innovation. roquechopdesign. com.

Roquebrune's El Brutalos is more than just intimidating. It has endless custom features, including dual magnetos to fire the tricked out "shovelhead" engine, a beefy single-loop frame with a swingarm suspended in the Vincent tradition, exotic brake components, and much more. Photo courtesy of Philip Roquebrune.

VTM SpaceSter

French bike shop VTM has created what can be described as a futuristic and artistic interpretation of the Sportster. Called the SpaceSter, this bike, designed by Bernard "Buck" Massart, goes contrary to most customs. It eliminates the focus on individual components, while stressing fluidity in design. Check out the firm's customs on its website. It clearly shows how American chopper design is alive and well in Europe. Photos courtesy of Bernard Massart, vtm-auch.com.

The Harley-Davidson Sportster engine is hardly recognizable with all the custom metalwork to create the elegant lines. Suspension comes from a set of Yamaha R1 inverted forks, attached to an 18-inch wheel.

This bike is all about aerodynamics. There are no visible cables, wires, or awkward protrusions. The custom-built frame stores the oil.

Bourget's Bike Works

Bourget's Bike Works has been around since 1993, producing a remarkable array of custom choppers and three-wheelers. The company was founded in Phoenix, Arizona, by Brigitte Bourget. They raised quite a few eyebrows over the years with radical designs, engineered and built within their modern 55,000 square foot facility. bourgets.com.

Three wheelers, with two wheels up front, are just as much open to interpretation as any other bike. This eye-catching custom "reverse trike" creation by Bourget's Bike Works seats two comfortably. It is powered by a 117 cubic inch S&S engine. Other unique Bourget creations are visible in the back at this show in Daytona.

Evil Eye

Steve Zagorski out of Long Island makes his living selling custom bike parts for a major supplier. This, however, did not mean he was going to build a bike out of a catalog. Instead, he started with a clean sheet of paper to design Evil Eye. Steve fabricated many of the bike's features himself. That takes a lot of time and patience, but the results are worth it.

Many of Evil Eye's components were shaped, machined, or welded by Steve himself, including the neat girder-type front forks. The bike is full of other unique and interesting features, like the snorkel-type air intake. Photo by Dino Petrocelli, dinopetrocelliphoto.com

Keeping with a vintage theme, Evil Eye sports a hand shift. Photo by Dino Petrocelli.

TPJ Customs

TPJ Customs is a Northern California shop that makes bikes from the ground up, or can supply machined components and accessories for your own creation. They have a remarkable variety of styles available for those looking for a custom ride. Photo courtesy TPJ Customs, tpjcustoms.com.

Pictured is the low and aggressive TPJ bike named Hazel. It is styled to reflect board track racers of the past.

Le Mani Moto

The creativity that surrounds custom motorcycles is unbounded. The melding of art, engineering, metalworking, and leathercraft reaches the highest levels of quality with the Le Mani Moto creations. Le Mani Moto says that it was, "Birthed in the heart and mind of a designer and artist with a love and affinity for all things vintage, classic, venerable and of fine quality." Well, that is certainly true in looking at their work. Photos courtesy of Gary Capone.

This Le Mani Moto creation encompasses vintage board track racer styling with elegant art deco touches, clever engineering, elaborate engraving, and rich paint. Photo by Dino Petrocelli.

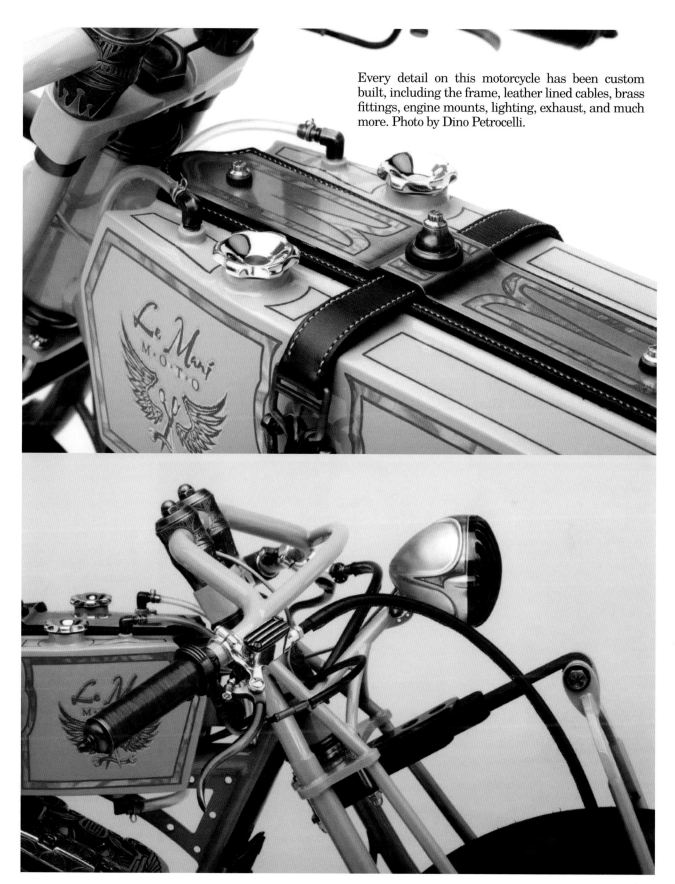

Every detail on this motorcycle has been custom built, including the frame, leather lined cables, brass fittings, engine mounts, lighting, exhaust, and much more. Photo by Dino Petrocelli.

Old Field Motorcycle

Old Field was started in 2008 in Long Island by three friends who love bikes. The brand truly deserves mention here because, unlike all the other bikes listed, these machines are powered by very humble industrial engines not typically used on motorcycles. Old Field's mission is not to create modern high-tech motorcycles, but rather focus on the look of earlier bikes. They incorporate modern components that assure dependability while keeping the finished product simple with the reliability that is expected in a modern-day bike. The company also offers to custom build you a frame to fit any motor you wish to install, be it an old dirt bike two-stroke, or a Honda engine from the 1980s. Photos courtesy of Old Field Motorcycle Mfg., oldfieldmotorcycle.com.

Old Field uses industrial motors like this 18 hp V-twin Koehler to power its bikes. They are fast enough to keep up with local traffic. The convenience of not having to shift makes these great bikes for new riders. They use a belt-driven torque converter.

Early motorcycle style is certainly visible in Old Field bikes, but things like electric start, overhead valves, hydraulic lifters, electronic ignition, DOT-approved lighting, and directionals are incorporated as well. This single-cylinder makes a great local runabout. Nearly everything, other than the motor, is handcrafted. They are street-legal, once blinkers and mirrors are added.

The Black Douglas Motorcycle Company

U.K.–based Black Douglas builds street-ready hand-built standard motorcycles reminiscent of classic 1920's flat-tank bikes. Quality is key here. The majority of parts are crafted by hand in Italy. Their Sterling Autocycle has no plastic components, except for the insulation on the electrical connectors that are hidden within the frame. These bikes are for the mechanical purist. Other than a CDI ignition system and modern three-phase alternator, everything else is mechanical and easy to maintain by a capable owner. They are infinitely more reliable than the bikes they emulate. To prove this, Black Douglas' co-founder, Fabio Cardoni, set off from Milan on bike number 003, the first production Sterling, on a journey in 2014 that proved the reliability of this modern classic. Three days and 1,400 kilometers later, not one issue. The efficient engine and the low overall weight of the vehicle allowed Fabio to complete the trip on picturesque roads on less than 12 gallons of fuel, obtaining an average of 70.5 miles per gallon at speeds averaging around 40 mph.

The Black Douglas Sterling Autocycle Countryman Deluxe pictured is available in 125cc and 230cc versions with a five-speed transmission. Both are certified road legal in Europe and in many countries overseas. Engines are modern OHV air-cooled four-stroke singles producing 11.5 and 14.3 hp respectively. Brakes front and back and good lighting make these bikes highly usable for everyday riding. The Black Douglas is sure to turn heads. Photos courtesy of The Black Douglas Motorcycle Co.

Parker Brother Choppers

Most people will immediately recognize this unusual motorcycle by Florida-based Parker Brothers Choppers as the bike from the movie *Tron*. The Lightcycle is a street-legal machine claimed to be able to hit 120 mph with its gasoline-powered TL1000R engine. An electric version is available, making it true to the bikes shown in the movie. As expected, the bike features neon lighting. Photo courtesy of Chris Perkins.

2010 CHRIS PERKINS

Leonhardt Gunbus 410

Following the bigger-is-better theme, German engineer Clemens F. Leonhardt took things to an extreme by creating the largest running motorcycle in the world. A custom fabricated frame houses the massive 6,728cc (410 cubic inches) V-twin derived from a nine-cylinder radial aircraft engine putting out 510 ft-lb of torque and a claimed 350 hp. The 1,433 pound bike has a three-speed transmission with reverse. Despite its large 38- and 42-inch tires, seat height is as on any other motorcycle. The bike was available for $350,000 back in 2013. There is absolutely no doubt that the appearance of this bike at any rally would instantly proclaim it as the biggest and baddest machine of them all. Photo © 2009 INA FASSBENDER/Reuters/Corbis.

Profile of a Custom Motorcycle Builder

Many custom bike shops utilize off-the-shelf engines, suspensions, wheels, and frames for their creations. They spend much of their time designing visually striking and intricate sheet metal and paint schemes. As the reader can see from many of the superb examples on the pages above, some builders take a more ambitious approach to building one-off mechanical marvels. One such creator is Allen Millyard, an engineer from Berkshire, England. Millyard's bikes are designed, engineered, and crafted with meticulous skill, much by hand. The common theme of bigger-is-better is immediately apparent, but in reality the more appropriate theme of bigger-is-more-challenging can be found behind his work. His focus on customizing engines is certainly unique.

Millyard started building custom machines as early as 15 years old when he managed to stuff an Austin Mini engine into a motorcycle frame. His first V-twin came at the age of 19. He states that his Kawasaki 415cc five-cylinder was his first "proper" project in 1996. This was followed by doubling up a 50cc Honda to create the SS 100 V-twin in 1999. The succession of machines that followed has brought him accolades from engineers and motorcyclists alike. Photos courtesy of Allen Millyard.

Pictured is Millyard's award winning Honda SS 100. This V-twin started off as a 50cc single. Photo by Stephen Millyard.

Who would not want to be seen on this stunning machine? This is Millyard's 1,600cc V-8 created from two four-cylinder KZ1000 engines. The engine utilizes a pressed together roller bearing crankshaft with side by side connecting rods. Pressing a crankshaft together in pieces versus a single forged unit allows builders the use of roller bearings for the lower end of the connecting rods. Normal connecting rods are split at the bottom to accommodate the use of shell (also called plain) bearings. Roller bearings are rugged and can run on less lubrication than the shell type. Photo by Roland Brown.

Making already fast bikes faster is another one of Allen's favorite undertakings. Pictured is a five-cylinder 850cc Kawasaki two-stroke that started its life as a triple. Photo by Roland Brown.

Millyard's 2,300cc V-12 Kawasaki is so well engineered and designed that at first glance it seems to be a production machine. The engine is comprised of two cylinder banks from Kawasaki's water-cooled KZ1300. Custom work abounds, including modified crankcase, crankshaft, stretched frame and tank, engine cooling, fuel intake, ignition, exhaust, and brakes. Photo by Roland Brown.

The V-12 has a pressed together roller bearing crankshaft that utilizes master and slave connecting rods like those that would be found on a nine-cylinder radial engine.

Two of Millyard's most radical bikes. The "Flying Millyard" on the left is a 5,000cc V-twin that utilizes two cylinders and heads from a nine-cylinder radial Pratt & Whitney airplane engine. Everything else, including the crankcase, frame, and many of the drive components had to be manufactured in his shop. Moving on to the "bigger is faster" theme, Millyard created a Dodge Viper V-10 powered motorcycle. The machine was clocked at 207 mph. Photo by Stephen Millyard.

Yamaha Motor Corporation, U.S.A.

KTM Sportsmotorcycle GmbH

Chapter 8

OFF-ROAD AND IN THE DIRT

It's more fun in the dirt. From all-out motocross to the versatility of dual-sports, this chapter takes a look at the many choices available for romping in the dirt and exploring the great outdoors.

Doing It in the Dirt

Motorcycles have always provided their riders with an unequalled sense of freedom and mobility. Nowhere is this more evident than when riders leave the tarmac and head for the mountains and deserts in search of new trails. Mostly referred to as dirt bikes, these surefooted machines have become highly specialized to meet a variety of off-road duties.

Small dirt bikes make ideal platforms for learning to ride a motorcycle. Clutch and throttle control on a forgiving 80cc or 125cc dirt bike is a lot easier to digest in the safety of a backyard than on the hard surface of a parking lot. Riding skills one develops on dirt tracks and trails translate well into road riding. Most of the great racers started on a dirt bike.

Every kid should have a small dirt bike to play with. It develops riding skills for bigger machines to come. The author picked up this 1973 Yamaha GT80 up for $100 twenty years ago. Another $75 in pistons, rings, and gaskets made the bike the one to learn on for his children and their friends. It is still in use today as a camp bike.

It's All in the Bounce

The popularity of off-road motorcycling escalated dramatically with the development of hydraulically dampened suspension units in the 1940s. This allowed the motorcycle to absorb significantly more bumps. As purpose-built off-road bikes evolved, so did their suspensions. These machines were typically called scramblers as they participated in off-road races called scrambles. Longer travel within the front telescoping forks combined with more powerful engines encouraged riding at higher speeds on harsh surfaces. Front and rear suspension units on the best off-road bikes today can easily handle a foot of compression. That absorbs a whole lot of impact.

Off-road bikes over sixty-five years ago were slightly modified street bikes. With hardly more than four inches of suspension travel, these heavy machines were hard on the rider. The addition of rear springs and shock absorbers, as seen on this 1950s-era Matchless, was a major step forward from the rigid-framed machines of the 1930s and 1940s.

The Last of the Big Brits

During the 1950s, several British motorcycle makers, like BSA and Matchless, offered a variety of purpose-built off-road scramblers and trials bikes in many sizes. The 250cc BSA C15S scrambler was a common sight on British weekly television shows airing scrambles racing. It had a good run between 1959 and 1965. These were real dirt bikes, with sturdy light frames, knobby tires, solo seats, alloy tanks, and void of any lighting. Larger 500cc machines competed in the senior classes. One of the best of these was the BSA Gold Star "Catalina" Scrambler.

The BSA Gold Star Scrambler was based on the famous 500cc DBD34 Gold Star road racer. This 1957 example was quite heavy compared to the light two-stroke machines Spain's Bultaco and Ossa were brewing up. It did, however, have tremendous power and torque that gave it an edge in the straights. Photo courtesy of Yesterdays Antique Motorcycles.

BSA's next generation of capable big bore off-road machines featured unit construction motors and improved suspensions. These were offered in 441cc and 500cc sizes, and started appearing in the 1960s. Unit construction engines saved considerable weight by combining the engine and transmission in one case. Continued development led to the highly capable but short-lived B50MX in 1971. The Japanese and European enduros were already dominating the off-road market by then.

This BSA B50MX is the British motorcycling giant's final effort at a motocross bike. It was offered between 1971 and 1973. They were sold as the Triumph TR5MX after BSA closed its doors. Photo courtesy of Baxter Cycle.

Triumph offered its little 200cc Tiger Cub in trials trim in the early 1960s. It had quite a presence in amateur events since it was most affordable and easy to maintain.

In order to encourage motorcyclists to explore off-road riding, variations of BSA's street roadsters were created to permit some light trail riding. Today we may call these dual-sports. BSA's 441cc single-cylinder Victor Roadster of the mid-1960s was offered with an aluminum alloy "Grand Prix" tank, skid plate, and high pipe to emulate its older brother, the B44GP Victor Scrambler. The frame, however, was the same as used on the street bikes. It is one of the best-looking motorcycles ever made.

By the 1970s, BSA's line included off-road capable road machines with 500cc and 250cc engines. These machines were the true precursors to today's dual-sport bikes. They were also sold under the Triumph marque. Pictured is a clean 1971 250cc Triumph T25SS that is being offered for sale at $3,000.

Far ahead of the larger British motorcycle makers in producing superb off-road bikes, Greeves introduced a Villiers-powered scrambler as early as 1953. This photo shows the unique leading-link front suspension as employed by the maker for its race-winning machines during the 1960s. The design offered over six inches of travel. This was significant compared to the four inches of most of its contemporaries.

The Booming 1960s and 1970s

Nearly every major motorcycle maker discovered the large market potential of off-road machines. The lighter dirt bikes offered by the Japanese makers during the late 1960s brought these machines to the attention of the masses, particularly baby boomers. The addition of lights allowed teenagers to use them as daily riders to go to school, work, or play. As engine displacement grew, many of these bikes initially considered "enduros" came to be known as "dual-sport" machines.

Yamaha's DT-1 brought off-road riding to countless people when it was introduced in 1968. The 250cc two-stroke engine produced a reasonable 18 hp. Street-legal lighting added tremendous versatility. Cost was a bit over $500; money well spent for so much fun. Photo courtesy of Mecum Auctions.

Yamaha used brilliant marketing to build a future base of loyal motorcycle buyers by introducing small dirt bikes like this 1971 60cc Mini-Enduro JT1 for kids.

Ducati offered scramblers between 1962 and 1974 in 125cc, 250cc, 350cc, and 450cc sizes. Scramblers are off-road capable machines with good street manners. Suspensions are not as radical as pure off-road dirt bikes. Ducati's new Scrambler line introduced in 2015 is clearly modeled after the original.

Ducati sweetened the pot with the highly affordable Scrambler Sixty2. It features the company's smallest L-twin at 399cc. Agile and with good ground clearance, it honors the scramblers of the 1960s. Photo courtesy of Ducati Motor Holding S.p.A.

By the mid-1970s European makers, like Spain's Bultaco, were making superb two-stroke-powered off-road machines. Light, nimble, and with plenty of suspension travel, these bikes took off-road riding to a higher level.

What Makes Dirt Bikes Different?

There are several key features on off-road machines that differentiate them from street bikes. Foremost is their extended suspension travel. They must be able to quickly absorb the energy of bike and rider bouncing over deep furrows. These hydraulically dampened suspensions tend to make the bikes high, improving ground clearance. They also make the ride quite soft on regular roads—a feature not so desirable when riding in a sporting manner on twisty roads. Most off-road machines today employ a single monoshock unit for the rear. It is composed of a shock-absorbing damper unit within a coil spring linked to the frame and swingarm. It allows for greater range in swingarm motion. Adjustability in damping, rebound, and pre-load is quite common. Damping may be by oil or pressurized gas.

Suspension technology kept improving significantly by the 1980s. This 1980 250cc Yamaha OW40 factory racer illustrates the advancements made to front suspension travel and the adoption of a monoshock rear unit—features that were already becoming popular on consumer dirt bikes.

Dirt bikes must have a strong frame that has the ability to take a beating and flex. Most modern dirt bikes use box section steel or aluminum frame components that give just enough to minimize any potential for breaking the welds or cracking the frame.

A naked view of a modern Kawasaki KXTM450F dirt bike shows the elegant simplicity of its aluminum frame and 12.4-inch travel suspension. The single shock suspension unit for the rear wheel hides directly behind the engine. This 449cc single-cylinder bike weighs less than 240 pounds. An equivalent street bike would weigh at least a hundred pounds more given additional equipment needed, such as lighting and instrumentation. Photo courtesy of Kawasaki Motors Corp., U.S.A.

The ideal off-road bike is also very light and has a powerful engine compared to its overall weight. Having a high power-to-weight ratio

allows the machine to navigate steep terrain with little effort, or launch easily over a mound to catch some air. Many off-road experts prefer a mid-sized engine over a larger one due to its superior power-to-weight ratio.

With a high power-to-weight ratio, the modern mid-sized off-road motorcycle can launch easily into the air given a proper incline. Long-travel suspension units help absorb the impact of a landing. Jumps like this with the Matchless previously pictured would have destroyed the machine's frame and hurt the rider.

Most dirt bikes made between the 1970s and the millennium were powered by two-stroke engines. Their light weight, combined with superior power compared to equivalent sized four-stroke engines, made them an ideal choice. The significant shift to four-stroke engines for off-road bikes over the last decade is not just in reaction to strict EPA regulations. Much of it was motivated by the improvements made to four-stroke power plants. Advances in electronic fuel injection and engine management systems have greatly improved smooth and controlled delivery of power while reducing overall engine size and weight. Many motocross racing categories have emerged strictly for four-stroke machines. Two-strokes are by no means dead, but they are seeing themselves limited more and more to smaller displacement motocross bikes.

332

Considered by many to be the ultimate dirt bike, Yamaha's YZ250 is still powered by a lively liquid-cooled two-stroke that can launch this 227 pound machine into the air for some exciting freestyle aerobatics. Mixing the oil with gas is automatic. It is slowly stepping aside to allow its four-stroke brother, the YZ250F, the opportunity to shine as it racks up numerous titles. Photo courtesy of Yamaha Motor Corporation, U.S.A.

The key difference between two- and four-stroke engines is in how they deliver their power. Two-strokes make their power at high rpms. This is often quite sudden and can startle the novice rider. Four-strokes deliver power more evenly across their rpm range. It is well recommended for beginners to start off on a smaller four-stroke machine. Bikes come in a broad variety of engine sizes, ranging from a tiny 50cc up to large 650cc. Most are single-cylinder in design. This reduces weight, and offers excellent torque for climbing.

It is never too early to start introducing our kids to the motorcycle. It won't be long before the little one is tearing up the backyard by himself. Get them used to wearing all the proper safety gear early on. No-Pedal balance bikes are effective for preparing toddlers for two wheels. Photos thanks to Brittany Adamczyk.

Entry-level dirt riders, such as five-year-old to eight-year-old kids, will benefit greatly from smooth four-stroke powered bikes. This Yamaha TT-R50E has an electric start 49cc SOHC engine. Photo courtesy of Yamaha Motor Corporation, U.S.A.

Just like with their shoes and clothes, kids will quickly outgrow their dirt bikes. The next step up can be a neat Kawasaki KLXTM110L. The 112cc four-stroke will provide a lot of fun for many years. Dad will surely sneak in as many rides as he can. Photo courtesy of Kawasaki Motors Corp., U.S.A.

Other features on most dirt bikes include knobby tires, a high exhaust, chain rear drive to minimize weight as compared to a shaft, a protective skid plate to keep the bottom of the engine safe from jagged rocks, rim locks to keep the tires from coming off the wheels, and lightweight plastic fenders.

Categories of Off-Road Machines

Specialization has created quite a few categories of off-road bikes.

Pure-Dirt

The term "pure-dirt" is often used to differentiate dirt bikes from other specialized types of off-road motorcycles. Pure-dirt bikes are strictly used off-road for free-riding, exploration, and just plain fun. These bikes are void of lights and unnecessary accessories. Many are now offered with electric start for convenience and to encourage newcomers.

Honda's superb CRF® line of four-stroke-powered dirt bikes come in a variety of sizes ranging from 99cc to 449cc. This CRF125F is ideal for teens and smaller adults looking for a low maintenance off-road machine. Photo courtesy of American Honda Motor Co., Inc.

At the high end of off-road bikes are Swedish makers Husaberg and Husqvarna, both known for their outstanding race-winning off-road bikes. Pictured is a Husaberg TE300 two-stroke. Both marques are now under the ownership of Austria's KTM. Photo courtesy of KTM North America, Inc.

Motocross

Motocross dirt bikes are the high-performance cousins to pure-dirt bikes. Famous makes have created a rich history for the sport. These include Penton, Greeves, CZ, Hodaka, Falta, Ossa, Bultaco, Husqvarna, Husaberg, Monark, Rickman Metisse, and all the current Japanese makes, to name a few. These bikes are made for racing, and include enhanced engines, suspensions, and sometimes even launch control systems to help get racers off the line without spinning their wheels. Gas tanks tend to be smaller to reduce weight.

The light weight and powerful engine of a motocross bike allows the rider to carve out serious dirt at the track. Photo courtesy of Suzuki Motor of America, Inc.

Honda's first production motocross bike was the CR250M Elsinore introduced in 1973. It was also Honda's first production two-stroke. It was a huge success and opened the doors for many would-be racers. Honda named several of its bikes after the famous off-road race held at Lake Elsinore, California.

By the time this 1978 Honda CR250R Elsinore came out, long-travel suspensions had evolved significantly. The CR250R made Honda competitive again after losing some ground to Suzuki years earlier. The bike still used dual shocks for its rear suspension.

A formidable motocross weapon today is Suzuki's RM-Z250. A sophisticated front fork system gives this bike an advantage in tight turns on the track. Suzuki was the first Japanese company to offer a production motocross bike back in 1968 with its TM250 model. Photo courtesy of Suzuki Motor of America, Inc.

At the high end of power are the 450cc motocross bikes like this race-winning Yamaha YZ450F. It is full of features its ancestors could not have envisioned. Included are electronics to manage launch control, speed sensitive suspension damping, and the ability to change the fuel and ignition engine control mapping for fine-tuning the bike to meet various track conditions. Photo courtesy of Yamaha Motor Corporation, U.S.A.

This motocross bike will certainly make onlookers doubt their hearing. Unlike the familiar ringing of a two-stroke, this Zero® MX runs a silent electric powertrain. Photo courtesy of Zero Motorcycles, Inc.

Enduro

Enduro motorcycles are street-legal dirt bikes. The addition of lights, license plate holder, and a horn allow the bikes to see use on and off the road. Enduro's are named after a racing category that has riders compete on longer courses than motocross. Rally enduro bikes have much larger gas tanks to accommodate long-distance off-road racing, such as the Paris-Dakar event. Many baby boomers had their first off-road experience on a Japanese enduro.

Husqvarna set the standard for high-quality enduros back in the 1960s. This 1969 Sportsman 360C is a superb example.

Husqvarna enduro bikes have come a long way since the 1960s. This 450 TE won the Enduro World Championship in 2014.

Trials

Trials bikes are about as specialized as they come. They are specifically used for slow riding in obstacle-laden environments. Their low center of gravity allows the rider to balance the machine while standing on the footpegs. Seats are almost nonexistent since the rider will hardly ever sit.

Spanish motorcycle maker Montesa dominated trials competitions back in the 1960s with bikes like this.

Modern trials bikes are ultra-light and maneuverable. There is no need for a seat since most of the riding is done standing up. Highly responsive and well-tempered engines are critical.

Trail

Trail bikes are not to be confused with trials bikes. Trail bikes are made for casual riding on dirt trails that require little expertise in handling. A favorite of campers, trail bikes are often seen strapped to the back of an RV.

The most famous trail bike of them all is Honda's CT70. The company offered these compact and reliable four-strokes in 50cc and 70cc sizes from the late 1960s through the mid-1970s. They are highly collectible today. The handlebars fold inward for easy transportation.

One of the most unusual trail bikes is the two-wheel-drive Rokon Trail-Breaker®. A patented front drive mechanism will get this machine out of the deepest mud. It is available today in a variety of configurations.

There is no doubt that the Russian IZH Samson trike is the clear winner in the extreme off-road trail category. This amazing machine is based on the water-cooled Jupiter two-cylinder two-stroke motorcycle. Chains are included. Photo courtesy of Kalashnikov Concern Press-Service.

Dual-Sport

Dual-sport motorcycles are street-legal machines that allow riders to enjoy extended trips on the highway, combined with off-road adventure. They tend to be heavier than enduros and a bit lighter than adventure touring bikes. The line gets fuzzy as new dual-sport machines come out within the adventure segment of a maker's catalog. Whatever the name, these bikes are the answer to the question, "What bike should I buy if I could only ever have one?" Used Suzuki DR650s and Kawasaki KLR650s from the late 1990s are very inexpensive today and allow exploration of this motorcycling segment before committing to buying a new one.

Dual-sports like the Kawasaki KLRTM650 can provide hours of comfortable road riding to bring you to special places accessible only to off-road machines. Photo courtesy of Kawasaki Motors Corp., U.S.A.

Suzuki's extensive line of DR® dual-sport bikes range from 199cc to 644cc singles today. The DR650 line has endured over twenty years, and features seat and suspension height adjustability. Photo courtesy of Suzuki Motor of America, Inc.

Triumph's Scrambler makes an excellent choice for those looking for a cool retro bike that has some off-road capabilities. The machine is styled after the 1960s desert racers (also called sleds) that people like Steve McQueen rode. Those bikes were stripped down Triumph 500s and 650s with high pipes and a skid plate. The Scrambler is sure to get a boost in sales due to its appearance in the 2015 film *Jurassic World*. Photo courtesy of Triumph Motorcycles.

Husqvarna's relationship with KTM has allowed it to enjoy development of new models. Pictured is the 401 SVARTPILEN concept bike that looks like a dual-sport on steroids. Photo courtesy of Husqvarna, KTM North America, Inc.

Where to Ride

It is not as easy to find places to ride off-road as one might imagine. Current efforts to restrict public lands from the use of motorcycles are threatening our ability to enjoy the remote areas of our country. Fortunately there are thousands of acres still available in the high plains states, Utah and Arizona. Off-road riding in the suburbs usually means trespassing on someone's property or paying to get into an off-road park. Off-road riding clubs usually hold title to their own land. This provides a safe environment to learn off-road riding skills. Many clubs hold regular motocross and trials competitions. Rider Planet's website is a great resource for finding parks and clubs in you area. Visit riderplanet-usa.com.

Joining the AMA and participating in some of their amateur off-road racing events is another excellent way to scratch the itch. There are also many dirt riding camps. A search on the Internet will reveal companies that offer weekend camps for riders of all ages. For a real special treat, you may consider traveling to New Zealand to take advantage of the rides that Pure-Dirt Tours offer. Visit puredirttours.co.nz.

Off-road riding is not limited to ATVs or two-wheeled bikes. Combinations like this Ural with sidecar are set up with a drive shaft to power the third wheel for excellent traction in the mud and snow. Photo courtesy of IMZ-Ural, imz-ural.com

Consider Trying Off-Road

Don't let the lack of off-road riding areas dissuade you from giving this great sport a try. There are plenty of places to trailer a bike to. As with many of the other motorcycle segments, there are countless used

bikes out there to minimize any strain on the wallet if you are not quite sure about purchasing a new one. Between Craigslist, cycletrader.com, and eBay, there should be no shortage of machines near you to choose from. Of course, two-strokes will smoke and body panels and gas tanks will have dents. As long as the bike shifts properly through all the gears, and the suspension components are not bent, loose, and don't leak, it is worth taking a risk. Re-boring a two-stroke cylinder and replacing the piston and rings is not an expensive affair to bring an old bike back to life. Once the bug bites, you are sure to take a look at many of the fantastic machines mentioned in this chapter.

Once a champion, this tired 1976 Bultaco 250cc Pursang has plenty of life in it to provide a spirited off-road experience to a loving owner. For only a few hundred dollars, there is little excuse for not trying off-road motorcycling.

This 1982 Honda CR125 two-stroke being sold at a swap meet at a fraction of the cost of a new one allows easy entry into the dirt bike scene. Despite its age, it is full of contemporary features, such as a monoshock rear suspension that can be upgraded with a modern unit.

The Little Harley-Davidsons That Could

Harley-Davidson through its relationship with Aermacchi introduced numerous off-road bikes. New for 1970, the 98cc Baja 100 was originally designed as a desert racer. Fitted with lights it became a great little enduro.

Using a clever play on words, Harley named its little 65cc trail bike the Shortster. Unfortunately it was only available in 1972. A larger version called the X-90 was also introduced. Photos courtesy of Ross Puleo.

Dirt riding is a skill onto itself. To get the most out of it consider a riding school like MX-Schools.com or Raines Riding University. Raines Riding University is led by six-time AMA National Champion Jason Raines and his wonderful wife Emily.

Photo courtesy of Raines Riding University.

Taking the term off-road to an extreme is world record stunt and FMX rider Robbie Maddison. "Maddo" is one of the most inexhaustible and creative freestyle motocross riders ever. He challenges himself constantly. When it wasn't enough to jump nearly 400 feet over the San Diego harbor, he took on his next project—to ride a dirt bike on water. With support from DC Shoes, Robbie built a bike that can literally ride on water. The rear wheel was fitted with a paddle type tire as used for desert dune riding. The front was fitted with a ski. Not without its endless challenges, the resulting images and video of him riding the waves in Tahiti called "Pipe Dream" are mind-blowing, to say the least. Photo courtesy of DC Shoes. Photographed by Milan.

Kawasaki Motors Corporation, U.S.A.

Ayres Adventure

Chapter 9

TOURING AND ADVENTURE

The American dream of the open road, from a weekend ride to the long-haul Iron Butt Rally, is the domain of the touring motorcycle. The variety of machines available today for exploring the world on and off-road is greater than ever, particularly with the many new adventure bikes being offered by nearly all major makers.

Indian Motorcycle International, LLC

The Need to Roam

Touring on a motorcycle is as old as motorcycling itself. If we take the literal definition of touring as "A journey where one travels from place to place," then most motorcycle rides are a tour of some sort.

Touring is typically associated with longer distance rides. That is certainly not a requirement no matter how tempting it is to emulate Emilio Scotto's ten-year, five-hundred-thousand-mile journey on a Honda Gold Wing or Danell Lynn's record for longest journey in a single country by traveling the US for 48,600 miles. Discovering a new part of the county on a long day trip might just as well be a tour. That can be done on pretty much any motorcycle, but some are just better at it than others.

Some bikes just make touring effortless and a lot of fun. Such is the case with the good-looking and good-handling Harley-Davidson Street Glide® Special. Photo courtesy of Harley-Davidson.

The real buzz in touring today is in "adventure touring." The premise is to use dual-purpose bikes that can travel off-road as well as on for the exploration of remote areas. Despite the popularity of the term, and the many highly specialized bikes available today, adventure touring has been going on for over a hundred years. The cross-country rides of Cannonball Baker and many others included hundreds of treacherous miles through sandy desert and muddy plains.

Modern touring bikes, be they cruisers or adventure tourers like this BMW R1200 GS parked on a side street in Manhattan, offer exceptional comfort for the long haul. The rising popularity and utility of the adventure bike segment is bringing them to the forefront as daily riders. We are seeing more and more of them in urban environments.

Touring bikes fall into five major categories:
1 - Pretty much any bike.
2 - A standard or a cruiser accessorized for touring.
3 - Purpose-built touring bikes.
4 - Sport touring (ST) bikes.
5 - Adventure (ADV) touring bikes.

We will refer to each of these categories throughout this chapter.

Any Bike Can Be a Touring Bike

Pretty much any motorcycle can be used for touring. It all depends on how comfortable you want to be. People tour on 50cc machines for hundreds of miles. Even the boys of *Top Gear* rode a 125cc Minsk, a Honda Super Cub, and a Vespa one thousand miles on their Vietnam adventure in

2009. Owners of 250cc Honda Rebels have recorded extensive cross-country trips exceeding 7,500 miles. It seems that size doesn't matter in touring, as long as the body and machine are willing and able.

My first long ride as a teen was on a 160cc Honda up and down the East Coast. At an average speed of 45 mph, I was content riding it all day long. Moving up to a 305cc Honda the following year allowed me to keep up with 60 mph traffic. By the age of twenty-one, I had graduated to a 650cc Triumph TR6R—my first big bike. It was no problem at all to ride four hundred miles a day as I was young, strong, and lived to ride. The bike's standard configuration made it easy on the back and neck, but not so much for the hands and feet. Extended high-speed riding produced some serious numbing vibration on all of these mounts. I learned to do what experienced riders had told me to do—look for that "sweet spot" in engine rpm that creates the least vibration in a particular gear. That may not always be at the speed you wish to travel, but nonetheless it is a good tip for when riding very old bikes.

Vintage enthusiasts still value the touring capabilities of Meriden-made Triumphs. This 750 Bonneville is accessorized with hard bags and a windshield.

Suzuki's silky smooth RE5 rotary-powered bikes were also offered in a touring configuration. This 1975 RE5M comes with all the accessories available, including exhaust pipe extensions to prevent the bottom of the panniers (bags) from melting from the hot rotary exhaust. Photo courtesy of Wayne Waddington.

Vibration, be it subtle or annoying, does limit one's endurance significantly. Pioneer bikes had no true suspensions other than some stiff springs mounted to the front forks and the pneumatic tires they rode upon. Engines were mounted directly to the frame and transmitted their vibration right through the handlebars and footpegs. Early American bikes had extended rubber handgrips to avoid the discomfort of severe vibration reaching the hands. Today's standards, such as a Triumph Bonneville, can easily take one many hundreds of miles a day without any real stress on the body. The balanced motors are silky smooth, and seating position is upright and comfortable. One would not think of a Triumph Bonneville as a touring bike, or for that matter any of the scores of comfortable standards or cruisers out there. Their limitations depend on one's expectations as they relate to long-distance riding. If day trips are all you are planning on doing, then any standard or cruiser will work just fine as long as the passenger is happy with their seat.

Day tours are a great way for couples to spend time together. Deciding on a destination is easy enough, but the real fun is to get lost on the back roads. One will be surprised at what can be discovered. Fill a backpack with some nice sandwiches and bottles of spring water to make it a perfect day.

Longer rides, particularly at highway speeds, may benefit from touring-oriented machinery. You may wish for a heavier bike that does not get tossed around so easily whenever a semi passes by. You may want an adjustable air suspension for a smoother ride for you and your mate, larger molded seats to cuddle your butts, footboards for a bit of wiggle room, highway bars to stretch your legs, a windshield to keep the bugs off your face, adjustable handlebars, cruise control, saddlebags for storage, easy mounting points for a top box, or even a stereo and built-in GPS. With so many great choices in touring bikes out there today, there is no need to limit yourself if long distance riding is what you really want to do. Go for it, but make sure you select the bike that matches your touring style.

Touring at the high end is expensive. This lucky rider is enjoying all the comforts and power of his BMW K1600 GTL. Be prepared to spend over thirty thousand dollars for a fully loaded rig like this.

The Van Buren Sisters Make a Point

Motorcyclists ventured on longer rides as soon as machines became reliable enough to risk traveling extended distances. That point came soon after the turn of the twentieth century. The story of the amazing Van Buren sisters presents an excellent example of how cross-country touring on a motorcycle did not wait for the comforts of a big bike with a cushy suspension and cup holders. These young ladies used the best standard motorcycle available in the United States at that time—an Indian.

Augusta and Adeline Van Buren were two adventurous women in their twenties living in New York City at the onset of World War I. They, like many, were not happy about the limited social rights women were subject to. Wages were significantly lower than that paid to men, and voting rights were nonexistent. Women were also restricted in their ability to support the armed forces. To demonstrate the capabilities of women, particularly in supporting the war effort overseas, "Gussie" and "Addie" decided to obtain a couple of Indian Power Plus motorcycles to ride across the United States during the summer of 1916. This took remarkable courage in that the heavy 1,000cc V-twin bikes themselves required great strength to handle—especially on the dirt and rutted roads they would be traveling on for long stretches of the trip.

The Van Buren sisters on the trail on their Indian Power Plus motorcycles with Firestone tires during their remarkable cross-country trip in 1916. Photo from The Van Buren Family Collection, courtesy of Robert Van Buren. vanburensisters.com

The sisters covered 5,500 miles during their two-month transcontinental journey from New York to California. This included a run up to the 14,109-foot summit of Pike's Peak and a side trip to Tijuana, Mexico. The conditions they faced would be considered unbearable to most of us today. Heavy rains, deep mud, drought, and getting lost in the remote wilderness certainly challenged their resolve. They not only endured, but did it with smiles on their faces. Confident that they proved the point that women can support the military effort, particularly as dispatch riders,

Addie, an English teacher, applied to the US Army after the trip. She was rejected. It must have been male insecurity to motivate that kind of a decision. Remarkably, the motorcycle media downplayed their accomplishment as well. Today we watch videos of "adventure tours" on television that show strapping men on their super-equipped adventure bikes making a big deal out of riding through talc-fine desert sand or crossing river beds with smooth melon-sized rocks that challenge their ability to balance the 500 pound bikes. They should keep a photo of Gussie and Addie in their tank bags as a reminder of how far we have come.

It has been one hundred years since the Van Buren sisters rode their Indians across the country. Today, Indian is back with several outstanding touring bikes available to eat up the interstate system. Pictured is the Roadmaster with electric adjustable windshield, keyless ignition, and 111-cubic-inch engine. Photo courtesy of Indian Motorcycle International, LLC.

Around the World in Eighteen Months

An equally remarkable story about long-distance riding on a standard motorcycle is about a young man who, on a whim, took a ride around the globe back in 1932. His name was Robert E. Fulton Jr.—related to the Fulton who developed the steamship. Young master Fulton took on the challenge based on his impromptu answer to a simple question asked by a young lady as to his plans for the summer after completing his first year at the University of Vienna. He had never ridden a bike, let alone owned one. Another guest at the dinner table had the solution. His family owned an interest in the Douglas Motor Works in Bristol, England. He offered up a 1932 Douglas twin cylinder, accessorized for touring with a special auxiliary gas tank, skid plate, and fitted with automobile tires.

Photo of the completely restored Douglas S6 as used by Robert Fulton Jr. on his historic round-the-world trip. Note the additional fuel tank on back. He ran out of gas only once, and that was in Munich. Fulton hid a 32-caliber Smith & Wesson pistol between the engine and skid plate of the bike. Photo was taken in Bristol, England, after the machine had been faithfully restored by the London Douglas Motor Cycle Club members. Photo courtesy of London Douglas Motor Cycle Club, douglasmcc.co.uk

Fulton was certainly not the first to ride a motorcycle around the world. People had been doing that since twenty years earlier. Carl Stearns Clancy was the first one to claim that title when he completed his 18,000-mile ride between 1912 and 1913. He rode a 934cc (57 cubic inch) 7 hp Henderson Four. Unlike the others, Fulton chronicled his trip in great detail with photographs, film, and a book. His book, *One Man Caravan*, is a remarkable tale of this motorcyclist's adventure through twenty-two countries lacking any real roads, fraught with bandits, corrupt police, and cuisine best imagined than tasted. The Douglas slogged through axle-deep mud more often than once, breaking chains and spirits. Fulton photographed and filmed most of his trip. It is a definite must-read for the adventure rider. There is also a DVD of his 40,000-mile journey. It is titled *Twice Upon a Caravan*, and is available from Searchlight Films, Bernardston, Massachusetts.

While Fulton was on his trip around the globe, motorcycle makers were experimenting with all sorts of configurations to make long-distance riding more comfortable. Perhaps the most colorful of these is the Czechoslovakian Böhmerland. This 1925 model at the Barber Vintage Motorsports Museum. Only a thousand of these bikes are said to have been made between 1924 and 1939. They were powered by a 598cc single-cylinder engine. Some models allowed three passengers in tandem, while this one features an elegant sidecar.

Wrenching Is Required

Motorcyclists like the Van Buren sisters and Fulton, traveling far away from home, had to be mechanically adept. Early machines were prone to the usual problems associated with pioneer technology and often required roadside repairs. These included broken leather drive belts or chains, fouled spark plugs, dirty ignition contact points, gummed carburetors, stuck valves, disintegrating clutches, and more severe mechanical malfunctions. Riders always had some basic tools to keep their machines running. Getting a puncture in the pneumatic tires and inner tubes was always a possibility. That is still the case today, although tires and tubes have come a long way in a hundred years. Bikes equipped with tubeless tires are easier to repair in the event of a simple puncture. Replacing a tube on the road is a skill that is slowly being lost to past generations of riders.

To get a feel for some of the problems early riders faced, we can look at today's Cannonball runs—those cross-country rides on antique motorcycles commemorating Erwin Baker's feats. An article in the January/February 2015 issue of *The Antique Motorcycle*® magazine recounted some of the breakdowns during the 2014 sixteen-day 3,939-mile run from Daytona Beach, Florida, to Tacoma, Washington. The list included electrical, carburetor, lubrication, clutch, distributor, magneto, head gasket, piston, chain, and tire puncture issues to name a few.

Riders of the Cannonball lining up to start their journey. Photo courtesy of Felicia Morgan, Cannonball Race 2010.

None of these issues are likely today when touring with any well-maintained bike made within the past twenty years, with the possible exception of a flat or an electrical glitch caused by a poor connection or shorted wire.

Bigger Bikes Mean Longer Trips

The introduction of larger cruisers in the 1930s offered greater comfort for extended road trips. The addition of saddlebags, windshields, and auxiliary lighting added convenience. More reliable motors with good electrical systems encouraged "roaming" as an American motorcycle pastime. By the 1950s the term "full dresser" meant a totally equipped big cruiser ideal for touring. The combination of the large V-twin cruisers with an emerging interstate system opened the doors to many motorcyclists looking to experience the adventure of long-distance riding. America was on the move. The trend has continued today with many offerings from American and Japanese makers of big V-twin touring cruisers.

This Harley-Davidson Hydra-Glide (hydraulic dampened front forks) was typical of a fully "dressed" American motorcycle made for the long haul during the 1950s. A comfortable "Buddy" seat accommodates a passenger, while saddlebags, windshield, auxiliary lights, and crash bars complete the package.

Maintaining its historic style, Harley-Davidson offers touring cruisers that clearly show their lineage to the full-dressers of the 1950s. This Road King® may be referred to as a "bagger." That term applies to bikes that have saddlebags, be they soft leather or hard plastic cases.

Harley-Davidson has quite a few touring models in its extensive portfolio of bikes today. Various configurations in frames, seating, luggage, engine cooling, and suspension offer options for pretty much any motorcyclists. The dashboard on this luxurious Road Glide® Ultra is well equipped with the latest technology while the Twin-Cooled® engine has liquid-cooled heads for optimum performance regardless of ambient temperature. The comfortable rear seat is sure to make any travel companion happy. Photo courtesy of Harley-Davidson.

A view of a fully-equipped touring Gold Wing's dashboard shows that this bike is made for the long haul. The powerful infotainment system integrates with other electronic devices, including Bluetooth® technology. Built-in GPS screen, cruise control, heated grips, optional CB radio and CD player, and adjustable headlights are features one would typically see on luxury automobiles.

Yamaha's Road Star® line is squarely targeted at the American buyer. This bagger comes with a 1,670cc (102 cubic inch) air-cooled 48-degree V-twin that has traditional pushrod-actuated overhead valves. The motor does have four valves per cylinder for better performance. Passengers always appreciate a backrest. Photo courtesy of Yamaha Motor Corporation, U.S.A.

America's "other" motorcycle company, Victory, offers several touring bikes as an alternative to those who want more contemporary styling and modern engine design. Victory motorcycles feature air/oil-cooled SOHC V-twins. This Cross Country® is considered a better handling machine on the twisties by many than its counterparts. Its hollow aluminum frame helps keep the weight under 800 pounds. Victory is made by Polaris, which also makes Indian motorcycles.

Victory styling can be extreme. The Vision touring bike is a real head-scratcher to most that see it for the first time.

Modern interpretations of the American touring cruiser are abundant among the Japanese motorcycle manufacturers. Motorcycle buyers will have many great choices to consider, such as this Yamaha V-Star 1300 Deluxe. Designed to compete squarely within the segment, it offers full technology integration with GPS, phone, and audio media at a notably lower price. Photo courtesy of Yamaha Motor Corporation, U.S.A.

Custom baggers are all the rage for specialty builders. Kawasaki offers an off-the-shelf option for those looking to ride rather than build. The Kawasaki Vulcan 1700 Vaquero® ABS is a great-looking machine that is powered by a 1,700cc (103.7 cubic inch) liquid-cooled SOHC, four valves per cylinder, 52-degree V-twin that puts out 108 ft-lb or torque at a lazy 2,750 rpm. Anti-lock braking is standard.

The European Option

While postwar Americans were enjoying their large, vibrating, and oil-leaking V-twins, Europeans were quietly developing their own interpretation of the touring motorcycle. The 1950s saw the final years of the wonderful big British Vincents. These relaxed machines made long-distance touring at high speeds most enjoyable. Philip Vincent introduced his enclosed Series D line in 1954 to accommodate those taking to the road in inclement weather. The public unfortunately did not see the benefit. Perhaps it looked too futuristic.

This photo shows the first and the last of the Vincent V-twin series bikes. The fiberglass bodywork of the Vincent Series D (left) offered superb weather protection for the rider. They, however, did not sell well. Weather protection is a common option today among big touring bikes. Leg shields, fairings, windshields, all protect the rider from direct exposure to rain, damp fog, or hail. The Series A Rapide on the right made a superb sport touring machine. Photo Mortons Archive.

By the 1960s, BMW 600cc flat twins with shaft drive were significantly more refined than what was available from either Harley-Davidson or the British makers. The engine was better balanced and vibrated less than a V-twin or parallel twin. Reliability was also a key to their success. Cost, however, was another issue. At a higher price than a Harley with twice the engine capacity, few could afford to buy a BMW in the United States. Motorcyclists riding them were considered elite and highly discerning.

The ultimate boxer-engined BMW sport touring bike, and certainly one of the best overall touring bikes ever made, is the current R1200 RT. It includes BMW's traditional ABS system, traction control, and a 125 hp air/water cooled flat twin. The bike even offers a heated seat option for both rider and passenger. Photo courtesy of BMW Motorrad USA.

The author purchased this 600cc 1969 R60/2 BMW from its one owner who clocked 232,000 miles on the bike before investing in a major rebuild of the engine. The bike provided him with a comfortable mount for over two-dozen trips across the country. The twin cylinder boxer engine balances out most of the vibration. A shaft-driven rear wheel eliminates any concern about a broken drive chain. BMW's flat twin/shaft-drive design was copied by several manufacturers, including Ural in Russia and Marusho in Japan in its Lilac model. The latter ceased production in 1967.

The MÜNCH Mammut was conceived in Germany in 1966. It is powered by a NSU four-cylinder automobile engine of 1,200cc displacement. In today's "bigger is better" culture, 1,200cc may not seem large. But the results were smooth and impressive power. It proved itself as a capable touring machine and may have inspired many of the large four-cylinder touring bikes that have followed since. Initially built until 1975, Munch has seen a revival since 2000 with ultra-modern versions of the bike being produced by MÜNCH MOTORRAD TECHNIK GmbH in Germany. Munch owners are in a very elite group.

European touring bikes in the 1970s, like this Moto Guzzi 850 Eldorado, brought luxury car comfort to two wheels. This bike features the company's iconic transversely mounted 90-degree V-twin engine, designed by Giulio Cesare Carcano in the early 1960s. The 90-degree angle offers good balance to quell vibration. Final drive is by shaft. Grand Touring had arrived.

Moto Guzzi continues offering touring bikes in pure Gran Turismo (grand touring) fashion. Pictured is its California 1400 Touring model. It is powered by a 1,400cc V-twin engine that uses ride by wire throttle control. ABS and traction control are also included. Photo courtesy of Moto Guzzi, Piaggio Group Americas, Inc.

Moto Guzzi's dynamic new MGX-21 Flying Fortress is aptly named. Full of aggressive styling cues and technology, this 1,400cc bagger is sure to make its mark on American roads. The bike was designed at the California-based Piaggio Advanced Design Center. It features lots of carbon fiber and a large 21-inch front wheel. Photo courtesy of Moto Guzzi, Piaggio & C SpA.

Jupiter's Travels

Considering the European bikes available for touring back in 1974, a Triumph may not have been the best choice for British journalist Ted Simon for circumnavigating the globe. He selected a 500cc Triumph T-100 Tiger for his four-year journey covering sixty-four thousand miles. The choice of bike was motivated by a sponsorship he had from a British newspaper to chronicle his trip. He would have been much better off with any of the more reliable BMWs available in 1974. The Triumph struggled with overheating and other issues that required repair, but managed to complete the trip.

Simons was in his forties when he undertook his extraordinary journey on his T100P Triumph. More remarkable was that he repeated the trip twenty-four years later. Photo Courtesy of Ted Simon. jupitalia.com

Simon's book, *Jupiter's Travels*, truly enlightens the reader on the value of exploring the world on two wheels. Local cultures, climates, and grand views are best experienced out in the open. The discovery of his inner self as a result of his trials underscored the connection between motorcycling and self-actualization. Simons repeated the trip in 2001, albeit on a flat twin air-cooled BMW R80GS. Simon had the engine enlarged from the standard 798cc to 1,000cc. This boosted horsepower without adding any extra weight. Other modifications included better brakes and a high-output alternator. He was seventy years old on his second trip and assures those of us nearing that age that motorcycle touring around the globe is not just for the young.

A modern BMW F800 GS that would have been an excellent choice for Ted Simon had it been available back in 2001. This dual-purpose bike packs 85 horses and is most capable on and off the road. The "Adventure" version sports a larger gas tank. BMW also offers a smaller 652cc single-cylinder in its extensive GS line. Photo courtesy of BMW Motorrad USA.

Inspiration for Adventure

Circling the globe on a bike is a luxury few of us can afford but dream of often. The current surge in adventure bikes (ADV) available from nearly all makers suggests that many of us love the idea of taking a few weeks off to ride in unforgiving landscapes. These bikes have longer travel suspensions, skid plates, high exhaust pipes, and knobby tires—all to deal with rough terrain. Inspired by Ted Simon's adventures, two well-known actors and motorcyclists, Ewan McGregor and Charley Boorman, fulfilled their dreams of taking a ride around the world. To give due credit, there was another rider, Claudio von Planta, the cameraman, who filmed most of the great off-road riding sequences while having to ride the same tough course. To fund the ride, they teamed up with a production crew that followed their trail and ultimately produced the documentary. The story is a wonderful tale of discovery that changed their perspective of the world and its people. As their predecessors had experienced, people are united in their hospitality, curiosity, and genuine love for life regardless of their state of wealth or poverty.

Ewan McGregor and Charley Boorman in the Rocky Mountains, Canada, with their BMW R1100GS motorcycles. Photo taken by Julian Broad, © 2004 Long Way Round.

The episode in Mongolia was perhaps the turning point in Ewan McGregor's and Charley Boorman's determination to carry on. The countless miles of riding in marsh and bogs tested their physical and mental endurance to the limit. Riding twenty feet, falling, and having to lift six hundred pounds of bike and gear countless times forced each of them to look far beyond the premise of their mission. Sharing a bowl of sheep and goat testicles with a welcoming Mongolian family also added a few credits toward building character. One learns hu-

mility and humanity on the road. Doing it on a motorcycle makes it rewarding beyond mere words. Their story, *Long Way Round*, and sequel, *Long Way Down*, are available on DVD, and well worth watching. The former is also available as a book. It often looks at the ride from a philosophical perspective.

Ewan and Charley chose the state of the art in adventure touring bikes, the BMW R1100 GS in the first film, and the R1200 GS for their trip down through Africa. These bikes are true road warriors, both on and off the tarmac. Their downside is their heft and height. Shorter riders like me can only dream of riding one through the sands of the Sahara.

There was another option that Ewan and Charley looked at—the KTM Adventure, available in a 950cc 75-degree V-twin then. It has evolved through several sizes to 1,195cc now. The KTM was a formidable contender. The decision to go with the "beemers" was motivated by the company's offer to supply the bikes for the trip. It would have been an informative comparison to see both machines on the journey.

The king of all adventure touring bikes is the fully equipped BMW R1200 GS Adventure. The powerful 125 hp engine is essential in moving the 573 pound bike plus gear and rider through rough terrain. The flat twin has been upgraded with liquid-cooling. While the Adventure model features more crash bars and a huge 7.9 gallon fuel tank, the regular R1200 GS has a 5.3 gallon tank. Photo courtesy of BMW Motorrad USA.

KTM's 1290 Super Adventure once again elevates the bar in adventure touring bikes. It features all the latest electronic controls to get the most out of the beast on and off the road. The impressive engine is based on the 1290 Super Duke® R, but configured for enduro duty. Photo courtesy of KTM North America, Inc.

Honda entered the adventure touring world before the term became popular. Its Transalp dual-sport was introduced in 1987, and came in several engine sizes, ranging from 400cc to 700cc. Their latest adventure bike, the Africa Twin, is squarely aimed at competing with BMW and KTM.

Yamaha's 1,199cc parallel twin–powered Super Ténéré ® ES competes head-to-head against the European adventure bikes. Easier to handle than many of its contemporaries, and loaded with electronic suspension control, ABS, and TC, this bike makes a compelling case. It is also quite a bit less expensive than many of its European counterparts. Photo courtesy of Yamaha Motor Corporation U.S.A.

Honda's new Africa Twin adventure bike comes with a 998cc parallel twin engine that is offered with either a six-speed manual gearbox or a new DCT transmission. The automatic transmission comes with selectable on- and off-road modes. Both versions have ABS standard with rear ABS on/off and Honda Selectable Torque Control (HSTC). Photo courtesy of American Honda Motor Co., Inc.

For those looking for a more exotic adventure touring bike, the Aprilia Caponord 1200 Rally may just fit the bill. The machine is loaded with electronic controls for suspension, traction, and braking. It is a bit lighter and a bit less expensive than its BMW counterpart. Photo courtesy of Aprilia, Piaggio & C SpA.

The nimble Suzuki V-Strom® DL650XTA opens this class of motorcycling up to many riders looking for a lower entry point in price and weight. The V-Strom 1000 ABS pictured is a good lower-cost alternative to those wishing for a narrow V-twin bike like the KTM 1190 Adventure. It features a 1037cc liquid-cooled, DOHC, 90° V-twin. Photo courtesy of Suzuki Motor of America, Inc.

Aprilia's Mana 850 GT has a bit of an identity crisis. It is called a sportbike by some, a maxi-scooter by others, and an adventure bike by the rest. The key to this confusion is that it has a fully automatic continuously variable transmission that can be pre-set for touring, sport, or rain riding. The bike handles like a well-mannered sportbike and does allow foot shifting through seven gears if you wish. Photo courtesy of Aprilia, Piaggio & C SpA.

Triumph's Tiger Explorer XC is a serious player in the adventure bike category. The 1,215cc three-cylinder DOHC, four valves per cylinder engine puts out 135 hp and enough torque at 86 ft-lbs to climb over pretty much the most rugged terrain. Final drive is by shaft. Triumph offers six model options in its XR and XC Tiger Explorer series. Advanced features abound, including traction control, ride modes, and the Triumph Semi Active Suspension System. Low seat options are also available. Photo courtesy of Triumph Motorcycles.

BMW's S1000XR has closed the gap between adventure tourer and sportbike. They have coined a new category called "Adventure Sport." The bike's 999cc engine is derived from the company's impressive S1000RR superbike. The machine offers a broad spectrum of advanced features, including Dynamic ESA semi-active suspension. With 160 hp on tap, adventure riding has become a whole new ballgame. Photo courtesy of BMW Motorrad USA.

Ducati entered the adventure touring space with its proven Multistrada. The 160 hp Multistrada 1200 Enduro is loaded with technology that makes it equally comfortable on the highway and off-road. The bike is available with a broad array of accessories, including aluminum cases and added impact protection. Photo courtesy of Ducati Motor Holding S.p.A.

Motorcycle adventure touring is certainly not limited to two wheels. The Russian-made Ural with sidecar makes a great companion on any off-road adventure. Not only does it allow the carrying of a lot of extra gear, but it has the traction to get over pretty much anything in its way with its two-wheel drive. A driveshaft links the rear wheel to the sidecar wheel.

Honda Redefines the Touring Bike

It didn't take long for Honda to recognize America's thirst for long-distance riding. The remarkable CB750 raised the bar considerably in 1969, but it was more of a super standard than a tourer. Quick to respond, Honda's development team introduced the remarkable Gold Wing in 1974. Available to consumers for 1975, the GL1000 featured an innovative flat-four water-cooled engine capable of an impressive 82 hp and 125 mph top speed. Anyone who knew anything about motorcycles recognized that this bike represented a whole new ball game—just like the CB750 had done six years earlier. The Gold Wing has evolved over the course of forty years to retain its title as the ultimate touring motorcycle. Current models are equipped with rider airbag. It is the industry's first production motorcycle airbag system. The bike's forks have sensors that detect a frontal impact.

Honda's GL1000 Gold Wing set a whole new standard for touring motorcycles back in 1975. The smooth-running water-cooled engine was coupled to the rear wheel by a near-maintenance-free shaft. This was all quite different from what was available from domestic makers. Well cared for examples like the one pictured will cost many multiples over the original $2,895 price.

Soon after its introduction, and immediate success, the Gold Wing began to morph into the ultimate touring machine. This 1985 GL 1200 sported all the amenities a modern touring rig could offer, including good weather protection, comfortable seats, stereo, and luggage. Despite its size, the bike was easy to handle. Photo courtesy of American Honda Motors Co., Inc.

The key to the Gold Wing's stability is its sturdy alloy frame chassis as seen on this 2001 model. Note that the radiators face outward just above the engine to save space. Photo courtesy of American Honda Motors Co., Inc.

The original Honda Gold Wing Valkyrie is an offshoot of the Gold Wing. It was brought onto the scene in 1996 as the GL 1500 C. It has the same plush seating and long-haul comfort. Like the original GL, it lacks a full fairing and has the radiator mounted centrally in front of the motor. Current Valkyries are much more futuristic in styling and sport a larger motor.

The Gold Wing has evolved to a 1,832cc liquid-cooled horizontally opposed six cylinder today. It represents the ultimate in luxurious touring. Rider airbag is standard.

Honda Gold Wings make great trikes. Numerous builders offer conversion kits. Check out MTC Voyager if you are interested.

Not a motorcycle anymore, this Gold Wing continues to serve its owner with four wheels.

Sport Touring Evolves

Sportbike riders were not about to stay behind as their buddies cruised the highways on their V-twins and Gold Wings. They were fully prepared to suffer some neck, back, and wrist discomfort. Many sportbikes allow some minor modifications to make things a bit easier on the body. Handlebar risers add an inch or two to reduce the stress associated with leaning forward. Footpeg relocation is more complicated. It requires new fittings for the brake and shift lever. All of the mods can have a dramatic effect on how many more miles one can ride before taking a break. The Europeans, however, introduced a better option forty years ago—the sport tourer.

Sport touring bikes are basically sportbikes with touring-friendly ergonomics. Footpegs and handlebars tend to be a bit more standard in their position. Seats are also a bit more comfortable, and as it is customary with most touring bikes today, fuel tanks are larger. Fairings add weather protection, while luggage-mounting points permit the use of hard cases for storage.

BMWs stunning R90S, introduced in 1973, became a model for other sport tourers to follow.

By 1983 BMW upped the game by introducing its K series. These liquid-cooled bikes had their DOHC engines set longitudinally in the frame, with cylinders lying horizontal. The original K100 featured a four-cylinder 1,000cc engine and monoschock suspension. BMW was the first to introduce ABS on a bike with its 1987 K100. By 1985 a three-cylinder 750cc was introduced as the K75. The K sport touring line continues today with its K1600 GT. Pictured is a K1100 LT, introduced in 1992. Note the addition of an extra footpeg on the crash bar to help relieve leg stiffness on long stretches.

Ducati's ST line offered the company's superb desmodromic L-twin in a sport touring configuration between 2003 and 2007. High-strung and high-maintenance cost limited the bike's life as consumers had other options.

Not to be overshadowed, Honda entered the sport touring segment in 1990 with its superb ST1100. Known also as the Pan European, it featured a new 1,085cc longitudinal 90-degree engine. The bike evolved into the ST1300, satisfying those who weren't quite ready for a Gold Wing but wanted something a bit more civil than the typical sport tourer. Photo courtesy of American Honda Motor Co., Inc.

Ducati's highly versatile Multistrada has clearly outsold its ST line. Introduced in 2003, the bike initially resembled a supermoto. The latest generation of the 1,200cc sport tourer includes the Multistrada 1200 S D|air®, the first motorcycle incorporating an intelligent system wirelessly connected with the airbags inside the special Ducati D|air® apparel by Dainese. This takes safety to a whole new level. Introduced in 2016 is the Multistrada Pikes Peak featuring many high-performance sportbike components. Photo courtesy of Ducati Motor Holding S.p.A.

MV Agusta is best known for its exotic sportbikes. It entered the sport touring segment in 2015 with its superb 798cc three-cylinder Turismo Veloce 800. Fast, nimble, and elegant in every way, it offers yet another great choice to motorcyclists and their mates looking to explore the world around them. Photo courtesy of MV AGUSTA Motor S.p.A.

The versatile Kawasaki Versys comes in a variety of configurations that may be categorized as standard, sport touring, or mild adventure touring. The bikes seem to do all of it well. Pictured is the 649cc parallel twin configured for sport touring. The Versys 1000 LT is a better choice if high-speed highway riding is part of the tour.

New categories seem to be born every year in motorcycling. The term "sports bagger" has entered the motorcycle lexicon. Yamaha's FJ-09® equipped with saddlebags is a perfect example of this breed. Light, nimble, powerful, and upright seating makes it an almost perfect sport touring machine. Photo courtesy of Yamaha Motor Corporation U.S.A.

Triumph has been making its superb three-cylinder Sprint ST sport touring bike since 1998. It is perhaps the best deal out there for a used sport touring machine that is aimed at the rider who wants a bit more sport than touring. Good used ones are available for under $5,000. Those interested in a new British sport tourer must take a good look at Triumph's Trophy SE.

Honda's latest entry into the sport touring segment is its stylish VFR1200F. The bike features an advanced 1,237cc SOHC 76-degree V4 engine, and is offered with an automatic dual-clutch transmission as an option. A padded top box makes for a good backrest for the passenger. Photo courtesy of American Honda Motor Co., Inc.

Kawasaki's enduring Concours® was first introduced in 1986 as the ZG1000. The 997cc DOHC four-cylinder bike defined the Japanese sport tourer. It saw tremendous success through 2006. In 2007, it was replaced by the larger Concours 14 with a 1,352cc VVT (variable valve timing) engine and shaft drive. Certainly one of the fastest sport tourers out there, it could get you across the country in less than a day if it weren't for speed limits. The bike comes in black in the event that the candy lime green color is not your style. Photo courtesy of Kawasaki Motors Corp., U.S.A.

Yamaha's FJR1300ES is one of the best values out there for a large displacement state-of-the-art sport touring machine. The electronic suspension system automatically manages damping and rebound on the go for numerous settings: solo, two-up, or with luggage. This allows fine-tuning of just the kind of ride you want on a particularly winding stretch of mountain road. The 1,298cc motor makes light of carrying a passenger and full saddlebags. Yamaha's FJR1300AS sport tourer features an electronic clutchless gear-shift system. Shifting is done by pushbutton on the left handlebar. Photo courtesy of Yamaha Motor Corporation, USA.

BMW's K line has certainly come a long way since 1983. The new six-cylinder K1600GT is pretty much the top-of-the-line in sport touring machines. Electronics abound in ride control, suspension, traction, and braking. At 718 pounds dry, this bike still offers sub-eleven-second acceleration in the quarter mile, and a top speed of 147 mph. Be prepared to pay over $26,000 for the privilege. Photo courtesy of BMW Motorrad USA.

New on the scene, Motus® Motorcycles is an American company making high-tech sport touring machines. In line with American muscle cars, their Baby Block MV4 uses pushrods to actuate the valves on the powerful V-four. Looking head on, the engine actually looks like a half-sized Chevy small block. Lee Conn, president, and Brian Case, VP of design, have added yet another great American motorcycle. Photo courtesy of Motus Motorcycles.

One should not count out any of the three-wheelers on the market for open cockpit touring. The Can-Am Spyder RT makes riding all day an absolute effortless event. The security of three wheels is a plus. Photo courtesy of Bombardier Recreational Products Inc.

Life on the Road

Touring at great distances requires some basic equipment and maintenance. Foremost is a thorough check of the bike way before the trip. Last minute fixes tend to be hasty and potentially dangerous. This check includes you. If you have any ailing issues, get them resolved. A nagging backache will not get any better on the road.

The Motorcycle Safety Foundation recommends a basic check of tires, tire pressure, controls, lights, oil, chassis, and stands as part of the process. Take care of anything that feels loose or leaks oil. Tires are paramount. A good tread is essential for riding in the rain. Sport touring tires may not last as long, but offer better grip on dry surfaces than high mileage ones.

Adjust and lubricate the chain. Adjust suspension preload to handle the extra weight of your gear. You may also want to attach a throttle assist device to help relieve wrist strain.

What to Bring

One can certainly over pack, but less is more. A credit card in the wallet will buy anything you may have forgotten. Essentials that should be stuffed into the saddle bags, top box, or tank bag include a motorcycle rain suit, water bottle, protein bars, small CO_2 tire patch kit, duct tape, electrical tape, JB Weld epoxy, zip ties, tire pressure gauge, a few feet of electrical wire, spare fuses, large and small trash bags, extra ear plugs, extra bungee cords, twenty feet of cord, a small fire extinguisher, a five-foot by seven-foot plastic tarp, and a small first aid kit with your personal meds, some ibuprofen, an anti-diarrheal, and antacid. The large trash bags come in handy as emergency ponchos, usually for other riders you may meet that have no rain gear. Some useful gear for any tour includes a waterproof handlebar-mounted smartphone/GPS case, a GoPro camera, and wireless communication system for chatting with your passenger or riding buddies. Bluetooth technology allows listening to music, speaking on the phone, or hearing directions from the GPS.

Keep cameras and other personal items in food storage bags. ALWAYS take your belongings with you. Clothing is bulky and should be kept to a minimum. A good riding suit with liner can always be made warmer with a couple of layers of clothing or a heated vest. I carry one heavy sweatshirt, a long sleeved T-shirt, pajama pants, and windproof motorcycle thermals. That combination covers most conditions. Pack a pair of khakis and a golf shirt for when dining out. Water-resistant or heated gloves and vest are optional. Some bikes come with heated grips and seats to help with cold mornings on the road.

A good motorcycle rain suit, waterproof covers for gear, and waterproof boots are essential for wet weather riding. A full-face helmet would do better than a skimpy half-helmet. Cold wet ears aren't much fun. ABS braking is a real plus when riding on wet surfaces.

The amount of tools you carry will depend on your ability to use them. The minimum you should take is a set of Allen wrenches that fit most of the fasteners on your bike and a Leatherman® tool. Handlebar controls will loosen over time. Other items include pliers and enough box wrenches to be able to at least remove the wheels in the event you need to have them serviced. I always carry a large crescent wrench for the axle nuts. It also serves well as a hammer or for protection. A spark plug wrench is always good to have if you can get at the plugs.

This Suzuki Boulevard M109R parked at 12,000 feet in the Rocky Mountains is well equipped with storage. The magnetic tank bag offers the convenience of a clear plastic pouch to hold a map and is easily removed for carrying when on foot. Soft luggage on the back is lighter than a plastic top box and doubles as an elegant suitcase when checking into a hotel.

Those looking to pull a heavy trailer for extended distance should consider one of the Voyager trike conversion kits by Motorcycle Convertible Kits. These kits adapt an independently sprung carriage to the motorcycles. Two wheels straddle the bike's rear wheel. The weight of a trailer will bear on the independent unit rather than on the bike's suspension. This offers much better control and stability.

Long-distance touring can be comfortable with the right gear. Despite its high cost, an Aerostich one-piece riding suit not only offers good rain protection, but includes armor at all critical points to protect the rider in the event of a fall. A full-face helmet is best for both protection and keeping dry. Aerostich offers excellent equipment for touring. aerostich.com

A trailer is an option for those who are planning to be on the road for a very long time. The trailer restricts handling but is quite useful for carrying everything that goes along with camping.

Where to Go?

The answer to this questions is simple . . . go wherever you want. One can plan all winter for the tour of a lifetime, calculating each pit stop based on estimated mileage and distance between gas stations. On the other hand, one can just load up the bike and head in any direction. This is particularly true if you are willing to sleep on the side of the road or at a rest stop in the event you find yourself in a remote part of the country. A small tarp comes in handy for those events when a rainstorm catches you off guard in the middle of the night.

The best advice for new touring riders is to start off locally first with some planned and unplanned day trips. Extend that to an overnight trip. After that venture farther. Smartphone mapping and GPS apps can help bring you back if you get lost. For more serious navigational tools, consider a high-end waterproof GPS unit, such as the Garmin zūmo®. The unit is much easier to manipulate with riding gloves than a smartphone and can manage all aspects of route navigation.

Depending on where you live, you may or may not have the benefit of beautiful riding roads. If you don't, you will have to ride to them. *Rider* magazine and *RoadRUNNER Motorcycle Touring & Travel*® magazine are great places to see photos and maps of wonderful destinations. Some of these destinations may be far away. Italy's annual *Motogiro D'Italia* event is a 1,637-kilometer ride that brings folks and machines from all over the world together to compete in a timed rally. Bikes of all sizes are represented. Experienced sport touring riders will find this event very exciting and challenging.

One of the great destinations for sport touring enthusiasts is the Tail of the Dragon, an eleven-mile stretch of road beginning at Deals Gap on the Tennessee/North Carolina state line. It is an internationally recognized stretch of road with 318 curves. This rider is recording his run with a GoPro® Hero mounted to the side of his BMW. Photo courtesy of Richard Adler.

The Guided Tour Option

One of the thrills of motorcycling is to tour with your friends and loved ones in faraway lands. This certainly includes Alaska, the Alps, Australia, Europe, and Africa. Several reputable tour companies will supply bikes and gear to make these rides events to remember. Check out the tours offered by Ayres Adventures, Edelweiss Bike Travel, and Globebusters Tours.

This stunning image of three riders participating in one of the Alaskan tours offered by Ayres Adventures is sure to inspire the notion of taking some time off to do the same. Photo courtesy of Ron Ayres, ayresadventures.com

If you and your buddies prefer to go on your own, then you should look at the great resources available on the Internet—in particular backcountrydiscoveryroutes.com. They offer detailed route maps and GPS tracking data for many exciting and challenging rides through some of this country's most beautiful places. Also check out whitehorsegear.com for an outstanding supply of touring guides, maps, accessories, and apparel

Adventure touring on your own in the Himalayas can take you to one of the highest passable roads in the world. The Khardung La (pass) in India's Kashmir region will bring you to an elevation of 17,582 feet. Electronic fuel-injected bikes will adjust the fuel/air mixture without a problem, while carbureted engines may need some tweaking to deal with the thin air. Photo by Tamara Hayden.

SKY IS THE LIMIT

54 RCC   16 TF

The Ultimate Challenge

As with anything we do, there are those who must take it to the extreme. This includes motorcycle touring. For those who want the challenge, and the badge that goes along with it, the Iron Butt Association manages a rally that requires participants to ride 11,000 miles in eleven days. It is held in the United States every two years. Each rally includes several side trips that can add an extra thousand miles and extra points for scoring. This is for serious riders who are in excellent physical condition. The patch that one receives after completing the tour is well respected by knowledgeable motorcyclists worldwide.

The Iron Butt Rally consists of checkpoints located around the United States. Riders must be present at each of these checkpoints within a two-hour window in order to be considered finishers. Photo courtesy of Iron Butt Association®

Hitting the Road

I could not wait to hit the road again on a long trip after writing this chapter. I hope that reading it has the same effect on you. Your choice of a touring machine will depend on an honest assessment of how you will be using it. Test rides are absolutely necessary. Most dealers will permit that, given you have proper licensing. It is even better to rent a touring bike before committing to buying one. A few words of wisdom before you head out:

1 - Be smart . . . take your time and don't take chances, especially at the end of a long day. There is no lousier feeling than being hurt hundreds of miles from home.

2 - Stay sharp. Don't crank the stereo or iPod so loud that you can't hear your environment.

3 - When tired, rest. It takes just twenty minutes of sleep on a roadside patch of grass to recharge the batteries and regain cognitive functions.

4 - Stay warm and dry. Hypothermia can creep up on you. Warm up by adding extra layers of clothing. If circumstances don't allow that, use a trick us old-timers have been using for decades—stuff newspapers inside your jacket and pants.

5 - Get off the bike and stretch every hour. We often get locked into a seating position, especially on sport touring bikes, which numbs our muscles. We don't even notice that circulation is slowing down. A two-minute walk around the bike will get the blood flowing and keep the muscles from cramping. Stretch a bit while you are off the bike.

6 - Hydrate! Long rides, especially at high altitudes, dehydrate the rider. This results in delayed reflexes and exhaustion.

See you on the road!

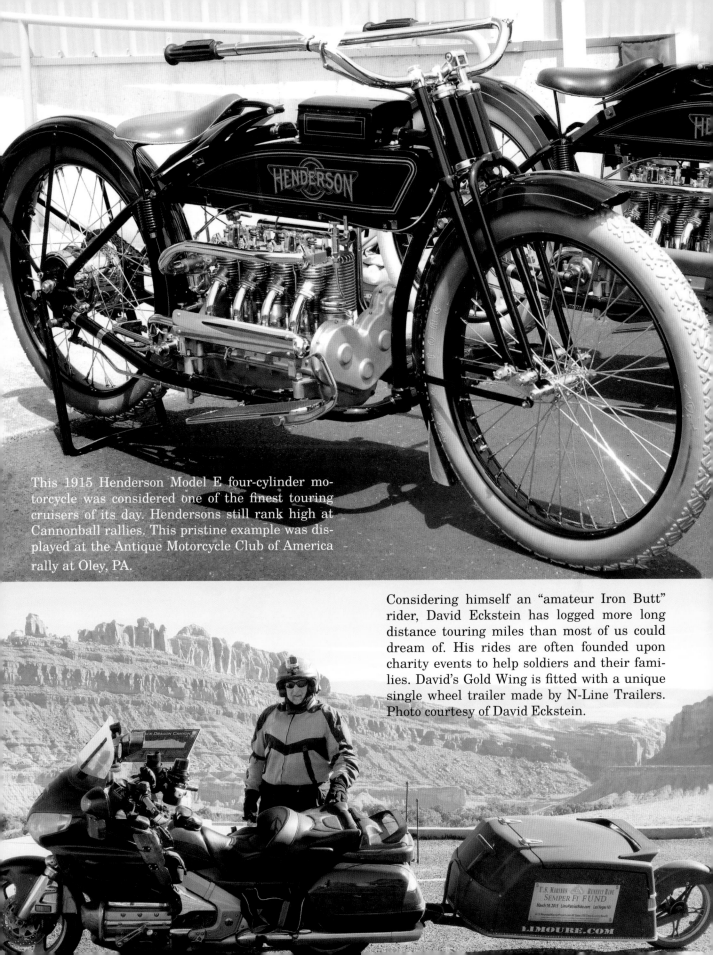

This 1915 Henderson Model E four-cylinder motorcycle was considered one of the finest touring cruisers of its day. Hendersons still rank high at Cannonball rallies. This pristine example was displayed at the Antique Motorcycle Club of America rally at Oley, PA.

Considering himself an "amateur Iron Butt" rider, David Eckstein has logged more long distance touring miles than most of us could dream of. His rides are often founded upon charity events to help soldiers and their families. David's Gold Wing is fitted with a unique single wheel trailer made by N-Line Trailers. Photo courtesy of David Eckstein.

Energica Motor Company S.p.A.

Sine Cycles

Chapter 10

ELECTRIC MOTORCYCLES

The quest to power motorcycles with electric motors began over one hundred and twenty years ago. The limiting factor was the battery. The dream never faded. As battery technology evolved, so did the reality that electric motorcycles are the way of the future.

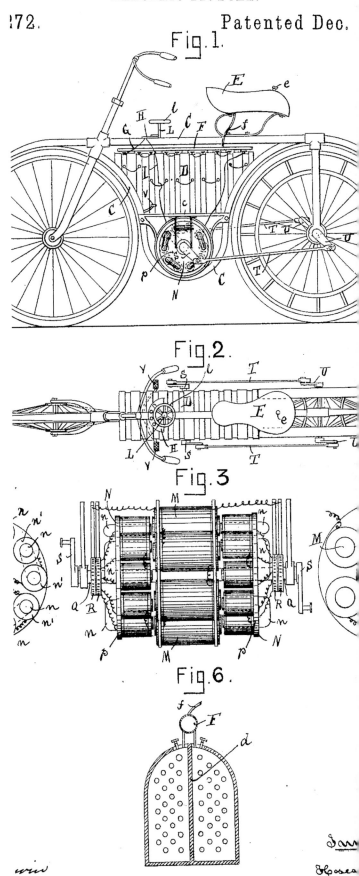

H. W. LIBBEY.
ELECTRIC BICYCLE.

172. Patented Dec.

Fig.1.

Fig.2.

Fig.3.

Fig.6.

A Long History of Development

Electric motorcycles have been around for as long as internal combustion engine–powered bikes. The concept began before our Civil War. The DC (direct current) electric motor had already been perfected to provide rotational power to machinery. Early motors were powered by lead-acid batteries. Battery-powered electric vehicles were being tested with great enthusiasm over one hundred and twenty years ago. Ogden Bolten patented his version of an "Electrical Bicycle" with a rear wheel–mounted motor as early as 1895. Hosea W. Libbey followed and was granted his US patent for an electric bicycle in 1897. That same year Humber motorcycle makers in England toyed with the idea and created an electric-powered tandem bike. Unfortunately, in all cases, the big bulky cells were not capable of holding a charge long enough for any sustained long-distance travel.

Developers waited patiently for battery technology to advance. Undaunted, electric bike prototypes appeared on a regular basis throughout the twentieth century. A major development was the lithium-ion battery. Able to be charged quickly, and with a good power-to-weight ratio, these cells became the preferred source of electricity for electric motorcycles. The cost of these batteries, however, is keeping the price of electric bikes high. This will no doubt change as manufacturing techniques improve and alternative sources of power are discovered.

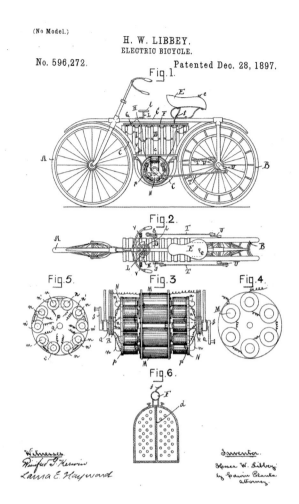

Libbey's 1897 US patent for an electric bicycle. The motor drives the rear wheel axle by connecting rods and cranks, much like that used by Roper on his steam bike.

Electric motorcycles have come a very long way since Libbey's patent. Major makers all see the potential for electric-powered bikes. Pictured is Honda's stunning RC-E racing bike concept. Photo courtesy of American Honda Motor Co., Inc

Watt's Legacy

Electric motorcycles rate their motors by kilowatts. Typically they range from 20 kW for small bikes to 150 kW for electric superbikes. Motors at the higher end generate a lot of heat and require cooling fins or liquid-cooling. Most makers will provide equivalent horsepower ratings, although this may be deceptive in that the torque of an electric motor tends to be much higher than an equivalent gas engine. Storage capacity is given in kilowatt-hours. The higher the number, the greater the battery's storage capacity. Think of it as having a larger gas tank. Typical range is between 10 kWh and 20 kWh. Voltage also makes a difference. The higher the voltage, the more power. Voltages vary from 20 volts for smaller bikes to over 500 volts for superbikes.

Today, nearly every major maker, including Harley-Davidson with its LiveWire™ bike, has thrown its hat in the electric ring. However, it is the innovative start-up companies that have brought the electric motorcycle to reality. The most successful is a California garage startup called Zero® Motorcycles. They introduced their first prototypes in 2006, and have continued to lead the market with lightweight on and off-road motorcycles for real-world use since 2009. Suspension and chassis design is very much in line with conventional motorcycles. Range has approached the magic 200-mile mark around town using auxiliary power modules, and continues to rise as efficient motor technology evolves. This will reduce the "range anxiety" typically associated with electric bikes. Recharging remains a downside, but quick-charging systems offered by many of the makers greatly reduces the wait. Zero's SR model, for example, will take at least nine hours to charge. This drops down to five hours using the optional quick-charger. Add another charger, and you are down to 2.4 hours. Separate chargers do require separate 15 amp circuits. New nanotechnology promises to recharge batteries in minutes rather than hours. Battery swapping makes machines likes the Zeros even more practical in urban environments where electrical outlets may be hard to find when parking on the street.

A common sight at bike gatherings today is to see an electric motorcycle being charged. Every little bit helps. Riders have learned to carry their own long extension cords.

The Plus and Minus

The benefits of electric motorcycles are self-evident. Besides their inherent "clean" low carbon footprint, they are quiet. I particularly love the electric off-road capable machines. They allow romping in the woods without annoying the campers and raising the attention of the anti-motorcycle crowd. Some models do introduce artificial engine noise to satisfy the senses. Another benefit is that batteries will typically last several hundred thousand miles—longer than most of us keep a bike for.

Electric motorcycles cost a lot more than comparable gas models. The motivation for buying one at this stage of the game is based more on the cool factor than return on investment. However, they do cost just pennies per mile to run. This is a great benefit for commuters. Another major benefit is that electric motors produce maximum torque at any rpm. This offers excellent acceleration and plenty of power at any speed. There is also no clutch to deal with on most models. The majority of electric bikes are driven directly off the motor and don't have a transmission. Coming to a stop does not require clutch action. The motor just stops. There is also very little to maintain on an electric motorcycle. Typically one would have to check the tires, drive chain, or belt, and the brake pads.

There are dozens of electric bike makers out there, with more on the horizon. Some makers like Honda are experimenting with hybrid technology. As with hybrid cars, a gas engine would power an electric generator to charge the battery that powers the electric motor. Hydrogen fuel cell technology is another option.

Britain's Intelligent Energy company developed a hydrogen fuel cell–powered motorcycle prototype named ENV (emission neutral vehicle). The bike was designed with a 6 kW 48-volt motor and introduced in 2005. The lack of hydrogen refueling stations has limited consumer interest for now in this promising concept. Photo courtesy of Intelligent Energy Limited.

On the Track

Electric bikes have proven to be formidable competitors. One of the fastest production motorcycles to-date is the Lightning LS-218, clocked at Bonneville at 218.637 mph. Even the prestigious Isle of Man TT has a zero emissions race category. There was some skepticism about electric race bikes from die-hard petrolheads during the inaugural race managed by eco-friendly race promoters TTXGP in 2009. TT organizers quickly recognized the great value in this class and decided to make it an official racing category for the following year's TT. It was aptly named TT Zero. The challenges faced by the entrants in creating motors, controllers, and battery systems capable of all-out performance are well documented in the 2011 Mark Neale documentary *Charge*. Brilliant independent developers, such as Cedric Lynch, were able to showcase their technologies on the unforgiving TT course. Lynch designed a unique permanent magnet brushed DC motor that powered Team Agni to first place for the one lap race. Other contenders, such as the American team lead by Michael Czysz, used Agni motors designed by Lynch. Despite some bad luck in 2009, MotoCzysz would see many podiums in the years to come. The first was in 2010 with US racer Mark Miller winning the TT Zero on the 37.75-mile course riding the MotoCzysz E1pc at an average speed of 96.82 mph. The list of record breaking continues as other notable electric bikes emerge from garages and factory R&D labs. Electric vehicle technology is very fertile territory.

The sampling below will offer the reader sufficient insight into this remarkable genre of motorcycle. New models are constantly emerging as older ones are improved. It is an exciting era in motorcycle history.

Electric superbikes, like those made by Lightning, approach Supersport race bike performance. Photo courtesy of Lightning Motorcycles.

Zero Motorcycles

One of the first generation Zero electric motorcycles introduced to market in 2009. The instrument cluster on early models was quite simple. There is a toggle to switch between sport and "easy" economy modes. Battery level indicator is standard on all electric bikes.

Zero produces great dual-sport electric models good for off-road riding. Photo courtesy of Zero Motorcycles, Inc.

Zero's SR "Max Performance" electric sportbike produces 67 hp (50 kilowatts), and a whopping 106 ft-lbs of torque. That's more torque than a typical V-twin. High-quality brakes combined with Bosch ABS provide secure stopping power. The Z-FORCE® motor generates electricity when braking. This bike, with optional extended range "Power Tank," lists for $19,840 as of 2015. Its sub-four-second 0–60 acceleration is sure to surprise most performance automobile owners revving their engines at a light. Photo courtesy of Zero Motorcycles, Inc.

Yamaha

Yamaha is planning on entering the electric bike market with the PES1 sportbike and the PED1 dirt bike. Pictured is the company's attractive sportbike prototype. Photo courtesy of Yamaha Motor Corp.

Oregon-based Brammo has been making impressive electric bikes for years. Its motorcycle business has been acquired by Polaris, makers of Victory and Indian. Brammo itself is staying focused on developing its electric traction motors and lithium-ion batteries. Brammo's first successful production bike was the Enertia Plus. The bike features many quality components, including an aluminum monocoque body, Marzocchi forks, Brembo brakes, and a Works Performance rear shock. It made for an ideal local runabout with an average of fifty miles in range.

Pictured is the Empulse® R sportbike release by Brammo in 2014. Unlike most electrics, the bike features an integrated six-speed transmission that gives the machine a middleweight sportbike feel. The AC motor draws a lot of current and is liquid-cooled. Range around town is about 100 miles.

Victory's acquisition of Brammo has allowed the resources to participate in the prestigious Isle of Man TT Zero race for 2015 with its special Empulse RR. The bike scored third place under rider Lee Johnston. Renamed as the Victory RR for 2016, William Dunlop rode the improved bike to a second place finish for that year's TT Zero. He achieved an impressive top speed of 165 mph. Victory is no doubt committed to electric superbike development. The bike's Parker GVM Water-cooled, 3-phase, IMP AC motor produces an impressive 174 hp. Photo courtesy of Victory Motorcycles, Polaris Industries, Inc.

As a result of its success at the TT, Victory has introduced the Empulse TT electric sportbike for 2016. It is marketed as a street-legal race bike. The price is an impressively reasonable $20,000. Brammo's acquisition by Polaris has paid off for both the company and the consumer. Photo courtesy of Victory Motorcycles, Polaris Industries, Inc.

Bultaco

Best known for their enduro bikes back in the 1960s and 1970s, Spanish motorcycle maker Bultaco returns with some exciting electric bikes. Pictured is the attractive Rapitan® prototype. Photo courtesy of Bultaco Motors.

Johammer

Austrian maker Johammer has brought its vision of a futuristic electric cruiser to market today. The bike features a twin-arm box-section front fork and an advanced torsion-resistant aluminum main frame chassis that houses both the battery and suspension components. The rear-wheel-mounted electric motor is neatly hidden beneath the sleek bodywork. This bike is sure to turn some heads. Photo by Zeidler G agency, courtesy of Johammer e-mobility GmbH.

Energica

For those who cherish the exotic beauty of Italian bikes, Modena-based Energica® offers two models that will stir the heart. Energica is the first Italian manufacturer of supersport electric motorcycles. The Energica Ego sportbike pictured produces an astounding 144 ft-lbs torque from 0 rpm to redline, an electronically limited 150 mph (240 km/h) top speed, and a 0–100 mph time of under three seconds. Other features include top of the line racing components, onboard chargers, and a range of approximately 120 miles of real world riding. A fast charge system brings the battery to 85 percent in just thirty minutes. All this exotic technology is not cheap. The Ego 45 retails for $68,000. The company also produces an equally sexy streetfighter named Eva. Photo courtesy of Energica Motor Company S.p.A.

Volta

Volta Motorbikes of Girona Spain offers two elegant models ideal for urban environments: the BCN City and the BCN Sport. Both feature a 25 kW (34 hp) motor and a battery that can be recharged in two hours given availability of a 220-volt outlet. Its BCN Sport, pictured, has some sportier components and a throttle map for sport riding. Photo courtesy of Volta Motor Company, s.l.

Quite a different environment from the assembly lines from motorcycle factories of the past, Volta electric bikes are assembled in pristine, well-lit workshops. Photo courtesy of Volta Motor Company, s.l.

Mission

Mission Motorcycles was an innovative California company that produces extraordinary electric superbikes. Its RS model, pictured, has a 120 kW motor that produces an astounding 160 hp at the rear wheel, with 120 ft-lbs of torque beginning at 0 rpm. It has a top speed of 150 mph, does 0–60 in under three seconds, and a quarter mile in 10.492 seconds. The 17-kWh battery is said to offer a 230-mile range in the city, but more realistically averages 140 miles in all-around riding. No expense has been spared, including exotic Italian suspension and brake components. The price for this magnificent piece of technology was just under $60,000. Unfortunately, financial troubles resulted in bankruptcy in 2015. There is hope that the brand will be picked up by someone else. Photo courtesy of Mission Motorcycles, Inc.

Lightning

As of this writing, the Lightning LS-218 claims to be the world's fastest production bike, gas or electric. Kawasaki's H2R is likely to take that title. The LS-218 was clocked at 218.637 mph at Bonneville. Its 200 hp liquid-cooled motor produces a massive 168 ft-lbs of torque. Drive is direct; there is no transmission. The 380-volt 20-kWh battery pack option offers a range between 160 and 180 miles. Prices start at a reasonable $38,888. Photo courtesy of Lightning Motorcycles.

Sora

The Sora electric bike is made by the Quebec, Canada, company Lito Green Motion. The bike is designed and marketed as a "luxury" electric. It has an innovative feature that allows the user to convert the bike's ergonomics from cruiser to full café racer. The $49,900 motorcycle has a continuously variable transmission and a regenerative breaking system. Other features include lots of carbon fiber, aircraft grade aluminum, key card ignition, touch screen GPS, and a top speed of 118 mph. Photo courtesy of Sora, soraelectricsuperbike.com

Brutus

Bell Custom Cycles (BCC) is a family-owned business that has its own take on electric bikes. Chris Bell started building and fabricating the original Brutus retro-sport motorcycle in 2010. The Brutus 2 sports a 10 kWh battery pack and a unique look that many custom bike enthusiasts will surely appreciate. Photo courtesy of Bell Custom Cycles, BrutusMotorcycle.com

Mugen

The 2016 TT Zero entry by Mugen named Shinden Go. Electric racing machines are relatively heavy for their horsepower due to the weight of the battery. This impressive bike is powered by a laminate-type lithium-ion battery and weighs about 550 lb. It produces over 160 hp. Photo courtesy of Mugen.

Mugen (M-TEC Co.,Ltd.) is a Japanese company manufacturing high-perfor-mance machines and parts. It was formed by Soichiro Honda's son Hirotoshi Honda back in 1973. They have participated in TT Zero since 2014 with great success, refining their machines each year. They also attract great riders, including John McGuinness and Bruce Anstey. Anstey won the 2016 SES TT Zero Race to produce his eleventh TT win. He lapped the Mountain Course at 118.416 mph.

Znug zecOO

The zecOO electric motorcycle is a remarkable piece of Japanese art and technology designed by Znug. It features hub center steering and a 50 kW motor.

Each zecOO is handcrafted from the ground up. Photos courtesy of Znug, zecoomotor.com

Sinecycles

It took the Swiss company Sinecycles to introduce an electric chopper. This bold design clearly shows that electric technology can enter the traditional cruiser market. Missing, of course, are the large chrome exhaust pipes. The 20 kW power unit and drive train is provided by Zero Motorcycles. A smartphone app offers detailed information about the motorcycle, such as charge time, average watts per mile, total charge cycles, and more. Photo by Ben Grna, courtesy of Bruno Forcella of Sinecycles.

The Killa Joule Landspeed Motorcycle

Swedish-born engineer and racer Eva Håkansson realized her dream of becoming the fastest female on a motorcycle in August of 2014. She still holds that title in the electric motorcycle category. She broke several records at the Bonneville Motorcycle Speed Trials with a top speed of 241.901 mph and a two-way average of 240.726 mph. The team beat the previous electric motorcycle speed record by 25 mph. The record also holds for the fastest sidecar. In September of 2014, the team bested their previous month's run by hitting an amazing 270.224 mph. Håkansson and her husband, Bill Dubé, both mechanical engineers, had worked on building the three-wheeled KillaJoule for five years. It is powered by two Rinehart Motion Systems PM100 controllers that, combined, produce 500 hp and 800 ft-lbs. It weighs about 1,540 pounds (700 kg) including Håkansson, and measures 19 ft (5.6 m) long, 21 inches (0.53 m) wide, and 38 inches (0.96 m) in height. Photo courtesy of Eva Håkansson.

The story behind the futuristic ROBRADY Vectrix motorcycle appearing on the cover of this book holds much history in the ongoing development of electric motorcycle engineering. Many individuals and companies have devoted all their resources toward the goal of providing us with environmentally responsible vehicles. This is one such story, providing details on how engineers turn concepts into reality.

A Case Study on the Evolution of Electric Vehicles

The following case study titled Vectrix Electric Vehicles & Technologies by Peter Hughes, former CTO of vectrix, serves as a good representation of the challenges companies looking to introduce new technologies face.

Vectrix Electric Vehicles and Technologies

Vectrix was a US company formed in 1997 with the intent of developing electric drive train technology focused on two- and three-wheel vehicles. These vehicles are referred to as scooters and fall into categories based upon top speed and power. For its initial product launch, Vectrix developed and brought to market the VX-1, which fell in the maxi class of scooters, with peak power of 20kW and peak torques of 65Nm. At the time of its introduction in April 2007, the VX-1 set the standard for electric two-wheel vehicles with a top speed of 68 mph.

Unlike traditional scooters, which use a belt/chain drive to transmit power from the engine to the rear wheel, Vectrix developed a motor/gearbox combination mounted within the rear wheel itself. This patented technology essentially moved the engine (motor) from the center of the vehicle to the rear wheel, thus eliminating the belt drive. This configuration freed up valuable real estate, which provided additional volume for the battery pack. In turn this resulted in extended vehicle range.

To successfully develop any transportation product, the drive train, structure, and energy source must be integrated in such a fashion as to provide superior user ergonomics as well as an appearance that adds value to the product. Fortunately, Vectrix was introduced to the ROBRADY product design and development team in February 1997 in Sarasota, Florida. A customer/client relationship was formed, which resulted in all of the Vectrix transportation products being styled by the ROBRADY team over the course of the sixteen-year history of Vectrix.

In all cases, ROBRADY developed "ideation" alternatives that defined options for vehicle styling details and features. Typically a baseline design was selected, after which ROBRADY reduced the selected design to a full clay model built around the structural components of the vehicle. Such clay models allowed for the development of vehicle ergonomics and the ability to rapidly make styling improvements, as well as integrate the latest components into the product. The clay model for the VX-1 was actually tested in a Lockheed-Martin wind tunnel in Marietta, Georgia, to refine the vehicle drag and aerodynamic properties prior to committing the styling to tooling.

Designers create clay mock-ups of concept bikes like the Vectrix Superbike as part of the design process. Photo thanks to ROBRADY.

Once the styling, design, and marketing teams agreed upon the results of the clay model, ROBRADY digitized the clay model and determined the break points for the exterior components. Individual component surfaces (fenders, side panels, etc.) were designed (A surfaces) as well as the back side (B surfaces) for all components. This resulted in a "jigsaw" puzzle of plastic and metal components that came together to complete the vehicle.

Thanks to the development of rapid pro-

totype technology, the later styling/design efforts benefited from the ability to print sample parts and check the details and operability before committing to hard tooling. The ROBRADY team also coordinated the development, manufacture, and first shot efforts of the tooling suppliers. For the VX-1 scooter the tooling team was US–based. For subsequent product development Chinese-based tooling sources were engaged to minimize costs and improve timelines.

The VX-3 was developed with two wheels in front using an I-shaped articulating front suspension.

Most electric vehicles include some form of regenerative braking, which recovers energy during braking mode by changing the field orientation of the motor such that it acts like a generator and puts braking load on the rear wheel. The challenge was engineering an effective and reliable user interface with the rider. Vectrix developed a unique bi-directional throttle that spring returns to neutral. The system uses a magnet that rotates in response to twisting the throttle and an integrated circuit, which translates magnet position into a digital throttle position signal. To drive forward, the rider simply rotates the throttle toward himself and to enable regenerative braking or reverse, simply rotates the throttle forward. The braking action/effect is proportional to the rotation of the throttle. The result is an intuitive throttle, which provides for forward, reverse, and regenerative braking. This was a key feature incorporated in every Vectrix product.

All electric vehicles need reliable and cost effective battery packs, which provide power for top speed and acceleration and energy for range. Vectrix worked with all of the major battery chemistries in pursuit of the best combination of battery characteristics. Vectrix was a battery system integrator, which included the development of charger and battery management system (BMS) technologies. The chemistry portfolio started at lead acid and advanced to nickel zinc, nickel metal hydride, lithium iron phosphate, lithium manganese, and nickel manganese cobalt (NMC). Each of these battery chemistries were tested and operated in vehicles to determine cycle life, performance degradation, peak power, regenerative capability, and sensitivity to environmental variations in temperature and humidity. In all cases the battery format was prismatic and the proprietary battery management system (BMS) was designed based upon the Linear Technology Company LTC 6800 series of multi-cell stack monitoring chips.

The Vectrix/ROBRADY team developed an electric Tall Wheel scooter designated the VT-1 in 2013, with a planned product launch in the summer of 2014. This 125cc equivalent vehicle incorporated sixteen-inch wheels front and rear. Its top speed was 62 mph, it out-accelerated the Honda SH150 gas bike, and it included removable batteries. The VT-1 platform was shared with Daimler/Smart as the core of the planned Daimler/Smart e-scooter. For both products the ROBRADY team styled the bikes and developed the part details.

Vectrix closed its doors in the winter of 2014, and these products were never completed and brought to market. To support its 2007 initial public offering on the AIM Exchange in London and to broaden its product line, the Vectrix Superbike was conceptualized and a full-scale model was developed by the ROBRADY Team. This electric motorcycle included an 80kW drive system and aggressive styling, which matched its incorporation of leading edge technologies. The Superbike concept model was the star of the 2007 EICMA show in Milan, Italy. It created a significant amount of interest, and Vectrix explored the opportunity to complete the development and make a limited production run of 100 vehicles. Unfortunately, the Superbike competed with engineering and financial resources needed to complete and introduce production vehicles. As such, the Superbike remained a concept and was never brought to market. To this day interest in this vehicle remains high.

Unsung Heroes

Electric motorcycle research and development is ongoing at a rapid pace. Major industrial concerns, such as Mugen and Victory, are devoting significant money to improve the power and efficiency of electrical systems. However, there are those unsung heroes that have been working quietly in the small labs and workshops of universities to add great knowledge and value to electric vehicle development. One such example is the team at London's Kingston University. With support from academia and numerous industrial sponsors, Kingston University London's science, engineering, and computing department has been creating landmark electric racing motorcycles since 2008. This is not without precedent. The university has supported motorcycle technology development for years using conventional petrol powered machines. Motorsport engineer Paul Brandon lead the Kingston team's electric bike entry in the 2009 TTXGP.

My introduction to Kingston University's electric bike team came as a bit of a surprise. Taking a daytrip to the small IOM seaside town of Port Erin I stumbled upon a small garage with two fellows working on a very high-tech machine. Dr. Robert Rayner, Senior Lecturer at the School of Mechanical and Automotive Engineering, and a student were preparing an electric racer for the 2016 TT Zero.

Dr. Rayner (left) and student Lewis Stroud working on The Ion Horse Mk2 electric TT racer for Kingston University London in a small garage in Port Erin, IOM.

The Kingston University electric bike team has had some major accomplishments over the years. These include:

- 2011 Ion Horse Mk1, Built and finished 3rd at TT Zero
- 2013 Ion Horse Mk2, Built and raced at TT Zero, fastest UK University, 4th place overall
- 2013 Ion Horse Mk2, British Land Speed record of 160 mph

Despite the gremlins that plagued the bike's electrical systems, the university team continues its enthusiastic dedication to electric motorcycle racing and engineering development. I commend these efforts as examples of how motorcycling is part of a much larger picture.

Close view of the massive battery pack shows the one hundred and forty individual lithium ion polymer pouch cells wired together.

The electric motor drives the chain sprocket directly. Note the large hose for liquid cooling the motor.

Photo courtesy of Rob Brady, robrady.com

Dan Mahony

Ducati S.p.A.

Chapter 11

RACING AND COMPETITION

Up a hill, on a trail, or around the track, there is always a challenge to be won. Motorcycle racing is a dynamic subculture of the sport that has a vibrant presence for those who follow it, but can be out of sight to many others who have not yet discovered its thrills. This chapter provides an overview of racing's history and its broad spectrum of events.

Man and Machine

Motorcycles are like horses. They are an extension of the rider. Racing them was a given from the onset. The machine empowers the rider to go faster than he could possibly run. With this power comes the need to compete. One can imagine the first time two motorized bikes met each other on the street. Someone had to take the lead, and racing began.

Motorcycle racing is a fast and furious world that offers great insight into what drives the development of the machines we ride. Photo by Dan Mahony, Mahony Photo Archives, mahonyphotos.com.

Motorcycle racing is a huge universe of history, machines, heroes, and famous racetracks. It is remarkable that out of the millions of motorcyclists, so few have ever been to a race. Interest in motorcycle racing has traditionally been more prevalent in Europe. It is a national sport, much like soccer. Americans compete in Europe to gain recognition as world champions.

Motorcycles as racing machines began with their use as pace vehicles for bicycle races. It was inevitable that bicycle racers would challenge the men on their machines. The first recorded instance of that was in England back in 1897. The bicycle won, but only because the motorcycle rider held back. It is said that he thought the noisy crowd was reacting to a problem elsewhere on the track.

Restriction on speed in England during the early years of the twentieth century forced many motorcycle racers to practice on bicycle tracks or cross the channel to participate in French street races. The three-and-a-half-mile Canning Town track in East London was one of the earliest motorcycle tracks built for racing in England. It became the scene for many exciting races a year before Harley-Davidson delivered its first bike to market in 1903. Indian had already been in the game for two years. Founder George Hendee recognized the racing potential of motorized bicycles from the beginning. He was a bicycle racer himself and was most impressed with Oscar Hedstrom's light and reliable pacer. He partnered with Hedstrom to build more pacers. The potential of Hedstroms's design shifted Hendee's business model toward making street motorcycles. The first Indian was built in 1901. Racing them was quick to follow.

The French enjoyed no restrictions, and happily held races on public roads. The honor of a racer's country was often at stake as early machines from throughout Europe competed. Long-distance races between Paris and Madrid made motorcycle racing international. Overzealous crowds numbered in the hundreds of thousands as spectators cheered on their countrymen. Speeds approaching 60 mph were wowing audiences. That was quite an accomplishment considering the machines of the day put out less than 3 hp. French rider Maurice Fournier broke new ground in 1903 with his giant 2,340cc twin-cylinder bike capable of putting out 22 hp. This was a massive machine and unyielding in handling. Engine size does not always guarantee victory. Smaller and lighter machines had the advantage on twisting and curvy roads.

Motorcycle racing in Europe was quick to get out of control. Rules were easily broken by racers looking to gain recognition in this new sport. The newly formed Fédération Internationale des Clubs Motorcyclistes (FICM) asked for support from the French Auto-Cycle Club in 1904 to manage its races. The first was the International Cup Race. Competing were Great Britain, France, Germany, Austria, and Denmark. It turned out to be a disaster. Excessive and unreasonable restrictions were placed on the contestants. One such restriction was the weight limit of 110 pounds for a racing machine. This resulted in frail frames and skimpy tires trying to cope with the heavy engines of the day. The International Cup Race was disbanded in 1906 and better venues were sought.

Harry and Charlie Collier at Canning Town in 1909. The Collier family began the famous Matchless marque. It later evolved to establish Associated Motor Cycles (AMC) that absorbed several brands of British motorcycles, including AJS, Francis-Barnett, James, and Sunbeam. Early Matchless bikes, as pictured on the left, used JAP-made engines. Photo Mortons Archives.

The British Go Off-Shore

Britain's Auto-Cycle Club desperately sought permission from the authorities to organize motorcycle races on closed public road circuits. It met with little hope. The answer was found on a small island off the coast of Ireland—the Isle of Man. This self-governing British Crown dependency, rooted in the Manx culture, welcomed the racers. They had no speed limits and offered the island's roads to become the most famous of all racing circuits. The first Isle of Man TT (Tourist Trophy) races were held in 1907. The term "tourist" referred to touring, or street, bikes of the time. The TT has since become the ultimate challenge for any motorcycle racer for a broad variety of categories. American manufacturers jumped on board to race the TT. It would create new markets for their bikes. Indian's remarkable victory in 1911 certainly proved that point. The company scored the first three places in the

Senior TT, and sales overseas followed.

Rem Fowler and his 1907 TT-winning Norton. It was powered by a French Peugeot V-twin engine. Standing behind him in the center is his pit attendant, James L. Norton. Norton started the famous brand in 1902. Fowler's average speed on the 158-mile race was 36.32 mph. Photo Mortons Archives.

While Europeans were racing at the Isle of Man, an American motorcycle maker and aviation pioneer achieved the astonishing speed of 136.36 mph on a motorcycle at Ormond Beach, Florida, in 1907. Glenn Curtiss used his 40 hp 4,410cc V-8-powered bike to set that unofficial world record. This motorcycle land speed record lasted for twenty-three years.

Racing in the United States

By 1904 the Federation of American Motorcyclists had become sufficiently credible to sanction events. Racing on public streets, however, was not as popular as it was in Europe. Motorcycle racing in the United States was focused more on city-to-city endurance runs, board track racing, and dirt track racing.

Endurance runs were very effective for creating publicity. Indian motorcycle designer Oscar Hedstrom took part in a 254-mile endurance run in 1902 between New York and Boston. It was a great way to advertise the reliability of his bikes. Despite Hedstrom's responsibilities at the Indian factory, he was an avid racer who held several championship titles. Walter Davidson used the same type of tactics to demonstrate

the ruggedness of his company's motorcycles. In 1908 he rode a stock single-cylinder Harley to victory at the Federation of American Motorcyclist endurance event in the Catskill Mountains.

Harley-Davidson president Walter Davidson in 1908 with his FAM endurance and economy event winning bike. He set a record of 188.234 miles per gallon. That feat would be considered remarkable today. Photo courtesy of Harley-Davidson.

No one captured the public's admiration more than "Cannonball" Baker. The remarkable endurance feats of Erwin Baker were always followed with great interest. Baker completed many cross-country rides on a variety of motorcycles, including Indian and Henderson. His run from San Diego to New York in 1914 on an Indian took only eleven days, twelve hours, and ten minutes. That may not seem fast today unless one takes into consideration that most of the trip was on terrible dirt roads.

A young Erwin Baker with his Indian Powerplus.

Today's Cannonball Endurance Run honors the long distance races of days past. Since 2010 dozens of riders have signed up to ride their antique motorcycles across the country. The 2014 Cannonball covered 3,938 miles between Daytona Beach and Tacoma, Washington. Bike entries ranged from 1914 to 1940. The winner rode a 1924 Indian Scout. Photo courtesy of Felicia Morgan, Cannonball Race 2010.

The Perilous Board Tracks

Bicycle velodromes quickly gave way to larger high-speed motordromes. Companies like Marsh, Orient, Excelsior, and Indian recognized early on that motorcycle racing of all sorts was good for generating sales. The sheer spectacle of board track racing was not lost on opportunists. Large real estate groups constructed half-mile and one-mile board track ovals all over the United States. Scores were built near urban areas to draw thousands of paying spectators. The track surface was made of two-inch by four-inch boards put on edge. This made a fast, slick, and dangerous surface as it aged and splintered. Steeply banked, these motordromes saw young men achieve speeds nearing 100 mph on machines hardly larger than a sturdy steel-framed bicycle. This was a formula for disaster.

This period photo shows the immense scale of board tracks. Many motordromes had one-mile-long ovals. The steep banks of the tracks allowed the machines to achieve high speeds while retaining traction. Photo courtesy of Harley-Davidson.

The sound and smell must have been intoxicating. The "total-loss lubrication" engines of the era burnt and spewed a lot of oil that made the track slick and filled the air with smoke. With no brakes and only an ignition kill switch, racers would use the track's steep banks to slow their bikes. Many brands appeared on the tracks as motorcycle makers found eager young men willing to take the risk. Merkel, Thor, Bradley, Emblem, Pope, and Cyclone were just a few.

Merkels were highly distinctive on the racetrack with their bright orange paintwork. Joseph Merkel began building bikes in Milwaukee as early as 1902. By 1909, his company was purchased by the Light Manufacturing Company of Pottstown, Pennsylvania. Initially called the "Light Merkel," the bike proved its race capabilities under Maldwyn Jones. Jones became a national champion and brought the "Flying Merkel" its reputation. Production of the Merkel brand ceased in 1915. It is a real treat to see one at vintage motorcycle events. An unrestored original sold at auction in 2015 at $423,000.

American-made Cyclone racers were produced between 1912 and 1917. They were noted for their astonishing 45 hp engines that could reach 110 mph on the board tracks. Unfortunately, uncertain reliability and high cost made them less popular. Excelsior, however, had good success with their overhead cam racers during 1919 and 1920. This 1915 Cyclone sold for over a half a million dollars at auction. Steve McQueen's 1915 Cyclone sold for an astounding $775,000 in 2015. Only a few of these magnificent machines still exist, and their value keeps going up. Photo courtesy of Mid-American Auctions.

The young age of board track racers is clearly evident in this photo taken in 1914. Heavy wool sweaters and leather helmets were all the protection racers had. Large cash prizes drew them to this dangerous sport. Top racers could earn over $2,000 a year. That is hundreds of thousands in today's money. It is interesting to note that the Excelsior is missing its chain in this posed picture. Note the steep banking of the track.

Board track racing lost favor with the public after a horrific crash at Newark's motordrome in 1912. Six people were killed, including two riders and four spectators. The track was closed down immediately as a grand jury investigation brought it to the nation's attention. Another tragedy occurred in 1913 at the Ludlow, Kentucky, motordrome. It killed a total of eight. An exploding gas tank contributed to the mayhem. Motordromes started to fade in the years that followed, as their boards dried up and audiences diminished. Racing in the United States focused on dirt tracks and the newly constructed race circuits.

Eddie Hasha rode an eight-valve Indian motorcycle like this one when he met his tragic death at the Newark motordrome in 1912. The large V-twin was a fast bike. A year earlier he reached 95 miles per hour, setting a record for the mile at the large Playa del Rey, California, motordrome.

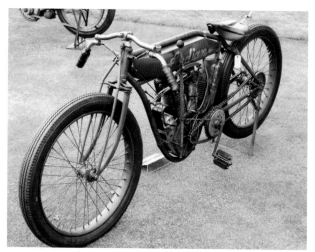

This unrestored 1912 Indian racer is valued more than the pristine restored example on previous page. Photo by Stephen Covell.

Fairground racetracks throughout the United States provided ideal racing venues after board track racing fell out of favor with the public. Dirt track, or flat track racing, was to become America's most popular motorsport in the decades to follow.

Harley's Unstoppable Wrecking Crew

Harley-Davidson entered the racing game a bit later than its competitors. It had banked on its reputation for producing reliable rather than fast bikes. Losing market share to Indian as a result of their racing success prompted the Motor Company to use its own racing efforts in advertising.

The years of 1914 through 1921 were the glamour years for Harley-Davidson's racing program. It assembled the best talent money could buy. The team was called "The Wrecking Crew." Their success in using the company's eight-valve V-twins changed the public's perception of the brand. Team member Ray Weishaar was the one responsible for giving Harley-Davidson motorcycles the moniker of "Hog." He celebrated victory laps with his pet pig. Spectators cheered the hog. Unfortunately, the Wrecking Crew was disbanded in 1921. Despite being the first to win a race at an average speed of over 100 mph that same year, the economic strain of supporting racing was too much for the company. Private racers, however, continued to carry the brand.

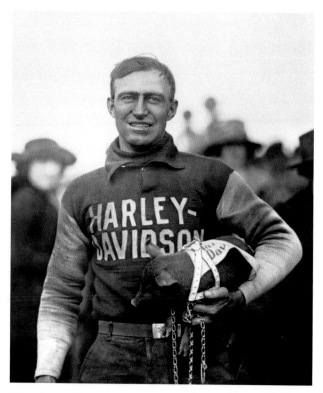

Wrecking Crew racer Ray Weishaar with his pet pig. The nickname of "hog" for Harley-Davidson bikes stuck. It even provided the acronym for the Harley Owners Group.

Racing machines like this eight-valve twin-cam gave Harley-Davidson's Wrecking Crew the tools they need-ed to compete and win races. Eight-valve Harleys were being built by 1915 and introduced to the market by 1916. Harley had no intentions of selling them though. They priced them at an astonishing $1,500; five times the price of a standard bike. These 53 hp 999cc (61-cubic-inch) V-twins were very formidable. Few true original examples exist today.

This 1915 eight-valve displayed at the Motorcyclepedia Museum, in New-burgh, NY, was used to win the Dodge City, Kansas, 300-mile races. Har-ley-Davidson won every one of them throughout the Wrecking Crew's run.

Race Circuits Evolve

Interest in automobiles and motorcycles flourished in the early 1900s. While the French led the world's production of cars, the English were hampered by a 20-mph speed restriction on public roads. Racing in England was limited to several shorter tracks, and the Isle of Man was only available for a few weeks a year. It was a matter of practicality that a large circuit be built. It would serve both the automobile and motorcycle industries.

The Brooklands

The famous Brooklands Motor Circuit, in Surrey, was therefore constructed in 1907 to meet this need. Brooklands was the world's first banked track designed for high-speed racing. It was a rough 2.75-mile course made of concrete. It took skill to keep motorcycles stable on its uneven surface. The track was a huge success. Over a quarter of a million spectators could line the course.

Brooklands was the scene of many dramatic races between American and British rivals. The most famous early match pitted British Champion Charlie Collier on his Matchless V-twin against American Jake de Rosier on his Indian during the summer of 1911. The series of races were extremely close. Average speeds of over 80 mph were recorded. At one point, one of Collier's spark plug wires came off. The racer didn't miss a beat as he reattached the high-voltage cable by feel alone. Tenths of a second differentiated these racers' lap times. Jake ultimately won, and Indian had yet another victory to boast about.

The wide Brooklands Motor Circuit hosted countless motorcycle racing events during its thirty-two-year reign. Photo Mortons Archives.

The Brooklands allowed the refinement of many specialized racebikes. This custom 1928 SS100 Brough-Superior, nicknamed *Moby Dick* by the media, was one such example. Its modified J. A. Prestwich engine displaced 1,142cc and produced 65 hp. It was capable of achieving 115 mph back in 1932. Photo courtesy of Bonhams.

Motor racing became very popular in the United States as well. A number of famous tracks attracted racers from all over the world. The Indianapolis Motor Speedway specifically was inspired by the design and success of Brooklands.

The Indianapolis Motor Speedway followed Brooklands' success and opened in 1909.

Daytona Beach

There was one racecourse that did not require any construction whatsoever—the Daytona Beach Road Course. It hosted countless races and scores of speed records during its fifty-six-year stay. The 3.2-mile course was first used in 1902. Hard-packed sand made it a good surface to test motorcycles for speed. The track was expanded to 4.2 miles in 1940. Racing was on two miles of pavement and two miles of beach. This may have inspired today's Supermotard racing. Nearly every well-known racer and motorcycle manufacturer made the pilgrimage to Daytona Beach during the winter months.

Aerial view of the Daytona Beach racecourse in 1937. Photo Mortons Archive.

The American Motorcycle Association, founded in 1924, got heavily involved in organizing professional and amateur racing events throughout the United States. These included local events at half-mile dirt track ovals to all-out road racing at major speedways popping up across the country. The most famous of these races is the Daytona 200. This intense race was first run on the beach circuit in 1937. "Iron Man" Ed Kretz won that race on an Indian.

Motorcycle Polo

Motorcycle Polo, or Motoball, as it is called in Europe, is essentially a soccer game where the players are on motorcycles. The ball is typically larger than a soccer ball and may be kicked or manipulated with the bike. Motorcycle Polo was very popular in the United States during the Depression years. It required extraordinary strength and skill. The bikes used were Harleys and Indians with foot clutches and hand shifts. The game is still played in Europe, albeit with smaller and more agile dirt bikes.

Pictured is Doc Batsleer on his Indian Sport Scout much like the one Ed Kretz used to race on Daytona's beach course back in 1937 to win the 200. This 45-cubic-inch V-twin is considered an exceptional handling bike—especially in its day. Doc is a champion vintage racer and has been racing Indians longer than anyone.

Motorcycle Polo played at American fairgrounds and horse tracks was a dangerous sport. There was little protection offered the players.

A newspaper clip from July 5, 1929, in the Philadelphia *Public Ledger* about the author's Uncle Harry after he was severely burned during a motorcycle polo match in Pottstown, Pennsylvania, when his gas tank exploded. Harry Manson was a national polo champion and the captain of the Philadelphia Ramblers.

The Great TT

Scores of notable motorcycle racetracks and races appeared in Europe over the decades to come. None had or has the impact of the Isle of Man TT. That was and is the place to be, and to showcase a company's engineering and riding skills. It is the most challenging course in all of racing. Riders face narrow streets through villages lined with stone walls, leading to open, twisting country roads that tempt very high speeds. The early rules of 1907 limiting fuel consumption to 90 mpg for single-cylinder machines, and 75 mpg for twins, would give away to more reasonable standards. Classes were developed based on engine capacity. The Senior TT focused primarily on 500cc bikes, while the Junior TT entrants raced 350cc machines. The 1920s brought the Lightweight 250cc class.

The Isle of Man course offers a tricky hairpin turn at Governors Bridge. Onlookers can get very close to the action, as is evident in this photo from 1949. Photo Courtesy of Iomtt.com/ fottofinders.com

Every established maker sought its share of victories from the TT. Where there were no rules, opportunities for success were found. BMW found such opportunity with its supercharged twins in the mid-1930s. They out-ran the best of the British without much effort. Au-diences were stunned. To put supercharging into perspective, Ernst Henne achieved 174 mph in 1937 on his supercharged 500cc BMW, while the best Norton singles had a top speed of 35 mph less. Supercharging was eventually banned as TT rules were fine-tuned to equalize the competition.

Stanley Woods, seated on a mid-1930s 500cc Velocette, was one of the great British racers between 1921 and 1939. He won a total of ten TTs. Photo Mortons Archive.

World War I put a stop to the TT for five years. Its return brought much development to the machines. Norton enjoyed many great victories at the TT with its bulletproof overhead cam singles. Works (factory) racers like Jimmy Guthrie and Stanley Woods became national heroes as they mastered the 37.75-mile mountain course with average lap speeds of 85 mph. Looming troubles in Europe, combined with economic restraints, caused Norton to retire its factory racing program in 1939. The marque would, however, be carried proudly by many privateers.

Norton's success at the TT between World Wars was based on its overhead cam singles. By 1937, a double overhead cam version of the 500cc International was developed. These factory racing bikes were made in 348cc and 499cc configurations. These new models were named Manx—a name derived from the Isle of Man's heritage, or as some would say, the island's bobbed-tailed cats. The use of Manx was, however, withheld until after the war in 1946. The large 500cc DOHC single-cylinder mounted within the sturdy twin-loop McCandless designed "featherbed" frame keep the bike competitive against faster Italian machines during the 1950s. The engine produced 47 hp at 6500 rpm. Norton also offered SOHC 348cc and 499cc versions of the Manx for private racers. Price was the same at £315. Pictured is world champion Geoff Duke aboard a 500cc Manx Norton 30M at the 1950 TT. Photo Courtesy of Iomtt.com/ fotto-finders.com

Postwar Racing

Racing after WWII took a while to recover. Rebuilding war-torn nations was a higher priority. However, motorcycle engineers were not idle during that time. They imagined new designs that would see the light of day within several short years on the race circuits that sprang up throughout Europe. These were important years for racing. Engines, frames, and suspensions started coming together to produce truly race-worthy machines.

412

Postwar racing brought out numerous remarkable machines from European makers. Italian Mondial offers a perfect example. Its small DOHC 125cc singles dominated the GP and TT circuit between 1948 and 1951. It is said that Soichiro Honda showed great interest in studying Mondial engines. Pictured is an ex–Mike Hailwood 1957 250cc Mondial Bialbero GP available for sale through Bonhams in 2015 at $100,000. Photo Stephen Covell.

Moto Parilla 175cc single-cylinder high-cam racers brought excitement to European race fans. Small displacement racing was affordable and surprisingly fast. Honda learned a lot from the Italian makers. Photo courtesy of Carollo Moto Classiche.

A prime example of wartime innovation was taking place in Stevenage, England, at the Vincent factory. The company was too small to supply motorcycles to the army, and therefore was converted to produce military components. Philip Vincent and Phil Irving were drafting the design for their next generation Rapide, the Series B. This 998cc 50-degree V-twin would represent a significant step forward from the original Series A. The team realized their vision and built this high-quality bike despite severe restrictions on postwar supplies and materials.

The new Rapide was introduced to market in 1946 and soon saw itself on the racetrack. True to Vincent's advertising slogan, this bike was the world's fastest standard motorcycle with a top speed of 110 mph. Vincent and Irving gave works test rider George Brown and his mechanic brother Cliff orders to custom modify a Rapide for racing. The sturdy engine offered many opportunities for performance modification. The results were impressive, and it was dubbed *Gunga Din*. This factory racer had polished internals, larger carburetors, special cams, doubled up valve springs, and larger exhaust pipes. It was just a matter of time that a production version of the bike would emerge. The Black Shadow was thus born. It was introduced in 1948 and brought the top speed to over 125 mph. It dominated the 1,000cc class endurance races of the day and would be the foundation for one of motorcylings greatest feats.

Lightning Appears

In the spring of 1948, Philip Vincent arranged a trip to the United States to meet potential clients. During his visit to California, he met John Edgar, a wealthy and avid motorsports enthusiast. Edgar had heard about the Black Shadow and asked Vincent if he could make a faster version of the bike to compete in the AMA National Class A flying-mile. The requirements would include breaking the previous 136.183-mph record held by Joe Petrali in 1937 on a modified Harley-Davidson 61-cubic-inch overhead valve machine. Class A racing utilized highly modified or purpose-built factory racing machines. Petrali was one of Harley-Davidson's best racers. He won every race during the 1935 Grand National schedule. Beating his record would be a real plus for Vincent.

Vincent accepted the challenge and went to work modifying a Black Shadow using many of the tricks learned from *Gunga Din*. Meanwhile, Vincent Martin, a Burbank, California, Vincent H.R.D. dealer, contacted famous American racer Rollie Free with an offer to ride the new machine. Free was most enthusiastic and would do it in between his hectic schedule of automobile racing.

The bike arrived at Edgar's in September of 1948. Within a couple of days, Rollie Free ran the machine at the Rosamond Dry Lake in California. He achieved 138 mph, breaking Petrali's record without much effort. Confidence was high that Rollie and the Vincent could hit the magic 150-mph mark at the Bonneville Salt Flats, Utah. After several attempts, Rollie Free and Vincent broke the world record for an unsupercharged motorcycle at 7:55 a.m. on September 13, 1948. A new bike was born—the Black Lightning.

Motorcycling's most iconic photo is of Rollie Free at the Bonneville Salt Flats breaking the 150-mph land speed record on John Edgar's Vincent. Free's previous runs were just shy of 150 mph due to drag from his loose leathers. He borrowed some sneakers and put on a bathing cap and swim trunks to cheat the wind. His average speed was 150.313 mph. Free's prone riding position was not unique to this run. He used this style frequently. Jerry Hatfield's book, Flat Out, chronicles in detail the remarkable history behind this story. Photo courtesy of Herb Harris, Harris Vincent Gallery, Inc.®

Harley-Davidson's top racer Joe Petrali won every race on the Grand National schedule in 1935. Photo courtesy of Harley-Davidson.

Only thirty-one Black Lightnings were built by Vincent. The Shadow engine with Lightning specs put out 70 hp. Magnesium castings and alloy fittings greatly reduced the bike's weight. Free's friend, Marty Dickerson, made many similar modifications to his Rapide and kept the name of Vincent alive in the record books for years to follow.

New Venues and Stars Emerge

Among the first tracks to debut new race machines after the war was the Assen TT track in Holland. The four-and-three-quarter-mile course was narrow and lined with dykes, which made riders appreciate the wider tracks elsewhere. Other notable tracks included Monza in Italy, Nurburgring in Germany, Spa in Belgium, Francorchamps in France, and Brands Hatch and Silverstone in England.

The combination of good racetracks and technically advanced machines prompted the restructuring of the FICM to become the French Fédération Internationale de Motocyclisme (FIM). Its first task was to organize a world championship road race series in 1949 called the Grand Prix. Strict rules governing engine size and other technical specification changed frequently as new machines entered the scene. The highest class today is the MotoGP 1,000cc class, featuring machines capable of exceeding 230 mph. There are as many as eighteen separate races spanning over thirteen countries in this championship series. Grand Prix racing has created heroes and legends since its inception.

German BMW Rennsport 500cc overhead cam racers were formidable contenders at the TT and on international circuits. The reliable boxer engine found its home in sidecar racing, dominating the category for decades. Photo Mortons Archive.

A great example of tracks and heroes took place in Florida back in the 1960s. The well-designed Daytona International Speedway replaced the Daytona Beach circuit in 1959. It filled the need of snowbird motorcycle racers while offering a great GP racing circuit. There were several course configurations to accommodate automobile, kart, and motorcycle racing. The Speedway was host to one of motorcycling's greatest racers—Mike Hailwood. In 1964 Hailwood achieved two outstanding victories in one day at that track. He not only managed to set a record time of 144 mph average speed for an hour endurance run, but then went on to win the US Grand Prix later in the day. Hailwood's reputation preceded these wins. He championed underdog Japanese motorcycle brand Honda at the 1961 Isle of Man TT and went on to win the 125cc, 250cc, and 500cc races all in the same week. British-born Hailwood would continue an illustrious career as a TT and Grand Prix world champion, representing Italian MV and Japanese Honda.

The remarkable and endearing world champion Joey Dunlop holds the record for the most TT wins. He won twenty-six times in a variety of classes between 1977 and 2000. Dunlop lost his life in a crash in Estonia in 2000. The outstanding 2014 movie *Road* chronicles the spectacular racing achievements of Joey, his brother Robert, and sons Michael and William. Photo Courtesy of Iomtt.com/ fottofinders.com

Not all GP circuits survived the evolution toward higher speeds. Faster lap times, particularly at the Isle of Man, created safety concerns among many racers. The island was part of the highly competitive Grand Prix series from 1949 to 1976. The high speeds on its public roads caused numerous accidents and deaths. Ten time TT winner and Grand Prix champion Giacomo Agostini led the charge on convincing officials to exclude the course from the GP race series. The TT continues to create heroes but also takes its toll in lives. Lap speeds have exceeded 130 mph today. Thousands of race fans make the pilgrimage to the small island annually to cheer their favorites and welcome newcomers. Numerous classes exist, ranging from small 50cc displacement machines to superbikes, from sidecars to pure vintage motorcycles.

A sleek replica of the four-cylinder Honda 250cc RC162 Mike Hailwood raced to victory in 1961. The engine was capable of rotating at 14,000 rpm, producing 40 hp.

Six Days of Torture

Competition was hardly limited to road or dirt track racing. Countless off-road events tested man and machine on muddy trails and rocky slopes. The most grueling of them was the International Six Day Trial (ISDT). This competition invited several hundred of the best off-road riders from all over the world to spend a total of six days racing against the clock, the elements, and nearly impossible mountain trails.

A few feet of the thousand-plus mile 1965 ISDT shows official observers and onlookers lining the trail as Jim Sandiford (BSA) leads Dennis Craine (Jawa). Eastern European two-strokes did particularly well during the 1960s and 1970s. Photo Mortons Archive.

The first ISDT was held in Carlisle, England, in 1913. Motorcycles were hardly capable of off-road racing like we envision today. However, competitors used the heavy, poorly sprung machines of the day to take to the hills and test their skills. Entrants faced many constraints. Perhaps the most challenging was the limited time and access riders had for maintenance. Tire punctures, for example, would have to be repaired in min-

utes in order to maintain position at the checkpoints.

Today, the ISDT has been renamed International Six Day Enduro, reflecting the nature of the competition and the type of bikes used. Over thirty countries compete to cover the 1,250 miles of trails within the six-day period. Only six hundred riders are allowed to compete. Prestigious gold, silver, and bronze medals are awarded to those who achieve high levels of riding skill, meet the strict time line, and have the fewest breakdowns. The clear majority of national wins are by European riders. American off-road icon Malcolm Smith won several gold medals during the 1960s and 1970s.

AMA Racing

Racing in the United States was starting to gain real public interest as more and more major motorcycle events were being hosted. A real boost came with the AMA's introduction of Class C racing in 1933. It allowed production (stock) motorcycles on the track. This was to encourage racing during a time when factory teams were dwindling. The Great Depression had taken its toll, and Class A racing was at an all-time low. Class B racing, allowing amateurs to race modified machines, wasn't doing much better. Few could afford it.

Class C racing brought new life to racing. It gave a lot of amateur racers an opportunity to compete on a national scale. They would often arrive at the track on the very bike they would be racing. Headlights were removed and rear fenders "bobbed" in an effort to reduce overall weight. Mile-long horse racing tracks became home to regular weekend events throughout the country.

Popularity of racing further encouraged the AMA to organize a new series named the AMA Grand National Championship in 1954. The championship series was based on the combination of five separate AMA racing classes in one series. Competitors would have to race on four dirt tracks and one road track. The first winner was Joe Leonard on a Harley-Davidson in 1954. The Motor Company had few competitors

on the flat-tracks. It's biggest rival, Indian, was out of business. After a long hiatus, Indian Motorcycle will be back on the flat track for the 2017 American Flat Track series. It will use the new liquid-cooled Scout FTR 750 four-valve V-Twin competition engine with a special dirt track chassis.

The AMA Championship series brought many great riders to the tracks in the 1960s and 1970s. Pictured is well-known American racer Dave Aldana on a BSA (38) tangling with Dave Sehl (21). Bart Marke (4) and Jim Maness (1) are taking the lead on KR750 Harleys. Photo by Dan Mahony.

British motorcycle makers took full advantage of AMA racing in the United States. Two-time AMA Grand National Champion Dick Mann raced Hondas and BSAs, including this exact 500cc BSA Gold Star single showcased at an AMA vintage racing event.

Triumph also saw many victories on the dirt with its 650cc twins in the late 1960s and early 1970s with champions like Gary Nixon and Gene Romero (pictured) at the controls. Photo by Dan Mahony.

The Harley-Davidson Advantage

Harley-Davidson would see great success in the Grand Nationals with its 744cc flathead KR750 racers. The bike was introduced in 1952 and competed through the 1950s and most of the 1960s. The KR750 was winning or placing high in nearly all Class C races during that time. Rules pitted 750cc side-valves against 500cc overhead valve British engines. The flathead was a bit dated from the onset compared to the alloy overhead valve British BSA, Matchless, Triumph, or Norton parallel twins, but kept up nicely on the dirt tracks. AMA National Champion Mert Lawwill rode a KR750 to claim the number-one plate for 1969, despite a full field of British machines. A well-tuned KR put out 48 hp at 7,000 rpm. This was achieved by a remarkably high 9:1 compression for a flathead. Large aluminum head fins helped cool the engine enough to prevent pre-ignition. In order to extract more power from its engines, Harley-Davidson would evolve its racers to overhead valves.

Harley-Davidson's flathead 750cc KR became the one to beat on the oval dirt tracks of America between the mid-1950s and most of the 1960s. Pictured is "Stan the Man" Engdahl's KR as exhibited at the Kansas Motorcycle Museum. He raced from the early 1950s all the way up into the 1980s. Stan was instrumental in bringing AMA amateur racing to the Midwest.

Harley-Davidson KRs are highly collectible today and set the model for many "street tracker" style bikes.

Harley-Davidson XLRs were limited run overhead valve racers used for specialized classes allowing larger displacement engines. The 883cc Sportster-based V-twin XLR was built between 1958 and 1969 for sprints and scrambles. It featured several improvements over a stock XLCH Sportster. These included a front-mounted magneto, ball bearings at the crankshaft, improved heads, flywheels, cams, valves, and pistons. Only about 500 XLR engines were produced. Factory riders like Mert Lawwill put the 80 hp XLR to good use. XLRs were also a favorite of drag racers.

The highly limited production 883cc XLR-TT was made through the 1960s for AMA Class-C racing for the 900cc category. It was capable of an impressive 82 hp. Sprinters and drag racers loved the bike for its quick launch off the line. This 1966 example was one of only twenty-five made that year. In addition to the iron head XLR engine upgrades, it featured Italian Ceriani forks and alloy wheels. XLR-TTs are highly collectible and will fetch over $50,000 today.

The Unbeatable XR750

Harley-Davidson introduced the 748cc overhead valve XR750 in 1970 to keep up with new AMA rules, and the latest 650cc and 750cc entries by British and Japanese makers. It was a homerun. The XR was capable of generating over 80 hp. Much of this was due to the less restrictive flow inherent to overhead valve systems. The company would upgrade its iron-headed XR engines to aluminum alloy heads for the 1972 season. Overheating was an issue with the iron heads. This design was a magic formula for the AMA series. Power was improved by 10 to 15 percent. Cal Rayborn brought immediate victories by winning the Indianapolis and Laguna nationals that same year with the road racing XRTT. The XR would eventually lose some ground to the fast Japanese two-strokes on road races, but continued to dominate dirt track circuits for four decades to come.

Harley-Davidson's all-alloy overhead valve XR750 remains a favorite for flat-track racers today. Its engine and transmission are unit construction and loosely resemble the Sportster motor it was derived from. Its shorter stroke allowed it to obtain higher rpms for more power. Large air filters keep the dirt from getting into the engine.

The most famous XR750 is clearly the one used by Evel Knievel for his famous jumps. This replica is proudly displayed at the AMA Motorcycle Hall of Fame. Photo courtesy of the American Motorcyclist Association.

AMA Motorcycle Hall of Famer Jay Springsteen won three consecutive AMA Grand National Championships from 1976 to 1978. He is pictured here aboard his winning XR750 Harley-Davidson racer at a vintage event in 2011 at the Barber Motorsports Park.

Harley-Davidson XR750 powered roadracers found themselves on the European circuits as well. Pictured (l-r) are dirt track legend Mert Lawwill, Doug Sehi, and the highly respected Cal Rayborn at the Trans-Atlantic Match races in the U.K. This would be one of Rayborn's last races using a Harley-Davidson. The pushrod V-twin was losing ground to the Japanese two-strokes. Rayborn joined the Suzuki team later that year. Photo Mortons Archive.

Multi-Cylinder Machines Take Over

Racing requires great rider skill, a solid chassis, compliant suspension, and a motor that offers exceptional power-to-weight ratio. It became evident early in the days of engine development that several smaller cylinders can breathe air and fuel faster than one large one. The result for the same overall displacement is higher revolutions per minute, equating to more horsepower. Multi-cylinder engines have more moving parts and were, therefore, at greater risk of failure on early highly tuned race engines. Metal fatigue was common, and alloys would have to be developed to withstand the high stresses. British makers like AJS experimented with multi-cylinder engines with limited success. The sturdy British single was therefore able to hold onto its titles before multi-cylinder engines became reliable. BMW twin-cylinder machines proved to be sufficiently reliable but focused mostly on sidecar racing. It was the four-cylinder Italian bikes entering the GP race circuit in the early 1950s that took racing to a new level, and pretty much put the singles to pasture.

British maker AJS experimented with DOHC two-cylinder racers. This magnificent 1954 AJS E95 parallel twin displayed at the fantastic Barber Vintage Motorsports Museum is such an example. The bike was derived from the earlier 499cc E90; a supercharged twin designed to compete against the prewar supercharged BMWs.

It was nicknamed *Porcupine* due to its long oil sump cooling spines. Banning of superchargers following WWII forced AJS to reconfigure the E-90 twin for normal aspiration, resulting in the E-95. The high cost of re-engineering the machine for non-supercharged use forced the designers to work with what they had. This greatly limited the motor's power potential. Combined with some reliability issues, this noble experiment in engineering eventually ended as the company left racing.

British single-cylinder overhead cam engines like on this Matchless G50, and the Norton Manx, made highly reliable racing engines. Their power limit was based on the heavy mass of long connecting rods and pistons moving up and down. In addition to being able to take in more air and fuel, the smaller and lighter pistons in multi-cylinder engines allow higher rpms, and therefore produce greater power. Photo taken at Barber Vintage Motorsports Museum.

The concept for a four-cylinder engine transversely mounted in the frame was the focus of two young Italian engineers back in the early 1920s. Carlo Gianini and Piero Remor saw this as a solution to the problematic uneven air-cooling inline fours of the day were experiencing. The importance of this design cannot be overstated, as it is the genesis of all high-performance four-stroke racing machines. The team built several motors, including a race-winning water-cooled four. Gilera, a motorcycle and scooter manufacturer founded in 1909, eventually bought the design for further development. They focused on an air-cooled 500cc machine to race in the Grand Prix.

Gilera Sets a New Standard

In 1950, Umberto Masetti surprised the racing world by winning the 500cc championship title on a Gilera-4 machine. That was the beginning of the end for the British singles. Norton held on for a while due to its superior frame and front suspension. Gilera hired British Geoff Duke, who was intimately familiar with Nortons, to help refine its bikes. The result was a race-winning design that would inspire motorcycle development for decades to come. Soichiro Honda took great interest in the Gilera-4 upon his visit to the European races in 1954. Inspiration gained from that visit would be seen in impressive four-cylinder Honda motorcycles to come.

Charismatic Geoff Duke on a Gilera-4 at the 1953 GP Des Nationes in Italy. The engine was capable of 57 hp at 10,000 rpm. Transversely mounted four-cylinder engines were clearly the way of the future. Gilera's double overhead cam design would be copied by many motorcycle and automobile engine makers. Photo Mortons Archives.

Gilera's decision to end its racing program in 1957 did not deter Italian engine development and presence on the podium. Gilera engineers joined Italian motorcycle maker MV (Meccanica Verghera) to keep their multi-cylinder concepts alive. Count Domenico Agusta, head of the firm, was determined to make a mark in GP racing. He would certainly achieve this. In the capable hands of racers like John Surtees, Mike Hailwood, and Giacomo Agostini, MV became the one to beat. MV Agusta refined its 500cc engines to three cylinders. This reduced the bike's weight to improve the power-to-weight ratio. By 1968 the MV 500-Triple was capable of 80 hp at an astonishing 12,500 rpm. This gave Agostini the right tool to win all ten GP races that year. MV's glory days lasted through the 1974 season. By 1975, Japanese two-strokes would dominate GP racing for decades to come. Multi-cylinder four-strokes, however, would find their place in other classes, including Superbike class and production class races.

Mike Hailwood racing in the Senior TT at the Isle of Man in 1965 on an MV Agusta 500-4. By this time the Gilera-rooted design was capable of putting out over 70 hp. Note the massive expanding shoe drum brakes that were common prior to the use of disc brakes in the early 1970s. Photo Courtesy of Iomtt.com.

Giacomo Agostini is considered one of motorcycling's greatest racers. He joined MV for the 1965 racing season. The rivalry between him and his teammate Mike Hailwood is legendary. Hailwood eventually left to race for Honda. Agostini won the coveted 500cc World Championship title seven times, the 350cc title for seven years, and ten TT wins. He stayed with MV until 1974, when he joined the Yamaha team. He became the first GP racer to win the championship on a 500cc two-stroke machine in 1975. Photo Mortons Archives.

Perhaps the most ambitious multi-cylinder racer was Moto Guzzi's 500cc liquid-cooled V-8 built for the 1955 GP season. The bike was capable of 172 mph. Unfortunate technical complications combined with the factory's withdrawal from racing limited its life to just two years. "Dustbin" fairings like the one on this racer were replaced by sleeker bodywork by the 1960s. The FIM banned them from racing in 1958 due to high-speed aerodynamic instability, especially on turns and through crosswinds. New rules required that the front wheel and rider remain exposed. Photo courtesy Motto Guzzi.

Kawasaki's Z1-inspired superbike first saw the track in 1976. The early four-cylinder inline air-cooled engines were prone to breaking under high stress, while frames suffered some weakness. With the help of tuner Rob Muzzy, the machine would dominate under the riding skill of Eddie Lawson, winning AMA Superbike championships in 1981 and 1982. Superbike racing allows high modification of production bikes. Kawasaki would move to a liquid-cooled inline 750cc four by 1989. Eddie Lawson continued on to win four 500cc Grand Prix championships. Photo of Herve Moineau on a Z1 in 1977 Mortons Archive.

Ducati's 1972 victory at the Imola 200 using this 748cc (45.6 cu in) two-valve per cylinder desmodromic air cooled 90-degree L-twin established the company in the sportsbike market. Raced by Paul Smart, a replica was made available to the public in 1974. By 2005, another updated replica was produced. It was aptly named the Paul Smart 1000 LE. Note the distinctive green frame. Photo by Stephen Covell.

This 1989 Yamaha FZR750 production racer photographed at the Barber Vintage Motorsports Museum is typical of the street-legal high-performance multi-cylinder machines Japanese motorcycle companies brought to market in the late 1980s. With a modest 750cc displacement and four-cylinders, the engine produced over 120 hp. It could achieve a stunning 170 mph. The bike competed squarely against Honda's RC30 and Suzuki's GSX-R, and was popular among private racers. Numerous great examples of historic racing machines can be seen at the Barber Vintage Motorsports Museum.

Honda Enters the Game

Motorcycle racing changed dramatically during the early 1960s. British machines were fading but held on strong in a few specialized circuits like flat track racing in the United States. Italians were still on top of their game in road racing.

This photo symbolizes the end of British reign on the tracks. Derek Minter on a 350cc Honda is ready to overtake Phil Read on a 350cc Norton at the1962 Thruxton 500-mile production race. Production races utilize motorcycles that are for sale to the public. Very few modifications are allowed. These typically include tires, seats, bars, and air filters. Photo Mortons Archive.

The combination of British and Italian riders on Italian made MVs was unbeatable. MV won world championships in 500cc, 350cc, 250cc, and 125cc classes for three years running between 1958 and 1960. That glory was to be short-lived as a hawk from Japan was circling above. Honda's factory racing team had quietly entered European racing in 1956. The company offered private racers low cost small displacement machines to break into the circuits. Within three years, its factory team made a strong showing with their twin-cylinder DOHC 125cc machines.

Honda's domination of the smaller displacement classes started with its entry into racing in 1959. Pictured is a typical 125cc start at the Isle of Man TT in 1964. Riders Ralph Bryans (left, Honda) and Frank Perris (Suzuki) push-start their machines. Photo Mortons Archive.

Honda learned a lot about Grand Prix racing during the late 1950s. It improved on its 125cc four-stroke DOHC engine for the 1960 season. The result was the RC 143—a 22 hp twin that, in the hands of expert riders like British born Jim Redman and Australian Tom Phillis, let the world know that Honda was a very serious contender. It was Honda's first World GP winner. Photo American Honda Motor Co., Inc.

Honda produced technically advanced and affordable small racers for the privateer in the 1960s. The 125cc CR® 93 twin's DOHC engine featured four valves per cylinder and produced 16.5 hp at 11,500 rpm in street-legal trim, 18 hp with a performance exhaust system, and nearly 21 hp with unrestricted pipes. Today it would make an exceptional café racer. The bike could exceed 100 mph. This pristine example is exhibited at the Barber Vintage Motorsports Museum.

The popularity and affordability of small displacement racers encouraged Honda to offer the Dream 50R retro-racer in 2004, this time with disc brakes. Photo courtesy of American Honda Motor Co., Inc.

The beginning of the end for Italian dominance came in 1960 when British rider Mike Hailwood joined Honda to win the title on a four-cylinder 250cc racer. By 1962 Honda dominated the 350cc and 250cc categories. Rhodesian rider Jim Redman was unstoppable. Honda's racing team would often place first, second, third, and fourth. Suzuki and Yamaha were soon to follow. By the mid-1960s, the three Japanese companies virtually owned international motorcycle racing from the ultra-light 50cc class all the way to the 350cc class.

Honda's technical mastery of multi-cylinder DOHC engines can be seen in its 297cc six-cylinder RC174 GP racer shown here at the 1967 Ulster GP. Mike Hailwood raced it in the 350 class. These engines could rev up to 17,000 rpm to produce 65 hp. Photo Mortons Archive.

Despite its success, Honda could not master the 500cc class during the 1960s. That was to remain MVs for a while longer, but only for a while. As Honda retired from racing in 1968, Yamaha went to work. By 1975 Yamaha won the Grand Prix World Championship with its four-cylinder water-cooled YZR500 two-stroke racer piloted by Giacomo Agostini. This was a first for a two-stroke machine. The next time an Italian maker would win the coveted GP was in 2007 for Ducati.

Japanese Two-Strokes Take Over

Motorcycle racing is expensive. Factory teams come and go as boardroom decisions are made about the return on racing investment. Privateers keep racing alive. With little or no sponsorship, these dedicated people prepare all week to race on weekends. They spend every dime they have on parts, oil, tires, and travel.

The advent of Japanese two-stroke engined racers in the 1960s and 1970s offered both professional and amateur racers something wonderful—a less expensive bike. Two-stroke engines have a lot fewer moving parts and can produce significantly more horsepower for their size and weight. They are also easier to maintain.

Yamaha, Suzuki, and Kawasaki offered many options. Their factory two-stroke racers were marvels of engineering. Between piston-port, reed-valve, and disc valve induction designs, there was always something new on the track. Everyone was experimenting to get as much power as possible out of a compact motor no larger than a breadbox. Honda followed with its own NS500 V3 two-stroke for the 1982 500cc GP season. US National Road Racing Champion Freddie Spencer had signed with Honda a few years earlier and brought home the GP World Championship for the brand in 1983. Two-strokes dominated GP racing up to the early years of the millennium. Rule changes by FIM encouraged the return of four-strokes. With power to spare and space-age chassis technology, the playing field was leveling.

The ultimate two-stroke was Honda's follow-up to their NS500: the NSR500. The company got very serious in 1984 with this remarkable liquid-cooled V4 two-stroke racing engine. Combined with a solid and assuring chassis, it brought them ten 500cc GP World Championships between 1985 and 2001. By the end of its reign, the engine was capable of putting out 180 hp. Engine technology had come a long way over the past 100 years.

Popularity of 1960s Japanese two-strokes, as this 1965 Yamaha, brought many racers to the ultra-lightweight 50cc class. So popular was this class that the Fédération Internationale de Motocyclisme (FIM) sanctioned it for GP World Championship racing. The class has since been replaced by 80cc bikes. Despite their tiny displacement and 10 hp, 50cc race bikes are capable of over 85 mph. Photo Mortons Archive.

Yamaha offered the entry-level racer the perfect bike in 1971. The twin-cylinder TA125 two-stroke was a simple and easy to maintain machine. Numerous examples of early Japanese racing two-strokes are on display at the Barber Vintage Motorsports Museum.

The 1970 Yamaha TD2 was the model made great by race champions Kel Carruthers, winner of the 1970 Isle of Man 250 TT, and Rodney Gould. Yamaha offered their over-the-counter road racers to the general public through their dealer network. Many privateers started racing aboard the TD2 and launched a whole new breed of racers aboard the twin-cylinder lightweights. These light bikes offered great handling and stopping via the highly developed four leading shoe front brake that Yamaha continued to use until the mid-1970s. Photo and text courtesy of Mecum Auctions.

Kawasaki's memorable 500cc H1 triple was offered in a racing version in 1970 as the H1-R, and in 1971 as the H1-RA. These piston-port two-strokes had some reliability issues on the track. The H2-R 750 triples followed in 1972. Their unwieldy power made them short-lived for racing. A new design was needed. Photo Mortons Archive.

Following the problems with their H series racers, Kawasaki went back to the drawing board to develop its KR250 and KR350 inline twins for 1975. The 250cc two-stroke KRs won five 250 World Championships for the green brand before it left that class after the 1983 season. Despite its modest 60 hp output, the bike was capable of 160 mph. The engines made peak power at 12,000 rpm and were known for very low vibration. Photo by author at the Barber Vintage Motorsports Museum.

Even Harley-Davidson got into two-stroke racers. For the privateer, it offered its RR250 twin for 1975 for AMA Class C racing. The bike was made by Italian Aermacchi. Exhibited at the Barber Vintage Motorsports Museum.

Honda's partnership with tobacco giant Rothmans resulted in three MotoGP titles using the formidable NSR500 engine. Photo courtesy of American Honda Motor Co., Inc.

Honda's NSR500 was replaced by the RC211V 990cc V-5 four-stroke in 2002 for the new MotoGP series. New rules, which would be changed later, allowed four-strokes up to 990cc to compete against the 500cc two-strokes. Many teams switched to four-strokes, including Honda. Honda Racing Corporation's partnership with Spanish energy company Repsol keeps the brand in the winner's circle. Many great riders enjoyed victory on the RC211V, including 2002 and 2003 world championships for Valentino Rossi, and 2006 for Nicky Hayden. Photo courtesy of American Honda Motor Co., Inc.

Homologation

This rather odd word is used frequently in racing. The term is defined as "to approve or confirm officially." This typically applies to racing events sanctioned by governing bodies that approve the specifications of bikes being raced. An example of that is in defining specs for what can be entered in a Superbike race. Rules may require a bike to be based on a production model. Even the number of vehicles produced is agreed upon. One example is the Harley-Davidson VR1000 Superbike. Only fifty were made to meet the minimum requirements homologated by the governing bodies. Many other examples of bikes exist that were made for limited production to meet homologation guidelines.

Harley-Davidson 1994 VR1000 in race trim. Photo courtesy of Mecum Auctions.

This Honda VFR750R RC30 racer used by Freddie Spencer back in 1992 required homologation by the FIM and AMA to compete in the World Superbike Championship. It was based on the V-4 VFR750 production bikes going back to 1986. Photo by Stephen Covell.

The American Who Shook Up the GP

Grand Prix motorcycle racing was always considered the domain of European riders. They scoffed at Americans trying to enter the game. After all, what do dirt track riders know about high-speed road racing? Well, after the 1978 season the whole world got the answer. A young man named Kenny Roberts from Modesto, California, took the prestigious GP World Championship title away from the European riders. Within a few short years, Roberts dominated the GP circuit. His aggressive dirt track style of riding combined with knee-dragging cornering won him the 500cc title in 1978, 1979, and 1980.

Kenny Roberts (right) with his arch rival and friend, Britain Barry Sheene. Roberts and Sheene competed fiercely on the track, with Sheene winning the 1976 and 1977 GP titles. Photo Mortons Archive.

Roberts started racing as a kid. He ultimately mastered the dirt ovals of America to win the AMA Grand National Championship twice. His success with road racing took off after Yamaha supported him by providing not only race bikes, but also the invaluable mentoring of famous racer Kel Carruthers. Roberts returned the favor by winning the company an AMA Grand National Championship in 1973. This was a first for any Japanese maker. He also helped Yamaha refine its machines. His feedback on the company's variable exhaust port system, called "Power Valve," allowed riders to have better control of the high revving four-cylinder two strokes the company was banking on to win. By the mid-1970s Roberts, was making a name for himself on American road racing circuits by breathing down the necks of the European legends. Roberts nearly beat the unstoppable Giacomo Agostini at the 1974 Daytona 200 race. The same played out at Imola, Italy. Agostini certainly recognized this young rider's extraordinary skills. Those skills went beyond riding a motorcycle. Roberts became instrumental in promoting professional motorcycle racing, fair treatment of the racers, and Grand Prix racing in the United States. His son, Kenny Roberts Jr., followed in his footsteps to win the GP World Championship in 2000.

Kenny Roberts on a Yamaha on the heels of Barry Sheene riding a Suzuki at the 1979 Belgian Grand Prix. Photo Mortons Archive.

The Sky Is the Limit

Professional and amateur motorcycle racing gains great popularity with each passing season. New riders discover the wealth of races locally as well as internationally. The AMA brilliantly sanctions highly specialized events for all ages in the United States. Youngsters can participate in racing as early as four. AMA Classes 3 and 4 allow less-experienced kids from four to eight years old, riding small 50cc dirt bikes for motocross racing. AMA Vintage racing encourages amateurs as well as former professionals to ride classic bikes in competition. Factory MotoGP teams continue to spend tens of millions on advancing their technology and high payrolls for superstar riders. Racing machines have evolved with horsepower unimaginable decades ago and razor sharp chassis controlled by electronics to help pilot the bike around tight turns at over 120 mph. Electronic technology is a serious point of discussion among veteran racers. Even though most will admit that crashes on the track have been reduced by more than half due to traction control technology alone, it does reduce the skill needed to handle a powerful machine at high cornering speeds. On the flip side, skilled riders take full advantage of this technology to push their machines to the limit.

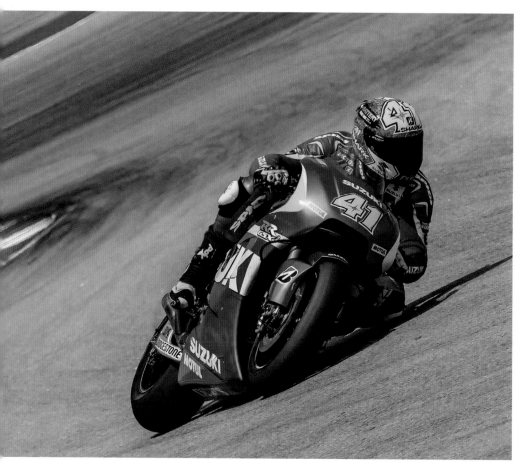

Photos like this capture the fluid beauty of motorcycle racing. Modern technology in engineering and tires has achieved performance unimagined by racers seventy years ago. Pictured is Suzuki MotoGP team's 2015 GSX-RR racer being testing at Sepang International Circuit in Malaysia with rider Aleix Espargaro. Photo courtesy of Suzuki Motor of America, Inc.

The next section in this chapter will outline the broad variety of major racing classes and events in the United States and internationally today.

Motorcycle Racing Categories

Over the decades countless motorcycle racing categories have been created based on the technical capabilities of the machines. The most enduring classes are the AMA flat track events, the Isle of Man TT, and the FIM's Grand Prix (GP) series. Many others have come and gone. One such venue was the Formula 750 road racing series originally started by the AMA and its British counterpart, the Auto Cycle Union, in 1971. The exciting series was picked up by the FIM from 1972 through 1979. Hopes were high that this class would become the premiere series, overtaking GP racing due to the extraordinary speed of the bikes. That did not happen. One reason was the overwhelming domination by one brand—Yamaha. Its TZ750 racer was simply unbeatable. This is remarkably similar to what happened with the Isle of Man Clubmans TT race that began in 1947 and was disbanded in 1956. BSA Gold Stars dominated. Clubmans racing is a category that came out of local racing clubs competing against each other with specific brands or configurations. BSA Gold Stars, Nortons, and Velocettes were favored among British racing clubs. Today, the American Federation of Motorcylists, founded in 1954 by a group of sport riding enthusiasts in Northern California, offers clubman road racing in several categories. It is an ideal entry point for those looking to enter racing.

The glorious 1979 Yamaha TZ750 on the right would be happier on the racetrack than being showcased at a country club event. Photo by Stephen Covell.

Even seasoned motorcyclists will be amazed to see the wealth of racing classes and categories listed herein. Although not a complete listing, it is the hope of the author that those not familiar with motorcycle racing will be inspired by at least one category and plan on attending its events.

The dedication of amateur racers cannot be overstated and must be seen to be appreciated. Racer #3 often finishes in the top two despite being handicapped by the lack of an arm.

AMA Racing

The American Motorcyclist Association is involved in one way or another with nearly all motorcycle racing events in the United States. It represents the FIM in international racing held on US soil. The AMA will partner with other organizations to promote and manage specific races. For example, the MotoAmerica North American Road Racing Championship racing series is sanctioned by the AMA and FIM for five specific production-based racing classes ranging in engine displacement from 373cc to 1,200cc. Each class has very strict rules about engine size, engine components, chassis, tires, and brakes. These classes mimic the FIM international ones and include:

SUPERBIKE: 750cc to 1,000cc three- and four-cylinder, or 850cc to 1,200cc two-cylinder, some engine modifications permitted.

SUPERSTOCK 1000: same engine sizes as Superbike, but with mostly stock engine components.

SUPERSPORT: 400cc to 636cc four-cylinder, 500cc to 675cc three-cylinder, 600cc to 750cc two-cylinder engines, with mostly stock components and some modifications allowed for compression and cam timing.

Superstock 600: 401cc to 636cc four-cylinder, 401cc to 675cc three-cylinder engines, and some electronic mods.

KTM RC 390: Cup open to racers fourteen to twenty-two years old, using 373cc fuel-injected single-cylinder engines with 38 hp. This is the same as the FIM's European Junior Cup class.

Unlike MotoGP machines, these highly modified bikes are closer to production sport-bikes, and thus offer great opportunity for attracting potential customers. The series also grooms American racers to compete internationally. Nine races are scheduled at major speedways across the country. Details are available at motoamerica.com.

Supersport racing utilizes slightly modified production bikes in the 400cc to 750cc range (depending on number of cylinders) and represents an ideal cost-effective entrée into professional road racing. Photo courtesy of Triumph Motorcycles.

AMA CLASSES

Under the AMA, over three thousand pro and amateur races a year are offered through its many local chapters, member clubs, and partners. The most famous is the AMA Pro Grand National Championship racing series. Its roots go back to the 1954 AMA National Dirt Track Championship. The AMA decided that same year to establish the Grand National Championship series. It consisted of eighteen points-paying races. It was mostly made up of flat track (dirt track) races, but a few road race nationals were added to demonstrate the variety of motorcycles and riders. Popularity of these races grew, and the AMA encouraged specialization of classes based on type of track and type of bike used. In 1986, flat track and road racing became two distinct AMA Pro Racing championships.

AMA Pro Racing announced in late 2016 the official rebranding of the AMA Pro Flat Track series to an all-new American Flat Track (AFT) series. This coincides with the great interest in the sport, and the revival of the historic competition between Harley-Davidson and Indian. Twin-cylinder motorcycles (650 – 999cc) will make up the AFT Twins class. These bikes will sport the latest technology available. The AFT Singles class allows newcomers to earn their wings on 450cc single-cylinder motorcycles.

The AMA Pro Road Race series is the country's most prestigious road race series. Even though its classes are similar to the MotoAmerica classes today, different tracks and rules apply. The foremost is the Superbike category with its awesome 200 hp, 190 mph 1,000cc bikes. This series started in 1976 and led the way to FIM-sanctioned World Superbike Racing (WSBK). AMA Pro Racing also includes a Motocross series and a Hill Climb series. Details about these races and schedules can be found at amaproracing.com.

Racing allows a mechanical canvas for the creative mind. Eric Buell brought Harley-Davidson an AMA Championship after many years with his 1125R racer in 2009. This bike is displayed at the Barber Vintage Motorsports Museum.

Other AMA pro and amateur racing events are listed herein. Many of them feature season-long, multi-event pro-am and amateur National Championship Series', while stand-alone events that recognize the country's best amateur racers are well represented in the many Grand Championship races.

- Vintage Dirt Track and DTX
- Road Racing
- Motocross
- Supercross
- Speedway
- Vintage Racing
- Youth
- Enduro
- Extreme Dirt
- Scrambles
- Hare and Hound
- Indoor Dirt
- Ice Racing
- Cross Country
- Hill Climb
- Land Speed
- Trial des Nations

One can clearly see the wealth of racing the AMA offers. There is truly something for everyone.

Flat track vintage motorcycle racing on traditional fairground ovals brings back the excitement of years past. Most racers will strap a steel "hot" shoe onto the left boot to help with sliding around the tight turns at high speeds.

Not all Harley-Davidson flat track racers were V-twins. This bike was built to compete in the smaller displacement classes. A 1972 350cc Italian-made Aermacchi engine is fitted to a 1962 Harley-Davidson rigid racing frame. Photo courtesy of John Adamczyk.

Another example of a non-traditional Harley-Davidson flat tracker. The bike pictured is a modified Harley MX-250 motocross bike introduced in the mid-1970s. The MX-250 was a very capable motocrosser made by Aermacchi until the Italian company was sold to Cagiva by Harley-Davidson in 1978.

Antique motorcycle racing is gaining in popularity with the good work done by the American Historic Racing Motorcycle Association. It is a not-for-profit organization dedicated to restoring and competing on classic motorcycles. The AHRMA is the largest vintage racing group in North America and one of the biggest in the world. They offer on- and off-road racing competitions. Their website will show a calendar of events throughout the country, ahrma.org

Vintage motorcycle racing events provide the rare opportunity to see historic motorcycles such as this Vincent 500cc single Grey Flash. What the Lightning is to the Black Shadow, the Flash is to the Comet. Only thirty-one of these original factory racers were made. Many reproductions have been created using Vincent Comets.

Isle of Man TT

Considered the premiere venue for road racers of all categories, the Isle of Man's 37.7-mile Mountain Course is also the most challenging. Unlike controlled racetracks, the course offers no forgiveness. Stone walls and hardwood fences provide little comfort in the event of a crash. Average lap speeds increase each year. During the TT's centenary in 2007, a lap record of 130.354 mph was recorded in the Senior TT by John McGuinness, a twenty-three time TT winner. In 2014, Bruce Anstey managed to run the course in 17:06.682 minutes, with a top speed over 206 mph. By 2015, John McGuinness broke that record and ran the course in 17:03.567 minutes at an average lap speed of 132.701 mph. That record was broken as well in 2016. Robert Dunlop's son Michael astounded onlookers and officials alike as he broke the 17 minute mark with a lap time of 16 minutes and 58.439 seconds. He clocked a lap record of 133.393 mph on his Hawk Racing BMW S1000RR superbike.

Anyone that has ever visited the island can appreciate these accomplishments, considering how many areas of the course require speeds under 80 mph. When it comes to racing, you can't get much closer to the action than at the TT. To get a sense of the speed and danger, look at the 2011 movie Closer to the Edge featuring the extraordinary TT racer Guy Martin.

Vintage motorcycle racing does not just mean old Indians and British makes. A number of classes exist where bikes from the 1970s and 1980s can be raced. These machines are relatively inexpensive and can easily be modified for amateur racing. Classic Superbike racing has stricter limits. It requires air-cooled engines with dual-shock rear suspensions made between 1973 and 1985. The lightweight class includes bikes like the Honda 350 pictured.

Sidecar racing can be unbelievably fast. Typically three laps are covered at average speeds over 110 mph.

Local residents watching superbikes screaming up Bray Hill.

Classic racing at Billown course near Castletown, IOM.

Junior class vintage racer at the TT.

William Dunlop taking the Victory RR electric superbike through it practice lap for the 2016 TT Zero. He achieved 158.3mph through the Sulby speed trap. Photo courtesy of Victory Motorcycles.

This memorial to Joey Dunlop was commissioned by Arai Helmet® and erected at the Bungalow section of the TT course near Mount Snaefell in 2002. It shows a contented racer overlooking the fast mountain course that he mastered so well. All twenty-six of his TT victories are engraved in stone at this revered site. It serves as a memorial to all racers who lost their lives to the sport. The Joey Dunlop Foundation established in 2001 supports disabled visitors to the Isle of Man.

The Isle of Man TT has been providing race fans with a beautiful venue since 1907. Pictured is Cameron Donald racing in the Dainese Superbike TT in 2012. Photo courtesy of iomtt.com.

The TT has two major events annually: the IOM TT that features contemporary machines and the Classic TT that features vintage machines. The TT racing categories include Superbike, Sidecar in a variety of sizes, Supersport, Superstock, TT Zero (zero emissions electric bikes), Lightweight bikes, and the famous Senior TT.

The Classic TT includes several categories based on engine size. The 500cc Classic TT features 351cc to 500cc machines. The 350cc Classic TT allows 175cc to 350cc machines to compete against each other. The Formula 2 Classic TT opens it up from 1,300cc to 351cc depending on year, while the Formula 1 Classic TT keeps it between 750cc and 126cc two-strokes, depending on year. You can get a lot of detail by visiting the IOM TT website at iomtt.com.

Sidecar racers Dave Molyneux and Patrick Farrance fly by one of many great places to view the TT. Photo courtesy of iomtt.com.

The Best TT Race?

Every TT since 1907 has offered unparalleled thrills. Among TT enthusiasts there is however one race that stands out above the others: the 1992 Senior TT. The race was the culmination of a week long battle between Steve Hislop and Carl Fogarty. The former rode a Norton RCW588 twin-rotor Wankel, while the later mounted a 750cc Yamaha. Both riders pushed their machines to the very limit as they exchanged the lead many times. Hislop ultimately won, but Fogarty's 123.6 mph lap record stood for an astonishing seven years.

Motorcycle Grand Prix

Grand Prix racing may be considered the most prestigious racing venue because of its high speed, high media visibility, and high investment in heavily funded teams. Superstar riders cost big money. The 2014 MotoGP World Champion Marc Márquez earned over $12 million a year. Advertising prestige is also a major plus despite the fact that most GP bikes have engines that have little in common with production machines. On the surface, covered with plastic bodywork, they do look similar to consumer models. Victory for a brand does sell bikes. One only needs to watch the first fifteen minutes of the 2011 documentary *Fastest* to understand MotoGP racing. The battle on the GP track in Catalunya, Spain, between teammates Valentino Rossi and Jorge Lorenzo in 2009 is astounding.

MotoGP racing is as exciting as it gets when it's in the rain. This is where traction control (TC) systems level the playing field. This race is at the Sepang racing circuit in Malaysia in 2009. Defending world champion Valentino Rossi (center with orange helmet riding a Yamaha) claimed his seventh MotoGP title while Australia's Casey Stoner (center front on the red Ducati) took first place. Photo Saeed Khan/Getty Images.

Grand prix racing has three distinct classes. The requirements and rules change frequently depending on new technology that enters racing.

MOTO3™ - This class features four-stroke, 250cc single-cylinder engines. It replaced the earlier 125cc GP category in 2012. Age restrictions apply. Maximum is twenty-eight, while minimum is sixteen.

MOTO2™ - This class has replaced the illustrious 250cc class as of 2010. Honda 600cc engines are used exclusively, producing around 140 hp. The minimum age is sixteen years old.

MOTOGP™ - This is the most demanding and challenging GP category. It is composed of eighteen races across four continents. As of this writing, maximum engine size is 1,000cc and must be four-stroke in design. The minimum age for riders is eighteen.

MotoGP champions are rock stars in the eyes of millions of fans. Nine-time GP World Champion Valentino Rossi has been racing motorcycles since 1993. He has won world championships in the 125cc, 250cc, 500cc, and MotoGP classes racing for Aprilia, Honda, Ducati, and most recently, the Movistar Yamaha team. Photo Mortons Archive.

Superbike Racing

The Superbike category is a very fast and powerful venue. Bikes are modified production motorcycles that must have the basic architecture of their consumer counterparts. Engines must be four-stroke, with displacement between 800cc and 1,200cc for twins, and between 750cc and 1,000cc for four-cylinder machines.

Kawasaki WSBK Championship rider Tom Sykes and the Ninja ZX-10R won the 2013 Championship. Sykes is the first Ninja rider since American Scott Russell to claim the World Superbike crown since 1988. Photo courtesy of Kawasaki Motors Corp.

Endurance Racing

Endurance racing tests man and machine for strength, perseverance, durability, and reliability. Races can last for twenty-four hours straight, over a great distance for days, or timed events to see how far a team can travel. Endurance racing has been going on since the early 1900s. It is a great way to promote the quality and reliability of a marque. It is also a proving ground for manufacturers to test their engines in real-world conditions.

Sidecar Racing

Sidecar racing is a sight to behold. The FIM Sidecar World Championship is the highest level for this category. Sidecar racing is also very popular at vintage racing events. The Germans, Swiss, and British clearly dominate this sport.

Sidecar racing can be on the track or off-road. In all cases, team effort between rider and passenger is essential in the performance and handling of the vehicle.

Motocross (MX) Racing

Motocross is all about racing in the dirt, mud, ruts, and jumps. Dozens of racers start side-by-side and often plow into each other at the first turn. The first one to get off the line usually makes it through the "hole" and takes the lead. This is referred to as a "hole shot." Modern off-road suspensions have prompted changes in course configurations over the years, featuring more extreme hills and valleys. The results are dramatic airborne jumps at high speeds. Classes range from youth 50cc to adult 250cc two-strokes, and up to 450cc four-stroke machines. AMA Motocross champion Ricky Carmichael is considered one of the very best in this racing category. FMX (Freestyle Motocross) is a derivation of MX, where high jumps with stunning aerobatics are the criteria for performance.

Motocross racing is a lot of fun to watch and even more fun to participate in. Vintage MX allows less expensive older bikes to be raced.

MX GP

International MX GP racing represents the FIM's Motocross World Championship events for motocross. The three classes, MX1, MX2, and MX3, are defined by specific engine sizes. Racing is grueling and just over a half-hour long.

Dominated by the European race teams, particularly from Belgium, MX GP racing is fast, furious, and high energy. KTM motorcycles consistently score high. Photo courtesy of KTM North America, Inc.

Supercross (SX) Racing

Supercross is indoor motocross with a lot more glitz and fanfare. Pop-star riders sponsored by high-profile beverage brands race on short indoor tracks riddled with jumps and washboards. It is noisy, fast, and exciting.

DTX

Dirt track cross racers use motocross machines on flat track ovals. It is a category first introduced by the AMA in 1989 to encourage flat track racing by allowing less expensive dirt bikes to compete. Few modifications are needed to a motocross bike to make it qualify. These are mostly confined to tires and suspension tweaks. Reducing the long suspension travel of the typical motocross bike works best for DTX racing. The low entry cost allows anyone to revive an old motocross machine for racing.

Supercross is a loud and exciting indoor event.
Photo by Diego Barbieri / Shutterstock.com

Trials

Motorcycle trials competitions are about as opposite to Supercross as one can get. These events are all about absolute finesse and control of the motorcycle in seemingly impossible terrain. Trials riders ride along a trail and are judged by observers who deduct points for poor maneuvers, placing a foot on the ground, or stalling out. Trials can be solo or with sidecar. Riders are standing on the footpegs while often balancing the bike at standstill to regain composure in preparation for a jump over a boulder or log.

Supermoto

Supermoto racing takes place on both paved and dirt road surfaces. The bikes look more like motocross machines but with street racing tires. Riding style, even on the tarmac, is more motocross style.

Supermoto's popularity has inspired many makers to offer street sportbikes in this style of motorcycle. Photo courtesy of KTM North America, Inc.

Trials are physically demanding and require great mental focus. Balance and surefootedness outweigh speed in these competitions. Riders stand on the footpegs while maneuvering the bike in near impossible terrain. Photo Mortons Archive.

Enduro and Cross-Country

Enduros are off-road events that test a rider's ability to meet timelines in difficult conditions through mountain and forest trails. Most events take several hours while others, like the ISDE and crazy Erzberg Rodeo, take days. Enduro bikes became very popular in the 1970s when Japanese makers like Yamaha offered street-legal off-road bikes equipped with lighting.

Bultaco was a Spanish motorcycle maker between 1958 and 1983. It was known for its outstanding two-stroke enduro bikes, such as this 1975 Alpina.

Hare Scramble

Hare scrambles are off-road races that take place on rough dirt courses, rocky terrain, open fields, and through dense forests. The track is clearly marked and may vary in length depending on the event. Racers may do multiple laps on the marked course. The one with the overall fastest time wins. One of the most grueling is the Red Bull Hare Scrambles in Erzberg, Austria. Of the 500 qualifiers, only a handful ever finish the race.

Hare and Hound

Hare and Hound races are a bit different than hare scrambles. Riders do not repeat the same track loop twice in a row. Races are typically forty miles long. The term "Hare and Hound" comes from the fact that the first rider is chased by the rest—the hounds. Since courses are unfamiliar to the riders before a race, the leader has the greater challenge.

Scrambling started in England back in the 1930s and continues to be a great amateur venue.

Cross-Country Rally

Cross Country rally races are larger enduro-type events spanning greater distances. These races are often run through deserts at high speeds with larger displacement off-road machines. The most brutal and competitive race is the Dakar Rally, formerly known as the Paris to Dakar Rally. A large portion of the race is through the Sahara desert heading toward Senegal. Races span over thousands of miles and can take weeks. They are well publicized by motorcycle makers. KTM has been the clear winning marque in this series, with BMW, Yamaha, and Honda following. The FIM sanctions other major championship rallies throughout the world.

The Baja 1000 is the most famous American cross-country rally. It is part of the Southern California Off-Road Experience circuit. The race takes place on Mexico's Baja California Peninsula. The grueling desert race can have teams of riders racing for over twenty-four hours straight. Seconds count at valuable pit stops to refuel and hydrate. Despite the cost associated with this race, amateurs number in the hundreds. Photo courtesy of Anthony Clarke.

Desert racing isn't confined to just gasoline-powered bikes. With their extended range, electric bikes have joined in on the fun. Photo courtesy of Zero Motorcycles, Inc.

Hill Climb

Hill climbing competitions have been going on for over a hundred years. It did not take long for bikes to achieve enough horsepower to race up a steep, muddy hill in an attempt to reach the top. Hill climbs have both professional and amateur venues. Some races are timed, where the winner is determined by the shortest time it takes to reach the crest. The Pikes Peak Hill Climb race, taking place on a 12.42-mile paved road in Colorado, is such an event. It has been running since 1916 and is the highest-elevation course in the world. Traditional dirt hill climbing venues often have colorful names such as Widowmaker and Devil's Staircase.

Hill climbing took off with the advent of more powerful motorcycles in the early 1900s, featuring a lengthened rear frame and chains on the rear wheel for traction.

Almost is not good enough in hill climbing. One can be inches from the crest and still not place.

The Pikes Peak International Hill Climb is a race against time. Pictured is a Ronin crossing the finish line at 14,110 feet elevation. Electronic fuel injection systems do a much better job of compensating fuel/air mixture at those altitudes than fixed carburetors. Photo courtesy of Ronin Motor Works. Photo by Ford McClave.

An indication of how serious Victory is about diversifying its line of motorcycles is their Roland Sands Project 156. The bike was designed to race at the Pikes Peak event for 2015. The name is derived from the number of curves on the mountain course. Several concept bikes have been developed from the 156 that should see production in the near future. The Victory Octane is an example. Photo courtesy of Polaris Industries, Inc.

Speedway and Grass Track

Speedway is a fast track race on either dirt or loose shale. Highly specialized single-cylinder bikes are used. These light machines have only one gear and no brakes. The term "powersliding" is most associated with this style of racing. Speedway has its roots in America going back to 1910 when horse racing tracks were recognized as great places to race motorcycles. American rider Bruce Penhall put the United States on top in speedway when it had previously been dominated by Europeans back in the 1970s and 1980s. He became 1982 FIM Speedway Champion, using a 500cc single Weslake motorcycle. Grass track racing is like speedway but takes place on longer courses. Since straights are longer, bikes may be equipped with two speeds.

The unmistakable silhouette of a speedway racer shows a narrow front wheel and a rooster tail of dirt following the sliding bike.

Ice Speedway

Ice racing is very much like speedway racing but on a thick layer of ice. Tracks are usually ovals of a quarter mile or less. It is popular in Canada, the northern United States, and Russia.

Drag Racing

Drag racing, or sprinting, is based on accelerating a machine in a straight line on a measured course. Quarter-mile tracks are most common. Winning may be based on the final terminal speed of the bike, or, in the case of drag racing, beating another opponent running parallel. Some sprints are based on "flying" speeds, taking the fastest speed at a particular point on the track.

Ice racing is nearly as fast as dirt track–based racing. Spikes screwed onto the tires keep traction but present a risk to riders upon a fall. Photo Mortons Archive.

Drag racing comes in all shapes and sizes, ranging from small stock street bikes to fully blown (super-charged) 1,000 hp nitrous-oxide breathing monsters capable of reaching 250 mph in a quarter mile. Photo courtesy of Scooter Grubb.

It is not uncommon to see dual-engine dragsters. This 1959 Triumph was quite fast in its day. Photo by Stephen Covell.

Land Speed Racing

Land Speed racing is all about attaining the fastest speed for a specific category of machine. Classes are based on naked or streamlined bikes, stock or super-modified, gas, diesel, jet, or electric, in every motor size imaginable. The AMA and FIM sanctioned Motorcycle Speed Trials held at the Bonneville Speedway on Utah's Bonneville Salt Flats represents the Mecca of this event. The straight-line course is ten miles long, allowing racers enough time to achieve terminal speed. Rollie Free achieved his 150 mph speed on a Vincent on the salt flats, while Burt Munro raced his antique Indian there in the 1960s to reach 205.67 mph in the flying-mile. Triumph set a number of speed records between the mid-1950s and mid-1960s. Johnny Allen achieved 214.47 mph in 1956 in a streamliner powered by a 650cc T110 engine. Triumph named their best-selling bike after the salt flats. It introduced the T120 Bonneville in 1959. As of this writing, Triumph will be back in 2015 to attempt to break the current record of 376.363 mph set by Rocky Robinson in 2010. The 1,000 hp Rocket III streamliner will be piloted by TT winner Guy Martin. The AMA and FIM sanction various championships at this venue. Racing usually starts in late August every year. Teams prepare all year and are occasionally challenged with damp salt that makes racing less than ideal.

The Triumph-powered *Gyronaut X-1* was built and raced by the team of Bob Leppan, Alex Tremulis, and Jim Bruflodt at Bonneville between 1965 and 1970. It achieved a top speed of 264.437 mph. Its twin Bonneville engines produced a modest 130 hp. As the name suggests, the streamliner incorporated a gyroscope for stability. Photo by Stephen Covell.

Racers of streamlined specialized motorcycles are exceeding speeds of 370 mph today. Denis Manning's "7" motorcycle streamliner set several world records at the Bonneville Salt Flats. The last record was won with a speed of 367.382 mph in 2009. The custom-built 3,000cc turbocharged, liquid-cooled, DOHC V-4 puts out 500 hp. This is the machine that Valerie Thompson rode to achieve 304.263 mph in September of 2016. Photo courtesy of Scooter Grubb. scootershoots.com

While big factory teams competed for records at the Salt Flats, independents like  Burt Munro inspired everyone with their feats. Pictured is the brand new *Munro Special* streamliner before it was shipped to the United States in 1962. Housed within is Munro's antique 1920 Indian Scout configured to 850cc. He achieved a record speed of 178.97 mph that year. He was 63 years old and continued to race at the Bonneville Salt Flats for years to come. Photo courtesy of John Munro.

Women racers make a very strong showing at the speed trials at the Bonneville Salt Flats. Photo courtesy of Scooter Grubb.

Eva Håkansson (right) is the fastest female on an electric motorcycle. She achieved a speed of 270.224 mph in September of 2014. Pictured is the KillaJoule team (l to r): Mike Stockert, Alicia Kelly, Bill Dubé and Eva. Kent Singleton not shown in picture. The electric-powered three-wheeler was crafted by the team from the ground up. See details in the Electric chapter. Photos courtesy of KillaCycle Racing.

Norton is eager to show that it has come back to racing after all these years. The British marque brought its new sportbike to the Bonneville Salt Flats to see how fast it will go. Photo courtesy of Norton Motorcycles, Ltd.

Profile of a Racer

Valerie Thompson is clearly an inspiration to women, particularly those who ride. As of this writing she is "World's Fastest Female Motorcycle Racer." She achieved this on September 1, 2016 at the Bonneville Motorcycle Speed Trials with a blistering one measured mile average speed of 304.263 mph (489.66 km/h) riding the famous Denis Manning designed "7" Racing streamliner pictured earlier in this chapter.

Valerie Thompson has been called "America's Queen of Speed." In addition to her remarkable 2016 Bonneville record of 304 mph, Valerie is a seven-time land speed record holder. She is also a lifetime member of the prestigious Bonneville 200 MPH Club, holds memberships in the Mojave Magnum 200 MPH Club, the ECTA 200 MPH Club, the Texas Mile 200 MPH Club, the Bonneville Motorcycle Speed Trials 201 MPH Club, and is the first female member of the Colorado Mile 200 MPH Club.

Valerie's interest in motorcycles began somewhat casually, as it does with most of us. In 1999, she was asked by a friend to go riding on the back of his custom bike. While she was checking the bike out, the owner noticed the back of her jeans. He apologized and said that her jeans would scratch the paint on the fender of his expensive custom. The passenger seat, according to Valerie's apt description, was "one of those fender stick-on seats." The fellow offered a good solution and told Valerie about how more and more women are riding motorcycles. This conversation inspired her to get her own bike. Soon after, they found themselves at a dealership at which Valerie bought her first bike, a 1999 Sportster. Within three months she upgraded to a Fat Boy, which she still has. It is the bike that she originally learned how to drag race on.

Her racing career started in 2006 drag racing motorcycles on quarter-mile tracks in the All Harley Drag Racing Association and NHRA Pro Stock Motorcycle series. Her desire to go faster, and break more records, led her to form her own land speed racing team, Valerie Thompson Racing, in 2012. Drawing from the hard work ethic she learned from her family, Valerie has developed the discipline all successful racers must embrace—to be the best one can be and compete at the highest levels. She certainly has done that.

Valerie and her team preparing for another run at the Texas Mile in March of 2015. Racers get very focused at the starting line and often develop certain rituals. Valerie's is to flip her kill switch back and forth a few times. Her personal best at the Texas Mile in 2014 was 217.7 MPH (350.53 KM/H) on a BMW S 1000 RR. Photo courtesy of Valerie Thompson Racing, valeriethompsonracing.com

Off the track, Valerie donates her time to charity with a specific interest in inspiring young girls and boys to reach their full potential. She earned the "American Women Riders Community Hero Award" in 2011 for her efforts to help kids achieve their goals. She participates in many events nationwide and is always willing to share advice with up-and-coming young racers.

Valerie will continue to seek new records, particularly at the NHRA Pro Stock Motorcycle racing class.

The two things all racers have in common are competitiveness and the need for speed. That was certainly the case with Marty Dickerson, shown with his modified Vincent Rapide in 1975 on the Bonneville Salt Flats. Photo by and courtesy of Seth W. Dorfler.

So Now You Want to Race

If all this reading about racing got your heart pumping, you should consider it. Learning to race is a gradual process. Most of the superstars started off as kids racing small dirt bikes or karts. Adults entertaining the idea have several good options.

1 - Check out local races. The AMA website is a good place to start. Local shops usually have a list of local and regional races. You can learn a lot by speaking with riders about the category and what it takes to get in. These races may be club races specializing in a certain class, size, or type of bike, ranging from off-road vehicles to all-out superbikes.

2 - Try your hand at an amateur event. There are plenty of AMA amateur motocross events throughout the year that will allow participation. Motocross is a great way to learn about racing of any type. Many of the great GP and Superbike champions started off on a dirt bike.

3 - If you ride a sports bike, consider going to the track. More and more major racetracks are offering track days. They will have certain rules as to safety specifications on the bike. It's usually easy stuff to do. Proper safety gear is also important.

4 - Consider attending a riding school. Keith Code's California Superbike School offers track training at various levels of expertise throughout the country. Freddie Spencer's High-Performance Riding School is another great way to get serious training for professional track racing. Local tracks may also offer riding instruction. An example is the Yamaha Champions Riding School (YCRS) located at New Jersey Motorsports Park (NJMP), Millville, New Jersey.

California Superbike School's founder Keith Code developed and patented this "Lean Bike" specifically for training riders on lean angles and braking on wet surfaces. Sophisticated training wheels will not allow the bike to fall, inspiring confidence while learning the limits of traction. Photo courtesy of California Superbike School.

There are just as many off-road schools. For the serious MX or SX rider, the Ricky Carmichael Race School will offer exceptional training to compete in motocross. Ontario, Canada–based MXSchools would make a fun summer vacation for the casual off-road rider looking to learn more about motocross riding. None of the classes are cheap, but they are worth the price considering the years of experience one can gain in just a weekend. Start hinting now about your next birthday present.

Happy Racing!

Chapter 12

WHERE TO SEE MOTORCYCLES

The motorcycle enthusiast does not have to travel far to see truly impressive collections of antique, vintage, and custom bikes on display. Museums, club meets, and national rallies offer endless opportunities to learn more about motorcycles and to see them firsthand.

Motorcycles Are All Around Us

If you have developed a deep passion for bikes, you will want to see more—many more. This includes all the old bikes from a hundred years ago, to obscure models made by folks who have come and gone. There are plenty of places to see them. The popularity of the motorcycle has even brought them into the prestigious Guggenheim Museum and the Museum of Modern Art in New York City.

Not quite the Guggenheim, but equally impressive, is singer-songwriter Billy Joel's personal collection on exhibit at his 20th Century Cycles in Oyster Bay, Long Island.

Finding rare motorcycles is always a treat when visiting museums throughout the world. This early 1920's V-twin was displayed against its original workshop setting at the Beamish Museum in Urpeth, England. The bike was built by Dene Motor Co. of Newcastle. Dene produced limited numbers of made-to-order British motorcycles between 1902 and 1924. The engines were typically sourced from proprietary engine manufacturers. This bike's two-cylinder engine was no doubt requested for sidecar duty. The bike also features rim brakes front and back. Photo courtesy of Laura Chisholm.

There Is No Place Like Home

The internet is certainly full of motorcycles. One could spend a lifetime perusing the countless websites that feature bikes and motorcycle lifestyle. *Jay Leno's Garage* is certainly one of the most fun sites to visit. His videos reviewing bikes of all types are both educational and entertaining. Leno has done a lot to promote the value of historic motorcycling. Online forums such as NYCvinMoto.com are great places to learn about local events and gatherings of motorcyclists who share a passion for vintage and classic bikes.

If you are willing to travel, there are many local places to see collections. One example may be a restaurant owned by a vintage bike collector. These restaurants will often feature a "bike night" where people gather to show off their rides. Trendy coffee bars popping up in urban areas use exotic Italian bikes and custom vintage café racers to decorate their shops. Clubs like the Philly Clan of the Brit Iron Rebels meet weekly at an old British-style pub. The event is called "Two Wheel Tuesday." One does not have to look far to find such venues.

The super trendy coffee bar at Jane Motorcycles in Brooklyn, New York, displays the custom vintage café racers they have built in their shop. Patron motorcyclists gather there on warm summer eves to enjoy a latte and meet fellow riders. It is a modern take on the "transport café" that launched the café racer scene. Photo courtesy of Jane Motorcycles, janemotorcycles.com

A common place to find old bikes is at a local bike dealership that has been around for a long time. They often exhibit a personal collection of machines. Another popular venue is the large annual manufacturer's bike shows held at convention centers. Many in the Northeast are held during winter months—at the height of motorcyclists' cabin fever. Even though most of the machines will be next year's models, these shows typically have plenty of vintage and custom bikes on display as well. Your local bike shop will know the dates.

Motorcycle tradeshows feature the latest offerings from top makers and accessory suppliers. Photo courtesy of Moto Guzzi, Piaggio & C SpA.

Vintage motorcycles will often hide quietly in places we may pass on our way to work. Located in Lower Manhattan, the New York City Police Museum displays a small but delightful collection of police bikes. The museum makes for a great lunchtime visit to learn more about New York's great history.

Newcomers to motorcycles are often surprised to find out about the many local events taking place in their area. These events are typically sponsored by local clubs focused on a particular brand or riding lifestyle. This can include pretty much any make of bike and riding interests, like café racing. Listings can be found in the free regional biker newspapers available at bike shops. These "rags" are full of in-formation on local specialty shops, suppliers, and events.

The Delaware Valley Norton Riders group has been holding one of its meets every April at Washington Crossing Historic Park. The event started off with a handful of Nortons but has now escalated to nearly a thousand bikes of all makes and models. It has become a popular family event for the Philadelphia-Trenton area.

Bigger Is Not Always Better

Annual bikefests, like those held at Sturgis, Daytona Beach, Laconia, and Leesburg, have plenty of new and old motorcycle eye candy to look at. However, some of these events are not the kinds of places you'd want to take your kids. They will be seeing too much adult eye candy as well. A better place for the family is a regional motorcycle show sponsored by one of the major organizations. Among the absolute best are those held by the chapters of the Antique Motorcycle Club of America. With fifty-eight chapters throughout the United States, there is always something going on. The AMCA typically has the best vintage American bikes on exhibit at these events. Check their schedule at antique-motorcycle.org.

AMCA events, such as this one in Rhinebeck, NY, feature hundreds of antique motorcycles. Their timeline exhibit is a wonderful way to experience the evolution of motorcycles over a hundred-year period.

Rolling the Dice

One of the best places to see bikes is at an auction. There you will be able to touch them as well. The larger ones feature a great variety of machines, while more specialized vintage auctions may focus on a particular historical segment. There are many local and national auctions running throughout the country, including those hosted by Bonhams. Local vintage events and swap meets typically will have a small auction as part of the venue. Mecum Auctions hold events in various parts of the country throughout the year. They host a huge one in Las Vegas every winter with over 750 superb bikes for sale.

Auctions are a great place to look at motorcycles. The temptation to buy a dream bike will be hard to resist. Mecum's large auctions allow a serious buyer the opportunity to examine bikes in detail and offer a very broad variety of machines all under one roof. Photo courtesy of Mecum Auctions.

Motorcyclists get cabin fever. The long winters in the Northeast require keeping busy to relieve the itch to ride. There are plenty of indoor swap meets if one looks around. They often feature small auctions for folks looking to turn their bikes. Local bike shops, bike papers, and national publications, like those offered by Walneck's, will typically list the ones in your area.

Vintage Motorcycle Days

The national Vintage Motorcycle Days meet at Lexington, Ohio, sponsored by the American Motorcyclists Association, is the best place to see a lot of bikes from the 1960s, 1970s, and 1980s. It is also a goldmine for anyone looking to find an old beat-up bike to restore. It typically happens in July and is about as much fun as one can have on two wheels. The swap meet alone covers fifty acres. Vintage groups gather there to show off their machines. Vintage racing is all part of the action. Family friendly, this event makes for a great weekend trip.

The AMA Vintage Motorcycle Days gathering in Ohio offers hundreds of acres of motorcycle fun. Bring a small dirt bike so you can ride around with tens of thousands of other happy bikers. The swap meet area is full of vintage bikes for sale.

Highbrow Venues

The popularity of vintage and antique motorcycles has brought them to some of the most prestigious country clubs throughout the United States. Part of the appeal is the audience—full of celebrities and well-heeled collectors. Annual events, such as the Vintage Motorcycle Concourse d'Elegance held at the World Golf Village near St. Augustine, Florida, feature the best in restored classics.

The high end of outdoor bike events includes concourse exhibits held at fancy country clubs, such as in Half Moon Bay, California. The best of the best in vintage machinery is exhibited. Pictured are Brough Superiors. These bikes are judged by experts on every little detail imaginable. Photo courtesy of Michael Schacht.

Motorcycle celebrities will often make an appearance at large gatherings. Pictured are racing legends Mert Lawwill and Gene Romero holding court at the Quail event. Photo by Stephen Covell.

Wherever You Go

It doesn't take long to find a really nice collection of motorcycles. On a recent cross-country trip, we saw a sign for a motorcycle museum in the middle of Kansas. Thirty miles off course, we stumbled upon one of the nicest small museums we had seen: the Kansas Motorcycle Museum in Marquette, Kansas.

The Quail Motorcycle Gathering in Carmel, California, offers an elegant environment for seeing some of the finest examples of classic motorcycles. Photo by Stephen Covell.

The Kansas Motorcycle Museum exhibits over one hundred superb bikes. Scores of early American bikes are presented.

Pristine examples of early twentieth century American motorcycles are within reach at the Kansas Motorcycle Museum. Pictured is an Emblem single-cylinder. The Buffalo, NY, company produced bikes between 1907 and 1925.

Going Abroad

If you travel overseas, consider checking out motorcycle rallies. The Ace Café hosts numerous large events in London. It is a good place to see the best café racers being built today. On the flip side, the gathering at Brighton Beach, England, will bring both bike and scooter enthusiasts together. While at the Isle of Man it is worthwhile to visit the fabulous Manx Museum. In addition to the rich exhibits recounting the island's Celtic and Viking heritage, special motorcycles are displayed during the TT. The island is also home to the private A.R.E Motorcycle Collection in Kirk Michael.

Mike Hailwood's 1978 TT winning Suzuki displayed at the Manx Museum in Douglas, IOM. That was Mike's fourteenth and final TT victory. He is justifiably considered one of the greatest motorcycle racers ever.

While in the U.K., consider seeing some real vintage British bike gems at several superb museums. The National Motorcycle Museum in Birmingham is one of the largest anywhere with over 850 classic bikes on display. For Triumph enthusiasts, the London Motorcycle Museum is a must. For off-road enthusiasts, visit famous trials rider Sammy Miller's museum in New Milton. It has a great variety of on- and off-road machines.

Museums in the United States

The following is a short list of some of the notable motorcycle museums throughout the country. Motorcyclists and their families should take advantage of visiting these institutions to learn about the various makes and the important role motorcycles have played in our social history.

AACA MUSEUM

The Antique Automobile Club of America (AACA) museum in Hershey, Pennsylvania, is simply a magnificent place to see countless examples of vintage automobiles. Sprinkled among them are dozens of fantastic examples of antique and vintage motorcycles. The kids will love this side trip when visiting the chocolate town. aacamuseum.org

The AACA Museum at Hershey provides a welcoming environment for the entire family to explore its large collection of vintage vehicles.

AMA MOTORCYCLE HALL OF FAME MUSEUM

The AMA Motorcycle Hall of Fame Museum in Pickerington, Ohio, is much like the sports halls of fame. Great exhibits surrounding well-known motorcycle racers and designers offer hours of education and pleasure. Major rotating exhibits feature specific marques, designers and historic events. motorcyclemuseum.org

The AMA Motorcycle Hall of Fame is a fitting tribute to motorcycling and those who have made their mark upon it.

Motorcycle racing history buffs will be delighted to see the actual machines raced by their heroes at the AMA Motorcycle Hall of Fame. Photo courtesy of the American Motorcyclist Association.

Rotating exhibits may feature famous designers, such as Arlen Ness.

BARBER VINTAGE MOTORSPORTS MUSEUM

The Barber Vintage Motorsports Museum, a not-for-profit organization located in Birmingham, Alabama, is the home of the world's largest collection of motorcycles. While many on exhibit are indeed vintage, the collection has many modern makes and models. Birmingham native George Barber began the collection in 1988 when his co-worker and friend Dave Hooper piqued his interest in the visibly exposed mechanics and artistry of motorcycles.

As Barber's motorcycle collection increased in size, it necessitated a larger location than its former Southside, Birmingham, location. In 2003, the museum and park opened to the public. The main portion of the Barber Museum is 144,000 square feet in size, with an expansion adding an additional 84,650 square feet of space.

The elegant and artful grounds of the Barber Motorsports Park offer a family-friendly vacation destination.

By 2015, there were more than 1,400 motorcycles in the Barber Museum's collection. The Barber Museum is located at Barber Motorsports Park, an 830-acre park with a 2.38-mile, seventeen-turn racetrack. People from around the world visit the park and museum throughout the year for a variety of reasons, including motorcycle and car racing events, and to see the vast array of vehicles on exhibit—many of which are exceedingly rare. The museum's collection, which includes a huge collection of vintage Lotus racecars and other vehicles, continues to grow by way of donations and acquisitions. Expansions and new construction take place at the museum and in the park continuously to accommodate growth and offer a first-rate experience for all.

Nowhere in the world will one see such an amazing display of motorcycles. The massive multistory structure on the right is a Christmas tree made of motorcycles.

Exhibits are diverse and designed to arouse interest at every turn.

Each fall the Annual Barber Vintage Festival draws tens of thousands of people of all ages for a three-day event that hosts motorcycles and riders from around the globe, a staggeringly large motorcycle swap meet, as well as entertainment for all ages. Many attend the Barber Vintage Festival every year, and it has often been described as a "bucket list" experience.

Text courtesy of Kelly Stewart, Barber Vintage Motorsports Museum, 2015. barbermuseum.org

Vintage racing at the Barber Motorsports Park allows racing fans to meet some of the greats. Pictured is world champion motorcycle racer Kevin Schwantz with his vintage Norton.

HARLEY-DAVIDSON MUSEUM®

The Harley-Davidson Museum in Milwaukee, Wisconsin, is an absolute must for any motorcycle enthusiast. It covers everything you could possibly want to know or see about the famous brand. More than 450 motorcycles and artifacts, dating back to Serial Number One, the oldest known Harley-Davidson motorcycle, are on exhibit. harley-davidson.com

In addition to seeing the complete historic line of Harley-Davidson motorcycles, touring the museum provides an informative view of twentieth century American history. Photo courtesy of Harley-Davidson.

KERSTING'S CYCLE CENTER

This collection of over one hundred nice antique and rare motorcycles in North Judson, Indiana, may be a bit off the beaten path, but owner Jim Kersting's private collection is worth seeing, even if you have to take that 100-mile ride from Chicago. kerstingscycle.com

MOTORCYCLEPEDIA MUSEUM

This museum, located in Newburgh, New York, offers an amazing array of motorcycles in its 85,000 square-foot space. Over 500 motorcycles, ranging from 1897 to the present, are on display. Any motorcyclist living in the New York Metro area must make the short trip. Coordinate it with the Antique Motorcycle Club of America's rallies in Rhinebeck for a real motorcycle overload. motorcyclepediamuseum.org

The Motorcyclepedia Museum is host to a very broad variety of motorcycles, spanning far over one hundred years.

One of the unique features of the Motorcyclepedia Museum is its Indian Motorcycle Timeline exhibit. Nearly every model year of the iconic marque is represented, starting with one of the first production bikes from 1901.

1901 Indian

1902 Indian
Single

1903 India
Single

NATIONAL MOTORCYCLE MUSEUM

The National Motorcycle Museum in Anamosa, Iowa, is a well-known institution among American vintage motorcycle enthusiasts. The fellows from the television show *American Pickers* have visited it more than once on their show. The collection holds over 400 bikes and an endless array of vintage engines, posters, and photos. Their online store has plenty of goodies for sale if you can't get there. nationalmcmuseum.com

OWLS HEAD TRANSPORTATION MUSEUM

For those in the New England states, Owls Head, Maine, will make a nice destination to see some really nice "pre-1940" bikes, cars, and airplanes. Even though the number of bikes is few, any motorhead will appreciate how the vehicles and planes are exhibited together, creating a great feel for the period. owlshead.org

THE ROCKY MOUNTAIN MOTORCYCLE MUSEUM

The Rocky Mountain Motorcycle Museum and Hall of Fame in Colorado Springs, Colorado, was established in 1992 as a venue for the general public to view, enjoy, and be educated by a well-rounded display of antique and classic motorcycles, photographs, and memorabilia. The museum is recognized as a publicly supported, non-profit, educational corporation. themotorcyclemuseum.com

THE SMITHSONIAN

The Smithsonian National Museum of American History in Washington, DC, has a nice collection of motorcycles on exhibit in its transportation exhibit. The most historic and valuable item is Sylvester Roper's steam Velocipede. Unfortunately, it's not always on display. However, Glenn Curtiss's remarkable eight-cylinder motorcycle is permanently on display at the National Air and Space Museum. si.edu

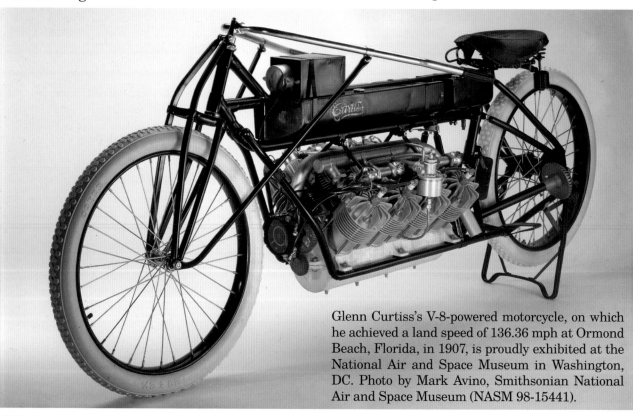

Glenn Curtiss's V-8-powered motorcycle, on which he achieved a land speed of 136.36 mph at Ormond Beach, Florida, in 1907, is proudly exhibited at the National Air and Space Museum in Washington, DC. Photo by Mark Avino, Smithsonian National Air and Space Museum (NASM 98-15441).

The Smithsonian's Work and Industry exhibits feature one very unusual motorcycle: the "Ghostrider." It is a completely automated robot motorcycle that drives itself and rights itself after a fall. It was developed by a team at UC Berkeley as part of a Defense Advanced Research Project competition in 2004. The bike is powered by a 90cc Yamaha racing engine. Photo by Anthony Levandowski, Division of Work & Industry, National Museum of American History, Smithsonian Institution.

SOLVANG VINTAGE MOTORCYCLE MUSEUM

The Solvang Motorcycle Museum, located in Solvang, California, displays a great collection of vintage and rare motorcycles. The collection is quite broad with something for everyone, ranging from a 1910 FN to the extraordinary Britten, and across all makes. The emphasis is tilted toward racing motorcycles. At the museum, you will find names such as AJS, BMW, Ducati, Gilera, Matchless, Moto Guzzi, MV, Norton, Triumph, Velocette, and Vincent. motosolvang.com

SPRINGFIELD MUSEUMS

Another great place to see Indian motorcycles is at the brand's birthplace: Springfield, Massachusetts. The Springfield Museums house two-dozen Indian motorcycles donated by Esta Manthos, co-founder and president of the former Indian Motocycle Museum. They also host "Indi-an Motorcycle Day" where one can see exceptional examples of the brand. springfieldmuseums.org

WHEELS THROUGH TIME

The Wheels Through Time Museum in Maggie Valley, North Carolina, offers one of the absolute best collections of rare and historic American vintage motorcycles. Located just five miles from the Blue Ridge Parkway, it makes for an ideal destination for anyone heading to the Great Smoky Mountains. Over three hundred bikes are on display. wheelsthroughtime.com

The displays at the Wheels Through Time Museum go far beyond bikes on pedestals. Each genre of motorcycle is beautifully staged against a fitting backdrop. Photo by Lori Weiniger.

Create Your Own Bike Event

Believe it or not, there are good people throughout this country who love motorcycles enough to test their neighbors' resolve to maintain good relationships. Bike enthusiasts may throw a breakfast for anyone who will show up. Upwards of one hundred motorcycles may come on an early Sunday morning. The key is to invite the neighbors and their kids. The latter will have a ball as they see and hear the toys adults play with.

An early morning biker breakfast may rock the neighborhood but is usually enjoyed by all once helmets come off and neighbors get to know the bikers.

Go to School

If you truly want to get in touch with motorcycles, old or new, consider one of the many vocational or trade schools that offer programs in maintenance and repair. Those lucky enough to go to a manufacturer's service school will learn the best service practices for a particular brand. Apprenticeships at a local shop offer a special experience. The owner typically has scores of years of knowledge relating to a very broad variety of bikes.

Professor Michael Littman at Princeton University's Mechanical & Aerospace Engineering department takes this to a whole new level with his The Art and Science of Motorcycle Design freshman seminar. The course includes a lecture series and accompanying hands-on lab that requires students to learn all aspects of motorcycle technology while completely rebuilding a vintage bike. This includes all engine, structural, and electrical subsystems. Learning about advanced computer aided technology and the use of a dynamometer is part of the course.

Student Alexander Walter putting the finishing touches on a1959 Triumph 200cc Tiger Cub restoration at Princeton University. Photo courtesy of Michael G. Littman, Ph.D.

Magazines, Books and Websites

Magazines are an ideal medium for those who can't travel or when cabin fever strikes mid-winter. The most popular magazines include *Cycle World, Motorcyclist*, the AMA's *American Motorcyclist*, Rider, and countless others specializing in custom, dirt, and adventure bikes. For the vintage enthusiast, there are several great periodicals, including the Antique Motorcycle Club of America's *The Antique Motorcycle* and *Motorcycle Classics* from Ogden Publications. Great websites include those by the American Motorcyclist Association (motorcyclemuseum.org), Antique Motorcycle Club of America (antiquemotorcycle.org), and the Antique Motorcycle Foundation (amf.foundation). Forums exist for pretty much any make or style of bike. Motorcycle Classics features vintage American, British, Japanese, and European bikes. Classic motorcycle magazines published in the U.K. offer readers a European view of vintage bikes, their history, and events. The most popular are those published by the Mortons Media Group. They include *The Classic MotorCycle, Classic Bike Guide,* and *Classic Racer*.

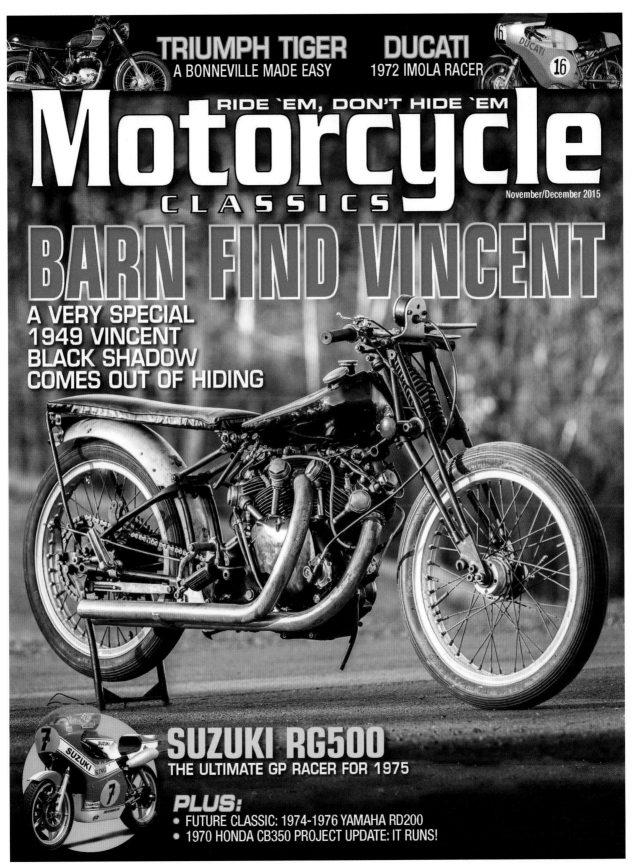

TRIUMPH TIGER
A BONNEVILLE MADE EASY

DUCATI
1972 IMOLA RACER

RIDE `EM, DON'T HIDE `EM

Motorcycle
CLASSICS

November/December 2015

BARN FIND VINCENT

A VERY SPECIAL
1949 VINCENT
BLACK SHADOW
COMES OUT OF HIDING

SUZUKI RG500
THE ULTIMATE GP RACER FOR 1975

PLUS:
- FUTURE CLASSIC: 1974-1976 YAMAHA RD200
- 1970 HONDA CB350 PROJECT UPDATE: IT RUNS!

Conclusion

If you have read this book in its entirety, you will have learned more about motorcycles than 98 percent of the people who ride them. This is sure to create a real sense of appreciation for every machine and every rider that passes by. You will look at the bikes in greater detail and study the riders within a social context.

The history of the motorcycle is clearly woven within the history of mankind itself. These machines provide an inexpensive means of transportation that has allowed workers to travel farther to earn an income to support their families. This helped the economic reconstruction of Europe after World War II and is the case in nearly all emerging economies today. Without motorcycles and scooters, millions would have to find a means of employment elsewhere, or relocate at great expense.

The motorcycle adds great value toward our quest for individual experience. It offers a means of recreation and self-expression that is unlike any other. The motorcyclist can experience travel without the confinement of an automobile, being able to smell the fragrances nature surrounds us with, and feel the subtle temperature changes we never noticed before when cocooned in a car. Whether its evolution, innovation, or destiny, this marriage between the wheel and the motor provides us with a remarkable vehicle for discovery that goes far beyond roads traveled—it goes deep within us. Just as those seeking to find inner peace with mindful meditation, motorcyclists can experience the same kind of focus and comfort. An early Sunday morning ride along an isolated stretch of beach has that effect. It insulates us from the harsh realities of the world and warms our hearts as we feel the freedom gifted to us by the machine itself. The popularity of motorcycling is directly associated

with the need to experience this type of freedom in an ever complex and restrictive world.

Motorcycling gives the rider a sense of accomplishment, as the machine does require some level of skill to maneuver. Riding also elevates the senses and provides therapeutic excitement. It is a sport many would not have considered, fearing for their safety and concerned with image. Those days are far gone as motorcycles of all types allow people to select a style of riding that makes them feel comfortable.

Motorcycling offers many other benefits. Practicing mechanical skills on an old bike is rewarding and a lot less expensive than working on an automobile. Racing a motorcycle for fun on weekends brings unrivaled thrills and a community of friends that provide respect regardless of place at the finish line. The social community surrounding motorcycling is endless. It is therefore imperative that future generations experience the benefits of motorcycling and understand its rich history. There are many organizations that are committed to keeping the flame burning and the wheels turning. Some fight for our rights to ride while others educate newcomers to the world of motorcycles.

If you haven't ridden, consider it. Take a MSF (Motorcycle Safety Foundation®) course. It will be one of the best investments you'll ever make. Expand your horizons by trying different types of motorcycles.

In all cases, whether you ride or not, be considerate of those who do. Respect the brand or style of motorcycle others may choose to ride, and support organizations like the AMA that promote safety and public acceptance of motorcycling. It is an expression of freedom that we do not ever want to lose.

Appendix A

Monocycles and Other Specialty Bikes

Monocycles

Clearly the most unusual motorcycle is the monocycle. This intriguing concept has been around for centuries as people would roll down a hill inside a tree-trunk, barrels, or wooden hoops. Advances in the nineteenth century would put pedal power to a single large wooden wheel. The 1930s brought gasoline-powered monowheels.

No one has championed monocycles more than inventor, engineer, and racer Kerry McLean. Pictured is Kerry on his 5 hp *McLean Wheel*.

McLean took the monocycle to an extreme with his Buick V-8-powered "Rocket Roadster." Kerry's passion for advancing this concept continues despite experiencing a serious crash. His website is a wealth of information and videos on this unique form of transportation. Photos courtesy of Kerry McLean, mcleanmonocycle.com

Three-Wheelers and Autocycles

Three-wheeled vehicles are nothing new. The earliest forms of the automobile ran on three wheels. Motorcycle makers offered them as well 120 years ago. Three-wheeled motorcycles, referred to as trikes, typically have their pair of wheels in the rear. This makes for less than perfect handling. Steering is quite the opposite of a conventional two-wheeled bike. High-speed cornering is an unstable proposition as well. Putting the pair of wheels up front made a big difference.

Can-Am's Spyder line of three-wheelers has carved out a nice niche within the motorcycling community. These machines created great public awareness of three-wheeled vehicles. They provide stability while still allowing tandem seating and handlebar steering. Can-Ams will most likely remain classified as a motorcycle.

Depending on seating position and steering mechanism, three-wheelers may be classified as motorcycles or autocycles, the latter being more like an automobile. Morgan Motor Company of England started building three-wheelers in 1910 to help customers avoid paying the tax imposed on four-wheeled automobiles. The vehicle used a conventional steering wheel and foot-operated brake and clutch. The company has endured, but something far faster than Morgans have emerged over the past two decades. These machines challenge the definition of a motorcycle.

Campagna Corporation, out of Canada, introduced its first production three-wheeled vehicle in 1995. It was powered by a Kawasaki motorcycle engine. The concept was like the Morgan in that the driver and passenger sit side-by-side in an open cockpit. A steering wheel is used to guide the vehicle.

Campagna T-Rex today comes in a variety of configurations. Pictured is the 20th Anniversary T-REX Special Edition powered by a 160 hp six-cylinder 1,649cc BMW engine. The machine is an interesting mix between car and motorcycle, offering the best of both. Contrasting with its high tech style and audio system are saddlebags over the rear wheel. Photo courtesy of Campagna Motors.

Toyota's i-Road is a very exciting concept initially available in Europe and Japan, but now making it to the US. The three-wheeled electric vehicle offers the stability of a car but handles like a motorcycle. A key selling point for commuters is that it is weatherproof. Pictured is the i-Road 002. Photo courtesy of Toyota Motor Sales, U.S.A., Inc.

For those looking to retain the handling qualities of a motorcycle in a three-wheeler, Tilting Motor Works offers a conversion for many Harley-Davidson models. The wheels tilt to retain the feel of riding a bike. This includes counter-steering. Photo courtesy of Tilting Motor Works, Inc.

Others have followed in offering exciting autocycles, including Can-Am, Polaris, Toyota, Elio Motors, and many custom builders. Can-Ams use handlebars, and seat rider and passenger in tandem. They will most likely stay classified as motorcycles rather than autocycles. The question facing the authorities on models with side-by-side seating and steering wheels involve vehicle classification. Unlike a trike, these machines behave more like automobiles. Newer models are partially or completely enclosed. Classified as motorcycles, these vehicles are exempt from many regulations imposed on automobiles. These include licensing, emissions standards, lighting, and other safety features, like bumpers. Most states right now require that occupants wear helmets. This could change if the vehicles are reclassified as autocycles. US Senator David Vitter (R-La.) introduced the Autocycle Safety Act (S. 685) in March 2015, which creates the new classification "autocycle" for enclosed motor vehicles with three wheels. This bill is designed to establish new safety requirements that are more in line with automobiles than motorcycles.

Taking the three-wheeled concept to the next level is the Polaris Slingshot, introduced in 2015. This impressive machine is closer to an all-out race car than a motorcycle. It does bring the thrill of high-performance motorcycling to a remarkably stable platform. It is powered by a 2,400cc four-cylinder engine capable of chest crushing acceleration and cornering. Polaris also makes the Victory and Indian line of motorcycles.

The Slingshot's cockpit is clearly automotive in design and layout.

Specialty Three-Wheelers

Three-wheelers make ideal vehicles for the handicapped. Several custom makers offer bikes and scooters allowing anyone the freedom to enjoy the open road.

This three-wheeler offers a wheelchair bound rider all the joys of motorcycling. Photo by Anthony Surber.

A simple ramp makes it easy to roll on and off the vehicle. This rider is not about to miss another rally at the Ace Café. Photo by Lisa Ensanian.

Eugene, Oregon, maker Arcimoto offers an exciting and highly affordable electric daily urban commuter in its SRK line. Weather protection is available in this tandem seater via optional side covers. Steering is by handlebars. Photos courtesy of Arcimoto.

The Enclosed Motorcycle

The Swiss company Peraves has created something a lot of people have talked about over the years—a totally enclosed two-wheeled motorcycle. The firm's innovative Monotracer® seats two in tandem and is capable of 155 mph using a BMW K1200 engine that averages 50 mpg. Outriggers allow the machine to stand on its own as one comes to a stop. Despite its Kevlar egg–shaped construction, the machine can lean 52 degrees on the track. It takes quite a bit of training to master one of these, but it is well worth it according to those who have. An electric version is also available. Air-conditioning and sound system are included. Handlebars are used to steer.

Appendix B

More on Horsepower

Horsepower represents the work an engine does. To keep horsepower in perspective, gears, pulleys, and levers are necessary to translate it into real-world work. No horse can lift 33,000 pounds with a single pulley in one minute. However, the use of several pulleys, or a series of gears, would allow the average draft horse the mechanical advantage to lift the weight one foot, given enough rope, in one minute. Of course any combination of feet and pounds will translate to the same value. For example, lifting thirty-three pounds one thousand feet in one minute produces the same result. So does lifting 330 pounds one hundred feet in one minute. The same is true of a motorcycle engine. A Yamaha YZF®-R1 engine, pumping out a whopping 178 hp, could never lift 5,874,000 (178 x 33,000) pounds one foot in one minute without highly reduced gearing. The engine could only achieve this by spinning at 11,100 revolutions per minute, producing its claimed 84.5 ft-lb of torque (twisting force about the crankshaft) to rotate small gears acting on larger ones connected to a hoist that would ultimately turn at a snail's pace to lift the object one foot in a minute. If you have ever used a winch to crank your boat onto the trailer, you can relate. Regardless of how it is done, one hp can lift 33,000 pounds one foot in one minute. A simple formula shows the relationship:

$$\textit{Power} = \frac{\textbf{Work}}{\textbf{Time}} \text{ or } \frac{\textbf{Force x Distance}}{\textbf{Time}} \text{ or } \frac{\textbf{33,000 lbs x 1ft}}{\textbf{1 minute}}$$

For the curious, 33,000 ft-lbs per minute equates to 550 ft-lbs per second, or 745.7 Watts. The Germans use the term pferdestarke (PS), an exact translation of horsepower. PS is often used as an indicator of power for engines when reviewed in European magazines. PS and hp are not exactly alike, but are close enough, and do not require conversion for the average enthusiast when reading the specs.

Torque Matters

Torque is actually a better indicator of an engine's power than horsepower. The two are directly related in that hp is derived after we measure an engine's torque while it is running. This is done on a dynamometer, or dyno. The instrument measures the rotational (twisting)

force created at the crankshaft or rear wheel at various rpms. The measure is typically in foot-pounds or Newton-meters. Early dynamometers were called "brakes" in that they provided resistance against the rotating crankshaft. The brake could be as simple as a fan rotating in water or oil. A scale measuring pounds was attached to the housing to measure the force acting on it. The term "brake horsepower," or bhp, is derived from this and typically reflects power at the crankshaft. This represents the engine's true horsepower before it loses some as it goes through the drive train to the rear wheel. Dynos today can use a variety of devices to provide resistance, including hydraulic systems, electromagnetic, or electric motors.

Horsepower can be calculated from torque by the following formula:

$$HP = \frac{\text{rpm x Torque}}{5252 \text{ (a constant)}}$$

Using the Yamaha as an example:

$$178\ hp = \frac{11{,}100 \text{ x } 84.5\text{ft-lb}}{5252}$$

Torque is what gives us that sensation of power, especially on long-stroke V-twin engines. The long connecting rods require crankpins that are further offset from the shaft's axis than short-stroke engines. This extra distance provides more leverage for turning the crankshaft, thus offering greater twisting force. Relate this to a longer shovel handle, which provides more leverage to move a large rock than a shorter handle one. Short-stroke engines, like high-revving two-strokes and high-performance multi-cylinder machines, make their torque at higher rpms. Bikes with lots of horsepower at higher rpms are good for going fast. Bikes with modest horsepower, but good torque at lower rpms, are ideal for hill climbing and trail riding in the woods. Motorcycle manufacturers design their machines with all of these considerations.

One of the most interesting new motorcycle engines to appear is the Motus V4 Baby Block®. It is a 1,650cc (100ci) liquid-cooled V4. It emulates the small block American V-8s found in muscle cars. Unlike most new engines, it uses traditional pushrod valve actuation with hydraulic lifters. This keeps maintenance simple, something to be considered when buying a motorcycle. Bore and stroke measure 88mm x 67.80mm and compression ratio is set at 11.5:1. The result is lots of torque and 160-plus horsepower. Photo courtesy of Motus Motorcycles.

Dyno Tuning

Unlike electric motors or steam engines, internal combustion engines produce their optimum torque at specific rpm ranges. This requires shifting into the right gear to maintain power to the wheel. Dyno charts detail an engine's performance by graphing torque and horsepower values against rpm. Dyno tuning allows one to adjust engine, ignition, and fuel specs using this tool to squeeze the most power out of an engine at a given rpm range. This "power band" can be redefined depending on adjusting cam and ignition timing, and a whole host of other variables.

DYNAMOMETER

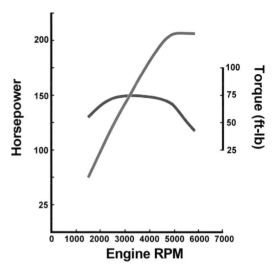

This dyno chart shows the relationship between engine rpm, horsepower, and torque. Maximum hp (red) for this engine is achieved at about 4,800 rpm, while maximum torque (blue) is hit at 2,800 rpm. This torque curve indicates that the bike has pretty good pulling power between 2,000 and 5,000 rpm. The "flatter" the torque curve, the less shifting is required.

Rear-wheel horsepower being tested on a dynamometer. Note the fan by the front wheel to help cool the engine. Photo courtesy of DYNOmite Dynamometer by Land and Sea Inc.

Appendix C

Air and Fuel

This section will provide a brief overview of how and what an engine breathes to make it run.

Most gasoline fueled engines require the liquid fuel to be mixed with air in proper proportions in order to be ignitable. It is the fuel reacting with the oxygen in the air under compression in the cylinder that provides the explosion that ultimately turns our wheels.

Achieving just the right mixture between air and fuel is critical for efficient combustion. Too much fuel vs. air creates a 'rich' mixture. This is typically seen on engines spewing black exhaust. Leaving the choke on after an engine has warmed up results in a rich mixture as well. Too lean of a mixture creates excessively high combustion chamber temperatures that could end up in melted piston crowns. The ideal mix between the two reactants is referred to as the correct stoichiometric air-to-fuel ratio. With gasoline this is 14.7:1 by mass. This means that the air mass (by weight) taken into an engine though the carburetor is 14.7 greater than the mass of the fuel taken in. This represents about 6.8% of fuel to air.

The job of creating the right mix is handled by two possible devices: a carburetor or an electronic fuel injection (EFI) system. More and more engines are fitted with EFI today as it is a more accurate method for achieving the proper air-fuel ratio.

The Carburetor

Carburetors, such as found on your lawnmower, have done a great job of supplying our engines with the correct air-fuel mixture for over one-hundred years. Their operation is simple in theory, but complex in execution. Their mission is to mix the air and fuel entering the engine at the proper proportions under various loads, speeds, and altitudes. Fuel flow is regulated through small openings called jets, while a needle meters just the right amount of fuel as it enters the airflow through the carburetor's restricted opening.

It all begins with the intake stroke. The piston creates a low-pressure area in the cylinder. The open intake valve allows the higher pressure air on the outside of the engine to push itself into the cylinder. As the air rushes in, it passes through the carburetor. In its center is a restricted section that is narrower than the entry point. This is called the venturi.

As air goes through the venturi, it speeds up and creates a low pressure area that draws up fuel from a small tube running up from a fuel reservoir. The fuel atomizes, like any perfume spray bottle, and enters the cylinder. The more air and fuel are allowed to enter the engine, the faster it will operate. The device that controls this is the throttle slide or a throttle butterfly. Illustration C-1 details some of these components.

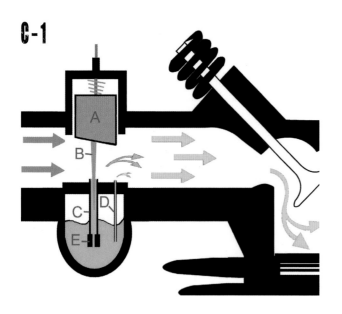

C-1

Air (blue) enters the carburetor. The throttle slide (A) is controlled by a cable going to the handlebar throttle grip. The gap between the bottom of the slide and the lower inside portion of the carburetor is the venturi. Fuel is drawn up from a reservoir via tube (C) as air passes by. On some carburetors, a needle attached to the throttle slide rides inside of this tube. The tube is then referred to as a needle jet. The needle (B) meters just the right amount of fuel as the throttle slide goes up and down. The taper and shape of the needle can be fine-tuned to achieve better results. At wide-open throttle positions, the fuel is regulated by the main jet (E). When the throttle slide is at its lowest position, fuel is introduced by a pilot jet (D) that is typically on the engine side of the carburetor. It draws fuel form the reservoir; normally referred to as the float bowl. The pilot jet influences mixture at smaller throttle openings as well. Most carburetors allow the air-fuel mix of the pilot system to be adjusted via an idle mixture screw. On some carbs this idle mixture screw regulates air intake, while on others it regulates fuel intake.

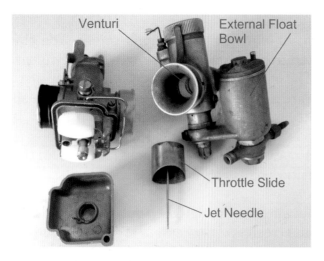

Carburetor components on a modern (left) and a seventy year old British Amal carburetor (right).

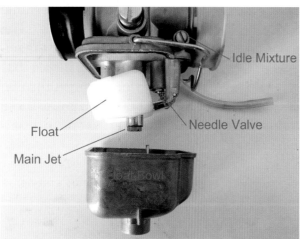

Close-up of a modern carburetor's lower half. It contains the float and needle valve mechanism that maintains the proper fuel level inside the float bowl. As fuel enters the bowl from the fuel tank, the float rises, forcing a needle to shut off the flow. Proper fuel level is critical for accurate fuel metering. Float levels must be set according to the maker's specifications. Also visible is the idle mixture screw and a large central screw. The latter sets the idle speed by adjusting the base throttle slide position.

While the basic design and function of a carburetor is as illustrated above, designs vary extensively. Some simple carburetors, as used on lawnmowers and old machines, use a fixed venturi. Flow is regulated by a circular disk placed within the carburetor's barrel. This disk has a central shaft used to rotate it. This is typically referred to as a butterfly valve or throttle valve. Opening the valve introduces more flow, which in turn increase engine rpm. These basic types of carbs were popular on American bikes prior to WWII.

Photo shows a CV carburetor with the top removed revealing the nitrile rubber diaphragm attached to the top of the throttle slide. The spring helps bring the throttle slide down. Note the butterfly valve in the carburetor barrel.

Other more advanced designs evolved as the need to meter air and fuel more precisely in high-performance engines arose. These designs controlled the raising and lowering of the slide valve via a vacuum diaphragm. They are referred to as CV or constant vacuum or constant velocity carbs. CV carbs are the most popular type of carburetors used on motorcycles that are not fuel injected. Some CV carbs use a large vacuum piston that is part of the throttle slide itself instead of a flexible diaphragm. Manifold vacuum raises the slide as the butterfly valve is opened. A jet needle meters the flow on both of these types.

This carburetor made by SU uses a piston housed within a large vacuum chamber to raise and lower the throttle slide as the butterfly valve is opened and closed.

The challenge facing carbureted bikes is to maintain the correct air-fuel ratio at various throttle openings and load conditions. Carburetor tuning therefore is an art in itself. Changing altitude, or anything in the flow of an engine, changes the mixture. Replacing a quiet stock exhaust system, for example, with a free-flowing louder one results in less restricted flow of gasses. A carbureted bike would have to have its mixture adjusted to compensate for the leaner condition created by this new system. This is referred to as re-jetting a carburetor, and typically involves changing the pilot and main jet. The same is true when installing free-flow air filters. A good shop manual will describe the workings of your particular bike's carburetor in greater detail.

Fuel Injection

Electronic fuel injection may not be popular with vintage bike die-hards, but it certainly has been a blessing for modern motorcycle owners. Gone is the need to re-jet, or adjust carburetors when riding in very high altitudes. The electronic system uses a variety of sensors to measure the current conditions to constantly set the proper air-fuel ratio. Figure C-2 shows a basic schematic of an electronic fuel injection system.

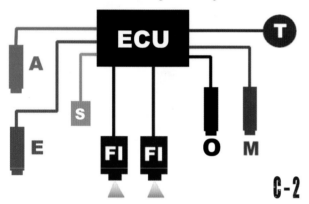

The Electronic Control Unit (ECU) is a small computer that receives input from several sensors. These include an air temperature sensor (A), an engine temperature sensor (E), a throttle positions sensor (T), a manifold pressure sensor (M), an engine speed (rpm) sensor (S), and an oxygen sensor (O) that resides on the exhaust pipe coming out of the engine.

A pre-programmed software 'map' stored in the ECU then tells the system how much fuel needs to squirted into the engine based on all the inputs from the sensors. Fuel injectors (FI) squirt just the right amount of fuel into the engine during the intake stroke to achieve correct stoichiometric air-to-fuel ratio. The results of changing an exhaust system or an air filter will be recognized by the sensors, and the ECU will adjust accordingly. Some ECUs allow re-map-

ping for high-performance tuning by plugging in a laptop or a mobile phone. There are third-party companies out there that may supply custom mapped ECUs for your particular bike. Regardless, EFI is a wonderful thing.

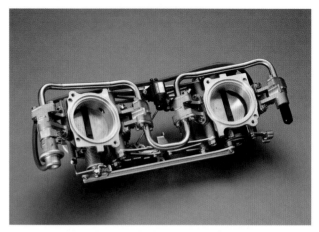

Some engines have the injector mounted to a throttle body, while others have the injectors attached directly to each cylinder head. The throttle body may look like a carburetor in that it serves as the main entry point for air, and typically has a butterfly valve in it to regulate air intake. The fuel is injected into the air stream of the throttle body, heading towards the cylinder. Pictured is a dual-throttle body from a Honda RC-51 racer. Note the large brass butterfly valves for controlling air intake. They are in a closed position. Also visible are four fuel injectors supplied by the (silver) fuel lines to feed the high-performance machine. Photo courtesy of American Honda Motor Co., Inc.

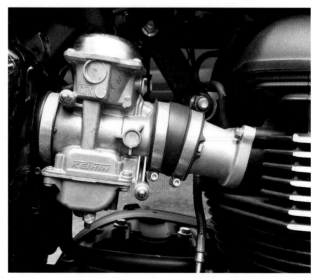

Looking remarkably similar to a CV carburetor, modern retro Triumphs like the Bonneville use fuel injection throttle bodies that resemble carburetors.

Motorcycling provides the opportunity to express individualism. Every rider develops their own image by what they wear and what they ride.

Index

S

Jo Ensanian